Anonymous

Papers and Proceedings Connected with the Passing of the Deccan Agriculturists' Relief Act Xvii of 1879

Anonymous

Papers and Proceedings Connected with the Passing of the Deccan Agriculturists' Relief Act Xvii of 1879

ISBN/EAN: 9783337812676

Printed in Europe, USA, Canada, Australia, Japan

Cover: Foto ©ninafisch / pixelio.de

More available books at **www.hansebooks.com**

SELECTIONS FROM THE RECORDS OF THE BOMBAY GOVERNMENT.

No. CLVII —New Series.

PAPERS AND PROCEEDINGS

CONNECTED WITH THE PASSING OF THE

DECCAN AGRICULTURISTS' RELIEF ACT, XVII. OF 1879,

From 6th April 1877 to 24th March 1880.

Bombay:
PRINTED AT THE GOVERNMENT CENTRAL PRESS.

1882.

CONTENTS.

	PAGE
Letter from the Secretary to the Government of Bombay, Revenue Department, to the Secretary to the Government of India, Department of Revenue, Agriculture and Commerce, No. 2202, dated 6th April 1877 ...	1
Minute by the Honourable A. Rogers, dated 29th May 1876, referred to in para. 12 of the above letter	19
Minute by the Governor of Bombay, dated 15th October 1877, on the effect of the new Civil Procedure Code on Indebted Ryots of the Deccan .	28
Do. do. dated 12th November 1877, on the special legislation for indebtedness of Ryots of the Bombay Deccan	30
Letter from the Chief Secretary to the Government of Bombay, Revenue Department, to the Secretary to the Government of India, Department of Revenue, Agriculture and Commerce, No. 308, dated 19th January 1878	35
Letter from the Secretary to the Government of India, Department of Revenue, Agriculture and Commerce, to the Chief Secretary to the Government of Bombay, Revenue Department, No. 404, dated 1st July 1878 .	40
Minute by the Governor of Bombay, dated 30th August 1878, containing further observations on special legislation for indebtedness of ryots of the Bombay Deccan	47
Letter from the Chief Secretary to the Government of Bombay, Revenue Department, to the Secretary to the Government of India, Department of Revenue, Agriculture and Commerce, No. 4579, dated 5th September 1878.	57
Despatch from the Secretary of State, No. 4 (Legislative), dated 26th December 1878, to the Government of Bombay	68
Letter from the Secretary to the Government of India, Home Department, to the Secretary to the Government of Bombay, Revenue Department, No. 222, dated 26th February 1879	78
Minute by the Governor of Bombay, dated 14th April 1879, containing further proposals for legislation regarding the indebted ryots of the Deccan	95
Letter from the Chief Secretary to the Government of Bombay, Revenue Department, to the Secretary to the Government of India, Home Department, No. 2056, dated 18th April 1879	104
Draft Bill referred to in above letter	113
Abstract of the Proceedings of the Council of the Governor General of India assembled on the 5th June 1879, in connection with the Bombay Indebted Agriculturists' Relief Bill	140
Do. do. dated 17th July 1879	142
Do. do. dated 18th July 1879	205
The Deccan Agriculturists' Relief Bill introduced into the Legislative Council of the Governor General by the Honourable Mr. T. C. Hope on the 5th June 1879	228
Letter from the Secretary to the Government of India, Legislative Department, to the Chief Secretary to the Government of Bombay, Revenue Department, No. 780, dated 26th July 1879	253
Letter from the Secretary to the Government of Bombay, Revenue Department, to the Secretary to the Government of India, Legislative Department, No. 4495, dated 27th August 1879	258
Report of the Select Committee on the Bill above referred to ...	270

	PAGE
Abstract of the Proceedings of the Council of the Governor General of India assembled on the 24th October 1879 in connection with the Bombay Indebted Agriculturists Bill	282
The Deccan Agriculturists Relief Act, 1879	361
Rules for regulating the procedure of Village Munsifs	387
Rules regarding Conciliators	391
Rules regarding Village Registrars and Registrations	394
Rules regulating the appointment, suspension, dismissal and remuneration of Village Registrars, and prescribing the fees to be levied by them ...	411
Notification No. 2109, dated 24th March 1880, declaring that the Rules regarding Registration made under Sections 61 and 63 of the Deccan Agriculturists Relief Act shall come into force in the four Collectorates of Poona, Ahmednagar, Sholápur and Sátára from the 1st April 1880 ...	413
Notification No. 1226, dated 19th February 1880, laying down a revised table of fees for instruments to be registered under Section 71 of the Deccan Agriculturists' Relief Act	413
Notification No. 7926, dated 31st December 1879, regarding reduction of Court fees and Stamp duties	414
Notification No. 89, dated 7th January 1880, republishing Government of India's Notifications Nos. 10 and 11, dated 3rd January 1880, remitting the duties on certain classes of instruments	415

No 2202 of 1877.

REVENUE DEPARTMENT.

Bombay Castle, 6th April 1877.

From
    THE SECRETARY TO THE GOVERNMENT OF BOMBAY,
To
    THE SECRETARY TO THE GOVERNMENT OF INDIA,
    Department of Revenue, Agriculture, and Commerce,
                                                     Simla.

Sir,

With my letter No. 3011, dated 20th May 1876, I had the honour, by direction of His Excellency the Governor in Council, to transmit to the Government of India seven copies of the report of the Commission which was appointed to investigate the causes of the riots which occurred during 1875 in the Poona and Ahmednagar Collectorates, together with its Appendices, marked A. to C., and two separate papers recorded by Messrs. Colvin and Shambhuprasád Lakshmilál. A similar number of copies of the volumes containing the Minutes recorded by the Commission, together with other papers which were not received with the report, were also forwarded on the 11th July 1876. I am now directed to submit the views of this Government.

2. The subject-matter of these papers divides itself into the following heads :—

1. The nature and extent of the riots themselves, and what was their immediate cause.

2. The extent to which defects, if any, in the revenue administration led to the riots, and whether any improvement in the system is required.

3. The state of the existing law relating to debt, and the action of Civil Courts.

1. *The nature and extent of the riots themselves, and what was their immediate cause.*

Nature and extent of the riots.

3. The riots commenced on the 12th May 1875. The object was in every case to obtain by force and destroy the bonds for money given by the cultivators to the village bankers. Actual disturbances took place in 11 villages in the Poona and 22 villages in the Ahmednagar Collectorate. Threatened riots were

u 862—1

arrested by the police in many other villages. The outbreak was over in about a month; but two cases happened afterwards in the Poona District, and another in a village of the Sátára Collectorate, 100 miles away from the affected tract, which showed that the feelings which had led to the riots were neither extinct, nor were they confined to Poona and Ahmednagar alone. The number of persons arrested was 951, of whom 501 were convicted. The absence of serious crime is a very remarkable feature in the outbreak. In many cases where the money-lenders themselves, at the ryots' demands, tore up their bonds, no further harm was done, and ferocity was shown in only one case where an attempt was made to burn a money-lender alive. Even in that instance, too, certain of the rioters themselves saved the banker's life.

4. It is clear that the feeling of hostility between the ryots and their creditors, which found open expression in the riots, had been increasing in strength for some time. Indeed, had it not been for a transient period of prosperity, the crisis which has occurred would have happened long ago. The affected districts are poor and in places sterile, and suffer much from scanty and precarious nature of the rainfall.

Causes which led to the riots.

The Ryots.

The ryots themselves, hardy and in many ways frugal race, have from the earliest time suffered from a load of ancestral debt, which they never think of repudiating, and is one of the main causes of their constant poverty. Devoid of education, and not possessed of much intelligence, the system of collecting the land revenue at fixed times and in fixed sums in cash necessitates constant recourse to the village banker for sums of ready money, against which is set the price of the produce sold to him. The social obligations which compel the expenditure of comparatively large sums at marriages and funerals also involve borrowing at very high rates of interest; and partly from the ryot's own carelessness about repayment, partly from the hardness and even fraud of the money-lender, small debts rapidly increase to large, so that once involved in debt a ryot is powerless to extricate himself. Formerly land in the Deccan was not the property of the ryot, and the ryot's credit was limited. The money-lender, therefore, advanced money with a stinted hand, and for some years after the conquest of the Deccan in 1818 seldom thought of having recourse to the Civil Courts to recover his debts, but was contented with taking all the ryot's produce, and leaving him only the bare necessaries of life. This state of things attracted attention as early as 1822, and from time to time the misery of the ryots and the danger of it to the State was represented to Government. From 1836-37, however, the land began

His original depression,

to be settled on terms which gave the ryots a proprietary title in it. Soon finding the value of this, they began to borrow money upon it, thus to live on their capital. At first the power of selling the land for money debts—a power unknown to native Governments, and foreign to the feelings of the people—was not exercised by the money-lenders. As soon, however, as the system of Civil Justice, introduced by the British, began to be better understood, and the ryots were getting to the end of their capital, suits became more frequent, and the people became familiar with sale of land for debt. Serious difficulties were foreseen; but the mortgaging of the land proceeded slowly, and about 1850 a period of good fortune dawned: the railway works were commenced, vast numbers of labourers were employed, and a great amount of money was spent amongst the ryots. Then came the American War, which diverted many millions of money to the Deccan to buy cotton. Prices of agricultural produce were greatly inflated, and the ryots' income was raised to an amount unconceived of before. Just about the same time a series of very extensive public works were commenced in Poona and the neighbourhood, which gave employment to those who needed it, and added to the money floating about the country. There is every reason to believe that at this time the ryots cleared off much of their former debts, but at the same time they learnt more expensive habits of living. From 1866 the tide of prosperity began to ebb. In 1866-67 the country suffered from severe drought, and in 1867-68 there was also a partial failure of crops. From 1870-71 the expenditure on public works was greatly reduced, and in that year prices, which had maintained themselves for some time after the cessation of the American War, began to fall steadily till, in 1875, an amount of grain could be bought for four annas which a rupee would hardly have purchased five years before. From 1867 the settlements of land revenue, made thirty years before, began to fall in, and the revision which took place in some of the disturbed tálukas, resulted in a considerable increase of the Government assessment. Population in the meantime had been increasing steadily, and its pressure on the land was much greater than it had been when the first settlements were made, and that in a part of the country where, considering the nature of the soil, the holdings are small, the average area per head of agricultural population ranging from 3 to 9 acres. All these circumstances contributed to contract the ryots' means; while it is possible they did not contract in the same proportion the more costly mode of living which high prices had justified. Again their debts began to accumulate, and they commenced mortgaging their lands more deeply than before.

Period of prosperity, 1850 to 1866.

Second period of depression.

Such of the sowkárs, and there are many, as come from other parts of India are hard, destitute of sympathy, and desirous of increasing their debtors' obligations in any manner possible. Their opportunity of enhancing their bond debts was much facilitated by a change in the Limitation Law which was made in 1859, putting an end to the old-fashioned, long-running accounts, and necessitating renewal of bonds at exorbitant rates every two years, or three years at the outside. As the ryots began to become once more deeply involved, the sowkárs began to press upon them. The result was that the mass of the people again became quasi-slaves, having to surrender all their produce to the sowkárs, and receiving from them only enough grain to live upon, as well as small sums of money, which served to increase their debts. In some places the sowkárs had recourse to the Civil Courts, and began to sell up the lands, which, as they were the only capitalists in the country, as well as for other reasons, were bought in by themselves for a mere song. These reverses naturally engendered discontent in the mind of the ryots, and discontent gradually ripened into hatred.

[margin: The Sowkárs.]

Evidence of the growing ill-feeling is shown by a number of outrages, where money-lenders were the victims, which occurred in the districts of Poona and Ahmednagar during the last three or four years, and by acts of open hostility, such as agreeing to deprive the Marwáris of the usual services which the various members of the village community render to one another, and molesting them in various disagreeable ways. What the actual cause of the outbreak was, will never be known. It appears, indeed, that one special cause of hatred was given by the sowkárs a month or two before the disturbances began. Government issued an order in February 1875 that moveable property should be sold before immoveable for arrears of revenue; in other words, that the selling up of a man's field should take place only in the last resort. One effect of this order was to protect the ryot's field, which was the sowkár's security, from being sold by Government as long as the ryot had any moveable property to seize. The sowkárs, therefore, knowing their security was safe, took advantage of the order to refuse advancing the second instalment of revenue for March 1875, although they had received all the produce of the fields. This must have exasperated the ryots beyond measure. It is probable, therefore, that when, as is stated to be the fact, the rumour spread that Government was inquiring into the ryots' circumstances, and that Her Majesty had ordered the sowkárs to give up their bonds, the ryots eagerly seized the pretext for taking the law into their own hands. But the precise manner in which

[margin: Supposed immediate causes of the outbreak.]

the fire was kindled is immaterial. The ryots are an especially quiet, law-loving race, and the causes to be probed are those which led to their inflammable condition, and not to the mere spark which began the conflagration. It may be noted, however, that there is no evidence to show that the ryots were urged to their excesses by persons of higher position and education, though they had the sympathy of many such.

2. *The extent to which defects, if any, in the Revenue Administration led to the riots, and whether any improvement in the system is required.*

5. The first and most important point to be considered under this head is whether or not the revision of the assessment, directly or indirectly, led to the riots. The Commissioners as a body are silent on the subject; but Government agree with Mr. Richey, the President, and Mr. Shambhuprasád, in considering that there is no reason to believe this to have been the case. The enhancement of the assessment was a mere trifle compared with the loss caused by the fall in prices. The tálukas in Ahmednagar, where so many riots occurred, have not been re-assessed, and the assessment will not be revised in any of them for three or four years to come. In the four tálukas of Sholápur which adjoin the affected districts, and which have been re-assessed, no attempts at disturbance were made. The táluka of Bhimthadi, where 6 cases occurred, was revised three years before the outbreak. In that of Indápur, which was revised seven years before, there was only one case. Not only were the villages where riots took place not those which had been most highly re-assessed, but the hostile movement against the sowkárs commenced in a village which has not been re-assessed at all. Government believe, therefore, with Mr. Richey that the movement was directed solely against the sowkárs, and that there was no further connection between the riots and the revision of assessment than that in individual instances the revised assessment may have been one, and that a small one, of the many causes which contributed to render a particular ryot's position intolerable.

Revision of assessments did not contribute to the riots.

6. Much discussion has, however, as the papers show, gone on as to the principles on which the revisions of assessment have taken place, and endeavours have been made to show that the new assessment, even though subsequently reduced, has been too highly pitched. The only papers which, in the opinion of Government, require remarks are the able minutes of Messrs. Carpenter and Colvin. Briefly put, Mr. Carpenter argues that the revisions in

Minutes of Messrs. Carpenter and Colvin.

certain tálukas were based on prices which were not a safe guide, and which obtained in a period when the assessment was not paid with ease and cultivation had not reached its fullest extent; that no allowance was made for the increased standard of comfort to which the ryots had attained during the currency of the late settlement, and which it is the object of Government to maintain; that the enhancement has been unequally distributed, and should in all cases have been lighter on land brought under the plough during the settlement than on land continuously cultivated; and that the system of classification of soils was faulty in that sufficient difference was not allowed between the best sorts and the worst. Mr. Colvin also, comparing the enhancements as carried out with those of the North-West Provinces, is of opinion that they are excessive, and that sufficient importance has not been attached to the growth of the population pressing on in a limited area, and to the admitted low and poor state of the population.

7. While His Excellency in Council must acknowledge the acuteness and justice of many of the criticisms which have been made, and which cannot fail to be of value to all Survey Officers, he does not feel himself called on to follow Messrs. Carpenter and Colvin through the details of their calculations and the conclusions they have educed. Settlements, whether original or revised, are matters requiring practical experience and knowledge of the country, and too great a reliance on figures and statistical tables is very apt to mislead. In the Bombay Presidency, as observed by Mr. Carpenter, data for ascertaining the true rent of land do not, and His Excellency would add, cannot exist. In revising the assessment, therefore, the precautions taken are to see that the soils be accurately valued, that the fields be accurately classed according to fertility and position, and that the villages be properly grouped. After this, the fixing of the maximum rates depends on a variety of considerations. The improvements which have been made in communications and in water-supply, the comparative wealth or poverty of the people, climate, the general fertility or sterility of the district, the ruling and probable future prices of agricultural produce, the benefits derived from the opening of new markets for the same,—are only some of the matters which have to be borne in mind, while the values of but few can be expressed in the form of tabular statements. Experience, therefore, and analogy of other tálukas and districts must be the Settlement Officer's guide in assigning their true weight to these various elements, so that he can fix an amount of assessment which it is not only just to Government to impose, but which will be easy for the people to pay. During

Principle of revisions of settlements.

this process allowances are always made to prevent encroachment on the increased standard of comfort which the people have reached, and to the continuance of which, as being the only evidence of true progress, the Government attach the greatest importance. It is thus quite possible that a revision may result in no increase at all, or even in the assessment being lightened.

8. As regards the revisions of assessment which have of late years been carried out in the Poona and Sholápur Collectorates, His Excellency sometime ago came to the conclusion that one factor on which the revisions were based, *viz.*, the prices of grain, had been over-estimated, and also that in revising the classification of fields (which was necessary owing to the faultiness of the early work of the Settlement Department) the medium and poorer soils had been valued at too high a scale. His Excellency in Council, therefore, lost no time in carrying out such reductions of assessment as were necessary. To prevent, moreover, for the future, increases which might bear with hardship on individual cultivators or villages, he laid down that without the sanction of Government no increase should exceed—

Precautions already taken against over-assessment at revisions.

In the case of an individual	... ...	100 per cent.
,, of a single village	... ...	66 ,,
,, of a single group of villages or of a single táluka	...	33 ,,

His Excellency in Council hopes that these orders will prove sufficient to prevent any hardship in future, and that no further change in the mode of carrying out revisions will be necessary. The Government of India are already aware that the re-classification of soils, which has been a chief cause of irritation, will not be undertaken again except where the original work is so erroneous—that is, so fraught with injustice to the great body of cultivators or to the State—that it is absolutely necessary to go over it again.

9. The Commissioners recommend that in future, when an increase of revenue, exceeding 25 per cent., is imposed at a revision, this increase should be imposed gradually; but they have not stated the detailed way in which they think this suggestion should be carried out. On the whole, His Excellency in Council is not inclined to view the proposal with favour. The revenue, as imposed in this Presidency, is never more than the people should be able to pay with ease, even in the first years after a revision, and there are many administrative objections to a change, not the least of which is the fraud to which the ryots

Government dissent from Commission's proposal to levy increased assessment gradually.

would be liable, and which is now prevented, owing to the demand on them being invariable. In poor tálukas, where it is possible that a difficulty may be felt by the people at first, the increase is never likely to exceed 33 per cent, and this is an amount but little beyond that which has been fixed by the Commission.

10. The rigid revenue system of this Government is alluded to, and the Commission observe that both Government and the ryots suffer by the fixing of the revenue at a certain sum, whatever the state of the season may be; and adding that, as Government has to give remissions in very bad seasons, it should share the profit in good seasons. His Excellency in Council, however, believes that it would not be possible to introduce "a more elastic system than the present, which should be governed by fixed principles, and avoid hap-hazard remissions," or that the "revenue could be fixed according to the quantity or timeliness of the rainfall." Any step which would render the ryots' payment variable, would re-introduce that element of uncertainty and gambling so dear to all natives, and be a pernicious and very retrograde measure. The ryot himself would not like it in the good years, as he would, under the system indicated, have to pay more heavily than at present. When assessing districts liable to drought, such as the Commission have in their mind, great care is taken to make allowances for bad seasons. And though the giving of remissions in the worst seasons is an evil, still it is preferable to the uncertainty and, Government may add, fraud which would follow the changing of the assessment every year according to the rainfall, which often varies in different parts of the same táluka. The old system of taking rent in kind would be the only effectual way to avoid the evil the Committee speak of, if it really be an evil, and this reversal of the policy of the past the Government are not prepared to recommend, although they can well conceive that the sowkárs' power of oppression might thus be materially reduced.

or to alter the assessment according to the nature of the season.

11. The Commissioners suggest an improvement in the rules under the Land Improvement Act. His Excellency in Council, however, could not assent to altering them in the sense of making loans easily available to ryots for purposes other than improvements; on the contrary, he concurs in the opinion, which the Commission have expressed in another place, that the State should, in this Presidency at least, make no attempt to take the place of the village banker. In times of great distress, to aid in the reclamation of a deserted village or for other special reasons, "takávi" is granted, and this His Excellency in Council

Improved rules under Land Improvement Act.

Government cannot lend money in place of the sowkár.

considers all that is at present required. The question as to the best mode of bringing loans for agricultural improvements still more within the reach of the ryots than at present is now under consideration, and the result of His Excellency's inquiries will be duly communicated to the Government of India. It may be observed, however, that as long as the population consists of small land-holders, most of whom are steeped in debt, there is little probability of the advantages of the Act being utilized much more than at present.

12. For the reasons stated, then, His Excellency in Council is not prepared to alter the revenue system of the country. He believes that it has had no appreciable effect on the ryots' fortunes, and that any change would be very much for the worse. Yet it is perfectly plain that the state of the ryots is in a most unsatisfactory condition. A perusal of the Report will show that for a long time past the indebtedness of the Deccan ryots has formed the theme of remonstrances against the law on the part of various eminent officers, such as the late Lord Elphinstone and Sir George Wingate; and, as has been said in paragraph 4, it is evident that, had it not been for the period of exceptional prosperity which ended with 1870, the present deplorable state of things would have come long ago. It is true that the boon of light and equitable rates of assessment and the conferring of a proprietary title on all holders of land—a title the value of which has only been appreciated in the last twenty years—gave a great impetus to cultivation, and placed the ryot in a far better position than ever he was before. But he commenced with a load of ancestral debt. The valuable property which was given him at the survey has been or is being squandered, and he is now worse off than on any one of the various occasions during the last forty years, when the matter of his indebtedness had been represented to Government. Formerly when he had no title in the soil he practically was not ejected for debt. But now this is possible under the present law. And although the money-lender who sells him up, usually allows him to remain on what was once his land, as a wretched rack-rented tenant, still he has lost the magic of property and is little better than a serf. The money-lender who obtains the ownership of the land is usually a stranger, a hard and unsympathetic landlord, grasping all he can secure for himself, and expending no capital whatever on the land. Even though only a small portion of the land has actually undergone formal transfer to the money-lenders, still there is evidence to show that some sowkárs have increased their holdings largely of late years; and from inquiries made in certain villages selected for the purpose, it appears that about one-third of the ryots are hopelessly involved, and lie practic-

ally at the mercy of the sowkárs. The Registration and Civil Court returns, too, show that the mortgaging and sale of fields has increased much of late years—that ruin is proceeding apace, which, if not arrested, will soon overtake the great body of the ryots. It cannot but be a matter of the greatest regret that this should be the end of all that Government have done for the ryots; and undoubtedly, if the law unduly conduces to this sad state of things, the law requires alteration.

13. For the purpose of considering what changes in the law are required, it will be convenient to enumerate the circumstances which attend an ordinary ryot's downfall from the commencement, and to see in what respects his position can be improved at the various stages of difficulty which impede his career. These stages may be divided into the following:—

I.—Difficulties of the ryot before he is taken into Court.
II.—While he is in Court.
III.—After a decree has been passed against him.

ALLEGED DISADVANTAGES OF THE RYOT.

I.—Difficulties of the ryot before he is taken into Court.

To begin with, the ryot is poor. This is an evil which no Government can cure, and all they can do is to make sure that his poverty is not enhanced by oppressive taxation. This is already done.

Poverty.

2. The ryot is ignorant. The remedy for this is to be found in the gradual extension of education. The utmost that lies in the power of Government in the meantime is to see that his ignorance is not made a vehicle for fraud on the part of others, and that, as far as circumstances admit, it is not allowed to work to his disadvantage when he is brought into Court.

Ignorance.

3. The ryot is said to be extravagant. This accusation the Commission show is to a great extent unfounded. Undoubtedly amongst the mass of the ryots, as amongst any other community, actual imprudence and extravagance are to be frequently observed, and the liability for the ultimate repayment of what they borrow has little weight with them. Expenditure, too, which was justifiable during the high profits of the American War, has, perhaps, not been reduced as times grew harder. Government, however, can by no direct action put a stop to extravagance. Expenditure on marriage festivals, for instance, is necessitated by the ryots' own social laws, and is by no means all money thrown away. Nor, on the other hand, is such expenditure so excessive that active measures, such as have been

Extravagance.

taken in regard to the Rajputs, who murder their daughters, could be adopted to reduce it.

4. The ryot is burdened with ancestral debt. Government can do nothing to relieve this, and they concur with the Commission in thinking that they should not be too ready to encourage him to disregard the religious duty, which Hindus cheerfully accept, of paying their fathers' debts, and which is one of the best traits in their character. Only when he is so desperately involved as to be beyond hope of extrication, he should be given the benefit of an insolvent law. (*Vide infra*, clause 19.)

Ancestral debt.

5. The ryots' bonds usually run at usurious interest, or what would be usurious interest in England. Here, again, Government are helpless. They are satisfied that no usury law would be of the slightest use, and that the grant of discretionary powers to Courts to reduce the rate of interest (which, as the Commission observe, is only another form of usury law) would be useless. Cases undoubtedly are of very frequent occurrence amongst the more unintelligent classes of Kunbis, Bhils, and aboriginal tribes, where the excessive amount of interest exacted really amounts to fraud and oppression. The High Court of Bombay, however, has decided that "inadequacy of consideration" when found in conjunction with any "other such circumstances as suppres-"sion of true value of property, misrepresentation, fraud, surprise, "oppression, urgent necessity for money, weakness of understand-"ing, or even ignorance, is an ingredient which weighs powerfully "with a Court of equity in considering whether it should set "aside contracts, or refuse to decree specific performance of "them." The High Court has pointed out to the Government that the wide scope of this ruling is binding on all ordinary Courts. If, then, the High Court and District Courts will see, as doubtless they will take care to do, that this ruling is acted up to, it would be useless to ask for anything more.

Usurious interest.

High Court's decision as to inequitable contracts.

6. At every stage of his money-dealing the ryot is defrauded by the sowkárs, and especially by the low class of sowkárs which has sprung up in the last generation. It may be taken as proved that the latter often declines to give accounts, refuses receipts, omits to give credit for payments or interest on payments, and declines to carry out his own stipulations in the bond.* Actual forgery, more-

Fraud on the part of money-lenders.

---

* At the end of Mr. Shambhuprasád's minute (page 82) an abstract of 29 original ryots' accounts, extracted from sowkárs' books, is given—some of the accounts having run for a very long series of years. The result is that out of Rs. 10,365 advanced, on which interest amounted to Rs. 8,561, only Rs. 9,759 in all were repaid. This points clearly to falsifying of accounts, as the sowkárs could not carry on business like this at a heavy loss.

over, is sometimes resorted to, and the ryot from ignorance is unable to prevent his creditor from taking advantage of these nefarious practices. To remedy this the Commission propose a system, of which the following are the main features :—

<small>Commission's proposals to prevent fraud approved.</small>

I.—All bonds shall be executed by notaries public, who will record whether consideration was passed or not in their presence.

II.—The ryot shall be entitled to receive a statement of his account at every year.

III.—Receipts to be given for every payment under bonds and payments to be endorsed on the bond.

IV.—Ryots to be given pass-books.

His Excellency in Council considers that these proposals are well considered, and should be adopted. Not only will frauds be prevented, but the ryot's pecuniary condition will be forcibly brought under his own eyes from time to time. This of itself, it may be hoped, will tend to make him more prudent than he is at present.

It is to be noted that the present state of the law is having its natural result on the ryot also, who is rapidly becoming demoralized, and given to tender false pleas and deny genuine obligations, and the measures proposed will have a good effect on him as well as on his creditor. The hereditary village writers will naturally be the notaries public, and will have the people's confidence. If notaries be appointed in sufficient numbers, there is no reason to fear that the system will not work well. The only objection is that it may make it more difficult for the ryots to raise money; but this will only be at first, and ought not, in the opinion of Government, to stand in the way of the scheme. Government propose, therefore, that a Bill be introduced to carry out the Commissioners' proposals at an early date.

7. Another way in which the ryot suffers is by the reduction, under the Act of 1859, of the time during which money bonds are current to the small period of three years. The Commissioners have carefully considered this question, and have come to the conclusion that, in the case of bonds entered into before a notary, the period of limitation should be six years. Mr. Shambhuprasád, indeed, thinks that the old period of twelve years should be reverted to. There is a vast consensus of opinion that the new law has affected the relations of creditor and debtor in the following way, viz., that whereas formerly an account was allowed to run on for twelve years on simple interest, now-a-days

<small>Hardship caused by the Limitation Act.</small>

a new bond must be entered into every three years, and the interest being added up and a new account struck, the amount of compound interest is swelled eventually to a very large sum.* In addition to the compound interest, however, the creditor usually, it appears, takes the opportunity of renewing a bond to extort fresh and burdensome stipulations under threats of suing his debtor in Court, all of which add to the total of the debt. His Excellency in Council concurs in think-

Alteration to six years proposed.

ing that, advisable in theory though it be that accounts should be struck and debtors forced to come to terms in a reasonably short time, still in a country where the majority of borrowers depend on a rather precarious rainfall, and where it has been the ancient custom to allow accounts to run on for an indefinite period, the time had not arrived in 1859, nor has it arrived at present, for restricting the period of limitation to three years. He concurs with Mr. Shambhuprasád that the twelve years' period should be reverted to, and he earnestly trusts, therefore, that His Excellency the Governor-General in Council will be pleased to make the necessary alteration in the law as soon as possible.

II.—*Difficulties while the ryot is in Court.*

8. When the ryot is sued in Court he is, it has often been alleged, met with fraud at the outset, in

Fraudulent non-service of summons.

that the service of a summons upon him is wilfully withheld by collusion between the creditor and the subordinates of the Court; and the Court being told that the summons has been served, gives a decree against him *ex parte*. There seems, from the evidence recorded by the Commission, much reason to believe that this is frequently the case;

Ex parte decrees.

and the enormous proportion of *ex parte* decrees passed in the Bombay Presidency when compared with other provinces, lends colour to the statement. There is no doubt, as the Commission state, that in the majority of cases the reason for the defendant's non-appearance is that he has no defence to make, or that he has no money to pay for a pleader, or that he is unwilling to lose the time involved in defending a suit, or that he is afraid of the subsequent vengeance of the creditor whom he has opposed. Still, although the Commission are of opinion that the provisions of the original Code of Civil Procedure as to the service of notices is sufficient, His Excellency in Council is satisfied that, even if there is not so much fraud of the kind as has been alleged, there is much room for it.

---

* *Vide* the accounts at page 84 of Mr. Shambhuprasád's minute. In one case an advance of Rs. 10 cash was made in 1863. Sums, amounting to Rs. 110, were paid from time to time, but at the end of ten years Rs. 220 were still due.

He is therefore very glad that the law, as recently altered, requires the Court to examine the serving officer on oath before substituted service is allowed.

9. The Commissioners are of opinion, on the whole, that sufficient chance is not at present given to a defendant to say his say: (i) because the Courts at present are far away; (ii) because the defence of a suit takes longer time than the defendant can spare; and (iii) because the Judge cannot now, should the defendant be unrepresented by a pleader, go into the rights of his case and make up to him the want of counsel as he could do if he had more time.

<small>Distance of Courts.</small>
<small>Length of time occupied in trying contested suits.</small>
<small>Inability of Judge to render ryot assistance.</small>

The Commissioners, therefore, recommend—

<small>Circuit Courts recommended, and appointment of more Subordinate Judges.</small>

(I.) That Courts should go on circuit.

(II.) That more Subordinate Judges should be appointed.

The proposal that Courts should go on circuit is, in the opinion of His Excellency in Council, one that should be carefully considered.

As regards the increase in the number of Judges, which the Commissioners have suggested, the measure is supported by numerous complaints: firstly, that the Subordinate Judges have now more work than they can compass, and could not try more disputed cases than now if they had them; and, secondly, that the income from Court fees is much larger than the expenditure on the Courts. Theoretically it no doubt is the case that the administration of justice should not be used as a source of revenue, and His Excellency in Council would be glad to learn that the Government of India are prepared to receive proposals for increasing the number of Subordinate Judges. But he is aware that from a financial point of view the scheme simply amounts to increased expenditure from the general exchequer, and it would be useless submitting the detailed requirements of the country unless the Financial Department were prepared to view them favourably.

<small>Financial aspect of proposal.</small>

His Excellency in Council would, however, remark that, next to peace and security of property, the good administration of justice is the principal benefit which the British are wont to boast of having introduced into India, and that, next to the Military and Executive Establishments, the Judicial Department is the last in which inefficiency should be allowed. He would point out that, over-

<small>Urgent necessity for more Judges.</small>

worked as the Subordinate Judges are now, they will, if their numbers be not increased, be unable to cope satisfactorily with the additional work which the new Civil Procedure Code will entail on them, and to a great extent the improved provisions which the Legislature has enacted will be inoperative.

Untrained and technical Subordinate Judges.

10. Complaints have also been made that the Subordinate Judges are untrained and technical, and unable to administer equity. The Commissioners do not say directly whether this is the case or not, but they are of opinion that, to administer the law properly, better men should be employed than can be obtained for Rs. 200 a month. His Excellency in Council, however, considers that the complaints as to the qualifications of the Subordinate Judges are unfounded, and that their pay, which ranges from Rs. 200 to Rs. 800 (Small Cause Court Judges drawing Rs. 1,000), and which was raised only recently, is sufficient. The proceedings of the Subordinate Judge are subject to the revision of the District Judge and the High Court, and this Government are not prepared to recommend more expensive establishments.

High cost of suits.

11. The high costs of suits are mentioned as another reason why the defendants decline to contest their cases; and the Commissioners add that there appears reason to think that some of the miscellaneous Court charges, fees for copying, attachments, processes, and the like, are unduly burdensome. The High Court will be moved to make an inquiry into this allegation, and favour Government with their opinion. No doubt there are many expenses, besides Court fees, which raise the cost of litigation, such as batta to witnesses and the like; but cheapened as justice undoubtedly ought to be, the finances of India could not possibly undertake the burden of items like these.

III.—*Difficulties of the ryot after a decree has been passed against him.*

Difficulties of the ryot after a decree has been passed against him.

12. The ryot's principal trouble begins when the money-lender has obtained his decree. For then the first and most objectionable measures of pressure may be put on him. He may be arrested and imprisoned.

Imprisonment for debt;

its abolition strongly recommended.

The Commissioners very strongly urge the total abolition of imprisonment for debt; but His Excellency is not prepared to commit himself to this very positive expression of opinion, as he considers it will be a very strong measure to deprive creditors of this security in respect to debts already contracted. There can, however, be no doubt that advantage is frequently taken of civil imprisonment to impose upon prisoners more severe terms than could otherwise be obtained, and the system in this country is peculiarly open to abuse. The Honourable Mr. Rogers is, however, in favour of the Commissioners' proposal, and he wishes that the minute which he wrote on the 29th May 1876 may be forwarded to the Government of India with this letter. A copy thereof accordingly is herewith sent.

13. The next hardship the agricultural debtor suffers is that all moveable property, of whatever kind or description it may be, can be sold without any reserve. The Government are very glad to find that the Legislative Council have forestalled the recommendations of the Commissioners in this respect, and that the houses of agriculturists, their necessary wearing apparel, implements of husbandry, &c., are to be exempt from sale in future.

Sale of all kinds of moveable property.

14. The next question to be approached is, perhaps, the most important of all, and the one that requires the most delicate handling, viz., the power of the Courts to sell land for money debts, the mode in which this power is exercised, and the effect it has on the rural community. And other cognate questions, such as the propriety of allowing ryots to be deprived of their land at all for debt, can be conveniently considered here. The position of affairs in this Presidency at present is as follows :—Government have converted the revenue-paying land into a transferable and heritable property. Some of those who lament to see the land passing rapidly from the kunbi to the sowkár, doubt, as Mr. Pedder puts it, whether Government have been right in making it as saleable as a bullock or a turban, and would apparently wish to recall the gift that has been made. This view, His Excellency in Council may at once state, he could not possibly accede to; it would be an act of confiscation, not justified even by the present state of affairs. Others, who do not go this length, would check or forbid the sales of land by the Courts for debt, but would allow the creditor to appropriate all the profits of the land. To this His Excellency may say that he does not see his way to making a man's land not liable for debts which have been fairly contracted (most of them, either actually or impliedly, on the very security of the land), and are proved to be justly due. If the proprietary right is allowed to continue, as it must, free and unrestricted dealing in land must be allowed too. Where, for instance, owing to the lightness of the assessment, the demand for

Sale of land by the Civil Courts.

Exemption of land from sale for debt not recommended.

produce, and other causes, the land acquires a saleable value which it had not before, the owner also acquires a power to raise money upon it. If he be resolved on thus raising money, Government are quite powerless to prevent him. They may, it is true, place artificial obstacles in his way, but these must all in the end be evaded; and as the only effect of them will be to raise the interest on the money borrowed, |it would be a shortsighted policy and against the interests of the ryot to create them; for if the ryot wants money, he cares not at what rate of interest he borrows. So, too, the proprietary right being given, Government are unable to prevent the ryot selling or leasing his property to whom he will; and any laws which would not directly convert the land into untransferable instead of transferable property would, as the Commission remark, also be evaded. It may, therefore, His Excellency in Council assumes, be held both impracticable and undesirable to interfere with a ryot's full power to mortgage his land or to alienate it privately, and if he can do this, His Excellency in Council can see no valid reason for preventing a Court also treating the land as liable for debt. The Commission's Report shows that, whether mortgaged land is left standing in the debtor's name by the Marwari, as is usually the case, or whether the latter obtains a decree and buys the land in at a trifle, he does not take the owner away from the field—the sting of total divorce from the soil is not added to the debtor's misery. It is not stated clearly whether, should a person other than the creditor buy the field, the new owner similarly permits the old one to remain as a tenant, but there is every reason for thinking he does. Under these circumstances there is not much real difference between the sufferings of a ryot whose field has been sold and one whose mortgages have not been foreclosed.

Mode of conducting sales should be improved. Government ought, however, to provide that when land is sold the sale shall be carried out in the manner best calculated to yield a good price; and, if the law is to take its ordinary course, this is about all they can do.

Reasons why Government should assist ryots whose fields are liable to sale. There are, at the same time, various reasons why the Government should, if they can do so, without violating the conditions of the property or deprecating its value, endeavour to assist ignorant and indebted ryots in recovering their solvency and to save them from the rigour of the law. It is a great economic evil that much of the soil should be cultivated by disheartened tenants who were formerly owners. The land produces less, and the wealth of the country is diminished; while the

n 862—3

new owners, as a body, decline laying out capital on the fields they purchase. The Commission point out how in one special degree the ryot's indebtedness affects the well-being of the country at large, viz., that they will not take water from irrigation canals, even when constructed by Government, as the labour involved in rearing irrigation crops is much greater than in raising ordinary dry crops, and the profit all goes to the Marwari landlord or mortgagee. Besides, it would be a pity to lose any effort for converting the ryots into a happy, independent community of small proprietors, or for securing to them the benefit of the boons Government intended for them. Another consideration is that crime increases in a country where the rural population is discontented and rack-rented; and, to say nothing of the political danger involved, the difficulties of administering such a province are much enhanced. For these reasons Government might, in the opinion of His Excellency in Council, provide, when the sale of land is decreed by a Court,

That should the profits of the land be found sufficient, if properly managed, to defray the debts in a reasonable time without divesting the owner of all proprietary right in it, the sale should be postponed, the amount of the debt should be raised or advanced by Government, and the land managed by an agency appointed for the purpose, till the debt should be gradually paid off.

14. It was the intention of His Excellency in Council to consider the proposals of the Select Committee on the Civil Procedure Code, and examine how far they provided for the measures above indicated. It appears, however, that the Code has actually been passed now, though a copy has not yet reached this Government. Under these circumstances, as His Excellency will very shortly leave India, and is anxious that his views should be placed before the Government of India, he has determined to forward this communication without any further delay. He is conscious of the extreme difficulty of the questions that present themselves in connection with the liability of land for debt, and the importance of striving by all the means in his power to benefit the rural population. But he is strongly of opinion that, as far as possible, nothing should be done tending to interfere in the trade of money, to lessen the value of land, or to exempt a man from the consequences of a legitimate contract. All that can be done is to prevent fraud, facilitate the course of justice among the ignorant and poor, and render such State assistance to the debtors as is consistent with absolute justice to the creditors. He trusts that these boons may in course of time be secured to all Her Majesty's Indian

subjects; and that the Civil Procedure Code just passed may be found to be of use in securing some of these benefits.

15. In conclusion, His Excellency in Council is sure that the Government of India will concur with him in thinking the Commission deserving of high credit for the way they have carried out their laborious task, and that Her Majesty's service has experienced a severe loss in the premature deaths of Mr. Carpenter and Mr. Lyon.

(Signed) I have the honour to be, &c.,

E. W. RAVENSCROFT,

Chief Secretary to Government.

Minute by the Honourable A. Rogers, dated 29th May 1876, referred to in para. 12 of the above letter.

It would be a work of supererogation to attempt to follow the Committee in the elaborate inquiries they have made into the condition of the Deccan ryot, and the various causes that have led to the late unfortunate outbreaks of violence which have resulted in the appointment of the Committee. Their general conclusions, and the remedies they would suggest, are contained in Chapter VII. of their report, and to these I will confine my remarks, taking the former in the order in which they stand printed.

Para. 122.

Under the head of "Poverty" it is admitted that the only possible means of mitigating this cause of the indebtedness of the Deccan ryots lies in the improvement of the conditions of agriculture by irrigation, and that the incubus of debt requires to be removed before they can be expected to avail themselves largely of such means. A suggestion, however, is thrown out, that the rules for carrying into effect the provisions of the Land Improvement Act might be modified in such a manner as to make it more easy for a ryot to obtain the advances authorised under that Act than under the present rules. These rules, however, have already been made as simple as they can possibly be, consistently with security for recovery of advances made. For all such small sums as a ryot can ordinarily require for the petty works of improvement he can undertake, he can always apply to the Assistant Collector in charge of his own táluka, and can obtain them without any more elaborate formality than is absolutely necessary to provide for re-payment. It is an undoubted fact, one already brought to notice in the Collectors' Annual Administration Reports, that the people do not avail themselves of these facilities; but the causes are not to be found in the absence of facilities. They probably lie in the fact that in most cases the people dare not forsake their old creditors, and that the latter discourage the contraction of loans which would in any way interfere with the realization of their own debts. It would, of course, not be practicable to make advances without security, and short of this I see no attraction that will lead the ryot to prefer public to private loans.

Para. 123. Passing over the heading of "Ignorance," the only remedy for which is, of course, education, but to counteract which to a certain extent other remedies, which will be adverted to presently, are proposed, we come to the pressure of population on the soil.

Para. 124. This, the Committee remark, can only be met by increasing the production of the soil or by emigration. Provision by the State of means of irrigation by canals will here and there mitigate the evil; but the palliative can only be partial, inasmuch as the construction of canals in most parts of the Deccan is a physical impossibility, and temporary, inasmuch as the increase of population will not cease (until at all events a Malthus revolutionizes the social customs of the country), and its pressure will soon overtake any increased production that irrigation may bring about. Emigration remains, and to this, in a modified form necessity has already driven the superabundant population of the Ratnágiri District, which supplies a large proportion of the recruits for our Native Army, as well as for the fortunately accessible labour market of Bombay. Localities suitable for agricultural emigrants are, however, in this Presidency but few, and may be summed up in the Panch Máháls in Gujarát (which I have no doubt will within the next 50 years be occupied by the superabundant population of the neighbouring districts), Khándesh, and to some extent North Kánara. But as yet the pressure in the Deccan has not reached the point at which emigration will be resorted to as a relief. The people are still, though in a very small way, peasant-proprietors, and it will not be till a large proportion of them sink from this to the position of day-labourers, and find it difficult to gain their bread even in that position, that they will think of emigrating. If any relief is to be afforded, then, it must be by much more immediate measures.

Para. 125. Under the head "Rigid Revenue System" a vague suggestion is put forward that there may be discovered some method of adjusting the Government demand to the ryots' capacity in a country of uncertain rainfall, which may not be open to the objection of uncertainty. Now, everything but a rent fixed in cash must be an uncertain demand, and even this must exercise an uncertain pressure upon the resources of the ryot, as it must in different years with varying prices of agricultural produce represent a larger or smaller proportion of the actual produce of the land. Setting on one side as obsolete and impracticable the system of the levy of an actual grain rent, the fixing of such a rent commutable into money, if practicable (which when the varieties of agricultural produce are taken into consideration it is not), would introduce a still greater element of uncertainty into the ryots' annual prospects. In a good year prices would probably be low, and the incidence of the rent would be lighter than in a bad year, in which prices would be high, and the commuted grain-rent would accordingly represent a larger amount of money. The result would be the very opposite of advantageous to the ryot himself, and the State would be benefited in a good year less in proportion than in a bad one. There would remain the system of a sliding scale of rent in cash or grain, commutable into money, varying according to season and the prices of produce, which it needs no demonstration to show would be more uncertain and more impracticable than either of the preceding, and would tend fatally to the discouragement of investment of labour and capital in the improvement of the soil.

It is difficult to understand what the Committee really mean by their suggestion. The statement of remissions under the ryotwari system in the Madras Presidency, given at page 289 of Appendix C., gives no clue to the principles on which remissions are granted; but it appears to have been ascertained that the rate depends on examination by local officers of a sufficient number of fields. This is objected to, and the fact that landlords in the North-West Provinces give remissions is then adverted to as an argument in favour of elasticity of demand. All this amounts to no more than that the demands of Government, for rent should not be exacted to the uttermost rupee, but that remissions should be given where found necessary without too minute inquiry into individual cases. That in this respect we have nothing to learn from the Committee, as this is precisely what is done, can be shown by reference to the remissions given in the current year in these very drought-stricken districts of Bhimthari, Indápur, &c.

There is a practical suggestion in para. 126, that where on revisions of assessment the Government demand is enhanced more than 25 per cent, the increase should be imposed gradually, according to the practice of the North-West Provinces. Now, this system is not now advocated for the first time, and has been after due consideration rejected in this Presidency. The probability is that in the North-West Provinces it is found advisable to adopt it in order to give time to Zemindárs or the representatives of village communities under various names to meet an increase in the demands of the State, by bringing more land into cultivation. This ground, however, does not apply in the case of individual ryots, who have no more land to bring under the plough. What their means are now for meeting increased demands they will be five or ten years hence, and the prospect of such increase must have the effect of unduly diminishing the value of land as a security in the future as well as at the period of first enhancement. If the full enhancement is made at once, the ryot at all events has learnt the worst, and can make his arrangements accordingly. If he wishes to raise money to improve his property, he can do so without hesitation, for he knows the entire profits will be his own. If he knows that five or ten years hence, and again in a certain number of years more, his rent will be increased, with what confidence will he set to work to improve his fields? Moreover, however theoretically correct a gradual enhancement may be, and however practicable in the case of large payments for villages or estates of considerable area, the system becomes unworkable when applied to the case of ryots with small holdings under our revenue survey system. Many men have holdings of only a few rupees in value, and these probably composed of small scraps of land here and there, forming only portions of survey numbers: to these of course the proposed system of gradual enhancement of rent would be quite inapplicable. Even in the case of men with larger holdings such a system is unnecessary, because the survey rules do not bind a man to maintain his holding entire: he can throw up any portion separately assessed in the village books, and need only keep and pay for as much as he may find it convenient to retain, so that in reality it depends a good deal on himself whether the enhanced assessment presses heavily on his means or not. Applying the proposal to the cases of the particular tálukas to which the Committee's report chiefly relates, there would be a great want of equity in carrying it out, even where it was practicable. The increase has arisen from various causes, *e.g.*, a general rise in the value of agricultural produce and in that of land in consequence of new markets and improved means of communication, relative under-valuation of land at the first survey settlements, cultivation of land wrongly entered at the time of those settlements as unarable, and actual encroachment on land not belonging to the holdings at all. Gradual enhancement could only be equitably carried out in the case of payments increased under the first of these causes only, and yet in the majority of holdings the increases would be found traceable to several of the causes combined. If the cases in which increase was due to the first cause were eliminated, the rest would be found to be very few in number, and the increases to be trifling. In a statement of increases in the 33 Pandharpur villages lately settled, sent up by the Survey Commissioner, the number of cases in which the combined causes of general increase of rates and the substitution of relative fair for former under-valuation of lands had led to enhancement were infinitesimal, and the enhancements in no case exceeded from 5 to 10 rupees on the holdings.

On the whole, then, I am opposed to the Committee's proposal for gradual enhancement of rents where the increase exceeds 25 per cent.

The more generally applicable remedies proposed by the Committee commence from para. 127, but before going into the questions of reform of the law contained in their Bills for the prevention of frauds and to limit the excessive powers given to decree holders, it will be advisable to follow the Committee in their proposals for reform in the conduct of judicial business. After showing that in the districts of Ahmednagar and Poona the suits for debt in the Subordinate Judges' Courts are in the proportion of about 93½ to all others, they show further that of the former about 91½ are for debts under Rs. 200 in amount, and consequently only about two per cent. involve sums above that amount.

Paras. 128 to 180. From these facts they urge the grant of Small Cause Court jurisdiction generally to all Subordinate Judges' Courts, and that these Courts should sit in different villages, in regular order, in such a manner as to render it generally unnecessary for litigants and their witnesses in such petty debt suits to be absent from their homes for longer than from morning to evening of a single day. The suggestion is, in my opinion, an excellent one; but it requires to be gone into in detail far more than I can in the course of this Minute, to determine whether the expense of carrying it out would be covered by the fees paid and stamps used in the litigation. I quite agree with the Committee that the Patels of villages should be made officers of the Civil Courts, to be present and to attest the execution of processes, &c., if not to execute them themselves. It will be remembered that a short time ago this principle was affirmed in our own Legislative Council by its being laid down that the village officers should be charged with the execution of processes under the revised Act for Mámlatdárs' jurisdiction in summary possession cases.

They also hope that the Subordinate Judges will be able, when their Courts become itinerant, to do without pleaders in a great measure, and get people to plead their own causes. I believe, however, the law with regard to the employment of pleaders would have to be a good deal relaxed to admit of this, and feel certain that in order to give the Subordinate Judges themselves the necessary time to sift cases thoroughly and endeavour to do real justice, the present high pressure system of judging their merits more by the quantity than the quality of their work, which leads them not to look with disfavour on *ex parte* suits, must be abandoned. A very striking commentary on the disfavour with which the method of procedure of the Civil Courts is looked upon in the Deccan is afforded by the fact of the private Courts of Arbitration that have lately been established in the Poona and Sholápur Districts, and which it is reported in the Native Press are largely resorted to by even Marwaris. I hope to see this movement spread, and to find arbitration more generally resorted to than it is at present. It would have been more convenient if, in discussing their proposed measures of relief, the Committee had first taken their proposals for the protection of the illiterate borrower against the preliminary wiles of the unscrupulous money-lender. I therefore pass at once to the draft Bill for the prevention of frauds.

To the proposals of the Committee for the appointment of Public Notaries, and generally as to the functions of these officers, I cordially agree. The difference in intelligence and education between the lender and the borrower in this country renders such a step not only necessary in the interests of the latter, but also one of great political importance. The Bill, which is merely a rough draft, will, of course, require considerable amplification; but all its provisions, especially those relating to the granting of receipts and copies of accounts, are desirable.

I observe that in para. 137 allusion is made to proposals submitted by a member of the Committee for dealing immediately with debt existing in the disturbed districts. These were, I presume, the scheme originated by Mr. Richey, under which Government were to advance money to clear off the ryots' debts by compromises with their creditors, and gradually recoup themselves from the produce of the lands, which were to be held as security for the repayment of the advances. I have already minuted very strongly against the adoption of any such proposals, and as I have heard nothing of them for a long time, I trust they have been finally shelved as impracticable, if not highly impolitic. In the course of my remarks on Mr. Richey's scheme, I suggested that what would at once restore confidence in the lately disturbed, but now perfectly quiet, districts would be a return to the old law of limitation, under which bond debts ran for twelve, instead of for three years, as under the present law. It would be equally effectual in preventing the recourse of creditors to the powers they possess under the existing laws against their debtors, which, the Committee fear, may be the effect of the discussion of the measures they have proposed : and I would strongly urge its adoption.

In most districts of this Presidency the provision of public notaries in sufficient numbers throughout the country could be effected without any great expense by the employment in that capacity of the village accountants, hereditary or stipendiary, already entertained. These men, as a rule, are intimately acquainted with the circumstances of the ryots in their respective charges, and as their employment would make the contraction of loans matters of public notoriety, additional security would be afforded to the ryot that all was fair and above board, and public opinion would be brought to bear on the petty money-lender in his original as well as his subsequent transactions with his debtor, so that there would be every probability of the system of extortion exercised by the more unprincipled among the former class described by the Committee being checked.

The main object of the draft Bill to amend the law relating to the execution of decrees is described to be the very reasonably one of reducing the creditor's power over his debtor to what may be sufficient for the protection of legitimate trading. It is a difficult matter to say what the particular limit of power shall be, but I consider that the Committee have fairly hit it off.

There can be little doubt of the abuse of the power of imprisonment for debt, in its being availed of, not for the original purpose meant under Act VIII. of 1859, which was to force a full disclosure of the debtor's property, but to hold a decree *in terrorem* over him for the purpose of further extortion. This appears abundantly proved by the fact of so few debtors being actually imprisoned, for whose apprehension warrants are issued. The object the power of imprisonment was meant to serve is to be effected by giving a creditor power to force his debtor to declare the whole of his property on pain of imprisonment for refusal, or for giving a false account of, or concealing or fraudulently making away with it.

The proposal to exempt necessaries from sale in execution of decrees is simply a return to the law as it existed before Act VIII. of 1859 was enacted, and I think I am not wrong in attributing the greater portion of the evils it is now proposed to take steps to remedy the enforced departure of the courts from the salutary old custom. A return to it is, in my opinion, as necessary in the interest of the creditor, as of the debtor, for it will prevent the former from, as he does now, killing his goose with the golden eggs. I heartily agree with this proposal.

With regard to the third proposal, that immoveable property should be sold only by order of the District Court and after inquiry, I see no reason why the power shall not be extended to the Subordinate Judges' Courts. I would, however, oblige the actual sale of the occupancy right in all land paying revenue to the State to be held after due notice before the Revenue authorities under the Collectors' instructions, and give power to the Collector to substitute for such sale a temporary attachment and management by himself in all cases offering a fair prospect of the liquidation of the debt by such means, say, within ten years.

I agree in the principle of the proposal to make a decree for debt obtained the *finis litis*. The possession of a decree is now, no doubt, a most potent means of extortion on the part of unscrupulous usurers, and to the abuse of the power thus obtained is due much of the mischief the committee have had to report upon.

Whether the object will, however, be gained by the simple proposal in Section 7 of the draft Bill, viz., that any agreement made by way of adjustment of a decree shall be carried into effect by the Court executing the decree, and not by a separate suit, appears to me very doubtful. There are so many causes that would tend to render nugatory the provision of Section 8, that any agreement extorted by the use of the Court's process in execution of a decree, or by a threat of such use, shall be void, that I suspect much more elaborate provision than this would have to be made, and that any provision that could be made would be liable to be evaded. The necessity of the debtor, and the willingness of the creditor would be the mothers of very complicated inventions in in such cases. I concur in the Committee's proposal that no application for the execution of a decree should be received after the expiration of six years from its date, or, where the debt decreed for is to be paid in instalments, from the date of the instalment of which payment is sought to be enforced, only as a compromise between the present limit of three, and the old limit of twelve years, the latter of which I am strongly in favour of for all transactions, whether of simply contracted or decreed debt. The short periods of limitation prescribed by the existing law were laid down with the philanthropic purpose of forcing men to look betimes to their position, and not allow themselves to drift out of their depth in debt, but that purpose has not been obtained, and never will be, as long as the people and their normal condition are what they are. Lifelong poverty and the continued struggle of existence, with the stolid apathy engendered by such a state of things, are inconsistent in their nature with any attempt at teaching the people forethought or care in such matters by legislation, and the sooner the attempt is abandoned the better, in my opinion. On the other hand, when a village-usurer lends money, he does not do it with the banker's idea of getting it back in order to turn it over again constantly, but by way of permanent investment on which he may live. Where his cupidity, therefore, has not been worked upon by the chance he sees the law has thrown open to him of indefinitely increasing his nominal capital by the constant renewal of bonds, short period of limitation is no object to him.

There is another forcible reason why the old limitation law should be restored, at all events in the districts to which the inquiries of the Committee have chiefly extended. The feelings of the two classes, the borrowers and the lenders, have been very much embittered towards each other. The former are only held back from open violence against the latter by the fear of punishment, and the latter are restrained from enforcing their demands through the Courts, and carrying matters to the bitter end, by fear of that violence. This state of matters, discreditable as it is to our rule, should, if possible, be put a stop to, or a spark may suddenly kindle a flame that it will take much more stringent measures to extinguish than those found efficacious hitherto. It may take years of discussion before the measures proposed by the Committee can be carried into effect, and we are in the meanwhile letting things slide. The money-lenders, however, cannot afford to wait while the law of limitation remains what it is: they must execute their decrees if they would not loose their capital, and this is a loss no one can be expected to put up with. Let the old law of limitation be reverted to for the Deccan Collectorates, and both parties will gain time during which to come to an amicable settlement. Each party is dependent on the other, and the ordinary ryot can no more do without the village money-lender than the latter can do without his dealings with the ryot by which to earn his livelihood. Where such is the case and where the source of the livelihood of both is the precarious outturn of the soil in uncertain seasons, it is bad policy to carry out laws which sow dissension between parties whose interests are identical, by not allowing time for them to settle their transactions to their mutual satisfaction.

The first and foremost remedy for the existing state of matters should therefore, I am convinced, be a return to the old law of limitation, and then the measures proposed by the Committee, combined with such modification of the laws under which the Civil Courts work as to enable them to act more as Courts of equity than as Courts of strict law.

29th May 1876. (Signed) A. ROGERS.

EFFECT OF NEW CIVIL PROCEDURE CODE ON INDEBTED RYOTS OF THE DECCAN.

Minute by the Governor of Bombay, dated 15th October 1877.

The report by the Deccan Riots Commission of 1875 will be fresh in the recollection of my Honourable Colleagues. The Commission found in certain districts (Ahmednagar, Poona, Sholápur, and part of Sátára) certain grievances on the part of the cultivating and land-holding classes to exist in respect of their indebtedness, and proposed various remedial measures. Regarding these proposals, however, it was not deemed practicable at the time to adopt any special action. And although the relations between these classes and their creditors may have somewhat improved, while the thoughts of all have been absorbed by the famine which has supervened—the law, the rules, the system respecting the indebtedness of the peasants under the ryotwári system in the districts specified have remained without change. A hope was, however, expressed at the time by the Government of Bombay in paragraph 14 of their letter No. 2202 of 6th April last, to the Government of India, that the new Code of Civil Procedure might do something towards the mitigation or removal of these grievances.

On examining the Commission's Report with the attention its importance merits, and comparing it with the new Code of Civil Procedure, Act X. of 1877, which has come into force from the commencement of the current month, October, after consulting also many authorities, European and Native, I find that considerable improvement has been made in the position of the ryot of the Deccan. And I propose to draw the attention of the Revenue Commissioners, the Collectors, and their subordinates of these particular districts to this subject, in order that they may be prepared for acting up to the several provisions of the law enabling them to protect the ryot, and to explain to the ryots generally those portions of the law which affect them especially. The ryots are comparatively ignorant, and may be slow to understand the significance of the changes introduced into the law, which changes may affect them materially, and, as we trust, beneficially. And as the public weal so largely depends on the prosperity of this most deserving class, it is proper that the revenue officers should take fair and legitimate opportunities of explaining the law to the ryots.

I will touch in the order of sections on those provisions which concern the very important subject.

First of all, a very important change has been made by section 266 of the Code in the law as to the exemption of certain property from attachment or sale in execution of decrees. Tools, implements of husbandry, cattle in sufficient number, to enable a judgment-debtor to earn his livelihood as an agriculturist, and the materials of houses and other buildings belonging to and occupied by agriculturists, are now no longer liable to be seized in satisfaction of a decree. The revenue officers should be instructed to make this widely known among the ryots.

In the next place, section 326 empowers a Collector in any part of the Presidency to represent to the Court that the public sale of any land which has been attached in execution of a decree is objectionable, and that satisfaction of the decree may be made by a temporary alienation or management of the land, and thereupon the Court may authorize the Collector to provide for the satisfaction of the decree in the manner which he recommends. The Collectors should have their attention called to this provision, and be told that Government expect them to avail themselves of it, on every proper occasion when the judgment-debtor is a *bond fide* ryot, and they should be desired to issue orders, through the Mámlatdárs, to the village officers throughout their charges, requiring them to inform ryots, whose lands are at any time attached by a Civil Court, that if it is possible for the decree to be satisfied by any means short of the actual sale of their land, they should at once apply to the Collector to intervene on their behalf.

Then, section 320 enables this Government, with the sanction of the Governor General in Council, to declare that in any local area, the execution of decrees of any particular kind in which the sale of land is involved, shall be transferred to the Collector. Sections 321—325 then invest the Collector with powers to manage or to deal with the land, as if it were his own, and to adopt one or more of several modes of satisfying the decree without selling the land except in the last resort. Rules under this section will require to be carefully considered; but steps may be taken at once to prepare such rules with a view to their being made applicable to the districts of Ahmednagar, Poona, Sholápur, and Sátára. The class of decrees to which they should refer would be those in which, or in execution of which, the sale of the interest of any occupant or his tenant is ordered to be sold.

I propose that we immediately request the sanction of the Government of India to our applying this section 320 to these four districts, forwarding simultaneously a draft of the rules which we propose, as we believe that the provision will prove very beneficial to the ryots.

Then by section 336, the Local Government may direct that every judgment-debtor brought before a court in arrest in execution of a decree for money, shall be informed by the Court that he may apply to be declared an insolvent. Then Chapter XX., sections 344 to 360, prescribe the manner in which the insolvent shall be treated. And by section 358 special consideration is shown to the debtor, if the debt be less than two hundred rupees. As these sections do afford some protection to the ryot against harassment, I would propose that an order under section 336 as applicable to these four districts be issued.

Though far from admitting that the sections alluded to in this Minute, all taken together, effect all that could be desired, I think that they will conduce to what may be termed the just interest of the ryot in these affairs. Even though we may desire more and may eventually have to propose more, still we may meanwhile make the most of these sections. For by them, a ryot's necessaries will be protected from sale for debt, his land instead of being inconsiderately sold in execution of decree will be brought under judicious management by the revenue officers, and he will be protected from arrest if he declares himself to the Court as an insolvent.

(Signed) RICHARD TEMPLE.

SPECIAL LEGISLATION FOR INDEBTEDNESS OF RYOTS OF THE BOMBAY DECCAN.

Minute by the Governor of Bombay, dated 12th November 1877.

On various occasions since assuming the Government of Bombay, I have been obliged to examine the matter of the indebtedness of the ryots of the Bombay Deccan, and to confer with the best informed persons to be met with, both European and Native. This matter seems to me to demand our further consideration, and I will now offer, for the consideration of my Honourable Colleagues, a brief outline of the conclusions arrived at by me provisionally.

2. The report of the Commission which sat on this subject in 1875 will be in the recollection of my Honourable Colleagues. The only authoritative deliverance which has been made on this report (so far as I know) is the letter of the Bombay Government of April last, which said in effect that no particular measures could be recommended and that the evils shown to exist were mostly beyond the power of Government to cure.

3. From my own enquiries I see no reason to doubt the accuracy of the conclusions formed by the Commission as to the existing evils. But I think we may devise some means of mitigating, if not of curing, these evils.

4. The evils described by the Commission probably are existing in a somewhat milder form now than, say, two years ago, when the Commission sat. The famine has turned the thoughts both of creditors and debtors into other channels. The disturbances of 1874-75 opened the eyes of the creditors as to the danger of pushing things too far. It is thought that the money-lenders are under the impression that the authorities are adverse to extreme pressure being applied to the ryots. It appears that from one cause and another the money-lenders are, in some degree, refraining from worrying the ryots.

5. Still these evils, though not exacerbated just now, exist, and will sooner or later break out again.

6. Meanwhile the new Code of Civil Procedure, which came into effect from the beginning of last month, October, has in several respects improved the condition of the indebted ryots.

7. While the emendation of this Code was pending I was in Bengal, and, together with my advisers, took much trouble in pressing various amendments in the interests of the people of Bengal. These very improvements will now, I find, stand us in good stead respecting the ryots of the Deccan.

8. I append for facility of reference a copy of a Minute recently prepared on the above points.

9. My colleagues will perceive that by the new Code a ryot's necessaries will be protected from sale for debt, his land, instead of being inconsiderately sold in execution of decree, will be brought under judicious management by the revenue officers, and he will be protected from arrest on a decree if he declares himself to the Court as an insolvent. And if his total debt does not exceed Rs. 200 (two hundred), he may be absolved by the Court from all future liability. But these improvements, which are considerable, leave several of the roots of mischief untouched.

10. There is, as shown by the Commission, much in the condition of the ryots which exposes them to temptation to run into debt. They are liable always to more than ordinary vicissitudes of season, suffering from drought and losses for a year or two years consecutively, and then having a bumper season to make up for all. They have sometimes had abundant employment and high prices together with abundant produce, and then they have suffered from a cessation, indeed from a reversal of these good conditions.

11. They have at present a fatal facility for obtaining cash from money-lenders, while the money-lenders have an equally fatal

facility for making the principal of the debt mount up by compound interest and the like to something fabulous, and then for recovering the whole principal and interest by processes, which drive the debtor from house to home till in despair he resorts to violence. If indeed, two parties, debtor and creditor, are resolved to embark on such courses as these we cannot prevent them. But we ought, I think, to see that our laws do not tend to bring about this state of things. At present they do actually so tend. Indeed, it is probable that unless this were the case people would not be treading such dangerous paths.

12. After much consultation with well informed persons, it seems to me that three things are wanted in the districts to which the report of the Commission refers.

13. Firstly, I think that the Civil Courts should be obliged to examine the merits of the debt for which they are asked to pass a decree. At present, if a bond duly executed and attested is presented, the Court must pass a decree, and the ryots, seeing the hopelessness of contention, seldom appear in order to put in any defence, and allow the decrees to be passed against them *ex parte*. But the bond may be utterly unjust—indeed, generally is more or less unjust. A fraction of it only consists of principal, the rest is all made up of interest. The bond itself is by no means the original one, but has been renewed three or four times, the sum total having been largely augmented at each renewal. Thus, for example, ten rupees borrowed mount up after a few years to an ostensible debt of a hundred rupees, and so on. Again, the debt may not have been incurred by the ryot himself, but by his father or grandfather. The man may know something of his own debts and of the interest thereon accruing. But he may be rendered liable for an ancestral debt of which he has but a vague idea, while he knows almost nothing of the manner in which the interest has been made up. With an ignorant, though industrious peasantry dealing with an acute and practised class of money-lenders these circumstances constitute real grievances. Therefore the Courts should be not only empowered, but directed to go into all these points to separate the real debt from the factitiously accrued debt. There should be a limit imposed to the accumulation of interest; it should be declared that the interest should not more than equal the amount of the principal (according to a local custom well known by the name of " dâm dupat "). There should be a distinction between a ryot's liability for his own debts and his liability for the debts of his ancestors. The present law, which renders him liable only to the extent of assets inherited, is found to afford him no protection whatever. He should not be liable for his father's or ancestor's debts until he has been asked whether he accepts them.

As a matter of custom binding on Hindus, he will accept the principal with, perhaps, a moderate interest, but he will naturally ask that the interest be reasonably scrutinized and taxed. And that is the very thing which we ought to desire to see done. If he declines to accept, the Court should ascertain the principal of the debt. If it was contracted by his grandfather, he should not be liable for any interest at all. If it was contracted by his father, he should be liable for simple interest during his father's lifetime only, provided always that the interest should not more than equal the amount of the principal. All these precautions will prevent the money-lender (who does not wish ever to be repaid in full) from turning the interest on an old debt into a permanent annuity payable by the debtor from generation to generation.

14. Secondly, I think that a ryot should have the right of coming forward *at any time* and claiming the benefit of the Insolvency Court, just like the citizens of capital cities, Bombay, Calcutta, and others. At present (as already shown in this Minute) he can do so *only* when, after the passing of a decree he is arrested in execution—then and not till then. I think he should be enabled to do so at any previous moment of his embarrassments which he may choose—even before a suit is brought at all.

15. Thirdly, a ryot's "ryotwári" land (revenue-paying land) ought not, I think, to be sold for debt unless it has been specifically pledged by him in a bond registered before a rural registrar or notary. In numerous cases land is sold for debt incurred many years ago before the ryot had been, by the Survey and Settlement, declared the virtual proprietor or (if the Survey and Settlement had been introduced) before either debtor or creditor had realised in their own minds the effect of the measure—when the creditor did not know that he would ever have such a security as the land for the loan, and when the debtor never knew that he would incur such a contingency as being sold out of house and home. Many a man will incur debt without reflecting that he runs the risk of losing his land to him one of the greatest of penalties. But he will hesitate if he is called upon to execute and register a bond pledging the land, and this will exercise a moral check upon his borrowing. It will render the money-lenders less facile than they now are in lending. It will also afford a just protection to many cases which are now quite unprotected.

16. These three proposals I make in regard to those districts only which are treated of in the Commission's Report. I have carefully consulted the late President of the Commission (Mr. Richey) regarding them. The districts are, as my colleagues will recollect, Poona, Ahmednagar, Sholápur, and a small

part of Sátára. I would propose a special law for the relief of indebted ryots in these particular districts, just as special laws were passed for insolvent debtors, or for special classes of them, in Oudh, in Western Bengal (Chotá Nagpore), in Sind, and in Gujarát. The case of the Deccan ryots needs special legislation quite as much as any of these cases, or more. The strict limitation of area to which such special legislation would be applicable smooths difficulties from the way of such legislation. And the case of these royts is harder than that of the ryots in other portions of the Bombay Presidency, for instance, indebtedness is notoriously less in the Southern Deccan and the Southern Marátha Country, less also in Gujarát, in all which territories the seasons are more propitious, the productiveness more abundant, and the conditions of rural life easier.

These three remedies are strong ones—they are not indeed perfect, because *no* legislation can prevent two parties from colliding and so running into danger if they are infatuated or resolutely minded, nor render people prudent who are bent upon imprudence. But they will remove some of the inducements which now allure people into trouble, and will supply counter-inducements to keep out of such trouble. They will have considerable effect. They will make the ryots more careful in borrowing and the money-lenders more chary in lending. They will diminish the ryot's credit without altogether destroying it, and they will certainly stop many cases of hard injustice which now continually occur under the very shadow of our Courts, and which naturally exasperate the people.

17. I bear in mind that the shortness of the term of limitation, recently prescribed by law, is assigned as one of the weapons put into the hand of the creditor for compelling the debtor to renew bonds at usurious rates. But if the remedies proposed in this Minute be adopted, I do not recommend that the term of limitation be lengthened, because it has the unquestionable advantage of ensuring short accounts and of preventing those long unsettled accounts so destructive to the debtors.

18. I have tried to propose moderate remedies, bearing in mind that the ryots cannot in *these* districts get on without *some* credit, without the means of obtaining a little accommodation in emergency, because the seasons are so uncertain. In proof of this there is the fact that in the Southern Marátha Country and in Gujarát where the seasons are more propitious and regular, this calamitous indebtedness hardly exists at all, or else is found in a less dangerous form. But besides this it is admitted on all hands that the Deccan ryots have of late years become extravagant in their habits, which habits were fostered by the advent of railways, the sudden rise of the cotton trade from 1862 to 1865, and the extraordinary

development of public works. Judicious legislation may indirectly rescue them from this dangerous tendency.

19. It would, I would add, be impossible to lay down that in *no* case shall land be saleable for debt—not even if it be pledged—for that would be breaking the land revenue settlement, which says that land shall be transferable as well as heritable property. I only say that it ought not to be sold except it be so pledged.

20. Nor do I wish to depress the money-lenders or to banish them from the Deccan. They have been specially useful during the famine of 1877 in advancing money and grain to the distressed peasantry. Even in ordinary times they have their uses and their legitimate functions in tracts so often afflicted by uncertainty of season. But the law has indirectly given them undue preponderance till they have multiplied and overshadowed the rural localities.

21. So far then the law should, I think, be modified, and it is to such modification that I have addressed myself in this Minute. If my Honourable colleagues concur, I would cause our Legal Remembrancer to prepare a Draft Bill for submission to the Legislature for the relief of indebted ryots in certain districts of the Bombay Deccan.

(Signed) RICHARD TEMPLE.

No. 308 OF 1878.

REVENUE DEPARTMENT.

Bombay Castle, 19th January 1878.

From

THE HONOURABLE E. W. RAVENSCROFT, C.S.I.,
Chief Secretary to the Government of Bombay,

To

G. H. M. BATTEN, ESQ.,
Officiating Secretary to the Government of India,
Department of Revenue, Agriculture and Commerce.

SIR,

I am directed to forward herewith, for submission to the Government of India, a draft *Bill for the relief of indebted agriculturists in certain parts of the Presidency of Bombay*, which it is the intention of

His Excellency the Governor in Council to introduce into the local Legislature, and to make the following remarks with reference thereto :—

2. The views of this Government as to the causes which led to the Deccan Riots of 1875 and the remedial measures to be adopted were expressed in my letter of the 6th April last, No. 2202. His Excellency the Governor in Council adheres to these views generally, and believes that many of the evils suffered by the people are beyond the power of Government to cure—being curable only by the people themselves. Still, further experience, combined with the lessons of recent events, have convinced him that some effort should be made by legislation to mitigate those evils even though they cannot altogether be prevented by Government.

3. The evils described by the Deccan Riots Commission are probably existing in a somewhat milder form now than, say, two years ago, when the Commission sat. The famine has turned the thoughts of both creditors and debtors into other channels. The disturbances of 1875 opened the eyes of the creditors as to the danger of pushing things too far. It is thought that the money-lenders are under the impression that the authorities are adverse to extreme pressure being applied to the ryots. It appears that from one cause and another the money-lenders are, in some degree, refraining from worrying the ryots. Still these evils, though not exacerbated just now, exist, and will sooner or later break out again.

4. Meanwhile the new Code of Civil Procedure, which came into effect from the beginning of October 1877, has in several respects improved the condition of the ryot. By it, a ryot's necessaries will be protected from sale for debt; his land, instead of being inconsiderately sold in execution of a decree, will be brought under judicious management by the Revenue Officers; and he will be protected from arrest on a decree if he declares himself to the Court as an insolvent. And if his total debt does not exceed Rs. 200, he may be absolved by the Court from all further liability. But these improvements, which are considerable, leave several of the roots of mischief untouched.

5. There is, as shown by the Commission, much in the condition of the Deccan ryots, which exposes them to temptation to run into debt. They are liable always to more than ordinary vicissitudes of season, suffering from drought and losses for a year or two years consecutively, and then having a bumper season to make up for all. They have sometimes had abundant employment and high prices together with abundant produce, and then they have suffered from a cessation or rather a reversal of these good conditions. They are thus tempted in bad seasons to incur debt which they hope

to pay off as soon as more favourable circumstances recur, and to urge them in their inclination they have at present a fatal facility for obtaining cash from money-lenders. Once, however, the money has been taken, the ryot is on the way to ruin, for the money-lenders have great facility for making the principal of the debt mount up by compound interest, and the like to something fabulous, and then for recovering the whole principal and interest by processes which drive the debtor from house and home.

6. It is, in the opinion of His Excellency the Governor in Council, the duty of Government to see that the laws do not tend to bring about the state of things just described. At present, they do actually so tend. To remedy this, His Excellency the Governor in Council considers, after much consultation with well informed persons, that three things are wanted in the districts* to which the report of the Commission refers, and in others similarly situated :—

(*a*). *Firstly.*—His Excellency the Governor in Council is of opinion that the Civil Courts should be obliged to examine the merits of the claim for which they are asked to pass a decree. At present, if a bond duly executed and attested is presented the Court must pass a decree ; and the ryots, seeing the hopelessness of contention, seldom appear in order to put in any defence, but allow the decrees to be passed against them *ex parte.* But the bond may be utterly unjust—indeed, generally is more or less unjust. A fraction of it only consists of principal, the rest is all made up of interest. The bond itself is by no means the original one, but has been renewed three or four times, the sum total having been largely augmented at each renewal. Thus, for example, ten rupees borrowed mount up after a few years to an ostensible debt of a hundred rupees. Again, the debt may not have been incurred by the ryot himself, but by his father or grandfather. The man may know something of his own debts and of the interest thereon accruing : but he may be rendered liable for an ancestral debt of which he has but a vague idea, while he knows almost nothing of the manner in which the interest has been made up. Therefore, the Courts should be not only empowered but directed to go into all these points to separate the real debt from the factitiously accrued debt. Compound interest should in no case be allowed, and it should be declared that in no case should the aggregate amount of interest exceed the principal. There should be a distinction between a ryot's liability for his own debts and his liability for those of his ancestors. He should not be made liable for his father's or other ancestors' debts until he has been asked whether he

---

* Namely, Poona, Ahmednagar, Sholápur, and Sátára.

accepts them. If he accepts, he should be rendered responsible, after reasonably scrutinizing and taxing his debt, for the full amount payable. If declines to accept, the Court should ascertain the principal of the debt, and, in case it was incurred by his father, award the principal with simple interest during his father's lifetime only—provided always that the interest does not more than equal the amount of the principal. In all other cases, he should not be liable for any interest at all.

(b). *Secondly.*—It appears to His Excellency the Governor in Council that a ryot should be given the right of coming forward *at any time* and claiming the benefit of the Insolvency Court, just like the citizens of capital cities, such as Bombay and Calcutta. At present, as already stated in paragraph 4 of this letter, the man can do so *only* when, after the passing of a decree, he is arrested in execution—then and not till then.

(c). *Thirdly.*—A ryot's 'Ryotwári' land (revenue paying land) ought not, His Excellency the Governor in Council considers, to be sold for debt, unless it has been specifically pledged by him in a bond registered before a rural registrar or notary, for it so happens that in numerous cases land is sold for debt incurred many years ago before the ryot had been, by the Survey and Settlement, declared the virtual proprietor, or (if the Survey and Settlement had been introduced) before either debtor or creditor had realized in their own minds the effect of the measure,—in short, when the creditor did not know that he would ever have such a security as the land for a loan and when the debtor never knew that he would incur such a contingency as being sold out of house and home. The present law does indeed require that all bonds for land over Rs. 100 in value should be registered, but this is not sufficient in the interests of the ryot, and registration ought to be extended to *all* bonds for land. If registration is required to give validity to bonds of Rs. 100, much more is it required for small bonds which are usually passed by a more ignorant and helpless class than that having larger transactions. Registration of *all* bonds for land is provided in the Code Napoleon, and similar provisions are to be found in nearly all the civilized Codes of Europe and America. In India alone is the ignorant man left unprotected from fraud, except in Oudh, where public notaries have been appointed and are said to be popular. If registration is extended to all bonds for land it will not indeed debar the ryot from executing any bond however improvident, but merely provide that he understands the conditions of the bond and that a copy of the document is kept as a precaution against fraud and forgery. Many a man will incur debt without reflecting that he runs the risk of losing his land--to him one of the greatest of penalties. But he will hesitate if he is called upon to execute and register a bond pledging the land, and this will exercise a moral check upon his borrowing, while it will render the money-lenders less facile than they are now in lending.

7. The three remedies spoken of in the last paragraph have been put into legal shape in the Bill now submitted. Special laws like this have been passed for insolvent debtors, or for special classes of them, in Oudh, in Western Bengal (Chotá Nágpur), in Sind, and in Gujarát. The case of the ryots of the Poona, Ahmednagar, Sholápur, and Sátára Collectorates needs special legislation quite as much as any of these cases, or more; and the strict limitation of area to which it would be applicable smooths difficulties from the way of such legislation. The area will probable be extended hereafter, should the experiment now about to be made prove successful.

8. The remedies are not indeed perfect, because *no* legislation can prevent two parties from colliding and so running into danger if they are infatuated or resolutely minded, nor render people prudent who are bent upon imprudence. But they will remove some of the inducements which now allure people into trouble, and will supply counter inducements to keep out of such trouble. They will make the ryots more careful in borrowing and the money-lenders more chary in lending. They will diminish the ryot's credit without altogether destroying it, and they will stop many cases of hard injustice which now continually occur under the very shadow of the Courts, and which naturally exasperate the people.

9. In conclusion, I am to request that you will be good enough to move His Excellency the Viceroy in Council to favour this Government with an early expression of his views on the subject of this letter. His sanction to the introduction of the Bill into the Bombay Legislative Council is also solicited.

I have the honour to be, &c.,

(Signed) E. W. RAVENSCROFT,
Chief Secretary to Government.

No. 404.

To

THE CHIEF SECRETARY TO THE
GOVERNMENT OF BOMBAY.

Simla, the 1st July 1878.

SIR,

In continuation of my telegram of the 3rd ultimo, I am now directed to reply to Mr. Ravenscroft's letters Nos. 308 and 584; dated respectively the 19th January and the 4th February last, on the subject of the measures necessary for the relief of indebted agriculturists in certain parts of the Bombay Presidency.

2. His Excellency the Governor in Council, in paragraph 4 of the first of these letters, reviewing the situation disclosed by the Report of the Deccan Riots Commission of 1875, observes that the condition of the ryot has been in several respects materially improved by the new Code of Civil Procedure, which came into force on the 1st October last : " By it, a ryot's necessaries will be protected from sale for debt; his land, instead of being inconsiderately sold in execution of a decree, will be brought under judicious management by the revenue officers; and he will be protected from arrest on a decree if he declares himself to the Court as an insolvent. And if his total debt does not exceed Rs. 200, he may be absolved from further liability." His Excellency in Council, however, considers that these improvements leave untouched many of the more important causes of the depressed condition of the people, and that further and special measures are necessary to enable these to be dealt with satisfactorily.

3. To this end legislation is proposed, to include provision for the following objects :—

(*a*.) To compel the courts, in cases where agriculturists are sued on bonds or for money due, to go behind the terms of the bond, to enquire into the justice of the claim, and to take into consideration the equity of the interest charged, even though it may have been distinctly agreed to by the defendant ;

(*b*.) To make it illegal to award compound interest, or more interest than the amount of the principal found to be due ;

(*c*.) To limit the liability of a ryot for debts incurred by his ancestors ;

(*d*.) To empower a ryot at any time to claim the benefit of the Insolvency Court, instead of, as at present, only when a decree has been passed against him ;

(e.) To protect a ryot's ryotwári land from sale for debt, except when it has been specifically pledged by him in a bond duly registered, and to require that all bonds for land shall be registered, whatever the value of the land pledged.

4. A Bill is forwarded with the letter to provide for these objects, and His Excellency in Council asks the sanction of the Government of India to its introduction in the Bombay Legislative Council. The Bill appears to be in general accordance with the principles stated in the letter; but the Government of India observe, with reference to head (d) mentioned above, that the Bill not only empowers an indebted agriculturist to apply for a declaration of insolvency, but also any creditor of such agriculturist to whom not less than Rs. 100 is owing, and that provision for the compulsory registration of mortgages of land [head (e)] does not appear to be included in the draft.

5. In the second letter under acknowledgment, the Governor in Council, referring to doubts which have been expressed regarding the power of the local legislature to deal with the subject, asks that, should the Government of India concur in these doubts, early steps may be taken for the introduction of the Bill into the Council of the Governor General for making laws and regulations.

6. The Government of India, I am to say, share in these doubts, and consider that while some of the objects sought to be attained by the Bill might, in their opinion, be secured by local legislation, the Bill, as a whole, could not be so dealt with, inasmuch as it affects several of the provisions of the Civil Procedure Code and other Acts of the Governor General's Council, which the local legislature is precluded from affecting by the provisions of the Indian Councils' Act. His Excellency in Council has therefore decided that legislation to carry out certain provisions of the draft Bill shall at once be taken in hand in the Legislative Council of India.

7. I am now to explain why it appears to the Government of India unnecessary to include in this legislation all the provisions enumerated in Mr. Ravenscroft's letter of the 19th January.

8. The action proposed under head (a) is considered by the Government of Bombay to be necessary, because "at present, if a bond duly executed and attested is presented, the Court must pass a decree." This appears to the Governor General in Council to be hardly an accurate statement of the case. On this subject I am to invite attention to the decision of the High Court of Bombay, quoted in clause 5, paragraph 13, of Mr. Ravenscroft's letter No. 2202, dated the 6th April 1877. His Excellency in Council

believes that it is the established practice of Courts in India to require, in the case of contracts, satisfactory proof that consideration has been actually received according to the terms of the contract, though mere denial of the receipt of the consideration stated is not in all cases sufficient to cast upon the plaintiff the burden of proving its payment.* Chief Justice Peacock, in a case† reported in 3 Bengal Law Reports, O. C. J., 130, held that a Hindu, who had given a promissory note for Rs. 1,200, of which he had received only Rs. 500, could only be compelled to pay as principal what he had received in cash. Mr. Justice Bayley, one of the Judges of the Bombay High Court, in a recent minute dated the 22nd February 1878, which is now before the Government of India, states that he has always acted on that case, and invariably refused to give in favour of a money-lender a decree for a larger amount of principal than the defendant has received from him. Lastly, I am to invite attention to Bombay Regulation V. of 1827, Section 9, which is still in force, and provides that " written acknowledgments of debt in any shape shall not be held conclusive in a court of law as to the amount, if the defendants show that a full consideration has not been received."

* See a decision of the Privy Council, reported in 2 Bengal Law Reports, 111 and 122, Rája Sáhib Prahlád Sen v. Bábu Budhu Singh.

† Ram Lál Mookerjee v. Haran Chandra Dhar.

9. The principles just stated would, it seems to the Governor General in Council, suffice to secure the objects contemplated by the Government of Bombay under head (a) in all cases in which there is any defence. It may be, however, that His Excellency the Governor in Council contemplates that even in cases where no defence is set up, the Court shall be bound to cast upon the plaintiff the burden of proving the actual receipt of the consideration stated in the bond and the absence of fraud. If this be the intention, I am to say that the Governor General in Council doubts the expediency of legislation in this direction at present. It would cast upon the Courts an amount of work which is seems very questionable whether they could, as at present constituted, get through: it would afford many opportunities for fraud and evasion to dishonest debtors, and might thus be an incentive to reckless borrowing; and finally, it would conflict with the provisions of section 102 of the Evidence Act regarding the burden of proof.

10. Respecting head (b), I am also to invite attention to the decision of Chief Justice Peacock in the case referred to in paragraph 8 of this letter. It will be seen that he held that Act XXVIII of 1855 did not repeal the Hindu Laws as to the rate of interest. Such rate is, in the case of Hindus, governed by the

strict rules of Hindu Law, which are notoriously in favour of the debtor. The Bombay High Court, moreover, in a series of cases cited at page 360 of Appendix B to the Report of the Deccan Riots Commission, have also held that that Act does not abrogate the rule of Hindu Law called *Dám-dupat*, whereby, amongst Hindus, the creditor cannot at any one time recover as interest more than an amount equal to the principal. I am also to solicit a reference to the opinion expressed by His Excellency the late Governor of Bombay in Council in paragraph 13, clause 5, of Mr. Ravenscroft's letter No. 2202, dated the 6th April 1877, which was unfavourable to the grant of discretionary powers to Courts to reduce the rate of interest.

11. This matter, however, is one which can be dealt with by the local Legislative Council, should His Excellency the Governor in Council, on consideration of these remarks, still think further legislation expedient; such legislation would not be beyond the powers of His Excellency's Council, inasmuch as it would not affect Acts of the Legislative Council of India passed subsequently to the date on which the Indian Councils' Act came into force.

12. The Government of India observe that no reference has been made, in the remarks in Mr. Ravenscroft's letter of the 19th January last under head (c), to Act VII of 1866 (Bombay Council). It seems possible that the application of that Act to the question of the liability of a ryot for his ancestor's debts may have been overlooked. The Act extends only to Hindus, and it may be that it does not even in their case secure to the ryots the amount of protection which His Excellency the Governor in Council considers necessary. If, therefore, His Excellency in Council should be of opinion that further legislation on the subject is necessary to extend the scope of the protection afforded by the Act, such legislation would also seem to be within the competence of the local Legislative Council.

13. It will be gathered from the above remarks that of the five points on which legislation is recommended by the Government of Bombay, the first three seem to the Governor General in Council to be altogether or in part provided for by the existing law. His Excellency in Council does not therefore think that it is necessary to include them in the measure which, as will be seen below, he proposes to introduce into the Legislative Council of the Governor General. I am, however, to suggest that, as it would seem possible that some of the *Mofussil* Courts in the Bombay Presidency may not be fully acquainted with the existing law, or may have overlooked its provisions, the High Court of Bombay should be moved by the Governor in Council to issue a circular to those Courts calling attention to the matter.

14. The other points, *viz.* :—
  (1) empowering a ryot at any time to claim the benefit of the Insolvent Court;
  (2) securing ryotwári land from sale in execution of any process unless it has been specifically pledged in a registered bond; and
  (3) requiring all bonds relating to land, without reference to its value, to be registered—

will be provided for in a Bill which will be at once introduced into the Legislative Council of the Governor General. The scope of the Bill will be limited to the districts named* by the Government of Bombay.

* Poona. Sholápur.
Sátára. Ahmednagar.

15. As will be seen from the draft Bill, of which I am directed to forward a copy for His Excellency the Governor in Council's consideration, it has not been thought necessary to insert any provision enabling the Government to extend the Act to any other portions of the Bombay Presidency by notification. *Primâ facie,* there would not appear to be any great object in taking such a power, and the more extended application of it might rightly be reserved to legislation; but on this subject the Government of India would be glad to learn the views of His Excellency in Council.

16. Certain other points in the draft Bill seem to require special consideration—

   1*st.*—Is the limitation of section 3 to "land paying revenue to Government, and belonging to any person earning his livelihood wholly or principally by agriculture," correct? Or would the Bombay Government prefer its extension to all land paying revenue to Government without reference to the status or character of the holders, and, if so, why?

   2*nd.*—Is the proviso in section 3, permitting sales of land by receivers in insolvency proceedings, correct? or is it essential to the success of the contemplated measure that the land should be protected from sale even in insolvency cases.

   3*rd.*—Is it necessary that section 4 should apply to all revenue-paying land? or would it not be more in harmony with the special scope of the Act to restrict its application, as that of section 3 is restricted?

   4*th.*—Is it quite safe, and is it essential to make section 4 applicable to transactions entered into before the passing of the Act? The section allows six months' grace in such cases, so that where transactions have been effected *in writing* no great hardships can result; but if in any of the districts to which this proposed Act will extend, *oral* mortgages have been customary (and this the Government of Bombay will doubtless ascertain) some modification of the section may be necessary.

17. In regard to all these points, as well as in regard to the provisions of the draft Bill generally, the Government of India will be glad if His Excellency the Governor in Council will favour them with his opinion at as early a date as possible, in order that there may be no delay in proceeding with the Bill.

18. In conclusion, I am to observe that the first and last of the three points mentioned in the 14th paragraph will demand the consideration of the Government of Bombay with reference to the establishment necessary to provide for the proper execution of the Bill when it becomes law. The limitations placed upon the action of the Courts in dealing with insolvency in the new Civil Procedure Code were thought necessary, because it was believed that the judicial machinery in the *Mofussil* was not sufficiently strong to work a complete insolvency law. Should the Bill when it becomes law make any considerable addition to the insolvency business of the Courts, it may be necessary to provide specially for its working. Similarly, if the provision making the registration of all bonds relating to land compulsory entails much additional work in registration offices, or if it is found that those offices are not sufficiently numerous, or are situated at too great distances from one another, it may be necessary to establish rural registration offices, a measure which, as the Governor in Council is aware, has been found of great advantage in the Lower Provinces of Bengal. This subject is discussed in clause 6, paragraph 13, of Mr. Ravenscroft's letter of the 6th April 1877.

19. I am to express the regret of the Government of India at the delay which has occurred in replying to this important reference, and the hope of the Governor General in Council that the Government of Bombay will consider the action about to be taken a satisfactory method of dealing with the questions at issue.

I have the honour to be, &c.,

A. O. HUME,
Secretary to the Government of India.

A Bill for the relief of Indebted Agriculturists in certain parts of the Presidency of Bombay.

Preamble.

Whereas it is expedient to relieve and protect indebted agriculturists in certain parts of the Presidency of Bombay; It is hereby enacted as follows:—

Short title.

1. This Act may be called "The Bombay Indebted Agriculturists Relief Act, 1878."

Local extent. Commencement.

It shall extend only to the districts of Poona, Sátára, Sholápur, and Ahmednagar; and shall come into force on the   day of   1878.

Indebted agriculturist may be declared insolvent.

2. Any person earning his livelihood wholly or principally by agriculture who is in insolvent circumstances, and who desires to be declared an insolvent, may apply in writing in that behalf to any Court empowered to entertain applications under Section 344 of the Code of Civil Procedure.

Every application under this section shall be made as nearly as may be in manner prescribed by Sections 345 and 346 of the said Code, and shall be dealt with as nearly as may be as if it were an application under Section 344 of the same.

Exemption from attachment and sale of revenue-paying land belonging to agriculturists.

3. No land paying revenue to the Government which belongs to any person earning his livelihood wholly or principally by agriculture shall be attached or sold in execution of a decree:

Proviso.

Provided that nothing herein contained shall prevent the sale of any land by a receiver appointed in any insolvency proceedings, or the enforcement of any mortgage, lien or charge of or upon any land.

Mortgages, &c., of revenue-paying land to be valid only when written and registered.

4. No mortgage, lien or charge of or upon any land paying revenue to the Government shall be valid unless it is created by an instrument in writing signed by the person creating such mortgage, lien or charge; and every instrument creating any such mortgage, lien, or charge, shall be deemed to be an instrument required to be registered by Section 17 of the Indian Registration Act, 1877.

Any such instrument executed before the passing of this Act, and which, but for the passing of this Act, would not have been required to be registered, may, notwithstanding anything contained in the said Indian Registration Act, 1877, be registered if presented for that purpose to the proper officer within six months from the passing of this Act.

FURTHER OBSERVATIONS ON SPECIAL LEGISLATION FOR INDEBTEDNESS OF RYOTS OF THE BOMBAY DECCAN.

Minute by the Governor of Bombay, dated 30th August 1878.

1. By our despatches of the 19th January and the 4th February last, we submitted to the Government of India a draft Bill for the relief of the indebted Ryots in certain districts of the Deccan, together with minutes and papers relating thereto, among which was a minute of my own, dated 12th November last.

2. By a despatch, dated the 1st July last, the Government of India sent for our opinion a Bill, which they proposed to substitute for our Bill, and which we are invited to accept as a satisfactory mode of dealing with the questions at issue.

3. While thankfully admitting the advantages proposed to be given to the ryots by the Bill of the Government of India, I am obliged to represent that this Bill is not sufficient to fulfil the objects which the Government of Bombay had in view when proposing legislation, and, therefore, cannot be regarded by us as a satisfactory mode of dealing with the questions at issue. In general terms it must be described as omitting the most essential of the several provisions which we devised for the protection of the ryots, and therefore as taking some of the heart, kernel and substance out of our measure. I am sure, therefore, that my Honourable colleagues will concur with me in submitting a further representation to the Government of India on the subject.

4. Our proposals are justly summarized in para. 3 of the despatch of Government of India of 1st July, thus:—

(*a*). To compel the Courts, in cases where agriculturists are sued on bonds or for money due, to go behind the terms of the bond, to enquire into the justice of the claim, and to take into consideration the equity of the interest charged, even though it may have been distinctly agreed to by the defendant;

(*b*). To make it illegal to award compound interest, or more interest than the amount of the principal found to be due;

(*c*). To limit the liability of a ryot for debts incurred by his ancestors;

(*d*). To empower a ryot at any time to claim the benefit of the Insolvency Court, instead of, as at present, only when a decree has been passed against him;

(*e*). To protect a ryot's ryotwari land from sale for debt except when it has been specifically pledged by him in a bond duly registered, and to require that all bonds for land shall be registered, whatever the value of the land pledged.

5. As regards (*a*) the first of the points, the Government of India do not agree to any fresh legislation; as regards (*b*) and (*c*) the second and third points, they consider that the Local Legislature of this Presidency may make provision if it sees fit; and as regard (*d*) and (*e*) the fourth and fifth points, they embody proposals in their Bill.

6. We may express our concurrence in this Bill, so far as it goes, as fully providing for our fourth and fifth points. We may declare our willingness to immediately introduce into our local legislature a Bill to provide for (*b*) and (*c*) the second and third points. But on the first point (*a*) we must, I submit, state our regret at its omission from the present legislation and make our earnest request that it may be included therein.

7. To recapitulate this, the most important point of all is stated by the Government of India (as seen above) thus : "To compel the Court in cases where agriculturists are sued on bonds or for money due, to go behind the terms of the bond, to inquire into the justice of the claim, and to take into consideration the equity of the interest charged, even though it may have been distinctly agreed to by the defendant." In my minute of the 12th November last, para. 13, it is stated thus :—

Firstly, I think that the Civil Courts should be obliged to examine the merits of the debt for which they are asked to pass a decree. At present, if a bond duly executed and attested is presented, the Court must pass a decree, and the ryots seeing the hopelessness of contention, seldom appear in order to put in any defence, and allow the decrees to be passed against them *ex parte*. But the bond may be utterly unjust—indeed, generally is more or less unjust. A fraction of it only consists of principal, the rest is all made up of interest. The bond itself is by no means the original one, but has been renewed three or four times; the sum total having been largely augmented at each renewal. Thus, for example, ten rupees borrowed mount up after a few years to an ostensible debt of a hundred rupees, and so on.

8. In our draft Bill it is stated thus :—

"In any suit brought for the recovery of money alleged to be payable on account of money lent, it shall be incumbent on the Court in which such suit is instituted, to ascertain and determine whether the defendant, or any one of the defendants, not being a surety merely of the actual debtor is an agriculturist.

"Whenever a court of first instance determines under this section or under any other sections of this Act, that any person is, or is not, an agriculturist, its decision on such point shall be final.

"If the court's decision under the last preceding section is in the affirmative, it shall be incumbent on it to ascertain the actual amount of money lent.

For this purpose the court shall—

(a) require the plaintiff to prove the origin of the debt, and the nature of each subsequent transaction, if any, in respect thereof;

(b) if any written acknowledgment of debt is relied on by the plaintiff, require him to prove to its satisfaction that the whole of the amount therein named was actually advanced to the debtor.

"If in any case the circumstances are, in the opinion of the court, such as to satisfy the court that some money has been lent, but the actual nature or extent of the transactions between the parties is doubtful, it shall be competent to the court to determine the amount of money lent upon an equitable estimate with reference to such considerations as the following namely :—

(a) the means and position of the lender;

(b) the means and position of the borrower;

(c) the amount of credit likely to have been given to the borrower by a person advancing money to him with the *bonâ fide* intention that it should be repaid with reasonable interest within a reasonable period;

(d) the occasion on which the money was borrowed and the amount likely to have been needed by a person in the borrower's station of life on such an occasion."

9. The point (a) as set forth in the foregoing quotations is the one upon which out of all our several proposals, we lay most stress. The Government of India remark that our statement that "at present if a bond duly executed and attested is presented the court must pass a decree" appears to be hardly an accurate statement of the case, and in support of their view refer us to several rulings of the Superior Courts, cited in para. 8 of their Despatch and to Bombay Regulation V of 1827, Section 9. They state that the principle contained in these Rulings and in the above Regulation seem to "suffice to secure the objects contemplated by the Government of Bombay under head (a) in all cases in which there is any defence," and that if it be our intention to cast upon the plaintiff the burden of proving the actual receipt of the consideration stated in the bond, and the absence of fraud in cases in which no defence is set up they "doubt the expediency of legislation in this direction at present," and state that "it would cast upon the courts an amount of work which it seems very questionable

whether they could, as at present constituted, get through; it would afford many opportunities for fraud and evasion to dishonest debtors, and might thus be an incentive to reckless borrowing, and finally it would conflict with the provisions of Section 102 of the Evidence Act regarding the burden of proof."

10. Our reply in the first place is that although our object may in some remote degree be indirectly provided for in the existing law, yet the law sounds so uncertain a note on this particular subject; its purport has to be gathered by legal learning from so many scattered sources; its meaning is so doubtful to the class of persons by whom civil justice is dispensed in the interior of the country,—that practically it is wholly inoperative in inducing the courts to "go behind the bond,"—that the practice really is as described by us, namely "at present, if a bond duly executed and attested is presented, the court must pass a decree"—that this practice is not remediable by rulings which may or may not be held under all future circumstances to have the force of law—that the difficulty is sure to continue unless there be positive legislation to the contrary—that this practice is at the bottom of all the admitted evils which we are trying to remedy—and that therefore it must be modified by positive enactment about which there can be no mistake and which will really be operative and effective in the administration of justice.

11. I will here quote some pertinent observations by our Legal Remembrancer, Mr. Naylor, C.S., an officer well versed in the actual working of our laws in the interior of the country. He writes :—

"Regarding point (a) The Government of India draw attention to certain rulings of the courts, and to Section 9, Bombay Regulation V. of 1827, and state their opinion that the principles laid down in them suffice to secure the objects contemplated by this Government in all cases in which there is a defence, and express doubts as to the expediency of throwing the burden of proof on the plaintiffs in undefended cases, and suggest that the High Court be moved to issue a circular to the mofussil courts calling attention to the existing law.

"The principles of the decisions and of the Regulation to which reference is thus made are :—

"(1) That 'inadequacy of consideration when found in conjunction with any other such circumstances as suppression of true value of property, misrepresentation, fraud, surprise, oppression, urgent necessity for money, weakness of understanding, or even ignorance, is an ingredient which weighs powerfully with a court of equity in considering whether it should not set aside contracts, or refuse to decree specific performance of them;' (III., By. H. C. R., 11, A. C. J.)

"(2) That 'it is the established practice of the courts in India, in cases of contract, to require satisfactory proof that consideration has been actually received according to the terms of the contract;' (II. Ben. L. R., III., P. C.)

"(3) That according to Hindu law the 'maker of a promissory note may show that there was no consideration,' and the holder of the note 'can recover no larger sum by way of principal than what the defendant received in cash;' (III., Ben. L. R., 130, O. C. J.)

"(4) That 'written acknowledgments of debt in any shape shall not be held conclusive in a court of law as to the amount, if the defendants show that a full consideration has not been received.' (Bom. Reg. V. of 1827, Sec. 9).

"It is worthy of remark that the first of the above decisions was passed so long ago as 1866, and the second and third in 1869; whilst the Regulation in which the fourth of the above principles is contained, has been in force in this Presidency since 1827. All three of the decisions are to be found in the published Reports and may be presumed to be as well known to the Judges and to the Bar as is, of course, the provision of Regulation V. Yet, notwithstanding this, it is an indisputable fact that for years past, thousands of decrees have been annually obtained by money-lenders against the ryots upon written acknowledgments for sums vastly in excess of the amounts ever actually lent by them.

"The causes of this state of things are not far to seek. With regard to the first decision a court of equity will, no doubt, interfere in any of the instances enumerated, provided that a case for interference is clearly established; but the reason why so few suits arise in which the courts have the opportunity of exercising their powers of interference is simply that ordinary defendants find it too difficult and too expensive to prove their case. With respect to the second and the third rulings a reference to II., Bengal L. R., 122, P. C., will show that in quoting, in para. 32 of his minute on the 'Negotiable Instruments Bill, 1877,' the 'head note' to the Report of the Privy Council's decision, the Honourable Mr. Justice Bayley does not seem to have quite fully conveyed the purport of the Privy Council's Judgment. The Sadar Court of Bengal had said that 'it is the established practice of the courts in India in cases of contract to require satisfactory proof that consideration has been actually received according to the terms of the contract,' but their Lordships of the Privy Council were of opinion that this proposition was 'too loosely expressed' and that the cases cited by Counsel showed that 'if it is to be taken as affirming that the mere denial of the receipt of the consideration stated is, in all cases, sufficient to cast upon the party relying on the instrument the burthen of proving the payment of that consideration, it is too wide.'

"Both the last two decisions had reference specially to the law in force in Bengal. In this Presidency the matter is governed by the express provision of Section 9, Regulation V. of 1827. The Honourable Mr. Justice Bayley would appear not to have had this provision in his mind—(vide para. 19 of his minute already referred to)—and also not to have had his attention drawn to a very important reported decision of the High Court of Bombay with reference* to it. There was a suit in
* V. By. H. C. R., 81, which the plaintiff sued to recover money on a
A. C. J. written acknowledgment of indebtedness signed by the defendant in his account-book, and the defendant pleaded want of consideration. The District Judge, following the Munsiff, held that the plaintiff must 'aver that the contract was made on good consideration, and must make good that allegation by proof.' But the High Court was of

opinion that the District Judge was 'in error in deciding that it lay upon the plaintiff to prove that consideration had been received. Regulation V. of 1827, Section 9,' it said, 'is the law which governs the case, and this declares that it is incumbent on the defendant to show that a full consideration has not been received.' Thus it may be said that in this Presidency the presumption is in favor of a defendant having received the full consideration stated in any written acknowledgment signed by him until he can show by satisfactory proof that he has not received the full consideration. And as a matter of practice in all mofussil courts the merest tittle of evidence as to the execution of a written acknowledgment is deemed sufficient proof on which, in undefended cases, to pass a decree for the full amount named in such acknowledgment, and a very large number of such decrees are awarded daily; whilst in defended cases, the mere denial by the defendant of the receipt of consideration is not deemed sufficient to throw the burden of proof on the plaintiff, for if the plaintiff has *prima facie* proved the execution of the written acknowledgment, the law is held to require the defendant to show that he has not received full consideration.

"I think, therefore, what has been said by the Government of Bombay is correct, *viz.*, that 'at present if a bond duly executed and attested is presented, the court must pass a decree; and the ryots seeing the helplessness of contention seldom appear in order to put in any defence, but allow the decrees to be passed against them *ex parte*.'

*   *   *   *

"Whatever legislative action has been taken for relieving the estates of tálukdárs and others from incumbrances, the *first* step thought necessary has always been to provide for the reduction of the claims against them to reasonable amounts. This is also one of the chief objects of Section 3—9 of the Bombay Bill, and I do not think that the ryots will ever obtain any adequate relief without some such provisions. When the borrower is an 'agriculturist' he is one of a class which, it is now generally admitted, needs protection against the craftiness and superior acumen of the lenders. It is, therefore, fair in such cases and quite in accordance with the Honourable Mr. Justice Bayley's and the Government of India's views, to throw the burden of proof, both in defended and undefended suits, on the lenders. The provision for the settlement of the amount due, in cases of doubt upon equitable considerations and for a reference to arbitration will, if adopted, simply lead to the matters in dispute being determined very much in the same way and by the same means that they used to be settled before we introduced the complicated and unsuitable machinery of Civil Courts, and in the same way they would be settled now if no courts existed, with this difference that the intervention of the courts will secure equal justice to rich and to poor, and punctuality in the discharge of their functions by arbitrators. Another very great advantage of these provisions will be that they will in time regulate the mutual dealings of the money-lenders and ryots in a manner equally beneficial to both, and will restore their relations to what they were in the olden time, when the money-lender knew that patience and considerate treatment of his debtor were the best, if not the only means of getting his money from him."

12. Such is the opinion of our Legal Remembrancer as quoted above in which I fully concur and probably my Honourable Colleagues will concur also.

13. The gist of the matter, then, is this. The Deccan Ryots were sued, still are sued, and will always be sued—unless there be fresh legislation—on bonds which are, in many instances, utterly unjust, though they may have been executed in due form. I mean by "unjust" repugnant to the sense of natural justice as between man and man, that moral sense which is present in the minds of all men whether educated or uneducated. The harassment therefrom arising drove these ryots in 1875 to commit agrarian outrages. A Special Commission showed after elaborate inquiry that the essential injustice of the majority of the bonds was the root of the mischief. It is clear that this injustice would be demonstrated by any judicial inquiry which might be had regarding the origin, progress, and circumstances of the debts. The existing law provides for judgment being given on the bonds only; that much is certain. Whether it provides for the Court by its own inquiries going behind the bond is, as we submit, uncertain. The Government of India seems to consider that it does so provide, while apparently admitting that the provision is indirect rather than direct, and must be gathered from scattered rulings and clauses, rather than learnt from positively clear enactment. We submit with deference that the uncertainty is such that the Courts practically do not go, can hardly be expected to go, and for the most part are sure not to go behind the bond. Therefore we urge that there ought to be direct and positive legislation, without which the existing evils must be perpetuated.

14. We may be encouraged to hope that the Government of India may be pleased to listen to our request, as they admit that policy of the law is or ought to be, that the Court should go behind the bond, the terms of their answer being that the law does, in some way, so provide already. But if we rejoin successfully that the provision is quite insufficient, is too uncertain to be of use,—then perhaps they will not object to make the law on the point clear by fresh legislation, to enforce a legal policy admitted to be right.

15. In other instances wherever the law is doubtful or inadequate on any point which ought to be clear, application is made to the Legislature to cure the defect to remove the doubt. That exactly is what we venture to solicit from the Government of India in the present case, the gravity and importance of which may constitute an excuse for our importunity.

16. I must next advert to the apprehension apparently felt by the Government of India lest we should by our point (a) (causing the court to go behind the bond) unduly throw upon the plaintiff the burden of proof in cases where no defence is attempted.

17. At present the indebted ryots seldom set up any defence to these claims. They see the futility of disputing the bonds in court, whatever they may think of the injustice. Indeed they have no chance whatever before the law of setting up any defence which the courts could be expected to act upon. But if our point (a) be passed into law, they would set up defences fast enough, and this too with some chance of equitable success. In this event it is manifestly just and reasonable that the burden of proof should fall upon the plaintiffs. But in the absence of defence in cases of this sort it seems to me but right that the plaintiff should have to satisfy the court that the bond is a just one. I am unable to follow the reasoning (as above quoted) to the effect that to cast on the plaintiff the burden of proving receipt of the consideration, and the absence of fraud,—would afford opportunities of evasion to dishonest debtors, and might thus be an incentive to reckless borrowing. Here we have educated, skilful, and wealthy creditors bringing claims against uneducated, unskilful and poor debtors. Is it unfair to cast upon such creditors the burden of proving such claims to be just, even if undefended ? On the contrary does not fairness demand that such burden should be cast upon them ? In fact, too, these ryot debtors are not, for the most part, evasive or dishonest debtors; they generally pay all, and much more than all, they really owe! It is this notorious circumstance which underlies the whole argument. The feeling of despair of ever getting out of the money-lenders' books makes them reckless in going on borrowing and borrowing, destroys all hope of independence. Our provisions will not be incentives to reckless borrowing, but will have the very reverse effect.

18. It may be, as apprehended by the Government of India, that our provisions will throw much work on the courts, more perhaps than they can conveniently get through. We are not indeed sure that this will be the result; but if it be so, then it ought not, in our judgment, to be allowed for a moment to prevent the measure being carried. If there were to be some temporary increase of judicial establishments in four districts (the bill will apply to four districts only and perhaps to some special localities in addition) we shall have to meet the cost from provincial finance, which we are most willing to do. Even then the cost would probably be counterbalanced by increase of stamp revenue. But the net cost, if any, would be so inconsiderable that we could not venture to urge it in the face of the clear considerations of justice towards so important a class of our peasantry.

19. No doubt, as justly observed by the Government of India, our proposal will conflict with Section 102 of the Evidence Act regarding the burden of proof. But we submit that this *per se* is

no prohibitive reason against our proposal. It certainly renders special legislation necessary, and therefore we have now to apply to the Legislature. The question is one of plain justice in these cases. Once that is determined, it becomes, we submit, the duty of the Legislature to frame a suitable law to supplement the general law.

20. We willingly acknowledge that either by the new Civil Procedure Code, or by the new bill, an indebted ryot may, by applying for the benefit of insolvency provisions, save himself from arrest and imprisonment, that his implements and agricultural cattle cannot be sold in execution of decree for debt, that his cottage, his land, his tenure, and rights therein cannot be so sold either—all of which constitute beneficial improvements in his condition, for which he may indeed be grateful to the Legislature, we now receive permission to provide by local legislation that he shall not be unreasonably liable for ancestral debts nor for an usurious rate of compound interest—all which constitutes a still further improvement; and a further cause of thankfulness.

21. Still we submit that despite these various provisions there may be, and will be, very many unjust bonds, to which the ryots will have to submit, unless the courts be not only empowered, but obliged to go behind the bonds.

22. No exclusion of ancestral debts; no restriction of usurious interest can prevent bonds being drawn up for a fictitious principal, or in acknowledgment of amounts which were never given by the creditor nor received by the debtor. And it is this concoction, this manipulation, as it were, of the principal, which is one of the strongest elements of injustice in these bonds, which injustice cannot possibly be remedied unless the courts be obliged to go behind the bonds.

23. Again, notwithstanding the humane provisions of the insolvency law, the merciful exemption of implements of land, and of cottages from sale, still there are many domestic articles which cannot be so exempted, which are of lesser importance, and more particularly the standing crop which is of great importance, as it supplies the food of the ryot and of his family. What arrangements an insolvent court would make for the subsistence of the ryot cannot exactly be foreseen. Possibly some arrangement would be made, though I am advised that the law does not compel the court to make any such arrangement. Still at the best the creditor would have a strong and tight grasp on the standing crop. I do not mention the garnered crop; because the creditor would never let it reach the stage of storage without his

interposition. He would attack it while it was standing on the ground. He would compel the Ryot to hypothecate it for the debt. He would leave to the Ryot such subsistence as he (the creditor) deemed fit. The standing crop, being the only food supply of the Ryot, is so essential a part of his little possessions that he must pay extreme deference to the creditor who is virtually master of that crop. Then comes the critical difficulty. The creditor presents to the Ryot an old bond, which must be paid off immediately, or else renewed on exorbitant terms. At present these bonds, as already stated, are often flagrantly unjust. This injustice will, we hope, be mitigated by legislation restricting usurious interest—even then there will remain but too much scope for injustice in these bonds. Restriction on usurious interest may be useful. Still they cannot prevent alterations in the amount of the principal as already shown. Thus the Ryot must "stand and deliver" to the bond, under penalty of having his crop attached and his food supply interfered with. The temptation to renew on some exorbitant terms will be generally irresistible. The creditors are notoriously ingenious in framing terms which, though exorbitant, will yet fail to show on the face of them usurious interest or anything else that may be illegal, and will yet evade the just intentions of the law. Then simultaneously with renewal of the arrangement, the old bond will be cancelled. The renewed bond will be executed, and will be *the* one formal valid bond, as between the parties, to be presented in court. And the Ryot will from time to time be obliged to pay upon that, or else will have his crop attached, and his food supply suddenly stopped. If, unfortunately, that bond be unjust, as it but too often will be, then the Ryot will be, to a considerable extent, the victim of injustice. He will not be indeed so helplessly a victim as he has been heretofore, as he will avoid paying a demonstrably usurious interest, he will be able to save himself from imprisonment and his land from sale. But for fear of his crop and his food supply he will still be, to some considerable extent, a victim.

24. From this oppression he may be saved altogether, and his liability may be limited to its proper proportions, by our proposal (*a*)—obliging the courts to go behind the bonds. That, at all events, is the most effectual provision that can be devised. And if well and carefully worked, as it probably would be worked, under a vigilant administration, it will be effectual. If this be enacted, then the Legislature will have done all it can for the ryot in this matter. But if this be not enacted, then the law notwithstanding the other improvements will be incomplete for this purpose; the remedies will be only half measures,—and much of the existing evils will remain. In that case we shall have undertaken legislation and yet have fallen short of our aim and have

failed to effect our purpose. Perhaps even an impression might arise that the existing evils are irremediable, whereas all the time they are remediable, as we believe. We have a fair ground for renewing our application to the Legislature—because we are asking not for the recognition of principles which the Government of India disallow, but for the enforcement of principles which they seem to allow.

25. For all these reasons I propose, with the concurrence of my Honourable Colleagues, to request earnestly the Government of India to allow the sections quoted in this minute as taken from our Bill to form a part of their Bill.

26. In conclusion, while exposing certain evils and suggesting their remedy, I am far from implying either that the money-lender is altogether blameable or that the ryot is altogether pitiable. With all his faults, the money-lender is a useful man, and often gives credit when it is most needed. With all his sorrows, the ryot enjoys many of those advantages which peasants most value.

RICHARD TEMPLE.

No. 4579 OF 1878.

REVENUE DEPARTMENT.

Bombay Castle, 5th September 1878.

FROM

THE HONOURABLE E. W. RAVENSCROFT, C.S.I.,
CHIEF SECRETARY TO THE GOVERNMENT OF BOMBAY,

To

A. O. HUME, ESQ., C.B.,
SECRETARY TO THE GOVERNMENT OF INDIA,
Department of Revenue, Agriculture, and Commerce,
SIMLA.

SIR,

I am directed to acknowledge receipt of your letter No. 404, dated 1st July last, forwarding copy of a Draft Bill which His Excellency the Governor General in Council proposes to introduce into the Legislative Council of India in substitution for "Bill for the relief of indebted agriculturists in certain parts of the Presidency of Bombay," submitted with my letter No. 308, dated 19th January 1878, and inviting the opinion of His Excellency the Governor in Council upon its provisions and upon sundry other points connected with its subject-matter.

2. In reply, I am desired to convey the thanks of the Government of Bombay to the Government of India for their ready acknowledgment of the need for legislation, and for the promptness with which it is proposed by them to take the necessary action in the matter, and to say that His Excellency the Governor in Council entirely concurs in the expediency of legislation in the direction suggested in the Draft Bill forwarded with your letter, and rejoices at the general concurrence of opinion which exists regarding the measures which the evils to be remedied call for.

3. But it appears to His Excellency the Governor in Council that unless the measures which may be adopted are sufficiently complete to give a reasonable hope of their securing success, it is to be feared that legislation will raise anticipations which cannot be realized, and may detract from the credit of measures which though good in themselves, are yet not calculated to meet all the evils for which Government have to provide. In proceeding, therefore, to discuss the various points raised in your letter under reply, and the requirements of the proposed enactment generally, His Excellency the Governor in Council's desire is to obtain the consent of the Government of India to the enlargement of the scope of the Draft Bill now received, by rendering its provisions more complete.

4. In the first place then the most important of the measures which His Excellency the Governor in Council is anxious to see included in the Bill is that described in para. 3 of your letter as "head (a)," namely:

"(a) To compel the Courts, in cases where agriculturists are sued on bonds or for money due, to go behind the terms of the bond, to inquire into the justice of the claim, and to take into consideration the equity of the interest charged, even though it may have been distinctly agreed to by the defendant."

5. The Government of India's observations upon this proposal may be stated to be—

(1) That so far as defended cases are concerned, the present state of the law renders it really unnecessary; and

(2) That as regards undefended cases its expediency is questionable.

6. Upon this matter I am directed to forward the accompanying copy of a Minute by His Excellency the Governor which has full concurrence of the other Members of this Government, and to state briefly that in the opinion of the Government of Bombay:

(a) It is not the present practice of Courts, at any rate in this Presidency, to require such proof as is really satisfactory that consideration has been actually received according to the terms of a written bond;

(b) The law in force in this Presidency also does not require the Courts to insist upon the production of such proof by plaintiffs, but on the contrary expressly throws the burden of proving the negative upon defendants;

(c) A clear declaration of the intentions of the law is necessary to bring the practice of the Courts of this Presidency into harmony even with the view, which is held alike by His Excellency the Governor General in Council and by this Government, that in defended cases the burden of proving receipt of the full consideration should be thrown strictly upon the plaintiffs;

(d) In cases in which the defendants are agriculturists such a declaration would, however, be insufficient, as owing to their ignorance and poverty and the trouble, annoyance, and loss of time involved in defending suits, they do not care, or have not the prudence to defend suits even when they often might do so successfully;

(e) It will not suffice merely to throw the burden of proof upon plaintiffs; it is still more necessary expressly to require the courts, when the defendants are agriculturists, to go behind the bonds, and not to rely upon the ordinary presumptions in favour of written matter, but to dispense fair justice as between man and man independently of the technicalities which have hitherto helped the moneylenders so effectually to ruin their debtors.

7. For these reasons I am to express the earnest conviction of His Excellency in Council that unless the proposed enactment should include provisions similar in effect to those contained in sections 3 to 8 (inclusive) of the Draft Bill submitted with my letter No. 308 of 19th January last, it will fail to touch the principal root of the evils which it is intended to remedy, though good so far as it goes, it will prove to be but a half-measure, and consequently will fall short of the expectations both of the Government which passes it and the people who may look to it to save them from some grave faults in the existing system of civil justice.

8. The inadequacy of the proposed extension of the Insolvency Law, without the simultaneous enactment of some such provisions as those to which I am adverting, has been very forcibly shown in the following passage of a Report by the Remembrancer of Legal Affairs to this Government which I am desired to quote:

"10. If an insolvent law is to be introduced unaccompanied by any such provisions, the ryot will not benefit much. He will be relieved from liability to imprisonment, it is true, but except in the rare case of the aggregate amount of his scheduled debts not amounting to more than Rs. 200, 'his* property whether previously or subsequently acquired,' will 'be liable to attachment and sale until the decrees against him held by the scheduled creditors are fully satisfied or become incapable of being executed.' And if the creditors are only vigilant the decrees cannot become incapable of being executed for 12† years from the date on which they were passed. Now when it is remembered that the ryot's land is only to be liable to attachment in execution, if it has been expressly hypothecated, and that under Section 266 of the Civil Procedure Code, his implements, cattle, and his own and his wife's and children's necessary wearing apparel and the materials of his house and other buildings are all exempt from attachment, it will be seen that in nine cases out of ten an insolvent ryot will possess scarcely any property out of which his creditors can be satisfied. On the other hand, each of his creditors will do his best to swell out his accounts against him and to get a decree which will entitle him to as large a proportion of the insolvent's small available assets as possible, and if no rules are provided for limiting the creditors' claims, they will experience no difficulty under the law as it is at present, in effecting their purpose.

* *Vide* Section 357 of the Civil Procedure Code.

† *Vide* Section 230, para. 4 of the Civil Procedure Code.

"11. This state of things will, I venture to think, not do much to improve that which it is sought to remedy. A country peopled by a mass of insolvent ryots whose very produce is not their own, and who are incapable of acquiring any property which will not be immediately seized and divided amongst a host of watchful creditors, will hardly fulfil the expectations which it is hoped to obtain by the present measures of relief.

*　　*　　*　　*　　*

What is wanted is rather a means by which the demands of the creditor may be, at any time, easily ascertained and fixed within reasonable limits, and that the debtor should be encouraged to pay the amount so ascertained and fixed, if possible, without being declared an insolvent, and that even when it is necessary for him to take the benefit of the Insolvent Act, he should still only be held liable for the payment of what is reasonable."

9. The provisions of sections 3 to 8 (inclusive) of the Draft Bill submitted with my letter No. 308, to which the foregoing remarks relate, include the remedies proposed by this Government which fall under the heads (*b*) and (*c*), as described in para. 3 of your letter under reply, namely—

"(*b*) To make it illegal to award compound interest, or more interest than the amount of the principal found to be due.

"(*c*) To limit the liability of a ryot for debts incurred by his ancestors."

To such of the provisions as are comprised in these two heads, His Excellency the Governor General in Council is understood not to object, but to purpose that such action as this Government may on further consideration deem necessary with respect thereto shall be taken in the local Legislature. Acting upon this permission the Governor in Council will by an early date introduce a Bill into his Legislative Council for the two objects above mentioned.

10. Adverting to para. 10 of your letter under reply regarding the necessity for interfering with the existing law as to interest, I am to state with regard to the rule of *Dám-dupat* that the Governor in Council fully recognizes the value of that rule as far as it goes, and that His Excellency's object is in fact (1) to make it generally applicable to *all* classes of agriculturists instead of its applying as at present, only when the defendant is a Hindu, and (2) to extend the rule itself by enacting that the amount of interest to be received by the creditor from any agriculturist debtor shall not exceed *in the aggregate*, the amount of the principal instead of thus restricting the amount of interest so recoverable at any one time merely.

11. The ruling of Chief Justice Peacock to the effect that Act XXVIII. of 1855, did not repeal the Hindu law as to the rate of interest, does not appear to this Government to be of any particular benefit to the ryot. The provisions of the written Hindu Code as to interest are shown by the Chief Justice himself in the Judgment* quoted to be far from precise, and His Excellency the Governor in Council is informed, and believes, that

* Bani Lal Mukarji Haran Chandra Dhar, 3 Bengal Law Reports, P. C. J., 130.

as a matter of fact this so-called "law" is not actually operative in this Presidency, and that amongst Hindus as amongst other people, the rate of interest is generally determined by whatever the rapacity of the lender will be satisfied with and the urgency of the borrower's need will induce him to consent to. In the few instances in which this is not the case the rate is settled by custom rather than by reference to the tenets of the written Hindu law.

12. The history of the past, at any rate, satisfies His Excellency in Council that there is no protection for the ryots from exorbitant interest in the rules of Hindu law, and he is very strongly of opinion that amongst other measures necessary for regulating the liabilities of indebted agriculturists, it is most essential that the Courts should be empowered to "take into consideration the equity of the interest charged even though," to use the words of your letter, "it may have been distinctly agreed to by the defendant." Ryots in their ignorance and helplessness will generally agree to any rate that may be asked of them trusting to the future to obtain easier terms, or to evade payment altogether; and where the object of the Judge is simply to ascertain what is reasonably due to the creditor, the agreement of the ryot cannot be regarded as of any importance. In a large number of cases indeed, it is believed that the ryot signs the bond without even knowing what rate of interest he has signed for or what other terms are contained in it.

13. The Governor in Council is aware, as pointed out in your 10th paragraph, that in my letter No. 2202, dated 6th April 1877. His Excellency the late Governor of Bombay in Council expressed an opinion which was unfavourable to the grant of discretionary powers to Courts to reduce the rate of interest. But when the settlement of the amount both of principal and interest is left (as is intended by the provisions of the Draft Bill submitted with my letter No. 308, and as is still recommended by the Governor in Council,) to the discretion of the Courts, or of the arbitrators to be appointed by them, this objection loses its force, and it would obviously be useless to empower the Courts to deal with the principal and not also with the interest.

14. With reference to your 12th paragraph, the provisions of Bombay Act VII. of 1866 were not overlooked by this Government, but that law was found even in the case of Hindus to whom alone it applies to afford no real protection to the ryot. With that Act, as one generally applicable to all Hindus, whether agriculturists or not, His Excellency the Governor in Council does not wish to interfere. But the special provisions which he has proposed for limiting the liability of a ryot for debts incurred by his ancestors go considerably further than does that Act, and these it is proposed should be applicable to all agriculturists within the dis-

tricts to which the Act will extend, whether they be Hindus or not. The principal object contemplated by these provisions is to prevent the money-lenders from turning the interest on an old debt into a permanent annuity payable by the debtor from generation to generation, and thus keeping the ryots in a perpetual state of indebtness and serfdom.

15. To recapitulate, then, the Governor in Council attaches the greatest importance to the provisions included under heads (*a*), (*b*) and (*c*) in your letter, and contained in sections 3 to 8 (inclusive) of the Draft Bill submitted with my letter No. 308, and is convinced that no measure for the relief of indebted agriculturists will be really adequate unless some such provisions form part of it. His Excellency in Council is willing to introduce a Bill by an early date into his Legislative Council embodying the requisite provisions under heads (*b*) and (*c*.)

16. The other points on which this Government suggested legislation are included in the heads (*d*) and (*e*) in your letter under reply, and have been provided for in the Draft Bill which the Government of India propose to introduce in the Legislative Council of the Governor General. These points, as more explicitly stated in your 14th para., are —

(1) Empowering a ryot at any time to claim the benefit of the Insolvent Act;

(2) Securing ryotwari land from sale in execution of any process unless it has been specifically pledged in a registered bond ; and

(3) Requiring all bonds relating to land, without reference to its value, to be registered.

17. The Governor in Council, while approving the proposed legislation on these three points, does yet, with a view to improving the details of the Bill so as to secure its more effectual operation, desire to offer the following suggestions, most of which, I am to say, were reserved by this Government for consideration when its own Bill should be before the Select Committee, under the impression that the local Legislative Council would have power to undertake the necessary legislation :—

(1) With respect to the insolvency provisions the Governor in Council deems it desirable that any creditor of an agriculturist to whom not less than Rs. 100 is owing, should be empowered to apply for a declaration of his debtor's insolvency, as well as the debtor himself. This point though not expressly mentioned in my letter No. 308, was provided for, with the concurrence of this Govern-

ment, in the Draft Bill submitted with that letter, and it is thought to be but equitable that the creditors should have equal rights with the debtors. The provision inserted in section 28 of the above Bill entitling an insolvent agriculturist to an absolute discharge from his debts if they were not incurred by himself as well if they do not exceed in the aggregate Rs. 200, is also thought to be a desirable one. But the Governor in Council will not press these proposed additions to section 2 of the Government of India's Draft Bill if that Government should not concur in the necessity for them.

(2) The provisions against the sale of land in execution of decrees should, His Excellency in Council thinks, extend to all land belonging to agriculturists, whether it pays revenue or not. A very large number of agricultural holdings in this Presidency are entirely exempt from land-revenue, and the political danger of depriving an agricultural population of its land is more serious when it pays no revenue to Government than when it is fully assessed. The land on which the ryots' houses stand is also, as a rule, not subject to payment of revenue, and it is desirable to include it in the exemption from liability to seizure in execution.

(3) The proposal embodied in section 4 of the Government of India's Draft Bill for making the compulsory clauses of the Registration Act applicable to *all* instruments relating to land, irrespectively of its value, might, His Excellency in Council thinks, be usefully extended so as to require the execution and registration of all instruments to which agriculturists are parties before a Public Notary, in the manner proposed by the Committee on the Deccan Riots at page 119 of their Report. Legislation in this direction was, as you have pointed out, approved by His Excellency the late Governor in Council, in clause (6) of para. 13 of my letter No. 2202, dated 6th April 1877, and it is suggested that some sections similar in effect to those which will be found in the Appendix to this letter should be substituted for section 4 of the Government of India's Draft Bill.

18. With respect to the local extent of the Bill, I am directed to state that His Excellency the Governor in Council would prefer that power should be taken in it to extend its operation by order of Government to any part of the Presidency. The circumstances of the ryots in some other places in the Presidency may be found to resemble those of the ryots in the four districts to

which it is proposed to apply the Bill in the first instance, and although the peculiar condition of these latter districts justifies the adoption of special tentative measures for the protection of the ryots in them, there appears to His Excellency in Council to be no good reason why they should be especially favoured, or why Government should not assure the ryots in the rest of the Presidency of their desire to extend the benefits of the measure to them also, if its operation in the four districts of the Deccan should, after some experience, promise to be successful.

19. To the questions raised in your 16th para., I am directed to reply as follows :—

1st.—The object of the Bill being to protect *bonâ fide* agriculturists only, this Government would desire to exempt only the land of agriculturists from liability to attachment in execution, but as I have already explained it would wish to see *all* land of agriculturists thus protected and not merely revenue paying land.

2nd.—The proviso to section 3 of the Government of India's draft Bill should, it is thought, be omitted, the intention of His Excellency the Governor in Council being, as shown by Section 26 of the draft Bill, submitted with my letter No. 308, that the exemption of land from liability to sale should continue *after* as well as before the debtor becomes insolvent. The protection to the ryot will otherwise be but very imperfect, and the advantage to him of being declared insolvent will be greatly reduced.

3rd.—The scope of section 4 should, in the opinion of this Government, be restricted in its application as that of section 3 is restricted, namely, it should apply to agriculturists and to instruments affecting their land only.

4th.—Oral mortgages are not customary in the Deccan of this Presidency, and there would be no hardship in letting the 2nd para. of section 4 stand as it is.

20. With reference to para. 18 of your letter I am to state that His Excellency the Governor in Council will be prepared, when the Bill becomes law, to make such arrangements as shall from time to time appear necessary for increase of establishment, whether in the Judicial or Registration Department, in consequence of the additional duties devolving upon those Departments. If these arrangements should involve some increase of expenditure, as it is probable they will, this Government will use its best endeavours to meet the same, feeling fully assured that the revenues could not be more legitimately or wisely employed than

in endeavouring to secure the happiness and prosperity of a loyal and contented peasantry.

21. In conclusion the Government of Bombay accept the Bill of the Government of India so far as the Bill goes, and will proceed to legislate locally on the points suggested by the Government of India— being thankful to see even this much of improvement introduced, although it falls considerably short of what is desired. But for the reasons assigned in these papers the Government of Bombay earnestly request that the additional provisions now recommended may be allowed.

I have the honour to be, &c.,

(Signed) E. W. RAVENSCROFT,
Chief Secretary to Government.

SECTIONS TO BE SUBSTITUTED FOR SECTION 4 OF THE GOVERNMENT OF INDIA'S DRAFT BILL.

Appointment of Public Notaries.

1. The Local Government may appoint such persons, whether public officers or not, as it thinks proper, to be Public Notaries.

Each such person shall be Public Notary for such local area as the Local Government shall prescribe.

Instruments to which an agriculturist is a party not to be deemed valid unless executed before a Public Notary.

2. No instrument to which an agriculturist is a party executed after the passing of this Act in any place in which this Act is in force shall be received in any Court of Justice, or by any persons having by law or consent of parties authority to receive evidence, as creating, modifying, transferring, or extinguishing or purporting to create, modify, transfer, or extinguish any right or obligation,

or as evidence in any civil proceeding,

or shall be acted upon in any such Court, or by any such person as aforesaid, or by any public officer,

unless such instrument is written by or under the superintendence of, and is attested by, a Public Notary.

3. When any persons, one or more of whom is an agriculturist, desire to execute any instrument, they shall present themselves before the Public Notary appointed by the Local Government for the area in which the said agriculturist, or any one of the said agriculturists resides, who after satisfying himself in such manner as he deems fit as to the identity of the parties, and receiving from them the prescribed fee, and the stamp, if any, which may be necessary, shall write the instrument, or cause the same to be written under his suprintendence and require the parties to execute it in his presence.

Instruments to be written by or under the superintendence of a Public Notary and executed in his presence.

Every instrument so written and executed shall be attested by the Public Notary, and also, if any of the parties thereto is unable to read and write, by two respectable witnesses.

Attestation of such instruments.

4. Every Public Notary shall keep a Register of instruments executed before him.

Registration of instruments by Public Notaries.

As soon as any instrument has been completely executed before a Public Notary, he shall make, or cause a copy of it to be made, in his Register. He shall deliver the original instrument to the party entitled to the custody of the same, and a certified copy thereof to the other party, or to each of the other parties, if there be more than one.

Previous to delivery the original instrument and each such copy shall be endorsed under the Public Notary's signature, with the date of registration, the name and residence of the Public Notary, and the volume and page of the Register in which the instrument has been registered.

5. In every instrument written by or under the superintendence of a Public Notary the amount and nature of the consideration shall be fully stated. If the instrument is to be executed in supersession, or partly in supersession, of previous instruments, such instruments shall be produced before the Public Notary and shall be fully described in the instrument to be executed, and shall be marked by the Public Notary, under his signature, for identification.

Consideration to be fully stated in every instrument executed before a Public Notary.

The Public Notary shall also endorse the instrument with a note, under his signature, recording whether or not the transfer of the consideration stated therein, or of any part thereof, took place in his presence.

6. Every instrument executed and registered in accordance with the foregoing provisions shall be deemed to have been duly registered under the provisions of the Indian Registration Act, 1877; and no instrument which ought to have been executed before a Public Notary, but has been otherwise executed, shall be registered by any officer acting under the said Act, or in any public office, or shall be authenticated by any public officer.

Registration under this Act to be deemed equivalent to registration under the Indian Registration Act, 1877.

7. Any person, not being a Public Notary, who writes any instrument which this Act requires to be executed before a Public Notary, otherwise than by direction and under the superintendence of a Public Notary, shall be punished for each such offence, on conviction before a Magistrate, with fine which may extend to one hundred rupees.

Penalty, if person not being a Public Notary, writes any instrument.

8. Nothing in this Act shall be deemed to require any instrument to which the Government or any officer of Government in his official capacity is a party to be executed before a Public Notary.

Exemption of instruments to which Government or any officer of Government is a party.

9. The Local Government may from time to time frame rules not inconsistent with this Act for regulating the appointment, duties, and remuneration of Public Notaries, and for prescribing the fees to be paid to Public Notaries.

Local Government may frame rules.

No. 4.

To

HIS EXCELLENCY THE HONOURABLE THE
GOVERNOR IN COUNCIL,
BOMBAY.

Legislative.

India Office, *26th December 1878.*

SIR,

I have to acknowledge the receipt of the despatch from your Excellency in Council, dated the 30th September last,

No. 11, transmitting for my information, copy of a " Bill for the Relief of Indebted Agriculturists in certain parts of the Presidency of Bombay," which has been introduced into your Legislative Council.

2. On the 16th November, I despatched to Your Excellency the following telegraphic message:—" Delay proceeding with Indebted Agriculturists Bill. Despatch follows."

3. I now proceed to state the reasons which induce me to doubt whether the provisions in the measure before me are at all adequate for grappling with the evils which have been so prominently brought to light in the report of the Deccan Riots Commission.

4. When that report arrived in this country in May 1876, Lord Salisbury was so deeply impressed with the distressing picture therein given of the agricultural population in the Deccan, that he awaited with great anxiety some communication from the Government of India as to the steps intended to be taken. But none such having arrived after an interval of nearly a year-and-a-half, His Lordship appointed a Select Committee of his Council to consider the report.

5. The Committee began to sit in November 1877, held several meetings, and examined some experienced witnesses well acquainted with the Bombay Presidency; but before they had terminated their inquiries, a despatch was received from Your Excellency in Council in February of the present year, enclosing the draft of a Bill for the Relief of Indebted Agriculturists in the Presidency of Bombay, and which you desired to have introduced into the Council of the Supreme Government.

6. That Bill contained three main principles :

(1.)—That the Court should be obliged to enter into the merits of every money claim, whether secured by bond or not, and should only award such sums, whether for principal or interest, as they deemed just, and should in no case give compound interest or a larger amount of interest than the principal sum.

(2.)—That the principle of the Insolvent Act, as prevailing in the presidency town, should be applied to the Deccan agriculturists.

(3.)—That land should not be sold in execution for debt, unless specially pledged in a bond duly registered.

Lord Salisbury, although not fully satisfied with all the principles contained in this measure, thought the occasion for attempting remedial legislation to be so urgent that he sanctioned by telegram the introduction of the Bill, being quite willing that the experimental legislation contemplated in the Council of the Governor General should be attempted. I also am of the same opinion.

7. Leave was accordingly given for the introduction of the Bill into the Council of the Governor General on the 28th June last, but, for reasons which have not been transmitted to me, the Government of India preferred, instead of one comprehensive Act, that your Government should pass a law dealing with some minor points relating to interest and to ancestral debts. The Bill which I have now before me is the result of the action of the Supreme Government.

8. I can well understand the difficulties which have deterred the Government of India from dealing with this subject as a whole, and which have induced them to leave minor points to be disposed of by the Local Government; but if the evils sought to be remedied are capable of being eradicated by legislation, I am clearly of opinion that they should not be dealt with piecemeal.

9. The very able report of the Commission, and the mass of valuable information contained in the appendices enable, us, I think, to draw the conclusion that some of the great causes which lie at the bottom of the poverty of the Deccan are wholly beyond the reach of the legislator, and are inherent in the national character and in the customs which have prevailed for countless generations. The Deccan ryots, like the general mass of the cultivating classes in other parts of India, are entirely without capital, and are driven on the first bad harvest into the hands of the money-lender, not only for the means to till their fields, but for food to keep themselves and their cattle alive till the crops of the next season are matured. This fact has created the system of borrowing at high interest, which prevails so largely amongst the agricultural population, and has made the existence of a money-lender in a Hindu village as essential as that of a ploughman.

10. The normal condition of a Hindu cultivator is much aggravated by local circumstances in parts of the Deccan: the soil is sterile, the climate is precarious, a good crop being in some parts obtained only once in three years; the fall of rain is scanty; the peasantry, though a sturdy and ordinarily a law-abiding people, are described as "utterly uneducated and with a narrow range of intelligence." It is obvious that the causes men-

tioned in this and the preceding paragraph are not to be easily modified by a legislative Act.

11. The districts in which the riots took place came into British possession in 1819, and at that period and for 20 years afterwards divers causes, such as the ravages of Holkar's army and the dreadful famine which followed his campaign,—a famine which was repeated two or three times during the first 20 years of the century,—the subsequent heavy fall of prices, and the consequently oppressive weight of the old Marátha rate of assessment, which was at first continued by the Government of the day; all these had produced an amount of poverty and ruin which the Settlement Officer writing in 1838 found it impossible to describe.

12. The Government of that day, however, made strenuous efforts to better this state of things. They reduced the assessment from an average rate of 13½ annas to 7 annas, they gave the cultivators for the first time fixity of tenure, and they abolished extra cesses.

13. A Resolution of the Government of Bombay, dated 30th August 1875, describes the satisfactory results of this new settlement of the land: "In 1838 more than 50 per cent. of arable land was waste; in 1871 only 1 per cent. Population increased during the term of the settlement 39½ per cent., agricultural cattle 19 per cent, ploughs 22½ per cent, carts 270 per cent; and wells 40 per cent. Government land was unsaleable in 1838; during the last five years of the settlement examination of the registration records showed that it fetched from 10 to 52 times its assessment. Thirty years ago there were no made roads, and communication was costly and difficult; the táluka is now traversed by the railway and by several excellent roads, and the increase in the number of carts indicates the extent to which the people avail themselves of the new facilities of communication with markets."

14. Satisfactory as this picture of progress is (and similar ones may be produced from all parts of India), there is undeniable evidence in the report before me that the very improvements introduced under our rule, such as fixity of tenure and lowering of the assessments, have been the principal causes of the great destitution which the Commissioners found to exist.

15. The saleable value of the land greatly increased the credit of the ryot, and encouraged beyond measure the national habit of borrowing, which I have before observed on. High prices led to extended cultivation, to more expensive modes of living, to larger outlay on the great stimulant to Hindu expenditure—marriage ceremonies. Recourse to the money-lender became then more

frequent than before, and the class of money-lenders competing for custom increased in most undue proportions. The first fall in prices, and the first bad harvests, both of which had occurred in these districts, found the cultivators as poor as ever, but encumbered with an additional mass of debt. Still no one would advocate as an amendment of the law that we should abolish fixity of tenure or increase the assessment on the land.

16. Up to this point, then, I can see no opening on which the legislator can enter with effect. In all civilized societies there is a vast amount of suffering and destitution, very lamentable to contemplate, but which it is wholly out of the powers of the State by any direct action to eradicate. All that Government can do is to take care that its own institutions shall not aggravate the misery which so often follows the spontaneous action of the population.

17. This last observation brings me to the consideration of the Bill now before me. Your Government has distinctly perceived that the Courts of Justice we have instituted, and the law they administer, operate most harshly, and frequently with great injustice, on debtors, who form the great bulk of the population. Here, therefore, is an opportunity for the beneficial interference of Government. Both the Bills which I have alluded to above have been framed with the view of mitigating the law, and of extending the powers of Judges to modify the contracts entered into between man and man.

18. I may say at once, after full consideration, that the Bill introduced into Your Excellency's Council appears to me to be so dependent upon the character of the Judge, and so likely to be defeated by agreements between helpless debtors and wily creditors, that I cannot suppose it will lead to any substantial results.

19. The question then remains as to what shall be done, for it is clear that some alteration in the existing law is imperatively called for. A fitting measure can only be properly prepared in India. For the consideration of the two Governments I proceed to notice the most salient points which have presented themselves to me on this head in the report and appendices of the Commissioners, and the lines of improvement which have suggested themselves. And I shall transmit a copy of this despatch to the Government of India, with the desire that they shall immediately apply themselves to the subject in a comprehensive manner.

20. Under Native Government, it seems no assistance was ordinarily afforded by the State to a creditor for the recovery of his debts. No Court of Justice was open to him, and he was left to his own devices to extort what was due, Government winking at very forcible measures that were occasionally employed. The result

was not so bad as might have been expected. It speaks well for the national character that contracts were rarely repudiated. And the Commissioners observe that in these proceedings "honesty was the best policy for the ryot, and caution was a necessity to the money-lender."

21. On the establishment of our rule, however, courts of justice were established everywhere.

22. It is abundantly manifest to me, on the evidence collected by the Commissioners, that no evil has been so loudly, and I must say so justly, complained of by the people as the action of the courts. The extreme severity of the law on debtors has been pointed out by the report.

23. The Judges are only the instruments for enforcing the law as it is, and no blame is imputable to them. But the extracts from the statements of the Judges themselves, cited by Mr. Colvin, demonstrate completely that, irrespective of the hardness of the law, they are incapable of administering justice between debtor and creditor.

24. One Judge says—" the Subordinate Judges in this district are much overworked, and really have not time to investigate cases properly and to weigh the evidence"; another says—" our Subordinate Judges are too hard-worked to allow, even if they were inclined to do so, of their going into the history of such cases. The court which was inclined to go into the old history of a case would have nothing but the sowkar's books to go upon if he produced them."

25. Another Judge enumerates the frauds perpetrated by the money-lenders, and states that they are practised with impunity. When "the deluded kunbi * * * is dragged into Court he is unable to answer the claims, or if he states a defence he is not in a position to prove it."

26. The Commission also assign another reason for our Courts being mere instruments in the hands of the money-lenders, namely, their great distance from the home of the debtor. A money-lender may easily instruct a pleader to take out process against a debtor in a court 40 or 50 miles distant at little cost to himself, but it is ruin for a cultivator, dependent on his daily labour, to absent himself for days together from his field, even if he has a valid defence.

27. Here then it is quite clear we have evils produced by the Legislature itself, and which it is within the competence of Government to extirpate.

B 862—10

28. I am extremely unwilling at any time, but especially now, to suggest any increase to the cost of administration; if it is made manifest that our courts of justice are inefficient in these special cases, and that our Judges admit they have not time to inquire into the real facts by a thorough investigation, I would suggest that although an addition to the cost of administration is very much to be deprecated, it is imperative to remedy the defects here pointed out. A re-distribution of expenditure might be made and I observe that it is stated in the Commissioner's report that 88 subordinate courts bring in a revenue of Rs. 16,89,744, and that the expenditure, including salaries of Judges, is only Rs. 6,90,717.

29. Evils such as have been depicted above, arising out of the costliness and inaccessibility of courts of justice, though of a much slighter character, existed in England also, and the remedy suggested was the establishment of Small Cause Courts. This innovation, after having been opposed sturdily for many years, was finally adopted, and has proved so eminently successful that nearly every year witnesses some extension of their powers. In India also the institution has been partially adopted. But it is from France that the most important evidence can be obtained as to the value of local courts. The agricultural population there is more akin than the English to that of India, inasmuch as French landed property is in the hands of inumerable petty owners, who cultivate with their own hands.

30. In that country small causes up to 100 francs are tried in every village before the Juge de Paix. The proceedings are summary, written pleadings are prohibited, and his decision is final on all sums not exceeding 50 francs. In the belief that a more detailed account of the proceedings of these courts than is to be found in the Code Civil might be useful to the authorities in India, Sir Frederic Goldsmid was requested to obtain some information on his late official visit to Paris, and I herewith transmit to Your Excellency the note he has furnished. It will be observed that the early meeting of the parties before the Judge in order to produce an amicable settlement of the suit, which is so strongly insisted upon by Mr. Bentham, is spoken of by the French authorities in the highest terms.

31. I cannot doubt that the existence of courts with summary jurisdiction and without appeal up to a limited amount, and possibly with the exclusion of professional pleaders, placed in ocalities within reach of the suitor's home would tend to remove many of the evils which have been brought to notice.

32. I am quite aware of the difficulties which intervene to prevent the entrusting of large summary powers to Subordinate

Judges, and that no portion of a Judge's functions requires more experience and self-control than the exercise of that large discretion over contracts which the High Court inculcates as belonging to Indian Judges under the law. For this reason it is obvious that the summary jurisdiction to be attributed to Subordinate Judges should only extend to a very limited amount.

33. But I am inclined to think that the principle of summary jurisdiction without appeal might be conferred experimentally on all civil Judges in the Deccan with great benefit, and the limit to be fixed would of course vary with the rank of the Judge. If the District Judge could devote one day in the week to the disposal of small causes up to, say, Rs. 500, as was the practice formerly of the Supreme Court at Bombay, he would, in my opinion, confer infinite benefit on the community; he would afford an example to the courts below him of the manner in which such jurisdictions should be exercised; and he would personally derive the benefit which experience in this country proves to result from a judge of appeal being occasionally employed in trying original causes.

34. How far these suggestions can be made applicable to the portions of India to which the investigations of the Deccan Riots Commission have extended, I leave it for the Supreme Government, in communication with Your Excellency in Council, to decide; but I am desirous that no time should be lost, and that a comprehensive measure should be at once proceeded with, founded on the principles which I have indicated, and on those which Lord Salisbury had previously sanctioned.

I have, &c.,
(Signed)   CRANBROOK.

No. 1.

Des Justices de Paix en France.

Paris, le 18 Décembre 1877.

Les justices de paix ont été instituées en France par la loi de 16-24 Août 1790.

[1] Il y a un juge de paix par canton, il est assisté d'un greffier et il lui est adjoint deux suppléants depuis la loi du 29 Ventôse, an IX. A Paris, il y a autant de juges de paix que d'arrondisse-

---

[1] There are 20 "arrondissements," which form so many "cantons" of juges de paix in Paris. The average population is about 90,000 —F. J. G. Average superficies marked at 390.

ments, quelques grandes villes de France en ont également plusieurs.

Nul ne peut être juge de paix s'il n'st Français et âgé de trente ans au moins (Art. 209 de la constitution de l'an-I II.), Il est nommé comme tous les fonctionaires publics, ainsi que les suppléants et le greffier, par Décret due Chef de l'Etat, et prête serment au tribunal de première instance. Aucun d'eux n'est inmovible.

Les juges de paix jouissent d'un traitement qui varie de 1,800 à 5,000, les fonctions des suppléants sont gratuites ; aussi ces derniers sont il choisis parmi les officiers ministériels (notaires, avoués, maires, &c.). Quant aux greffiers, ils jouissent d'un traitement fixe de 600 fr à 2,400 fr, et touchent, en outre, des droits d'expédition pour les actes de leur ministére.

Les juges de paix ont une triple mission :—

1°. En *matière penale*, ils connaissent des contraventions de simple police (Code d'Instruction Criminelle, Art. 137 et suivant) et prononcent des peines variant de 1 à 19 francs d'amende et de un à cinq jours de prison (C. P., Art. 461 et suivant). Ces jugements sont susceptibles d'appel lors qu'ils infligent une pénalité supérieure à cinq francs d'amende ; l'appel est portè devant le tribunal correctionnel (Code d'Inst^{on} Cr^{lle}, Art. 172 et suivants).

2°. En *matière civile*, ils statuent,—

En dernier ressort, sur toutes actions personelles ou mobiliéres jusqu'à la valeur de 100 francs.

A charge d'appel devant le tribunal civil, sur tontes demands, contestations, &c., excédant cette somme selon les distinctions de la loi du 29 Mai 1838, modifée le 2 Mai 1855.

3°. En *matière de conciliation*, ils doivent s'efforcer de mettre d'accord les parties en cause, de façon à prévenir le proces par un arrangement aimable dont ills dressent procés-verbal.

Cette démarche est le préliminaire obligatoire de tout procès entre parties capables de transiger et hors le cas d'urgence ; toute demande en matière commerciale est reputée urgente, et dispensée, par suite, du préliminaire de conciliation. (Code de Procédure Civil, Art. 49.)

N. B.—The appointment of the juge de paix, I am told, is held pending the pleasure of the governing authorities, and is in no way limited to a certain number of years.

(Signed)   F. J. GOLDSMID.

No. 2.

Hotel de Louvre, Paris.
24th December 1877.

My dear Sir Erskine Perry,

The authorities tell me they cannot give me a fair average of a rural canton, as they vary so considerably in extent, and a large extent may sometimes have but a small population; but a highly instructive and useful volume called "Statistique de la France,"* of which the first volume has been lent me, shows that this country has a superficies of 52,857,675 hectares, and that there were in 1872 no less than 2,857 "justices de paix" for a population of 36,102,921. This book published by Guillaumin 14, Rue Richelieu, in 1875, might be doubtless procured at Hachette's or Baillière's, in London. In the meanwhile, I make an extract to the point:—

* Par Maurice Block.

"Le traitment des juges de paix, réglé par la loi du 21 Juin
"1845, et por l'ordonnance du 2 Novembre 1846, est le même que
"celui des juges de tribunaux de première instance, dans les villes
"oú siegent ces tribunaux; dans les autres localités, il est ainsi
"réglé par l'ordonnance du 2 Novembre 1846, et par trois décrets,
"du 23 Août 1858, du 22 Septembre 1862, et du 12 Novembre
"1868; 3,000 fr. dans les cantons composant les arrondissements
"de St. Denis et de Sceaux; 3,000 fr. dans les villes de 39,000 âmes
"et au-dessus (Roubaix, Tourcaring); 2,700 fr. dans les villes de
"20,000 âmes et au-dessus (Arles, Cette, Elbeuf, Le Creusot, et
"Mezières, chef-lieu de département); 2,400 fr. dans les chief-
"lieux d'arrondissement où ne siége pas de tribunal de premiére
"instance, et qui ont mois de 20,000 âmes (Argelés, Bonnac,
"Commercy, la Palisse, la Tour-du-Pin, Manléon, le Puget Mhes-
"siers, et Poligny, &c., &c.)", i. e., briefly, 2,100 francs for a minimum population of 3,000; 1,800 francs where less than 3,000. It appears, moreover, that 2,051 "juges de paix" belong to the last class, and 248 to the penultimate. Paris "juges de paix" (there are 20) have 3,000 francs, besides an office allowance of 1,500 franc=9,500 (380*l*).

As regards the average size of a rural canton, I take the letter "A" in the Directory of Departments, &c., and strike an average of cantons coming under that letter,* I then find the average of hectares in 11 Departments (speci-

	Cantons.			Cantons.
* Ain ....having	36	Ardennes......having		31
Aisne............ „	37	Ariège......... „		20
Allier .... „	28	Aube .... „		26
Alpes Hautes . „	24	Aude .... „		31
Alpes Basses... „	30	Aveyron ...... „		42
Ardèche ...... „	31			

fied in margin). The result is that there are about 30 cantons in 1,560,000 acres (634,458 hectares). Each "juge de paix" would then have an extent of 52,000 acres.

On again looking over Block's Book of Statistics, I find 91 Departments with—

   363 arrondissements.
   2,850 cantons.
   37,386 communes.
   38,067,094 population in 1872 (an average of 13,346 to the canton).
   36,472,031 do. in 1866.

Believe me,

Very truly yours,

(Signed) F. J. GOLDSMID.

P. S.—I make the hectare$=2\frac{1}{2}$ acres, less $\frac{1}{8}$th of a rood. The "Annuaire" of the "Bureau des Longitudes" makes it 247,114,316 acres.

As regards "conciliation," it is considered here to work admirably. They have endless arguments in its favour; but their higher Judges have not the power of using it as ours in England (which my informant seemed to lament). It is the special privilege of the "juges de paix."

No. 222.

To

  THE SECRETARY TO THE GOVERNMENT OF BOMBAY.

Fort William, the 26th February 1879.

SIR,

  I am directed to communicate for the information and guidance of His Excellency the Governor in Council, Bombay, the following observations and instructions on the subject of the Despatch No. 4, under date the 26th December last, addressed by Her Majesty's Secretary of State to the Government of Bombay, regarding the measures to be taken for the relief of the ryots in the Deccan with reference to the facts stated and the opinions expressed in the report of the Deccan Riots Commission.

2. The report in question was reviewed at length in your letter of the 6th April 1877, No. 2202, in which the subject was dealt with under three heads, namely—

(1) the nature and causes of the riots themselves;
(2) the defects in the revenue administration which may have contributed to cause the riots, and the remedies advisable; and
(3) the effect of the civil law and civil courts on the Deccan peasantry, and the measures advisable for altering the law or reforming the courts.

Under the first head, the Bombay Government showed that the riots were confined to an arid tract of the central Deccan, comprising parts of the four Districts of Poona, Sátára, Ahmednagar and Sholápur. There was comparatively little serious crime or violence. The hostility of the ryots towards their creditors, the money-lenders, lay at the bottom of the disturbances. This feeling had been increasing in strength for some time. The peasantry are poor owing to the sterility of the soil and the extreme variableness of the seasons. They habitually contract debts beyond their means; most of them are said to be "steeped in debt." Since 1836 the ryots have been able to give a lien on their lands to their creditors, who consequently gained more and more power over the ryots. From 1850 to 1866 there was a period of great good fortune for the Deccan ryots. Railways and roads were made through the country; other public works were constructed; money was spent largely; and the cycle of prosperous years culminated in the era of the American war, when Deccan cotton fetched three to six times its usual price, and the market price of other agricultural products rose enormously. But after the close of the American war, a great fall of prices took place. During the period of plenty the ryots had, many of them, paid off their debts; but they had contracted costly habits of life; and these habits they could not (or did not) suddenly discard. Thus, the peasantry soon became involved in debt again. The money-lenders, most of whom belonged to an alien race whose home was in Rajputána, had little sympathy for the peasants. Civil Courts had been multiplied, and their procedure had been rendered prompt. Creditors took their debtors into court, obtained decrees, sold up the ryots' land, and reduced the ryots to the position of serfs. Hatred towards the money-lenders became more bitter, discontent with the procedure of the courts was engendered, and in March 1875, the popular feeling found expression in attacks and outrages on village bankers. One feature of these outrages was that the account books and bonds found in the money-lenders' possession were destroyed by the rioters.

3. On the second head, the Bombay Government, differing from the opinion of two members of the Commission, considered that the recent revision of the land revenue assessment in the Deccan, the principles on which that revision was conducted, and the results of that revision, had no share in causing the riots of 1875, or in causing the depressed condition of the peasantry. The Bombay Government showed that before 1875 they had, in consequence of the great fall of prices, made considerable reductions in the land revenue demand recently imposed on parts of the four districts where the riots occurred; and they had laid down restrictions on future increases of the land revenue assessment. The Bombay Government saw no sufficient reason for acting on the Commission's recommendation that large increases of the land revenue should be made leviable gradually, instead of being carried out *per saltum* in one year as at present. And they did not see their way either to the Government usefully taking the place of the village banker and lending money to the ryots, or to any arrangement for altering the land revenue year by year according to the variations of the season. The Bombay Government concluded their review of this part of the subject by stating that the state of the ryots of the Deccan was most unsatisfactory; that one-third of the ryots were hopelessly involved and were little better than serfs, practically at the mercy of the bankers; and that ruin, if not arrested, would soon overtake the great body of the ryots.

4. Under the third head, namely, the action of the civil law and of the civil courts, the Bombay Government grouped the difficulties of the ryot in three classes. Before a ryot was taken into court by his creditor, he was at a disadvantage by reason of his poverty, his ignorance, his extravagance, the load of ancestral debt which weighed upon him, the usurious interest charged, and the fraud occasionally practised by the money-lender, and also by reason of the shortness of the term of limitation which entailed the frequent renewal of bonds at usurious interest. When a ryot was taken into court by his creditor, he was at a disadvantage by reason of fraud practised by court subordinates in collusion with the creditor, whereby a summons was often returned as served when the ryot knew nothing whatever about the suit or summons; by reason of the *ex parte* decrees which followed upon such fraudulent returns to summonses; by reason of the distance of the courts, the long duration of contested suits, and the inability of the Judge to help the ryot to put his case properly; and by reason of the high cost of litigation. After a decree has been passed against a ryot, he is under great difficulties, because he is liable to be imprisoned for debt; because his property of *all* kinds was (but is not now under the new Code of Civil Procedure) liable to forced sale; because his ancestral lands are liable to a forced sale cou-

ducted under circumstances which (until the new Procedure Code was passed) were generally very disadvantageous to the ryot. For the purpose of relieving the ryot from some of these difficulties the Governor in Council, proceeding on the recommendation contained in the report or Minutes of the Commission, proposed—

    (a) that all bonds between ryots and money-lenders should be executed by notaries public;

    (b) that the ryot should be entitled to receive from his banker a yearly statement of his account;

    (c) that receipts for a ryot's payments should always be entered on the bonds;

    (d) that ryots should have pass-books, wherein their dealings with their bankers should be entered;

    (e) that the period of limitation for money bonds should be altered from three to twelve years;

    (f) that Civil judges should go more frequently on circuit;

    (g) that the number of judges should be increased;

    (h) that the High Court should instruct the Subordinate Courts to act up to the law which binds Judges to weigh equitably the incidents to a disputed contract before it decrees full performance;

    (i) that the High Court should take steps to keep the miscellaneous costs of litigation as low as possible;

    (j) that Government should be enabled to advance money to insolvent ryots whose holdings were put up to auction by the civil courts, and should gradually recover through an agency for the management of such holdings.

The Governor in Council felt unable to support the recommendations of the Commission to the effect that—

    (k) imprisonment for debt should be abolished;

    (l) sales of land in execution of money decrees should be abolished.

5. With this letter from the Bombay Government was forwarded a Minute by the Honourable Mr. Rogers, a member of that Government, who advocated the abolition of imprisonment for debt, on the ground that the power to apply for execution against the person is seldom used by creditors, save as a means of extorting fresh and more usurious bonds from creditors.

6. Owing to the famine and other causes, the recommendations made by the Commission and by the Local Government were not formally dealt with by the Government of India during the year 1877; but in the Code of Civil Procedure passed early in that year, before the receipt of your letter of the 6th April, but after the report of the Commission had reached the Government of India, certain provisions were introduced, the effect of which was to afford great protection to the ryot as regards the sale of his land under decrees of court.

7. His Excellency Sir Richard Temple having, in the meantime, succeeded to the office of Governor, the Bombay Government took up the question again in their letter of 19th January 1878, No. 308. In this letter the Bombay Government stated that, although the evils on which the Commission had reported were less actively felt, still there was every reason to apprehend that they would sooner or latter break out again. The Governor in Council admitted that the new Code of Civil Procedure (Act X. of 1877) had improved the condition of the ryot; for his necessaries were now protected from sale; his lands, instead of being subjected to forced sale, might be placed under the management of revenue officers for the mutual advantage of his creditor and himself; he might protect himself from arrest by showing himself to be insolvent; and if his total debts did not exceed Rs. 200, he might, after his insolvency had been proved, be absolved by the court from all further liability. Nevertheless, the Bombay Government held that some of the roots of the mischief, on which the Commission had reported, remained untouched. The Governor in Council proposed early legislation on five separate matters, and forwarded a draft Bill to provide—

(1) that in money suits against ryots the court should be compelled to go behind the bond, into the facts and incidents of the transactions which led up to the bond;

(2) that in suits against ryots compound interest should not be decreed by the courts, and that simple interest in excess of the principal of a debt should not be allowed;

(3) that a ryot should be bound to pay more than the principal of, and certain limited interest on, ancestral debts;

(4) that a ryot should be entitled at any time to claim the benefit of the insolvency law, without waiting (as the present law compels him to do) until he is arrested in execution of a decree; and

(5) that a ryot's lands should not be sold in execution of a money decree unless they have been specifically pledged to the decree-holder by a registered bond.

83

8. The Bombay Government subsequently, in their letter of the 4th of the following month, adverting to the possibility that the Local Government might not be legally competent to legislate on such a matter, recommended that the necessary legislation should take place in the Council of the Governor General.

9. The representations of the Bombay Government, of which the above is a summary, as well as the report of the Commission, received the most careful consideration from the Governor General in Council, and on the 1st July 1878, the Government of India, in a letter from the Department of Revenue, Agriculture, and Commerce, No. 404, stated the conclusions at which they had arrived. Fully recognizing the great importance of the matter, and accepting the view taken by the Government of Bombay that a special remedy should be provided for the evils now weighing upon the ryots of the five districts embraced in the report of the Commission, the Government of India reviewed the five recommendations submitted by the Government of Bombay. Taking these recommendations in the order given above, the Government of India pointed out that Bombay Regulation V. of 1827, as well as decisions of the High Courts of Calcutta and Bombay, certainly authorise, if they do not absolutely require, the courts to demand satisfactory proof that the consideration set out in a bond has really been received by the defendants. And the Governor General in Council doubted the expediency of further legislation in that direction. In regard to the award of usurious interest, it was observed that the old Hindu law called *Dám-dupat* still obtains in the Deccan, and that under its provisions the creditor cannot, among Hindus, recover as interest a sum more than equal to the principal of a debt; but that, if the existing law on the subject was insufficient, the Bombay Legislature were competent to deal with the matter. In regard to the 3rd point, attention was invited to Act VII. of 1866 of the Bombay Council, whereby the liability of a Hindu for his ancestor's debts is restricted. At the same time it was said that if the provisions of that law did not give sufficient protection to ryots, the local Council would be competent to amend their own law on the matter, on the other points, namely, (4) a provision empowering a ryot to claim the benefit of the Insolvent Court, and (5) a provision exempting a ryot's land from sale save under a registered bond pledging the land in security for the debt, and requiring all bonds relating to be registered, a Bill was prepared for submission to the Governor General's Council, and a draft of that Bill was forwarded to the Bombay Government for their opinion.

10. The Government of Bombay in their letter of the 5th September 1878, No. 4579, accepted, subject to certain suggested modifications, the Bill which the Government of India proposed

to introduce into the Council of the Governor General in regard to points (4) and (5) described above. The Government of Bombay considered that the existing law and rulings of the High Court did not in practice suffice to protect the ryot from usurious compound interest, or from being unduly saddled with ancestral debts, and they remarked that the law, as it now exists on this point, applies only to particular classes of the community. His Excellency in Council expressed his readiness at once to act on the suggestion of the Government of India that a Bill to amend the law on the subject of points (2) and (3) above-mentioned should be laid before the local Legislature.

11. The Bombay Government again urged strongly that fresh legislation was needed to *require* not merely to *enable* the courts to go behind the bonds on which bankers sue ryots. They stated that at present it was not the practice of the civil courts of Bombay to require satisfactory proof that the consideration named in a bond had been actually received. They represented that any legislation in behalf of the Deccan ryots which did not fulfil this requirement would be a half measure, and must, therefore, be unsatisfactory. Further, the Local Government advised that the proposed legislation should provide for the establishment of local notaries public, as suggested by the Commission; and requested that power might be taken for extending the special legislation to other parts of the Bombay Presidency outside the four districts to which the enquiries of the Commission were mainly directed.

12. The Government of India, in replying to the foregoing representation in their letter of the 27th November 1878, adhered to the view that it was not expedient to legislate on point (1), in order to enable, or to require, courts to go behind the bond. The Governor General in Council held that the existing law enabled courts to do this, whenever the defendant contested the *bonâ fides* in a bond, and could support his objection. Any further legislation in that direction would practically be transferring to the plaintiff in suits for money due on a bond the burden of proof, which according to the Evidence Act lies upon the defendant. The Government of India were not prepared to assent to special legislation for the purpose of shifting the normal incidence of proof, as between the indebted agriculturist of the Deccan and those to whom his debts are due. The proposal to extend the insolvency clause of the Bill beyond Rs. 200 in the case of ancestral debts seemed to the Government of India unnecessary. As the Indian Registration Act provided sufficiently for the registration of deeds to which agriculturist were parties, and as the number of registration offices could be increased at the discretion of the Local

Government, it was deemed undesirable to create a second system of registration offices, under notaries public, side by side with the registration offices under Act III. of 1877.

13. Shortly after this letter was sent to the Government of Bombay, the Government of India received a telegram from the Secretary of State, desiring that the Bills referred to should not be proceeded with pending the receipt of a despatch from Her Majesty's Government. With that despatch, which bears date the 26th December last, the Government of India have been furnished with a copy of the despatch bearing the same date, No. 4, addressed to the Government of Bombay, in which the subject is fully reviewed and the conclusions are stated, at which the Secretary of State has arrived as to the objects that should be aimed at in the proposed legislation. It should be noted here that when this despatch was written, the Secretary of State was not in possession of the letters addressed by the Government of India to the Government of Bombay, under date the 1st July and the 27th November 1878. In regard to the procedure which is to be adopted, the Secretary of State has decided that evils which it is sought to remedy, so far as they may be capable of being eradicated by legislation, should not be dealt with piecemeal, but should be provided for in a single comprehensive enactment. It follows, therefore, that the whole of the legislation must be comprised in one Bill to be passed in the Council of the Governor General. One of the conclusions which Lord Cranbrook draws from the Report of the Commission is that—

some of the great causes which lie at the bottom of the poverty of the Deccan are wholly beyond the reach of the legislator, and are inherent in the national character and in the customs which have prevailed for countless generations

The grounds of this conclusion are stated in the following paragraphs :—

(9.) The Deccan ryots, like the general mass of the cultivating classes in other parts of India, are entirely without capital, and are driven on the first bad harvest into the hands of the money-lender, not only for the means to till their fields, but for food to keep themselves and their cattle alive till the crops of the next season are matured. This fact has created the system of borrowing at high interest which prevails so largely amongst the agricultural population, and has made the existence of a money-lender in a Hindu village as essential as that of a ploughman.

(10.) The normal condition of a Hindu cultivator is much aggravated by local circumstances in parts of the Deccan. The soil is sterile, the climate is precarious, a good crop being in some parts obtained only once in three years, the fall of rain is scanty, the peasantry, though a sturdy and ordinarily a law-abiding people, are described as 'utterly uneducated, and with a narrow range of intelligence.' It is obvious that the causes mentioned in this and the preceding paragraph are not to be easily modified by any legislative Act.

(11.) The districts in which the riots took place came into British possession in 1819, and at that period and for 20 years afterwards divers causes, such as the ravages of Holkar's army and the dreadful famine which followed his campaign, a famine which was repeated two or three times during the first 20 years of the century, the subsequent heavy fall of prices, and the consequently oppressive weight of the old Marátha rate of assessment which was at first continued by the Government of the day, all these had produced an amount of poverty and ruin which the Settlement Officer writing in 1838 found it impossible to describe.

(12.) The Government of that day, however, made strenuous efforts to better this state of things. They reduced the assessment from an average rate of 13½ annas to 7 annas, they gave the cultivators for the first time fixity of tenure, and they abolished extra cesses.

(13.) A Resolution of the Government of Bombay, dated 30th August 1875, describes the satisfactory results of this new settlement of the land. In 1838 more than 50 per cent. of arable land was waste; in 1871 only 1 per cent. Population increased, during the term of the settlement, 39½ per cent; agricultural cattle 19 per cent; ploughs 22½ per cent; carts 270 per cent; and wells 40 per cent. Government land was unsaleable in 1838; during the last five years of the settlement, examination of the Registration records showed that it fetched from 10 to 52 times its assessment. Thirty years ago there were no made-roads, and communication was costly and difficult; the táluka is now traversed by the railway and by several excellent roads, and the increase in the number of carts indicates the extent to which the people avail themselves of the new facilities of communication with markets.'

(14.) Satisfactory as this picture of progress is (and similar ones may be produced from all parts of India), there is undeniable evidence in the report before me that the very improvements introduced under our rule, such as fixity of tenure and lowering of the assessments, have been the principal causes of the great destitution which the commissioners found to exist.

(15.) The saleable value of the land greatly increased the credit of the ryot, and encouraged beyond measure the national habit of borrowing, which I have before observed on. High prices led to extended cultivation, to more expensive modes of living, to larger outlay on the great stimulant to Hindu expenditure, marriage ceremonies. Recourse to the money-lender became then more frequent than before, and the class of money-lenders competing for custom increased in most undue proportions. The first fall in prices, and the first bad harvests, both of which had occurred in these districts, found the cultivators as poor as ever, but encumbered with an additional mass of debt. Still no one would advocate, as an amendment of the law, that we should abolish fixity of tenure, or increase the assessment on the land.

(16.) Up to this point, then, I can see no opening on which the legislators can enter with effect. In all civilized societies there is a vast amount of suffering and destitution, very lamentable to contemplate, but which it is wholly out of the power of the State by any direct action to eradicate. All that Government can do is to take care that its own institutions shall not aggravate the misery which so often follows the spontaneous action of the population.

The Secretary of State then proceeds to state his opinion as to the nature of the remedies that should be applied. His conclusion is that these remedies mainly consist in the adoption of measures for mitigating the harshness with which the courts of justice and the law operate on the debtors who form the great bulk of the population. He remarks that the civil judges are so few, and their courts are so distant from the homes of the ryots; that they are incapable of administering justice between debtor and creditor. And while reluctant to suggest, especially at the present time, any increase of the cost of administration, he deems it imperative that these defects should be remedied, either by a re-distribution or by an increase of expenditure. He remarks that the status of the agricultural population of India is much akin to that of France, and he suggests that it might be possible to establish in the rural districts of India, and of the Deccan especially, tribunals similar to those of the *juge de paix* in France and in Switzerland. In each of the rural *departments* of France there is a *juge de paix* on a salary of £72 a year and upwards, with an average jurediction over 80 square miles and of 13,300 souls. His decision is final up to a limit variously stated at £2 and £4 sterling. In all cases, which are not urgent or do not involve questions of mercantile law, he is bound to confront the parties together, and to attempt to secure an amicable settlement between them, before he brings the case on his file for formal trial. Lord Cranbrook suggests that "the existence of courts with summary jurisdiction and without appeal up to a limited amount, and possibly with the exclusion of professional pleaders, placed within reach of the suitor's home, would tend to remove many of the evils which have been brought to notice." He admits that the circumstances of Indian society require that only a very limited summary jurisdiction should be given to subordinate judges, more especially in the exercise of discretion as to the enforcement of the terms of written contracts. But he suggests that "summary jurisdiction without appeal might experimentally be conferred on all civil judges in the Deccan with great benefit," and he adds that "the limit to be fixed would of course vary with the rank of the judge." His decision is that a comprehensive Bill for relieving the Deccan agriculturists should be framed, as soon as possible, on the principles set forth in the despatch, and also on those which Lord Salisbury had previously sanctioned.

14. The Governor General in Council has very carefully considered the observations and instructions contained in the Secretary of State's despatch. The suggestion that the number of courts of justice in the interior should be increased, and that all judges should be invested with a final jurisdiction in petty

cases, points to a very considerable change in the procedure of our civil courts. The propriety of limiting the right of appeal in petty civil cases has been discussed in India for many years past. At present the decisions of Courts of Small Causes are practically final up to a limit of Rs. 500, in what are known as cases of the Small Cause Court type. In Madras the decision of a village headman is final in suits for personal property up to Rs. 10, and if the parties consent, he can determine similar suits up to Rs. 100 in value, with or without the assistance of a pancháyat (local jury). The regulations under which these village courts exist, set out that powers were given to village courts, among other reasons, in order "to diminish the expense of litigation in petty suits, and to promote the speedy adjustment of such suits without subjecting people to the inconvenience attending a long absence from their homes." The returns of 1877 show 44,163 suits decided by village headmen out of a total of 196,343 suits decided by all courts in the Presidency. The District Munsiffs in the Madras Presidency are invested under a local Act (No. IV. of 1863) with a final jurisdiction "in suits of a nature cognizable by a Court of Small Causes when the debt, damage or demand does not exceed in amount or value the sum of fifty rupees." It has been on occasions held by authorities conversant with Indian life that the people greatly value the privilege of appeal. Very recently in Bengal, when a scheme for improving the courts in the interior of the country was, after long discussion, submitted to the home authorities, it was decided that final appellate jurisdiction could be only given to benches of two Judges (one European and one Native) up to a limit of Rs. 200 in value. And it was held that the majority of suitors would not be satisfied with any final appellate jurisdiction short of the High Court in suits of higher value until the new appellate benches to be established in the interior gained for themselves the confidence of the people.

15. It is desirable that these facts and these considerations should be kept in view in framing a scheme for remodelling the system of judicature in the districts to which the correspondence reviewed in this letter has reference; but the Governor General in Council readily admits that the circumstances which have occurred are such as to justify the experimental legislation which has been sketched out in the despatch of the Secretary of State. It will be for the Government of Bombay to consider how far it will be expedient to give jurisdiction in petty suits to the headmen of villages, to what extent and at what cost to the Provincial revenues the existing judicatories require to be increased, and how far a summary jurisdiction, not open to appeal, should be conferred on each grade of judicatory. The Bill will deal not only with

the civil courts but with the other points for which it was intended to provide in the Bill which the Honourable Mr. Cockerell obtained leave to introduce into the Council of the Governor General in June last, and in the Bill which was to have been passed into the Council of the Governor of Bombay under the authority conveyed in the letters from the Department of Revenue, Agriculture, and Commerce, of the 1st July and 26th November 1878. In order that no avoidable delay may occur in carrying out this measure, the Governor General in Council has resolved to entrust the duty of preparing the draft of a Bill for the purpose of giving effect to it, to the Honourable T. C. Hope, C.S.I., who will be instructed to perform this duty in communication with the Government of Bombay and with the Home, Revenue, and Legislative Departments of the Government of India. Each Department will be instructed promptly to furnish Mr. Hope with all papers he may require, and with such assistance as may be necessary for preparing a Bill for submission to the Council of the Governor General for making Laws and Regulations. Mr. Hope will visit Bombay to consult with His Excellency the Governor in Council on the details of the Bill, as soon as he is prepared to do so.

16. There is one point, however, which, although it may possibly not involve legislation, appears to the Governor General in Council to demand further consideration from the Bombay Government, viz., the possibility of adapting the assessment of the land revenue to the variations in the season. This question is discussed in paragraph 10 of the Bombay Government letter of the 6th April 1877. The Governor General in Council fully agrees in the view that, in ordinary cases and where the land revenue is moderate, it would not be good, either for the ryots or for the public treasury, that the land revenue demand should fluctuate. But the system, which is best for districts enjoying an ordinarily regular rainfall, may not be the best for the arid tract of the Central Deccan, where (it is said that) a good rainfall comes only once in three years. In view of the very great fall of prices, and the vicissitudes of season in the Deccan during the last few years, it would be desirable that the present Government of Bombay should consider whether the recent (1873-75) revisions of the revenue have given sufficient relief from an assessment, which was based, in part, on an unduly high estimate of the normal value of field produce in the Deccan. And, further, the Governor General in Council would wish the Government of Bombay to consider whether in these four districts, or in parts of them, it would not be wise to have a varying scale of revenue demand to be applied in unfavourable seasons, whereby the normal assessment might be reduced by a certain percentage over an entire district, or divi-

sion of a district, in the event of a failure of rain or other cause of serious damage to the crops.

I have the honor to be, &c.,

(Signed)   C. BERNARD,

Offg. Secretary to the Govt. of India.

No. 977, dated Allahabad, the 8th November 1878.

From—C. ROBERTSON, Esq., Secretary to the Government of the North-Western Provinces and Oudh.

To—The Offg. Secretary to the Government of India, Home Department

In reply to your letter No. 1958, dated 22nd October last, I am directed to forward herewith a full translation of the article on the revival of village pancháyats which appeared in the *Akhbar-i-Anjuman-i-Panjab* of the 27th September last.

THE REVIVAL OF VILLAGE PANCHA'YATS.

[Translation of an article from *Akhbar-i-Anjuman-i-Panjab*, dated the 27th September 1878.]

Syed Ahmad Khán Báhádur, C.S.I., Editor of the *Aligarh Institute Gazette*, has published a leader in his paper of the 7th September, page 290, refuting the arguments of a Native of Punjab for the revival of the village pancháyat. The Syed sayes that the pancháyat is an oppressive institution of the dark ages, quite unsuited to the present state of civilization, science and art. He is unquestionably an educated and enlightened gentleman, but his love of Western civilization has produced in him a strong dislike for everything Native, whether it be Native ideas, associations, arts or manufactures. He seems to forget that the very same Western enlightenment which has so much influenced him is advocating the revival of such useful institutions. As his eloquence has reached to the Legislative Council and secured for him a seat there, he has given his opinion beforehand, so that it might be taken as that of the educated Native community and have weight in the Council.

We beg to refer the Syed to Section 6 of the Act X. of Civil Procedure Code for 1877, Madras. The village pancháyats and munsifs have been established all through the Madras Presidency agreeably to this Act. We beg to ask him whether they are doing real good to the country, whether they are composed of the enlightened Europeans, and whether Madras is a portion of India? When they are doing their work satisfactorily in the Madras Presidency, there seems to be no *primâ facie* reason why the institution should not succeed in other parts of the country. We don't think that the village munsifs and the members of panchâyats in Madras are all well educated men and thoroughly acquainted with all the laws and regulations in force in the country, but it is not essential that they should have such an elaborate training. They may be intelligent and clever men, and such can easily be found in every part of the country. Some simple rules and regulations can with ease be framed for their guidance. But the technicalities of the law are quite different things from justice. The panchâyat can very fairly decide the cases of its own village, as it fully knows the particulars. Syed Ahmad Khán remarks that although the law recognizes the decisions of panchâyats as legal, the people hardly resort to them for the settlement of their disputes. The cause of this is that in the present times of freedom and liberty, when even children do not obey their parents the village headmen have no authority and influence over the inhabitants of the village. On the contrary, they are themselves afraid of *badmashes*. They hear false evidences given in the courts, but cannot breathe a word. If their authority were restored, the *badmashes* would fear them, and the people would refer their disputes and private quarrels to them for decision. On account of their having no legal authority at present, they are not held in honour by the people.

Syed Ahmed Khán has served as Judge for him long time. We beg to ask him how many intricate cases he has referred to private panchâyats and commissions every year for decision. If the working of the civil courts of a Presidency were well considered, more than one-fourth of all the cases decided might be referred to panchâyats for final decision. One would have many occasions to admire the penetration of such panchâyats in intricate cases. We ask Syed Ahmed Khán whether the following kinds of cases would not be better disposed of by a village panchâyat than by a court of justice—

(1.) In a village which is situated 25 miles from the nearest court of justice, A's cattle injure B's crops. Now B has to seize the cattle and take them to the nearest police station, which is, say, ten miles distant from the village. He then goes to the court, which is 25 miles distant from his house, to sue for damages, pays the court fee and the expenses of the witnesses, and his work also suffers during his absence from house. In spite of all this trouble and expense he may not be able to produce sufficient evidence for the conviction of the accused, and, therefore, the accused may be acquitted by the court.

(2.) In the same village a quarrel takes place between A and B, and A slightly hurts B. B goes to the court, which is 25 miles from the village, and submits a plaint, charging A with causing simple hurt. Four or five witnesses, both for the prosecution and defence, are then summoned to the court. Their dispute is ultimately settled by private compromise. Thus they are unnecessarily put to a great deal of trouble and expense which would be avoided if there were a legally constituted panchâyat in the village.

(3.) In the same village A borrows Rs. 2 from B, and afterwards does not repay the amount to the creditor. B applies to the court for the recovery of his money, and the debtor and the creditor are each put to an expense of Rs. 5 before the latter obtains a decree for the amount against the former.

(4.) In the same village A holds a decree for Rs. 2 against B, and applies to the court for the execution of the decree. But before the decree is executed and B's property attached, B pays the amount of the decree to A. A, the decree-holder, must then go to the court to certify to the fact of the payment. Suppose he is unable to walk 25 miles, he will have to hire a carriage. If there were a village pancháyat, he might certify the payment to it.

We do not mean that every caste such as barbers, potters, kahars, &c., should have their different pancháyats. In every large village or town a pancháyat should be established, consisting of two, three, five or more respectable and influential persons of the village or town. When there are three or four small villages at a short distance from one another, a pancháyat should be established in one of those villages, and its jurisdiction should extend over all of them. A few simple and short rules should be prescribed for the guidance of such pancháyats. They might be entrusted with powers to hear and decide the following kinds of cases—

(1) Suits for damages for injury done to crops, trees, &c., provided the damages do not exceed Rs. 20;
(2) Suits for the recovery of debts up to Rs. 20;
(3) Disputes connected with marriage or caste matters;
(4) Disputes arising from the closing of thoroughfares;
(5) Cases of causing slight hurt;
(6) Cases of abusive language; and
(7) Offences against sanitary rules.

In all cases the plaints submitted to the pancháyat might be on plain paper, and copies of judgments might also be granted by it on plain paper to the contending parties. If any party is dissatisfied with its decision, he might appeal to the regular court of justice within one month after the date of the judgment delivered by the pancháyat. Otherwise the decision of the pancháyat would be considered final and taken as that of a legally constituted court. In cases of marriage, relations and caste disputes the pancháyat would have simply to ascertain whether the party made outcaste is really guilty. If the wronged party has a valid claim for damages thus sustained, he might then be authorized to file his regular suit in the civil court, if it be beyond the pancháyat's power to decide. The pancháyat might also be entrusted with the duties of village marriage registrar. In every civil suit in which the value of the claim is above one rupee, the pancháyat should levy a fee of eight annas from the party who loses the case. When a court executes a decree for money against the judgment-debtor, and the judgment-debtor pays the amount of decree to the decree-holder, the decree-holder should certify the payment to the village pancháyat. In criminal cases the pancháyat might fine up to Rs. 5. It might be also entrusted with the duty of exercising a check over the village *badmashes*.

If such village panchayats be established all over the country by the Government, the people will be spared a great deal of inconvenience and expense, and the courts will be greatly relieved from much miscellaneous work and from the trouble of deciding numerous petty cases.

The Local Government might be authorized to increase the power of such panchayats whose working is found quite satisfactory, and to decrease the powers of others where the working proves irregular and unsatisfactory in any way.

By the constitution of such panchayats the influence of the village headmen will be legally established, the *badmashes* will be kept from mischief, petty disputes and quarrels will be amicably and fairly settled, and courts will not be overworked with petty cases as is the case at present.

(True Translation.)
(Signed)   KASHI NATH,
Officiating Government Reporter.

The 2nd November 1878.

FURTHER PROPOSALS FOR LEGISLATION REGARDING THE INDEBTED RYOTS OF THE DECCAN.

Minute by the Governor of Bombay, dated 14*th April* 1879.

I have given my best attention to the Despatch of the Secretary of State of the 26th December last, regarding legislation in respect to the indebted ryots of the Deccan (including the districts of Poona, Sátára, Ahmednagar, and Sholápur); and to the letter from the Government of India, of the 26th February last, upon the same subject. I have, as directed by the Government of India, carefully consulted Mr. T. C. Hope, who, as member of the Legislative Council of the Governor-General, will presumably have charge of any Bill which may now be introduced into that Council. I have now to record the following observations for the consideration of my Honourable colleagues.

The previous proposals by the Government of Bombay on this subject are stated in my previous Minutes of the 12th November 1877 and the 30th August 1878. These proposals are thus summarised in para. 6 of the Secretary of State's Despatch abovementioned, as quoted below:—

" A Despatch was received from Your Excellency in Coun"cil, in February of the present year, enclosing the draft of
" Bill for the relief of the indebted agriculturists in the Pre-

" sidency of Bombay, and which you desired to have introduced
" into the Council of the Supreme Government.

" That Bill contained three main principles—

" (1). That the Courts should be obliged to enter into the
" merits of every money claim, whether secured by bond or not,
" and should only award such sums, whether for principal or
" interest, as they deemed just, and should, in no case, give
" compound interest or a larger amount of interest than the
" principal sum;

" (2). That the principle of the Insolvent Act as prevailing
" in the Presidency-town, should be applied to the Deccan
" agriculturists;

" (3). That land should not be sold in execution for debt,
" unless specially pledged in a bond duly registered."

" Lord Salisbury, although not fully satisfied with all the
" principles contained in this measure, thought the occasion for
" attempting remedial legislation to be so urgent, that he
" sanctioned by telegram the introduction of the Bill, being
" quite willing that the experimental legislation contemplated
" in the Council of the Governor-General should be attempted.
" I also am of the same opinion."

After adverting to the sufficiency of our Civil Courts for the
satisfactory disposal of the litigation between the indebted ryots
and the money-lenders, the Secretary of State proceeds thus in
paras. 28 to 31 :—

" I am extremely unwilling at any time, but especially
" now, to suggest any increase to the cost of administration,
" but if it be made manifest that our courts of justice are in-
" efficient in these special cases, and that our Judges admit
" that they have not time to enquire into the real facts by a
" thorough investigation, I would suggest that although an
" addition to the cost of administration is very much to be
" deprecated, it is imperative to remedy the defects here pointed
" out. A re-distribution of expenditure might be made, and I
" observe that it is stated in the Commissioner's Report that
" 88 subordinate courts bring in a revenue of Rs. 16,89,744,
" and that the expenditure, including salaries of Judges, is only
" Rs. 6,90,717.

" Evils such as have been depicted above, arising out of
" the costliness and inaccessibility of Courts of Justice, though

"of a much slighter character, existed in England also; and
"the remedy suggested was the establishment of Small Cause
"Courts. This innovation, after having been opposed sturdily
"for many years, was finally adopted, and has proved so
"eminently successful that nearly every year witnesses some
"extension of their powers. In India also the institution has
"been partially adopted. But it is from France that the most
"important evidence can be obtained of the value of local
"courts."

"   *   *   *   *   *

"It will be observed that the early meeting of the parties before
"the Judge in order to produce an amicable settlement of the
"suit, which is so strongly insisted upon by Mr. Bentham, is
"spoken of by the French authorities in the highest terms."

The Secretary of State then seems to sum up his wishes on this matter thus, paras. 31 to 33 :—

"I cannot doubt that the existence of Courts with summary
"jurisdiction and without appeal up to a limited amount and
"possibly with the exclusion of professional pleaders placed in
"localities within reach of the suitor's home would tend to
"remove many of the evils which have been brought to notice."
       *   *   *   * It is obvious that the summary
"jurisdiction to be attributed to Subordinate Judges should only
"extend to a very limited amount.   *   *   *   * The
"principle of summary jurisdiction without appeal might be
"conferred experimentally on all Civil Judges of the Deccan with
"great benefit."

Lastly, the Secretary of State directs, para. 34, that "a comprehensive measure should at once be proceeded with, founded on the principles which I have indicated, and on those which Lord Salisbury had previously sanctioned."

From the foregoing quotations I gather that in this proposed legislation, the main principles for which the Government of Bombay have contended are virtually approved on the condition that the judicial machinery be strengthened, the number of Civil Courts augmented, and the procedure in some respect improved. It is to this condition, then, that I have to apply myself.

There is no doubt that the number of the Civil Courts ought to be augmented in the Deccan, and that the existing Courts are often too far from the homes of the people, as will be seen from the table given below :—

Table showing the distances at which villages in the territorial jurisdiction of the Subordinate Judges of the Deccan are situated from the Courts to which they respectively appertain.

Name of District	Name of Court.	NUMBER OF VILLAGES.												
		Within 5 miles.	Within 10 miles.	Within 15 miles.	Within 20 miles.	Within 25 miles.	Within 30 miles.	Within 35 miles.	Within 40 miles.	Within 45 miles.	Within 50 miles.	Within 55 miles.	Within 60 miles.	Total
POONA	1st Class Sub-Judge's Court, Poona	29	76	32	44	24	41	12	51	2	..	..	..	312
	2nd Class Sub-Judge's Court, Junnar	31	60	43	16	9	2	..	..	..	..	..	..	161
	Do. do. Khed	20	54	44	41	34	25	8	6	..	..	..	..	232
	Do. do. Talegaon	9	45	31	23	5	5	..	..	..	..	..	..	118
	Do. do. Patas	4	21	44	19	40	19	20	14	13	14	6	4	218
	Do. do. Wadgaon	15	63	35	50	1	1	..	..	..	..	..	..	165
SATARA	Sub-Judge, 2nd Class, Sátára	26	76	29	..	..	1	..	..	..	..	..	..	132
	Do. 1st Class, Wái	18	50	47	34	50	61	58	40	25	..	..	..	383
	Do. do. Karad	10	42	17	20	96	42	..	..	..	..	..	..	227
	Do. do. Rahimatpur	5	45	40	42	26	12	..	..	..	..	..	..	170
	Do. do. Vitta	5	47	34	29	13	2	..	..	..	..	..	..	130
	Do. do. Ashta	4	14	38	36	25	21	..	..	..	..	..	..	138
	Do. do. Tasgaon	5	20	17	7	..	..	..	..	..	..	..	..	49
	Do. do. Dahiwari	15	39	52	20	..	..	..	..	..	..	..	..	126
	Mootalik Inámdár of Karád	..	1	..	..	..	..	1	..	..	..	..	..	2
AHMEDNAGAR	1st Class Sub-Judge's Court, Ahmednagar	23	42	14	39	27	26	23	3	..	..	..	..	247
	2nd Do. do. Sángamner	25	41	48	45	39	10	1	..	..	..	..	..	255
	Do. do. Nevasi	18	56	66	53	35	16	..	..	..	..	..	..	244
	Do. do. Kade	5	1	8	26	52	50	37	22	9	..	..	..	210
	Do. do. Ráhuri	7	12	42	32	55	30	26	28	13	5	..	..	250
	Do. do. Shrigonda	12	27	42	52	26	6	3	..	..	..	..	..	168
SHOLAPUR	2nd Class Sub-Judge's Court, Sholápur	15	65	38	28	3	1	2	..	..	..	..	..	152
	Do. do. Bársi	16	40	38	28	24	12	12	14	1	..	..	..	185
	Do. do. Mádha	8	23	14	54	42	23	4	11	4	1	..	..	184
	Do. do. Pandharpur	8	33	25	27	41	21	8	17	7	5	..	..	192

I would submit however, at the outset, that improvements in the substantive law relating to the indebtedness of ryots is quite as essential as the multiplication of Courts. If that law be improved, as we propose, then its administration will be all the better for more Courts. But if it were not so improved, then the multiplication of Courts might not prove an advantage—indeed, might even prove a disadvantage; for in that case the money-lender, who is generally the party to invoke the action of the Courts against the ryot, would enjoy increased facilities. If the Courts are, in the present unimproved state of the law, in any degree engines of oppression against the ryot, then their augmentation would only have the effect of bringing the oppressor nearer to the oppressed.

But anticipating improvement of the law respecting indebtedness, I would recommend the early augmentation of the Civil Courts in these four districts by fifty per cent. There are now 24

Subordinate Civil Judges (Natives) employed in these four districts I would increase them by 12, bringing their number up to 36. The additional cost is shown in a table, of which an abstract is given in the margin:* it amounts approximately to Rs. 48,000 per annum; which charge will have to be borne by the provincial finances of the Bombay Presidency. Although, as the Government of India are aware, it is hard for our provincial finances—reduced as they are by the recent famine, and with continued demands upon them by reason of the still existing distress—to bear additional burdens; still this much of extra cost must apparently be borne. I am far from saying that the proposed augmentation is sufficient for the needs of the people; but it seems to be as much as we can afford at present: and it is susceptible of further expansion hereafter according as our means may permit.

* Twelve 2nd Class Sub-Judges at Rs. 150 per month each ... ...Rs. 1,800
Ditto Establishments for at Rs. 180 per month each ... ...Rs. 2,160
Cost per month...Rs. 3,960
Cost per year ... „ 47,520

I think that two Assistant Judges or Subordinate Judges ought to be appointed to aid the District Judges in these four districts (Poona, Sátára, Ahmednagar, and Shólapur) in supervising and inspecting the Courts of the Subordinate Judges thus augmented in number. Such officers might be called Supervising Assistant Judges or Sub-Judges, and would be chosen from among the Assistant Judges or Subordinate Judges, and would be added to these establishments. The cost of that measure is noted in the margin,* it also would have to be borne by our provincial finances.

* Two officers, one at Rs. 600 and one at Rs. 500 per month ... ...Rs. 1,100
Cost per year ... ... „ 13,200
Travelling allowance for ditto at Rs. 100 per month each for eight months in the year ... ... „ 1,600
Total Cost per year...Rs. 14,800

The total proposed cost would be annually ... ...Rs. 47,520
14,800

Rs. 62,320

This is the least which we can propose. Hereafter, if circumstances shall be favourable, we may be able to propose more.

I have considered the possibility of appointing Native Civil Judges, of a lesser status than the present Subordinate Judges, for the disposal of cases between money-lender and ryot. But I am clearly and strongly of opinion that this is not advantageously possible. After long experience and much labour we have succeeded in securing Native Civil Judges of good general education, sound legal training, trustworthy character, fair social position, and promising prospects. These several circumstances, as factors acting in combination, have brought about a considerable degree of judicial efficiency, which efficiency would be sacrificed exactly as any or all of the abovenamed factors should be lost. Now these factors would be all either impaired or relinquished if inferior natives of lesser status were to be appointed Judges. Whatever may be the opinion regarding our civil law and procedure, there is general acknowledgment of the comparative purity and trustworthiness of the administration of the law by the present civil courts; and this is, *per se*, a vast gain in comparison with the results of former times. This gain we should lose if we appointed inferior judges on scales of salary materially less than those now allowed. It were easy to enlarge on this subject; but probably the foregoing mere abstract of considerations will indicate the reasons why I should most earnestly deprecate any attempt to supplement our existing judicial agency by inferior native judges.

I then come to the important point of Conciliation Courts somewhat on the model of those in France. I would take power to appoint selected native gentlemen to be conciliation judges. Such persons would have to be very carefully chosen. Some would certainly be found, perhaps even many might be found; the possible number of them could not be exactly stated beforehand without actual trial of the system. We should have to proceed tentatively and judiciously. But if the plan at all succeeded, then many suitable persons would be soon forthcoming. The reasons for carefulness are manifest. If good and faithful men are chosen, then there will be no abuses, and the conciliation will answer. But if, as might easily happen, men thus appointed were to prove unfaithful to their trust, then conciliation would be worse than a failure; abuses would spring up, new evils would be added to any evils which might have previously existed; and some scandals would occur to bring discredit on the scheme. While some of the Natives in the Deccan, whose names might suggest themselves for selection, would be good men, many might be otherwise. Without any disparagement of the Native gentry of the Deccan, I only adduce what is known to every one when I remark that there are many Marátha Brahmins, who, though intelligent and influential, would not ordinarily be selected for an honorary office like that of Conciliation Judge, which affords great scope for intrigue to those who might be minded to exercise it. Moreover, in the present social state of the Deccan, much temptation would unavoidably surround the position of a Conciliation Judge, mediating between money-lenders and ryots. The money-lenders form a powerful class; many individuals among them are wealthy and influential. They often have on their books, not only the peasantry, but also many of the Native gentry. They are better acquainted than any other unprofessional class with the mode of bringing the law and its agencies to bear on debtors. Unless therefore the Conciliation Judges were well chosen, suspicion would soon become rife regarding collusion on their part with the money-lenders. At the best, the fidelity of Conciliation Judges can be ensured only by the moral effect of local opinion on the spot, and the vigilance of supervising authority.

The question then arises as to what functions should be entrusted to the Conciliation Judges? In the first place it appears to me that every money-lender who has a claim against a ryot should be obliged to bring that claim to the notice of a Conciliation Judge before instituting a suit in a Civil Court. Such suit should not be entertained by the Court, except on production of a certificate signed by the Conciliation Judge to the effect that both the parties had appeared before him and had been unable to agree; or that the claimant having preferred his claim, the ryot had either declined to attend, or after having been warned to attend had neglected to do so. By these means the money-lender would not only have an opportunity of settling his claim out of Court, if so disposed, but will be actually obliged to try to do so, if it be possible. The ryot will also have the opportunity of so settling, if he chooses to do so. But if he prefers that the case should be tried by a regular Court, he should not be compelled to attend before the Conciliation Court. He should be warned to attend, and every possible precaution should be taken to make sure that the warning shall reach him. If then he does not attend, it must bo that he has reasons for deliberately preferring the formal tribunal of the Civil Court. It would be better in that case that he should be heard by the Civil Court; and having declined the offices of the Conciliation Court, he cannot complain of the procedure of the Civil Court by whom he has elected that his case should be tried.

Having carefully considered whether the ryot should be compelled to attend before the Conciliation Court against his will, I think that he should not be so compelled. If the Conciliation Judge had the power of compelling the attendance of the ryot to answer the money-lender's claim, he, the Judge, would have a power which would be liable to abuse. Though he would not have the power of deciding or enforcing his decision, if he formed one, still he would, by compelling attendance, be able, if so disposed, to put great pressure on the ryot to compromise the claim. Such power of applying pressure—by an educated man of position upon an uneducated and humble man, on a claim preferred by a man generally of some education and wealth—is a power that ought not to be conferred upon honorary Conciliation Judges in the present state of society in the Deccan. I state this with confidence, appealing to the knowledge of those who are acquainted with the Native gentry of the Deccan, from among whom the Conciliation Judges would have to be selected.

For the same reasons I would not give the Conciliation Judge the power of summoning witnesses of his own motion. He should, however, not only be empowered, but bound, to hear any witnesses whom either party might bring forward.

Similarly he would be bound to inspect any papers or documents which either party might adduce.

He would record any decision at which he might induce the parties to arrive. And he would keep such registers and records as might be prescribed; the records would, however, be of brief and simple character.

Thus he would be a Conciliation Judge in reality as well as in name, without reaching the authority or status of a Judge. If persons of this description were to be made virtual Judges; were to be vested with portions of judicial authority, such as summoning the ryot and the like, they would be exposed to temptations to them sometimes irresistible; they would then become unpopular with the peasantry; and the Government would find that in trying to do good, it had in result done harm. But if they be retained as Conciliation Judges, and nothing more; if the extent to which the peasantry shall elect to come before them shall depend on their commanding public confidence; if their power to settle cases shall rest on their moral influence with the parties;—then they may prove very useful, may dispose of many cases which would otherwise have remained standing disputes between the parties, may often save the ryot from the process of the law, or may relieve him from the anxiety caused by claims hanging over his head.

I have given particular attention, as requested by the Government of India, to the system which has long existed in the Madras Presidency, whereby village headmen are empowered to decide summarily without appeal small civil claims. From my own experience in that Presidency I am not sure whether local opinion is unanimous as to the value of the work thus performed, a value which cannot be well tested, as no detailed record is kept. Nevertheless, nominally a great amount of work is thus done, measured by the number of suits returned as decided, as well as by the proportion which such return bears to the aggregate returns of civil litigation in the Presidency. And after making every reasonable abatement, I do not doubt that much real work is thus done, to the great convenience of the people, and that the status character of the village headmen are hereby raised, generation after generation. I am willing, indeed anxious, to attempt the gradual introduction of this plan into the Bombay Presidency.

The introduction, however, would be very gradual, for many of the village headmen in the Deccan are not deemed trustworthy by our District Collectors; many also are illiterate. Still out of a large body of men some will be good, even though the general standard of the body be low. And as education shall spread from one generation to another, more and more good men will be forthcoming. Moreover, the vesting of them with this limited degree of judicial responsibility will have an elevating effect on these men, and will tend to make them trustworthy.

Mostly, the persons selected would be the village headmen, who represent an ancient and established institution. The selection need not be limited, as in the Madras Presidency, to the village headmen; but might fall upon any fit person in or near the village.

The safeguard, in constituting these petty honorary courts, is really this, that the value of the cases thus entrusted to such village tribunals would be small—ten rupees in each case. Such cases would be between ryots and farm-labourers, or shopkeepers, or artisans and the like. The disputed transactions between money-lenders and ryots would not be included in this category—most of these cases would be for amounts exceeding ten rupees. Thus these village tribunals would have nothing to do with affairs between ryots and money-lenders—a class of cases with which they would be utterly unfitted to deal, inasmuch as the money-lenders would have undue influence with them. But they would dispose of much petty business which now goes to the Civil Courts, occupying some of the time of those Courts, which time might be given to more important cases. About one-sixth of the civil suits in the Deccan are understood to be for values under ten rupees; though the statistics do not enable us to discriminate the exact proportion. From this may be estimated the relief which would be afforded to the Civil Courts by the establishment of these village tribunals, if they could be established overywhere.

Their procedure would be summary, and there would be no appeal. But the District Civil Judge would have power, *ex proprio motu*, to revise any of their decisions which he might have reason to think unjust.

As the value of these cases is so small, I think a power might be entrusted to these unpaid tribunals, which in larger civil causes could not be entrusted to any honorary tribunal.

Professional pleaders should be excluded from appearing before conciliation judges and village tribunals. After some consideration, I think they should be excluded from the regular Civil Courts in cases below one hundred rupees in value; power being reserved to the Judge to admit a pleader in any case, recording his reasons for the admission.

Thus I hope that the augmentation of the number of Subordinate Judges; the establishment of Conciliation Courts for the voluntary settlement of claims out of Court; the empowering of village headmen or other selected persons on the spot to decide summarily all the pettiest sorts of suits; the strengthening of the agency for inspection of Civil Courts in the interior of the country by appointing two supervising Assistant or Subordinate Judges—will improve and enlarge the means of disposing of civil causes, and will enable the Subordinate Judges to give more time to those questions between money-lenders and ryots which cannot be settled out of Court. And I think that all this may be done, if not to the full extent desirable, still to a considerable extent, without imposing on our provincial finances a burden greater than they can bear.

The increase of the establishment of Subordinate Judges is a matter of executive arrangement and does not require legislation. But for all the other arrangements above-mentioned, legislation is required.

Then as regards summary jurisdiction, on which so much stress is justly laid by the Secretary of State, it is to be remarked that already we can by law invest the Subordinate Judges with powers of Small Cause Courts: some Subordinate Judges are thus invested, and the remainder can be so invested. It is therefore better at once to declare by law that all these Judges shall have these powers. The Small Cause Court jurisdiction covers generally those cases between money-lenders and ryots which do not involve mortgage or other transfers of land. It can, by legislation, be made to cover these transfers also. And for the lower grades of Native Judges the limit of value of suits may be raised from 50 to 100 rupees.

In some respects the procedure of the Small Cause Courts may be improved in order to suit the cases between money-lenders and ryots; and for this also legislative provision can be made.

As the operation of Small Cause Courts, with summary powers and without appeal will be extended, I think that there ought to be with the District Civil Judge a power to revise of his own accord the decision in any case where he might think that injustice had been done. For this we shall make provision.

The provisions already proposed regarding insolvency for the relief of indebted ryots and other improvements in law, will render imprisonment for debt extremely rare, except in case of fraud. If it be thought desirable to abolish imprisonment altogether as regards indebted ryots, I see no objection.

The amount of debt which should entitle a ryot to the benefit of the insolvency-law should, I think, be at least Rs. 50. For that amount and upwards the insolvency principle may be well applied; but not for petty amounts below Rs. 50.

I would insist that every instrument to which a ryot puts his hand should be written by a village registrar, who would register the same under the supervision of the Registration Department.

I have considered whether it would be practicable to declare the ryots in a particular district, or part of a district, as generally insolvent, and to treat them and their landed tenures in a manner similar to that adopted by several existing laws regarding encumbered estates and indebted zemindárs in certain parts of India. My opinion is decidedly adverse to any such declaration being made respecting ryots. They are a large general class very different from the limited and special classes to whom the several Encumbered Estates Acts have been applied. Such a declaration and the proceedings consequent thereon would lead to grave complications and serious embarrassments, affecting probably the collection of the land revenue, and encouraging claims being made on Government to advance money for paying off the debts of ryots. The indebted ryots are not confined to any one locality, but are scattered all over the Deccan. It would be impracticable in the first place, and it would be in the second place impolitic, even if it were practicable, for any Government to undertake to deal with the debts of a whole peasantry.

I have thus endeavoured to touch upon all the points mentioned in the Despatch of the Secretary of State, namely, the augmentation of the Civil Courts of the interior, the formation of Courts of Conciliation, the establishment of village tribunals, the extension of summary jurisdiction without appeal, the exclusion of professional pleaders in some classes of cases, I trust that our draft Bill herewith to be submitted will be found to duly embody all these points.

In these and all other points relating to this subject, both I and my colleagues in the Government have had the advantage of conferring with Mr. T. C. Hope, whose assistance and advice were commended to us by the Government of India by their Despatch of the 26th February. The opinions of Mr. Hope, as an eminent member of the Civil Service of this Presidency, and as an officer of much experience will always receive our best consideration. We have formed our own opinions after conferring with him. The Bill has been prepared in consultation with him on the basis of the principles set forth in the foregoing paragraphs of this Minute. It embodies all that I and my colleagues are able to propose. We trust that it has the concurrence of Mr. Hope. And we beg to submit it for the favourable consideration of the Government of India with a view to their introducing it into the Legislature if they see fit.

The executive proposals regarding increase of establishment, as apart from the legislative proposals, have been considered by myself and my colleagues in Council, and we are prepared to make the necessary financial provision.

(Signed) RICHARD TEMPLE.

No. 2056 OF 1879.

REVENUE DEPARTMENT.

Bombay Castle, 18*th April* 1879.

From
    J. B. PEILE, Esq.,
        Acting Chief Secretary to the Government of Bombay;

To
    C. BERNARD, Esq., C.S.I.,
        Officiating Secretary to the Government of India,
                Home Department,
                        Simla.

SIR,
I am directed to acknowledge receipt of your letter No. 222 of 26th February 1879, reviewing past proceedings in connection with the subject of the proposed legislation for the relief of the indebted ryots of the Deccan, and communicating the intention of His Excellency the Governor General in Council to depute the Honourable Mr. T. C. Hope, C.S.I., to confer with the Govern-

ment of Bombay for the preparation of a fresh Bill of the nature contemplated in the Despatch of the Right Honourable the Secretary of State to this Government, Legislative, No. 4, of 26th December 1878.

2. In accordance with the instructions of the Government of India a new draft *Bill for the relief of indebted agriculturists in certain parts of the Presidency of Bombay* has now been prepared, which I am desired to forward herewith for submission to the Government of India. In the preparation of this draft the Governor in Council has had the valuable co-operation of the Honourable Mr. Hope, who has recently visited Bombay and discussed with the members of this Government the various important points relating to the contemplated legislation, and it is believed that the Bill now submitted has his general concurrence.

3. The questions involved in the considerations of this matter have been very fully dealt with in a Minute, dated the 14th instant, by His Excellency the Governor, which is entirely concurred in by the other members of this Government, and of which I am therefore desired to append a copy to this letter.

4. The point to which attention is most especially directed by the abovementioned Despatch from the Right Honourable the Secretary of State is the evil arising from the action of the Civil Courts and from the great distances at which those Courts are held from the ryots' homes.

The methods by which the Governor in Council proposes to remedy this grievance are:

(1) by increasing the number of Subordinate Judges' Courts so as to place every village within as reasonable a distance as possible from the seat of the Court in whose jurisdiction it lies;

(2) by appointing, whenever convenient, two or perhaps more places for each Subordinate Judge to hold his court at on different days in the week or month;

(3) by extending the summary and final powers of the Subordinate Judges;

(4) by entertaining two or more Assistant Judges or Subordinate Judges for the special duty of inspecting and supervising all subordinate courts, and giving to them, as well as to the District Judges, certain express powers to stay any subordinate court's proceedings and arrange for cases being transferred or tried by a Bench;

(5) by simplifying the procedure of Subordinate Judges in cases which they are empowered to try summarily;

(6) by appointing Village Munsifs, wherever possible, to try summarily and without appeal, suits for money up to Rs. 10;

(7) by appointing Conciliation Judges for the amicable settlement of disputes between agriculturists and other persons.

5. It will be observed that the first six of these proposals do not affect the ryots exclusively. Their object is to improve the system of civil judicature generally and thereby to enable the ryots, who form the bulk of the population of the four districts in question, to obtain cheaper and speedier justice, and with less trouble to themselves than they are now able. The seventh remedy, the appointment of Conciliation Judges, it is proposed in the first instance to limit to ryots' cases, because the experiment will be a novel one in India, and it is thought prudent to watch the result of it in a special class of cases before extending its scope.

6. Legislation is unnecessary for the purposes of the first and second of the above proposals, as sections 21 and 23 of the Bombay Courts Act, 1869, already enable Government to take the requisite steps. But both of these proposals, as well as the fourth proposal, will necessitate a very considerable additional outlay on the civil administration of the Deccan, which the Governor in Council is compelled to admit is absolutely necessary, however much he could wish, for financial reasons, that it were not so. As at present advised, he is of opinion that it will suffice to increase the number of Subordinate Judges in the four districts in question by 50 per cent., *i. e.* from 24 to 36. The probable cost of this addition is shown in the table appended to this letter. In the establishments therein estimated for, there are two kárkúns (one on Rs. 25 and one on Rs. 12) less than in the smallest of the existing establishments, but it is thought that when 36 Courts are employed to do the work at present performed by 24, some such reduction of establishments will be feasible.

7. With the regard to the extension of the summary powers of Subordinate Judges, I am to explain that this Government already possesses the power, under section 28 of the Bombay Courts Act, of investing any Subordinate Judge of the 1st or 2nd class with the jurisdiction of a Court of Small Causes in suits up to the amount of Rs. 500 and Rs. 50, respectively. This jurisdiction has indeed already been conferred upon several Subordinate Judges in the Deccan, but the system of conferring it from time to time by special notifications in the official Gazette is productive of considerable inconvenience and uncertainty, and it is thought better that every Subordinate Judge should, as such, possess the jurisdiction. After full consideration, the Governor in Council has also come to the conclusion that Subordinate Judges of the 2nd class may

safely be entrusted with summary powers in suits up to the amount of Rs. 100, and that it will be advisable thus to extend their powers in order both to increase the number of cases which will be decided summarily and to give the Subordinate Judges more time for the disposal of other work. And for the benefit of the ryots, it is proposed (section 4 of the Bill) that suits relating to a mortgage transaction in which the mortgagor is an agriculturist and any suit for an account brought by an agriculturist shall be added to the class of suits which under Section 6, Act XI. of 1865, are already cognizable by Courts invested with Small Cause Court powers.

8. But, whilst wishing thus to extend the number and the importance of the cases which may be disposed of summarily, and without appeal, by Subordinate Judges, the Governor in Council thinks it necessary to make special provision in the Bill for a constant supervision and control of their proceedings, either by an Assistant Judge, or by a good Subordinate Judge, specially selected for the purpose. This forms the fourth of the above proposals, and it is anticipated that it is one which will effect much good. At present the subordinate courts are, it is thought, too little subjected to examination and scrutiny. District Judges, being also Sessions Judges, are only able to visit them at rare intervals, and owing to various reasons no inspection of them takes place sometimes for two or three years together. It is proposed therefore (section 7 of the Bill) to appoint two officers (either Assistant Judges or Subordinate Judges), each of whom shall, during the fair season, be employed in visiting and examining into the work of the subordinate courts of two districts, and during the rains, when travelling is impossible, shall perform the usual duties of an Assistant, or Joint Subordinate Judge in one of such two districts, as may be required. To carry out this proposal, it will be necessary to add either two Assistant Judges or two Subordinate Judges of the 1st Class to the existing establishments. The pay of a Third Grade Assistant Judge is Rs. 600 and of a Third Grade 1st Class Subordinate Judge Rs. 500 per month. Assuming that Government find it expedient to appoint one Assistant Judge and one Subordinate Judge, the additional cost will be Rs. 1,100 per month for twelve months in the year, and Rs. 200 per month for travelling allowances Rs. 100 each for eight months in the year, in all Rs. 14,800 per annum. But although the two additional officers, whom it will be necessary to retain, will be entertained on the lowest salaries of their class, Government will not of necessity appoint them to the duty in question. The best Assistant Judge or First Class Subordinate Judge available in any grade will be selected for the purpose, and the vacancies thus created will be filled by the two additional appointments.

9. In order further to augment the usefulness of the officers who will be selected for this duty, it is proposed (section 7 of the Bill) to invest them, if the District Judge so directs, with the power at present possessed only by the District Judge himself under section 25 of the Civil Procedure Code, of transferring suits to their own file, or to other subordinate courts and also to confer upon them and upon the District Judges a new power of forming Benches of two or more Judges—in whom they may, if they think fit, include themselves—for the disposal of important cases (sections 6 and 7 of the Bill). As a further safeguard against hasty or illegal decisions, a section has been inserted (section 22) rendering Subordinate Judges' unappealable decisions liable to revision and correction by the superior courts, in the same way that the decisions of Criminal Courts are revised, and it will be a standing instruction to the Supervising Assistant or Subordinate Judges to go carefully through the records of the subordinate courts and bring to the notice of the District Judge every case in which his interference appears to them to be called for.

10. A considerable share of the dissatisfaction caused by the Civil Courts as at present constituted is believed by many to be attributable to the intricate rules of procedure by which they are bound. The Governor in Council thinks therefore that the experiment may be tried of introducing a more simple form of procedure based, to a great extent, on the local Mámlatdárs' Court Act (Bombay Act III. of 1877). In carrying out this idea, it became necessary to consider whether it would be advisable to limit the applicability of the new procedure to agriculturists' cases, and to create special Courts, or to invest the existing Courts with special jurisdiction, for the trial of such cases. To the creation of a new class of courts the Governor in Council thinks there are weighty objections. The salary which could be offered to the Judges would not be attractive enough to command the services of men of the same class as the present Subordinate Judges, and it seems to the Governor in Council to be most undesirable to lower the standard of qualification for admission to the subordinate grades of the judicial office. The establishment of a special Civil Court for the benefit of one particular class of the community would also form a precedent of very questionable expediency. On the other hand, it would be obviously inconvenient for the Subordinate Judges to have to follow one law of procedure in cases to which the Code of Civil Procedure applies, another in small-cause-courts' cases, and a third in agriculturists' cases; and it would be unreasonable to require the Judges to apply one law of procedure in a suit if an agriculturist is a party to it, and quite another law if the parties are not agriculturists. If, therefore, it be admitted that a simplification of the existing procedure in summary cases is necessary,

the only course seems to be to make the amended law apply to all such cases which a Subordinate Judge may have to try, whether an agriculturist be a party thereto or not. This is therefore the reason why by the provision of sections 8, 20, 30, and 31 of the Bill it is purposed to supersede the present small-cause-court procedure law entirely.

11. With regard to the sixth of the above-mentioned proposals, I am desired to say that the Madras Reg. IV. of 1816, under which Village Munsifs are appointed in that Presidency, contains many provisions which are unsuited to this Presidency and to this time. The village headmen in this Presidency could not now, as a general rule, be entrusted with judicial powers. But the knowledge that such of them as show themselves by superior education and good character fitted for the office will be invested with such powers, may in time induce them to qualify themselves, and there are some on whom a very limited jurisdiction might even now be conferred with advantage. Here and there, too, a good district hereditary officer or an Inámdár or a retired Government servant may be found to whom similar honorary powers might be given. Wherever any such jurisdiction existed, it would *pro tanto* exclude that of the Subordinate Judge, and so relieve the latter of a number of petty suits. But to ensure success, the procedure required of such honorary Village Munsifs ought to be of the simplest possible character, and the sections in the Bill which deal with this matter (Nos. 21—28) have been framed with an express view to this end. And as the appointment of such Munsifs would be at first purely experimental, the Governor in Council is not prepared to recommend that they should have jurisdiction in suits exceeding Rs. 10 in amount.

12. His Lordship the Secretary of State having signified his approval of some attempt being made to introduce Courts of Concilliation, on the French model, into the Deccan Districts, the Governor in Council has given this matter his most careful consideration, and the provisions which he is, in consequence, prepared to support have been embodied in Part VI. of the Bill. The success of Courts of this class in this country will depend mainly upon the character and local position of the persons appointed to be conciliation-judges. It does not seem desirable that the office of conciliation-judge should be associated with that of an ordinary civil judge. Such an office might be greatly abused by a judge anxious to diminish the amount of his judicial work, and there would be great danger of his contracting a bias during the informal proceedings before him in his capacity of conciliation-judge which he would be unable to shake off when he came to try the matter in dispute judicially. It seems, therefore, necessary that courts of

conciliation should, with perhaps rare exceptions, be entirely dissociated from the ordinary courts; and that the persons to be appointed conciliation-judges should be specially selected with reference to their local standing and personal influence with the people. The Governor in Council proposes, therefore, merely to take power to appoint such judges wherever it may be found practicable, and is of opinion that the appointment should be an honorary one.

13. The above comprise all the new proposals, which the Governor in Council deems it necessary to submit for the purpose of ameliorating the civil judicial administration of the four districts in question. But the Bill contains substantially the same provisions regarding (1) insolvency and (2) inquiries into money-claims against agriculturists and limitation of their liability for interest and for ancestral debts, and (3) the sale of land in execution of decrees as were contained in the draft Bill forwarded with my predecessor's letter No. 308 of 19th January 1878. Those principles have, it appears, been virtually approved by their Lordships the present and the late Secretaries of State, and Lord Cranbrook in his despatch already adverted to, has desired that the measure now to be introduced shall be founded upon them.

14. It will be observed, however, that the procedure in insolvency-cases has been somewhat simplified in the present Bill (Part V.) and that the Government of Bombay now proposed that the minimum amount of debt which shall qualify an agriculturist to be declared an insolvent shall be reduced from Rs. 100 to Rs. 50. Simultaneously with the introduction of a complete insolvency-law it appears to the Governor in Council that the agriculturists to whom it will apply may be exempted from liability to arrest or imprisonment for debt. This has accordingly been provided for in section 40; and in sections 57—60 certain new provisions have been introduced, which it is believed will be found to be peculiarly suitable to the circumstances of the agricultural class.

15. The sections relating to inquiries into money-claims against agriculturists have been carefully re-considered with reference to the correspondence ending with your letter No. 696, dated 27th November last, and the Governor in Council trusts that in the shape in which they now appear (*vide* sections 33 and 34, and also section 3 of the Bill) they will be found less open to the objections which were entertained to them by the Government of India in their original form.

16. The Government of Bombay are of opinion that it is essential to the success of their proposals with regard to courts of conciliation and Village Munsifs that the court-fees chargeable upon their proceedings or processes should be either remitted entirely,

or fixed at very low rates, sufficient only to cover the actual cost of maintaining these courts. This Government would also gladly see some reduction allowed in the court-fees leviable in suits of the nature which it is proposed to empower Subordinate Judges to try summarily. But it has not been thought necessary to insert anything in the Bill on this subject, as the Government of India have power under the existing law to remit court-fees whenever they deem fit, and a new Bill relating to court-fees generally is already, it is believed, under their consideration.

17. With regard to the question of the exclusion of pleaders, the Governor in Council is clearly of opinion that legal practitioners should be barred from appearing on behalf of any party before a Conciliation-Judge or a Village Munsif. But with respect to proceedings in the ordinary Civil Courts the question is one of some difficulty, and upon the whole, whilst not prepared to advocate their absolute exclusion in any case in those Courts, the Governor in Council has arrived at the conclusion that the experiment may be tried of disallowing their appearance in cases under Rs. 100 in amount except with the special permission of the Court. In order, however, to prevent these provisions with respect to legal practitioners (Part VII. of the Bill) from operating detrimentally in the case of illiterate parties who have no knowledge of law or of the ways of the Courts, it is proposed to allow any relative, servant or dependent of a party to be employed either conjointly with, or in lieu of such party ; and a suggestion, to which reference is made by the Deccan Riots Commissioners in para. 130 of their Report, has been acted upon so far as to empower the Subordinate Judges to require the Government Pleader to undertake the defence of the debtor in any case in which the creditor is allowed to appear by counsel and the debtor is to poor too pay for a similar advantage.

18. The Governor in Council has deemed it desirable to introduce into the present Bill (Part VIII.) the sections relating to Public Notaries, which were suggested in para. 17, clause (3) of Mr. Ravenscroft's letter to your address, No. 4579, dated 5th September 1878. In your reply to that letter No. 696, dated 27th November 1878, para. 12, you pointed out certain objections to the sections in question, but these have, it is hoped, been obviated by denominating the officers whom it is proposed to appoint "Village Registrars" instead of "Public Notaries," and by placing those officers under the orders of the Inspector-General of Registration, and empowering the latter (section 77) to supervise and regulate their proceedings and to provide for the custody of their records. I am to add, in further explanation of the necessity for these sections, that although section 34, clauses (*a*) and (*b*) and section 58, clause (*c*) of Act III. of 1877, do already provide for

inquiry being made by Registering Officers into the fact of the execution of such instruments as come before them and into the identity of the parties, and to record any payment of consideration made in their presence in respect of any such instruments, the class of instruments to which that law applies is a limited one, whereas the object of this Government's proposal is that *every* instrument to which an agriculturist is a party shall fall within its purview (*vide* section 72 of the Bill), and that such instruments shall not be merely registered by the Village Registrars, but shall also be written by them.

19. The VIIIth Part of the present Bill is based upon sections 8 to 11 of the Draft Bill for the prevention of frauds submitted along with the Deccan Riots Commissioners' report (pp. 119 121). It is thought that the necessity which it is thus intended to throw upon creditors of giving their debtors receipts, or pass-books or statements of account whenever demanded, on pain of penalty in case of default, will strengthen the hands of the ryots and enable them to obtain written evidence of their transactions with their money-lenders.

20. With reference to the concluding paragraph of your letter, I am desired to say that the Governor in Council has given his best consideration to the question of the possibility of superseding the fixed rates of land-revenue assessment at present in force in the four districts in question by a scale of rates varying, as suggested by the Government of India, with the favourableness of the seasons, the proposal is one which it is anticipated there would be very great difficulty in adopting, but the Government have the matter still under their consideration, and should it be found feasible to recommend any alterations in the existing system of settlement of the nature suggested, a separate communication will be addressed to the Government of India on the subject.

I have the honour to be, &c.,

(Signed) J. B. PEILE,
Acting Chief Secretary to Government.

Table showing the probable cost of entertaining twelve additional Second Class Subordinate Judges. (*Vide* para. 6 of the accompanying letter).

	Rs.
Salary* of each Subordinate Judge per month	150
Establishment for ditto :	Rs.
One Názar...	45
One Kárkún	30
One „	20
One „	15
One „	12
One Naik...	9
Three Peons at Rs. 6 each	18
One Menial	6
Contingencies	25
	180
Total monthly cost for each ... Rs.	330
„ „ „ twelve ... „	3,960
Annual cost for twelve ... „	47,520

* *Note.*—The lowest salary of a Subordinate Judge is at present Rs. 200, but it is thought that with the good prospects of promotion before them which the Department now offers there will be no difficulty in obtaining twelve new men of the same class as the present Subordinate Judges to begin on a pay of Rs. 150. All the new men will, of course, not necessarily be posted to the Deccan Districts.

A Draft Bill for the Relief of Indebted Agriculturists in certain parts of the Presidency of Bombay.

Whereas it is expedient to relieve the agricultural classes in certain parts of the Presidency of Bombay from indebtedness; It is enacted as follows :—

PART I.

PRELIMINARY.

Short title.
1. This Act may be cited as the "Bombay Agriculturists Relief Act, 1879."

Extent and commencement.
It extends only to the Districts of Poona, Sátára, Sholápur, and Ahmednagar and shall come into force in those districts on the   day of   18   ;

but it shall be lawful for the Local Government, with the previous sanction of the Governor General in Council, from time to time, by notification in the *Bombay Government Gazette*, to extend all or any of its provisions to any other local area within the said Presidency.

Definitions.

2. In this Act, unless there be something repugnant in the subject or context :

"Agriculturists".

(1) the word "agriculturist" means a person who earns his livelihood wholly or principally by agriculture ;

" Money."

(2) the word "money" includes grain and any other agricultural produce.

" Pleader."

(3) the word " pleader" has the same meaning as in the Code of Civil Procedure.

Repeal of Bombay Regulation V. of 1827, Section 9, Clause 1.

3. Clause (1) of section 9 of Bombay Regulation V. of 1827 is repealed so far as regards any suit to which section 33 of this Act applies.

PART II.

OF THE CIVIL COURTS.

Subordinate Judges to exercise the jurisdiction of Court of Small Causes in certain cases.

4. Subordinate Judges of the first and second classes shall exercise within the limits of their ordinary local jurisdiction, the jurisdiction of a Court of Small Causes for the trial of—

(a) suits cognizable by such Courts up to the amounts of five hundred and one hundred rupees respectively, and

(b) suits between mortgagors and mortgagees for the foreclosure or redemption of mortagages, or for the possession or profits of the land mortgaged, where the mortgagor is an agriculturist, and the value or amount of the claim does not exceed five hundred or one hundred rupees, respectively, and

(c) suits by agriculturists for an account as hereinafter defined without limit as to value or amount.

Distribution of business between a Court of Small Causes and a

If the territorial limits of any Court of Small Causes established under Act XI. of 1865 shall be coincident or partly coincident, with the local limit of the jurisdiction of the Court of a Subordinate

Subordinate Judge having co-ordinate jurisdiction. Judge, the District Judge to whom the said courts are subordinate may from time to time make such orders as he shall deem fit for regulating the cognizance of the suits in which the said Courts have co-ordinate jurisdiction.

Appointment of Village Munsifs. 5. The Local Government may from time to time

(a) appoint any person to be a Village Munsif, and

(b) cancel any such appointment.

Extent of jurisdiction. Every Village Munsif so appointed shall be subordinate to the District Judge, and, subject to his general control, shall take cognizance of suits for money lent, or advanced to, or paid for the person sued, or due on an account stated, or on a written or unwritten engagement to pay up to the amount of ten rupees within such local limits as shall from time to time be determined by the Local Government.

6. The District Judge may stay the proceedings in any suit **District Judge may sit with one or more Subordinate Judges as a Bench for trial of any case.** or other matter pending before any court subordinate to him, and sit together with the Judge of the said court, or with the Judge of the said court and the Judge of any other court subordinate to him, as a bench for the disposal of the same. If the members of such bench differ in opinion, the opinion of the District Judge shall prevail.

7. The Local Government may appoint any Assistant or **Assistant or Subordinate Judge may be appointed to inspect subordinate courts.** Subordinate Judge to inspect and supervise, subject to the orders of the District Judge, every court subordinate to such Judge, and every Conciliation-Judge's court within the local limits of such judge's jurisdiction.

One such Assistant or Subordinate Judge may be appointed for two or more districts, if the Local Government thinks fit.

Any Assistant or Subordinate Judge so appointed may, if the District Judge so directs, exercise the powers of a District Judge, under section 6 of this Act, or under section 25 of the Code of Civil Procedure.

PART III.

OF PROCEDURE.

Subordinate Judges.

8. Every suit instituted in the Court of a Subordinate Judge, **Suits to be commenced by a plaint.** under section 4 of this Act shall be commenced by presenting a plaint to the Court, or to

the Clerk of the Court, if any have been appointed. The plaint shall contain the following particulars :—

(a) the name, religion, caste, profession, and place of abode of the plaintiff and the defendant ;

(b) a plain and concise statement of the circumstances constituting the cause of action, and when and where it arose ;

(c) the amount or other relief claimed, or the nature and situation of the property of which, or of the profits of which possession is sought, as the case may be ;

(d) a list of the documents and of the witnesses, if any, the plaintiff wishes to adduce, and whether the witnesses are to be summoned to attend, or will be produced at the time and place appointed for the hearing.

9. If the plaint do not contain the several particulars hereinbefore required to be specified therein, or if it contains particulars other than those specified, or if the statement of particulars be unnecessarily prolix, or if the amount or value of the claim be undervalued, or the stamp insufficient, the Court shall, at its discretion, order the necessary amendment to be made then and there, or within three days from the date of such order.

Amendment of plaint.

10. When the plaint is in due form, the Subordinate Judge shall require the plaintiff to subscribe and verify it in his presence in open court in the manner following, or to the like effect :—

Plaint to be subscribed, verified and endorsed.

" I, A. B., the plaintiff, do declare that what is stated in this plaint is true to the best of my information and belief."

The Subordinate Judge shall endorse the plaint to the effect that it was duly subscribed and verified in his presence.

If the plaintiff cannot write, the verification may be written for him in open court, and the Subordinate Judge shall in such case record that the verification was made in his presence, at the request of the plaintiff who affixed his mark to his name in token of the authenticity of the verification.

11. The Subordinate Judge shall reject the plaint if it appear upon the face of it, or after questioning the plaintiff, or on summary enquiry, as the case may be, that—

Rejection of the plaint.

(a) no cause of action is disclosed ;

(b) the subject of the plaint is not within the jurisdiction of the Court;

(c) the suit is barred by any positive rule of law.

The reason of rejection shall be written on the plaint by the Subordinate Judge with his own hand.

Procedure on admission of plaint.

12. If the Subordinate Judge admit the plaint, he shall receive and register it and shall appoint a convenient day and place for the trial and final disposal of the case. The day to be fixed shall not be earlier, except by the consent of both parties, than ten days, nor except for unavoidable reasons later than fifteen days from the day when notice of such appointment issues.

Notice shall be given verbally to the plaintiff to appear with his documents and witnesses on the day and at the place appointed.

A summons shall at the same time be issued to the defendant.

Attendance of witness.

13. If either party require his witnesses to be summoned to appear on the day and at the place appointed, the Subordinate Judge shall issue summonses for that purpose.

Effect of default of plaintiff.

14. If the plaintiff fails to attend with his documents, or omits to adopt measures to procure the attendance of his witnesses on the day and at the place appointed, and fails to satisfy the Court either on such day or within fifteen days afterwards, that he was prevented from so doing by some unavoidable circumstance, the Court shall reject the plaint, and may award to the defendant such compensation as it thinks fit for any expense and loss of time he may have suffered. Such rejection shall bar a fresh suit.

No suit to be decided ex parte.

15. No suit shall be heard or determined *ex parte*.

If the defendant fails to attend, the Court shall adjourn the hearing and take steps to secure his attendance by the issue (a) of a fresh summons, or (b) of an order that he be arrested and brought before the Court.

Upon the defendant's appearance, the case shall proceed.

Hearing of the case.

16. Upon the day originally appointed, or any day to which the case may be adjourned as aforesaid, the Court shall proceed to fix such issues as it may deem proper, to hear the evidence, and to pass judgment and issue its decree.

The proceedings may be, from time to time, adjourned for sufficient reason.

17. In cases in which the matter at issue is of smaller amount or value than ten rupees, it shall be discretionary with the Court to take the depositions of the witnesses in writing or not.

Record of evidence.

In cases in which the matter at issue is of the amount or value of ten rupees or upwards, it shall not be necessary to take down the evidence of the witnesses in writing at length ; but where the evidence is not so taken, the Subordinate Judge, as the examination of each witness proceeds, shall make a memorandum of the substance of what he deposes, and such memorandum shall be written and signed by the Subordinate Judge with his own hand, and shall form part of the record.

18. No written statement other than the plaint shall be received unless required by the Court, or with its permission.

Written statements.

19. After the evidence has been taken, and the parties have been heard, the Subordinate Judge shall pronounce judgment in open court, either at once or on some early future day.

Judgment.

In any case in which the evidence of the witnesses has been recorded in writing at length, or in substance by a memorandum made by the Subordinate Judge, the judgment need not contain more than the points for determination and the decision thereupon.

In other cases, the judgment shall also contain the substance of the evidence, with a concise statement of the case and of the reasons for the decision.

20. The chapters and sections of the Code of Civil Procedure hereinafter mentioned extend (so far as they are applicable and not inconsistent with this Act) to Subordinate Judges exercising jurisdiction under section 4 or Part V. of this Act, that is to say,—

Partial application of Code of Civil Procedure.

PRELIMINARY.—Sections 1, 2 and 3.

CHAPTER I.—Of the jurisdiction of the Courts and *res judicata*, except section 11.

CHAPTER II.—Of the Place of Suing, except section 20, paragraph 4, and sections 22 to 24 (both inclusive).

CHAPTER III.—Of Parties, and their Appearances, Applications and Acts.

CHAPTER IV.—Of the Frame of the Suit.

CHAPTER V.—Of the Institution of Suits. Sections 49, 59 and 60 to 63, (both inclusive).

CHAPTER VI.—Of the Issue and Service of Summons, except sections 64 to 71 (both inclusive).

CHAPTER VIII.—Of Written Statements and Set-off. Section 111, section 112, paragraph 2, sections 113 to 116 (both inclusive).

CHAPTER IX.—Of the Examination of the Parties by the Court.

CHAPTER X.—Of Discovery and the Admission, &c., of Documents.

CHAPTER XIV.—Of the summoning and attendance of Witnesses. Sections 163 to 167 (both inclusive), section 168 (substituting in the last paragraph " Subordinate Judge" for " Court of Small Causes") to 173 (both inclusive), section 174 except the Explanation, section 175 to 178 (both inclusive).

CHAPTER XV.—Of the Hearing of the Suit, &c. Sections 179, 180, 181, 186, 187, 188, 190, to 193 (both inclusive).

CHAPTER XVII.—Of Judgment and Decree. Sections 199 to 202 (both inclusive), 205 to 212 (both inclusive), 216 and 217.

CHAPTER XVIII.—Of Costs. Sections 220, 221 and 222.

CHAPTER XIX.—Of the Execution of Decrees. Sections 230 to 258 (both inclusive), section 259 (except so far as it relates to the recovery of wives), 263, 264, 266 to 335 (both inclusive).

CHAPTER XXI.—Of the Death, Marriage, and Insolvency of Parties.

CHAPTER XXII.—Of the Withdrawal and Adjustment of suits.

CHAPTER XXIII.—Of Payment into Court.

CHAPTER XXIV.—Of requiring Security for Costs.

CHAPTER XXV.—Of Commissions.

CHAPTER XXVI.—Suits by Paupers.

CHAPTER XXVIII.—Suits by Aliens and by and against Foreign and Native Rulers, except the first paragraph of section 433.

CHAPTER XXIX.—Suits by and against Corporations and Companies.

CHAPTER XXX.—Suits by and against Trustees, Executors and Administrators.

CHAPTER XXXI.—Suits by and against Minors and Persons of unsound mind.

CHAPTER XXXII.—Suits by and against Military men.

CHAPTER XXXIII.—Interpleader.

CHAPTER XXXIV.—Of Arrest and Attachment before judgment. Sections 483 to 490 (both inclusive), and section 491 (so far as relates to attachments).

CHAPTER XXXV.—Of Temporary Injunctions, &c. Sections 492 and 494 to 497 (both inclusive).

CHAPTER XXXVII.—Reference to Arbitration.

CHAPTER XLVII.—Of Review of Judgment.

CHAPTER XLIX.—Miscellaneous. Sections 640, 641, 642, 643 645, 647, 648 (so far as relates to attachments), and 651.

Except as is in this Act otherwise specially provided, the provisions of the said Code or of any other enactment now in force for regulating the procedure of civil courts, shall not apply to the proceedings of Subordinate Judges under the said section or Part of this Act.

Village Munsifs.

21. Every suit before a Village Munsif shall be instituted by presenting a plaint to such Munsif signed or attested by the mark of the plaintiff, and containing the particulars prescribed in section 8 of this Act.

<small>Suits before Village Munsifs to be commenced by a plaint.</small>

22. Upon receipt of any such plaint, the Village Munsif shall, by verbal summons through the village officers, or in such other manner as he deems fit, require the defendant to appear before him in person within two days or such longer period as he shall deem reasonable.

<small>Procedure on receipt of plaint.</small>

The Village Munsif may from time to time extend the period for the defendant's appearance if the defendant is absent from the local limits of his jurisdiction, or for any other sufficient reason.

If the defendant fails without reasonable cause to attend, the Village Munsif may adjourn the hearing and secure his attendance either by the issue of a written summons, or by an order that he be arrested and brought before him.

Notice shall be given verbally, or, if in any rule made under section 85, the Local Government shall so direct, in writing, to the plaintiff to appear on the day appointed for the defendant's appearance.

Plaint to be explained to the defendant.

23. Upon the day originally fixed, or any day to which the case may be adjourned as aforesaid, the Village Munsif shall explain the nature of the plaint to the defendant in the presence of the plaintiff.

If defendant objects to the claim inquiry to be held.

24. If the defendant shall object to the claim the Village Munsif shall proceed, either immediately or on some other day as soon after as the business before him will permit, to inquire into the truth of the claim and of the defendant's objection thereto respectively.

Decision may in certain cases be given without examination of witnesses.

If the parties are willing to dispense with the examination of witnesses, the Village Munsif shall give his decision on consideration of the statements of the parties and of any documents which they may produce for his perusal; or if either party shall consent in writing to let the case be settled by the evidence of the other on oath or solemn affirmation in any form common amongst, or held binding by persons of the race or persuasion to which such other party belongs, and not repugnant to justice or decency, and not purporting to affect any third person, the Village Munsif may, if he thinks fit, tender such oath or affirmation to such other party, and if he agrees in writing to make the same shall give his decision in accordance with the evidence which the said party shall give on such oath or affirmation.

Examination of witnesses.

25. The Village Munsif shall receive such evidence as may be tendered by the parties, and for this purpose shall have power to summon any person residing within the local limits of his jurisdiction or within a distance of ten miles from the place where he holds his court, to give evidence or to produce any document in his possession or power. The depositions of the witnesses may be taken in writing or not, as the Village Munsif shall in each case think fit.

Any witness duly summoned by the Village Munsif who shall refuse to attend, or attending shall refuse to answer, and any witness or party refusing to produce any document required, may be fined by the Village Munsif a sum not exceeding one rupee, or may at the instance of such Village Munsif, be proceeded against by a Subordinate Judge under section 174 of the Code of Civil Procedure.

Punishment of recusant witnesses.

Any fine inflicted by a Village Munsif under this section may be recovered by the Collector under the law for the time being in force for the recovery of arrears of land revenue.

26. When the parties have been heard, and the evidence, if any, on both sides taken and considered, the Village Munsif shall pass his decree, which shall be written and signed by himself, and shall bear date the day on which it is passed, and shall contain the number of the suit and the names of the parties, and shall specify clearly the amount awarded, or other determination of the suit.

Contents of Decree.

27. In every such decree the Village Munsif shall also specify such period, not exceeding six months, as he shall deem fit to allow for the satisfaction of the same by the parties amongst themselves.

Execution of Village Munsif's decrees.

If at any time within one month after the expiry of the period so fixed, the judgment-creditor shall prove to the satisfaction of the Village Munsif that the decree has not been satisfied, or has not been fully satisfied, the Village Munsif shall forward a certified copy of the said decree to the Court of the Subordinate Judge having jurisdiction in the place where the judgment-debtor resides, together with a certificate setting forth the extent, if any, to which satisfaction of the said decree has been obtained.

The Court to which a decree is so sent shall deal with it as it would deal with a decree sent to it for execution under section 224 of the Code of Civil Procedure.

28. Every Village Munsif shall keep a register in which he shall from time to time enter with his own hand the names of the parties in every case which comes before him, the dates of all their appearances, the names of the witnesses examined for either party and, when their depositions are not taken in writing, the substance of their evidence, and a concise statement of the points at issue, and of the reasons for the decision.

Record.

General Provisions.

Court of first instance to determine, when necessary, whether party is an agriculturist.

29. Whenever under any provision of this Act, the jurisdiction or procedure of a court, or the nature of its decision depends upon any party to a suit or application being an agriculturist, it shall be the date of the court in which such suit or application is brought to ascertain and determine whether such party is an agriculturist.

The decision of any court of first instance that a party is or is not an agriculturist shall be final.

No appeal in cases tried under this Act.

30. No appeal shall lie from any decision or order of a Village Munsif or Subordinate Judge or of a District Judge, or Assistant Judge in exercise of any jurisdiction conferred by this Act.

Reference of questions.

31. If before or on the hearing of any suit or other matter by any such Munsif or Judge any question of law or usage having the force of law or the construction of a document, which construction may affect the merits, arises on which the Court entertains reasonable doubt, the Court may draw up a statement of the facts of the case and the point on which doubt is entertained, and refer such statement, with its own opinion on the point, for the decision of the District Judge, or, if the District Judge be dealing with the case, of the High Court. Pending the receipt of a decision upon such reference, the proceedings shall be stayed.

Of revision.

32. The District Judge may call for and examine the record of any suit or other matter tried under this Act for the purpose of satisfying himself of the legality or propriety of any decree or order passed, and as to the regularity of the proceedings, and may pass such order thereon as he thinks fit.

The Assistant or Subordinate Judge appointed under section 7 may similarly call for and examine the record of any such case, and if he see cause therefor, may refer the same, with his remarks, for the orders of the District Judge:

Provided that no decision or order shall be reversed or altered for any error or defect, or otherwise unless a failure of justice shall be deemed to have taken place:

Provided also that nothing herein contained shall authorize the reversal of the decision of any court of first instance that any person is, or is not, an agriculturist.

PART IV.

OF SUITS AND OTHER PROCEEDINGS TO WHICH AGRICULTURISTS ARE PARTIES.

33. If in any suit brought for the recovery of money alleged to be payable on account of money lent or advanced to, or paid for the defendant, or on an account stated, or on a written or unwritten engagement, or for the redemption or foreclosure of a mortgage, or for the possession or profits of mortgaged land, the defendant, or any one of the defendants, not being a surety merely of the actual debtor, or the mortgagor, or any one of the mortgagors as the case may be, is an agriculturist, the Court shall ascertain the actual amount of money lent, advanced, paid or due. For this purpose the Court shall, irrespectively of the provisions of the Indian Evidence Act,—

Actual amount of money lent, &c., to be ascertained when the debtor is an agriculturist.

(a) inquire into the origin of the debt, and the nature of each subsequent transaction, if any, in respect thereof;

(b) if any written acknowledgment of debt is relied on by the plaintiff, ascertain whether the whole of the amount therein named was advanced to the debtor.

The Court shall further enquire into the history and merits of the case, with the view of ascertaining whether there is any defence to the suit on the ground of fraud, mistake, accidents, undue influence or otherwise.

34. If in any such suit a doubt arises as to the actual nature and extent of the transactions between the parties, the following shall be relevant facts, that is to say—

If not ascertainable, may be fixed equitably.

(a) the means and position of the lender at the time the debt was incurred;

(b) the means and position of the borrower at such time;

(c) the state of the borrower's credit at such time, and the prospect at such time of his repaying a loan of the alleged amount;

(d) the circumstances under which the money was borrowed; and

(e) the requirements of a person in the borrower's station of life under such circumstances.

35. The Court may of its own motion, and if both parties so desire shall, refer the question of the sum to be allowed on account of the principal of the debt to arbitration.

Reference to arbitration in certain cases.

When any such reference is made by desire of the parties, nomination of the arbitrators shall be made in accordance with section 507 of the Code of Civil Procedure. When the reference is made of its own motion by the Court, it shall appoint three arbitrators, who shall be residents of the same village, town or city in which the debtor and creditor reside, if they both reside in the same village, town or city, and if, in the opinion of the Court, fit and proper persons can be thus obtained.

The provisions of sections 508 to 521 (both inclusive) of the Code of Civil Procedure shall apply to every reference to arbitration under this section.

36. The interest, if any, to be awarded upon any sum ascertained to have been actually lent or awarded as aforesaid, shall be—

Reasonable interest to be allowed,

(a) the rate, if any, agreed upon between the parties, unless such rate be deemed by the Court to be unreasonable; or

(b) if such rate be deemed by the Court unreasonable or if no rate was agreed upon, such rate as the Court deems reasonable:

Provided always that—

(a) all payments already made by or on behalf of the debtor to the creditor, and all profits of any kind whatever enjoyed or realized by the creditor in satisfaction of the debt shall be brought to account, and credited, as far as they go, in cancelment first of the interest, if any, due at the rate allowed by the Court at the time or times at which such payments were made or such profits enjoyed or realized, and next in reduction of the principal amount of the debt;

but payments, &c., already made to be deducted;

(b) if the agreement between the parties expressly so provides, no interest shall be allowed;

and interest not to be allowed if agreement so provides;

(c) compound interest shall not, in case, be allowed.

and compound interest not to be allowed;

(d) the amount of interest received or to be received by the the creditor shall not in any case exceed, in the aggregate, the amount of the principal debt;

and aggregate amount of interest not to exceed the principal;

(e) if the debt, or any portion thereof, was not contracted by the person from whom the creditor seeks to obtain recovery, but by such person's father or other ancestor, the said person shall be called upon to state whether he is willing to accept the full responsibility for such debt, or for such portion thereof; and if he accepts such responsibility, shall be held liable for the full amount payable on account of such debt or of such portion thereof, subject to the other provisions of this Act, or of any law for the time being in force relating to liability for ancestral debts; but if he declines to accept such responsibility, shall be held liable only for the principal amount of such debt, or of such portion thereof, with interest up to the date of the death of the person who incurred such debt or such portion thereof if such person was related to him in the first degree, and otherwise only for the principal amount of such debt or of such portion thereof.

and in the case of ancestral debts interest to be disallowed or limited.

37. It shall be competent to any agriculturist at any time to sue for an account of monies respectively lent or advanced to or paid for him by a creditor and paid by him to such creditor, and for a decree determinative of the amount, if any, still payable by him to such creditor.

Agriculturist debtors may sue for accounts and settlement of amount of their debts.

When any such suit is brought, the amount payable by the plaintiff shall be determined under the same rules as would be applicable, if the creditor sued for recovery of the debt; and the provisions of Chapter XXIII. of the Code of Civil Procedure relating to payment into Court shall be applicable as if the plaintiff were a defendant in a suit to recover the debt, and the defendant the plaintiff in such suit.

Amount of debts in such cases to be determined according to foregoing provisions.

In any decree passed under this section, the Court may order that the amount due shall be paid by instalments with or without interest.

Decree may provide for payment by instalments.

The plaintiff may pay the amount of the decree, or the amount of each instalment fixed by the decree as it falls due into Court, in default whereof execution of the decree may be enforced by the defendant in the same manner as if he had obtained the decree in a suit to recover the debt.

Execution of decrees under this section.

38. At any time after a decree has been passed under which any money is recoverable from an agriculturist the Court may, whether in the course of execution of the said decree or otherwise—

Part payment and discharge.

(a) direct the payment of a portion of the amount decreed, and after satisfying itself as to the means of the debtor and other claims upon him, if any, and of his inability to pay the balance grant him a discharge from such balance; or

(b) if the debtor's liabilities amount to Rs. 50 direct proceedings to be taken with respect to him as if he had applied to be declared insolvent under Part V. of this Act.

39. The Court may, at any time, direct that the amount of any such decree or such portion of the same as aforesaid, shall be paid by instalments with or without interest.

Payments by instalments.

The Court may, when such instalments do not extend over a period longer than seven years, direct that they, or any of them, all be recovered by the Collector as a revenue demand and paid to the decree-holder.

40. Except as provided in section 60 of this Act, no agriculturist shall be arrested or imprisoned on account of debt.

Arrest and imprisonment for debt abolished.

41. No agriculturist's land shall be attached or sold in execution of any decree or order unless it has been specifically pledged as security for the re-payment of the debt to which such decree or order relates, and the mortgage lien still subsists.

Land exempted from attachment and sale unless specifically pledged.

42. If, upon application being made for the execution of a decree for the payment of money against an agriculturist, it appears that the person against whom execution is sought is not the person made liable by the decree for the amount thereof, but the heir of such person, the amount recoverable under the decree shall be determined by the Court in accordance with the provisions of clause (e) of section 36 of this Act.

Ancestral debt.

PART V.

OF INSOLVENCY.

Chapter XX. of the Civil Procedure Code not to apply to agriculturists.

43. Nothing in Chapter XX. of the Code of Civil Procedure shall apply to any judgment-debtor who is an agriculturist.

Power to apply to be declared an insolvent.

44. Any agriculturist who is in debt and whose debts amount to fifty rupees or upwards, and any creditor who claims a sum of not less than fifty rupees from any agriculturist, and any two or more creditors who claim an aggregate sum of not less than the said amount from any agriculturist, may apply in writing to the Court of the Subordinate Judge of lowest grade having jurisdiction in the place in which such agriculturist resides, to declare such agriculturist an insolvent.

Every such application shall be subscribed in the manner prescribed in section 10.

Contents of application by debtor.

45. If such application is made by the debtor, it shall set forth—

(a) the amount and particulars of all pecuniary claims against him;

(b) the names and residences of his creditors, so far as they are known to, or can be ascertained by him;

(c) the amount, kind and particulars of his property, and the value of any such property not consisting of money;

(d) the place or places in which such property is to be found; and

(e) his willingness to put at the disposal of the Court all such portion thereof as is by law liable for debt.

Contents of application by creditor.

46. If such application is made by a creditor or creditors, it shall set forth—

(a) the name and residence of the alleged debtor;

(b) the amount and particulars of his or their claims against the alleged debtor;

(c) the name and residence of any other persons to whom the alleged debtor is believed to be indebted; and

(d) the grounds on which it is sought to have the alleged debtor declared an insolvent.

47. When the application is made by the debtor, the Court shall cause a copy thereof, together with a notice of the time and place at which it will be heard, to be stuck up in court, and to be served on each creditor named therein.

Notice to issue on debtor's application.

48. If upon perusal of an application made by a creditor or creditors, and after such examination of the applicant or of any of the applicants, as the Court thinks fit, the Court deems that there is not sufficient *prima facie* reason to believe that the alleged debtor is in insolvent circumstances, it may reject the application.

Creditor's application how to be dealt with.

If the Court deems that there is such reason, it shall fix a day for the alleged debtor to produce a statement, verified in the manner prescribed in section 10 of this Act, setting forth the particulars specified in clauses (a), (b), (c), and (d) of section 45, and to show cause why he should not be declared an insolvent, and shall cause a copy of the application, with a notice in writing of the time and place at which such cause is to be shown, to be served on the said debtor.

49. In the case contemplated by section 45 or by section 46, the Court may, by proclamation or otherwise, as it thinks fit, publicly invite the appearance on the day fixed of all persons having claims against the debtor.

General invitation to other claimants.

50. If at any time after an application has been made, the Court is satisfied that the debtor has already removed, concealed, or destroyed, or is about to remove, conceal, or destroy any books, papers or property, with the intent to avoid examination in respect of his affairs or otherwise to delay or embarrass the insolvency proceedings, the Court may, by warrant, cause any books, papers, or property in the possession of such debtor to be attached and to be safely kept so long as the Court directs.

Attachment in certain cases.

51. On the day fixed for hearing the application, the Court shall examine the alleged debtor, in the presence of such of the creditors as appear, as to his circumstances and present or future means of payment and shall hear any creditors opposing the application.

Procedure at first hearing.

52. If the Court is satisfied that the debtor's liabilities amount to Rs. 50 or upwards, and that he is in insolvent circumstances, it shall declare him to be an insolvent.

Declaration of insolvency.

53. Upon such declaration of insolvency, the Court shall proceed, upon such day as it may fix, to hear such evidence as the alleged creditors may produce regarding the amount and particulars of their respective claims, and any reply and evidence which the insolvent may offer in opposition thereto, and to ascertain the available assets of the insolvent.

Inquiry into debts and assets.

The Court shall determine, in accordance with sections 33 to 36 (both inclusive), the amount of the insolvent's several debts, and shall frame a schedule specifying such debts, the names of the persons to whom they are due, and the order in which they are payable and also the available assets of the insolvent.

A copy of such schedule shall be stuck up in the court-house.

54. Any person claiming to be a creditor of the insolvent who has not appeared during the previous proceedings may, within one month from the publication of the schedule, apply to the Court for the amendment of the schedule by the insertion of his name and claim therein. If the Court is satisfied that he was prevented by unavoidable causes from previously appearing, it shall hear any evidence the applicant may produce and the defence of the insolvent, and then comply with or reject the application.

Amendment of schedule.

Any creditor mentioned in the schedule may, within one month from the publication thereof, apply to the Court for an order altering the schedule so far as regards the amount, nature particulars or precedence of his own debt or that of another creditor or striking out the name of another creditor. The Court after hearing the insolvent and any other creditors concerned, shall comply with or reject the application.

Any creditor mentioned in the schedule may, within one month from the publication thereof, apply to the Court for the addition to the schedule of any available assets mentioned therein, and the Court, after hearing the applicant and the insolvent and any other parties concerned, shall comply with or reject the application. The Court may, at any time, of its own motion or on the application of the insolvent, so amend the schedule.

55. *Fraudulent transfers.* The Court may, at any time, annul any transfer of the insolvent's property, or of any part thereof, which shall be shown to have been made by the insolvent with intent to defraud his creditors or to give an unfair preference to any of them, and may direct that the property so transferred shall be entered in the schedule as available assets and dealt with accordingly.

56. *Liquidation of debts.* Upon the final settlement of the schedule of debts and assets the Court shall proceed—

(*a*) to pay debts, fines, and penalties (if any) due by the insolvent to Government;

(*b*) to pay such costs of the insolvency proceedings as may be due under any rule made by the Local Government under section 85 of this Act;

(*c*) to distribute the balance of available assets among the scheduled creditors rateably according to the amount of their respective debts, or according to any order or preference fixed in the schedule.

57. *Conversion of moveable property into money.* In order to make the payments specified in section 56, the Court may convert into money such portion of the available moveable property other than money as it thinks fit.

58. *Specific properties may be assigned to particular creditors, or their annual proceeds devoted to payment of insolvents' liabilities.* In order to make the distribution required by clause (*c*) of the said section, the Court may, in its discretion, assign specific properties at such respective valuations as it deems equitable, to individual creditors, in lieu of converting the same into money.

The Court may likewise direct payment to be made by the insolvent by instalments out of the annual proceeds of specific properties, in lieu of so assigning or converting the same.

59. *Powers of court if assets insufficient.* If the debts cannot be fully liquidated in manner hereinbefore provided, the Court may—

(*a*) direct that the balance be paid by the insolvent by instalments out of the annual proceeds of his immoveable property; or

(*b*) direct that a portion of such balance be so paid and grant the insolvent an absolute discharge as to the remainder; or

(*c*) grant the insolvent an absolute discharge as to the whole of such balance.

60. When the instalments fixed under section 58 or 59 do not extend over a period longer than seven years, the Court may direct that they, or any of them, shall be recovered by the Collector as a revenue demand be levied and paid to the creditor.

Recovery of instalments.

Until such instalments have been paid—

(*a*) the property shall not be transferable by the insolvent or his heirs; and

(*b*) the insolvent or his heirs shall not receive a final discharge with respect to any balance of such instalments;

(*c*) the insolvent or his heirs shall be liable to be arrested and imprisoned in the civil jail for a term which may extend to one year, in the event of their fraudulently neglecting or refusing to cultivate or let for hire or cultivation, as the case may be, any or all of the said property:

Provided that the insolvent or his heirs may, at any time, pay up the full amount of any instalments due, and shall thereupon receive a final discharge.

61. If at any time previous to the grant of a final discharge, it is shown to the satisfaction of the Court that in the course of the insolvency proceedings—

Procedure in cases of fraud.

(*a*) the debtor has wilfully made any false statement as to the debts due by him, or as to the property belonging to him, whether in possession or expectancy or held for him in trust, or has fraudulently concealed or removed any property; or

(*b*) a creditor has wilfully made any false statement as to the amount, particulars or precedence of his claim, whether such statement affect the debtor or other creditors; or

(*c*) either debtor or creditor has concealed any fact material to the issue, or committed any other act of bad faith regarding the matter in issue;

the Court may send the offender to a Magistrate to be dealt with according to law.

PART VI.

OF CONCILIATION-JUDGES.

Appointment of Conciliation-Judges.

62. The Local Government may, from time to time,—

(*a*) appoint any person to be a Conciliation-Judge, and

(*b*) cancel any such appointment.

Every Conciliation-Judge so appointed shall exercise his functions under this Act, at such place and in respect of matters affecting agriculturists residing within such local limits as the Local Government shall, from time to time, determine.

63. When any dispute arises between two or more parties
Disputes may be brought before Conciliation-Judges. one of whom is an agriculturist as to any matter within the cognizance of a Civil Court, or when any decree to which an agriculturist is a party passed before the date when this Act comes into force has remained unexecuted, (1) any party to such dispute or decree may apply to the Conciliation-Judge having jurisdiction in the place where the said agriculturist resides, or (2) both or all the parties may jointly so apply.

64. If the application be made by one of the parties only,
Procedure thereupon. the Conciliation-Judge shall take down, or cause to be taken down in writing a general statement of the applicant's contention, and shall thereupon by summons, or by such other means as he deems fit, invite the person against whom such application is made to attend before him upon a day to be fixed for this purpose, on which day he shall direct the applicant to be also present.

If the said person fails to appear on the day first
Day for attendance may be, from time to time, postponed. fixed, the Conciliation-Judge may, if he thinks fit, from time to time, extend the period for his appearance.

65. Whenever all the parties are present, the Conciliation-
When all parties appear, Conciliation-Judge to endeavour to reconcile them. Judge shall call upon each in turn to explain his contention regarding the matter in dispute or the claim under the decree and shall use his best endeavours to induce them to agree to an amicable settlement or to submit the question at issue between them to arbitration.

66. The Conciliation-Judge shall hear the statement of any
Conciliation-Judge to hear statements of witnesses, &c. witness and peruse any book of account or other document produced by the parties; and if any party or witness shall consent in writing to affirm any statement upon oath or solemn affirmation

in any form not repugnant to justice or decency and not purporting to affect any third person, shall arrange for such oath or solemn affirmation being duly taken in the presence of all the parties.

67. If on the day on which the case is first heard by the Conciliation-Judge, or on any subsequent day to which he may adjourn the hearing, the parties shall agree to terms for the settlement of the matter in dispute, the said terms shall be forthwith embodied in a decision, or in an agreement for reference to arbitration, or in *aráznáma*, as the case may require, which shall be read and explained to the parties and shall be signed or attested by the marks of the Conciliation-Judge and of the parties, or their representatives respectively.

Procedure on conclusion.

68. When a decision has been so framed and signed or attested, the Conciliation-Judge shall forward the same in original to the Court of the Subordinate Judge of lowest grade having jurisdiction in the place where the agriculturist who is a party thereto resides.

Decision duly signed or attested to be forwarded to Civil Court, and

The Court which receives the decision shall order it to be filed, and it shall then take effect as if it were a decree of the said court passed on the day on which it is ordered to be filed and from which no appeal lies.

to be filed in the Civil Court and given effect to as a decree.

69. If the person against whom any application is made before a Conciliation-Judge cannot be found, or if he refuses or neglects, after such period as the Conciliation-Judge thinks reasonable shall have been allowed for his appearance, to appear before the Conciliation-Judge, or if he appears, but the attempt to reconcile the parties or to induce them to resort to arbitration fails, the Conciliation-Judge shall on demand give to the applicant, or, in the case of a joint application, to either applicant, a certificate under his signature to that effect.

Certificate to be given to applicant if conciliation fails.

No suit and no application for execution shall be entertained in any Civil Court in respect of any matter or decree which ought under the foregoing provisions to have been brought before a Conciliation-Judge, unless the plaintiff or applicant first produces a certificate as aforesaid.

Suit, &c., not to be entertained by Civil Court unless such certificate is produced.

PART VII.

OF PLEADERS.

Pleaders to be excluded.
70. No Pleader shall be permitted to appear on behalf of any party to a case before a Village Munsif or a Conciliation-Judge, or in any case cognizable by a Subordinate Judge under section 4 of this Act, in which the value or amount of the claim does not exceed one hundred rupees:

Provided that—

(a) any party to any such case may be permitted on reasonable cause being shown to the satisfaction of the Conciliation-Judge, Munsif or Subordinate Judge to employ any relative, servant or dependant, who is not, and has not previously been a pleader, or a mukhtyár or law-agent, to appear either conjointly with or in lieu of such party;

(b) a Subordinate Judge may admit a pleader to appear before himself for any party in any such case as aforesaid in which for special reasons, which he shall record at the time in writing, he deems it desirable that the party should have such assistance;

Appointment of counsel for debtor in certain cases.
(c) in any case in which a creditor is so permitted to appoint a pleader to appear on his behalf, and the Subordinate Judge is of opinion that the debtor is not in such pecuniary circumstances as to admit of his obtaining similar counsel, the Subordinate Judge may, with the consent of the debtor, direct the Government Pleader, or some other competent person, to undertake his defence.

If in the case provided for in clause (a) of this section a relative, servant or dependant appears in lieu of a party, he shall be furnished by him with a *mukhtyárnáma* defining the extent to which he is empowered to act.

PART VIII.

REGISTRATION BY VILLAGE REGISTRARS.

Appointment of Village Registrars.
71. The Local Government may appoint such persons as it thinks proper, whether public officers or not, to be Village Registrars.

Each such person shall be Village Registrar for such local area as the Local Government shall prescribe.

The Local Government may appoint any person by name or in virtue of his office to exercise all or any of the powers conferred on it by this section.

72. No instrument executed after the passing of this Act, to
<small>Instruments to which agriculturist is a party not to be deemed valid unless executed before a Village Registrar.</small> which an agriculturist residing in any place in which this Act is in force is a party, shall be received in any Court of Justice, or by any person having by law or consent of parties authority to receive evidence, as creating, modifying, transferring, or extinguishing, or purporting to create, modify, transfer, or extinguish any right or obligation;

or as evidence in any civil proceeding;

or shall be acted upon in any such Court, or by any such person as aforesaid, or by any public officer,

unless such instrument is written by, or under the superintendence of, and is attested by, a Village Registrar.

73. When any persons, one or more of whom is an agricul-
<small>Such instruments to be written by or under the superintendence of a Village Registrar and executed in his presence.</small> turist, desire to execute any instrument, they shall present themselves before the Village Regitsrar appointed by the Local Government for the area in which the said agriculturist or any one of the said agriculturists resides, who after satisfying himself in such manner as he deems fit as to the identity of the parties, and receiving from them the prescribed fee, and the stamp, if any, which may be necessary, shall write the instrument, or cause the same to be written under his superintendence, and require the parties to execute it in his presence.

Every instrument so written and executed shall be attested by
<small>Attestation of such instruments.</small> the Village Registrar, and also, if any of the parties thereto is unable to read and write, by two respectable witnesses.

74. Every Village Registrar shall keep a register of instru-
<small>Registration of instruments by Village Registrars.</small> ments executed before him in such form as shall from time to be prescribed by the Inspector-General of Registration under section 77 of this Act.

As soon as any instrument has been completely executed before a Village Registrar, he shall make, or cause a copy of it to be made, in his register. He shall deliver the original instrument to the party entitled to the custody of the same, and a certified copy thereof to the other party, or to each of the other parties, if there be more than one.

Previous to delivery the original instrument and each such copy shall be endorsed under the Village Registrar's signature with the date of registration, the name and residence of the Village Registrar and the volume and page of the Register in which the instrument has been registered.

Consideration to be fully stated in every instrument executed before a Village Registrar.

75. In every instrument written by or under the superintendence of the Village Registrar, the amount and nature of the consideration shall be fully stated.

The Village Registrar shall also endorse the instrument with a note, under his signature, recording whether or not the transfer of the consideration stated therein, or of any part thereof, took place in his presence.

If the instrument is to be executed in supersession, or partly in supersession of a previous instrument, such instrument shall be produced before the Village Registrar and shall be fully described in the instruments to be executed, and shall be marked by the Village Registrar under his signature for identification.

Registration under this Act to be deemed equivalent to registration under the Indian Registration Act, 1877.

76. Every instrument executed and registered in accordance with the foregoing provisions shall be deemed to have been duly registered under the provisions of the Indian Registration Act, 1877; and no instrument which ought to have been executed before a Village Registrar but has been otherwise executed, shall be registered by any officer acting under the said Act, or in any public office, or shall be authenticated by any public officer.

Village Registrars to be subordinate to the Inspector-General of Registration.

77. The Inspector-General appointed under the said Act shall exercise, by himself and through his subordinates, a general superintendence over all Village Registrars and shall have power from time to time to make rules consistent with this Act for regulating their proceedings and for providing for the custody of their records.

Penalty if person not being a Village Registrar writes any instrument.

78. Any person who, not being a Village Registrar, writes otherwise than by direction and under the superintendence of a Village Registrar, any instrument which this Act requires to be executed before a Village Registrar, shall be punished for each such offence, on conviction before a Magistrate, with fine which may extend to one hundred rupees.

79. No mortgage, lien or charge of or upon any land belonging to an agriculturist shall be valid unless it is created by an instrument in writing signed by the person creating such mortgage, lien or charge.

Mortgages, &c., to be valid only when written and registered.

80. Nothing in this Act shall be deemed to require any instrument to which the Government or any officer of Government in his official capacity is a party to be executed before a Village Registrar.

Exemption of instruments to which Government or any officer of Government is a party.

PART VIII.

OF RECEIPTS AND STATEMENTS OF ACCOUNT.

81. Every agriculturist who makes any payment of money in liquidation of debt shall be entitled to receive at the time of such payment a written receipt from the person to whom such payment is made.

Agriculturists to be entitled to written receipts,

If such payment is made under any instrument written, under section 73 of this Act, by a Village Registrar, the said receipt shall, if the agriculturist so require, be endorsed on the copy of the said instrument furnished to him under section 74 of this Act.

82. Any agriculturist by whom any money is due under any instrument shall be entitled to receive from the person claiming under such instrument, within one month after the date on which by local custom annual accounts are balanced, a statement of his account up to that date.

and to own annual statement of account.

The Local Government may, by notification in the *Bombay Government Gazette*, declare what date shall in any district or portion of a district be taken to be the date on which annual accounts are balanced for the purpose of this section.

83. Any agriculturist in whose name an account is kept by any trader or money-lender shall be entitled to receive from such trader or money-lender, on demand, a pass-book, and to require from time to time that his account up to date be written therein and attested by the signature or mark of the said trader or money-lender.

And to have his account made up from time to time in a pass-book.

An entry so made in any such pass-book of any payment made to the trader or money-lender shall be deemed to be equivalent to the grant of a receipt for the amount so entered.

84. Any person who, in contravention of sections 81, 82 or 83 of this Act, refuses or neglects to give a receipt, or a statement of account, or a pass-book, or to write, or cause to be written any account or any part of an account in a pass-book, or to attest the same when so written, shall be punished for each such offence, on conviction before a Magistrate, with fine which may extend to one hundred rupees.

Penalty for contravention of sections 81—83

PART IX.

MISCELLANEOUS.

85. The Local Government may from time to time make rules consistent with this Act—(*a*) regulating the proceedings of Village Munsifs and Conciliation Judges in matters not provided for by this Act;

Local Government to frame rules.

(*b*) fixing the charges to be made by Conciliation-Judges for any thing done by them under this Act;

(*c*) determining what record and accounts shall be kept by Conciliation-Judges, and what returns shall be framed and furnished by them;

(*d*) regulating the appointment, suspension, dismissal, duties and remuneration of Village Registrars, and prescribing the fees to be levied by them;

(*e*) generally for carrying out the provisions of this Act.

All such rules shall be published in the *Bombay Government Gazette*, and shall thereupon have the force of law.

Abstract of the Proceedings of the Council of the Governor General of India, assembled for the purpose of making Laws and Regulations under the provisions of the Act of Parliament 24 & 25 Vic., cap. 67.

The Council met at Government House on Thursday the 5th June 1879.

PRESENT:

His Excellency the Viceroy and Governor General of India, G.M.S.I., *presiding*.
His Honour the Lieutenant-Governor of the Panjáb, C.S.I.
His Excellency the Commander-in-Chief, G.C.B.
The Hon'ble Sir A. J. Arbuthnot, K.C.S I.
Colonel the Hon'ble Sir Andrew Clarke, R.E., K.C.M.G., C.B., C.I.E.
The Hon'ble Sir John Strachey, G.C.S.I.
General the Hon'ble Sir E. B. Johnson, R.A., K.C.B.
The Hon'ble Whitley Stokes, C.S.I.
The Hon'ble Rivers Thompson, C.S.I.
The Hon'ble F. R. Cockerell.
The Hon'ble Sayyad Ahmad Khán Bahádur, C.S.I.
The Hon'ble T. C. Hope, C.S.I.
The Hon'ble B. W. Colvin.

BOMBAY INDEBTED AGRICULTURISTS RELIEF BILL.

The Hon'ble Mr. Hope moved for leave to introduce a Bill for the relief of indebted agriculturists in certain parts of the Presidency of Bombay. He said :—

"The Council are already aware that during the monsoon of 1875 agrarian outrages of a serious nature took place in certain districts of the Deccan forming a part of the Bombay Presidency; that a commission appointed by Government reported very fully upon the causes of these outrages, and the remedial measures they thought desirable; that the Government of Bombay, in April 1877, before Sir Philip Wodehouse's departure, submitted their general views upon the question to the Government of India; and, finally, that Sir Richard Temple's Government sent up in January 1878 the first definite proposals for meeting the case by legislation. The origin, nature and causes of the difficulty, and the various proposals for its removal, were explained so fully and clearly by my

Hon'ble friend Mr. Cockerell, in his speech of the 20th June last, that it is not necessary for me to go over any part of the ground again, at least on the present occasion.

"The course of procedure at that time considered desirable was that some of the Bombay Government's proposals should be dealt with in this Council and others in that of Bombay. Leave to introduce Bills was accordingly granted by this Council to Mr. Cockerell on the date already mentioned, and by the Bombay Legislative Council to Mr. Ashburner on September 13th, 1878. It happened, however, that, during the discussion of the details of the measures thus decided on, a telegram from the Secretary of State was received on December 3rd, requesting that further definite action might be postponed pending the arrival of a despatch he was about to send. The despatch arrived towards the end of January last, and showed that the Secretary of State, while approving of the proposals of the Bombay Government, considered that they should be supplemented by further provisions for increasing the efficiency of the Courts of Justice, and also that the subject could be better dealt with by one 'comprehensive measure' than by two passed in different legislatures.

"The Government of India, concurring in these views, and finding that, owing to various Acts passed in the Governor General's Council being affected, that Council alone was competent to enact one measure disposing of the whole subject, entrusted to me the duty of conferring with the Government of Bombay as to the provisions which such a measure should embrace, and of introducing into this Council the Bill as finally determined upon. I accordingly visited Bombay in April last, and the result was that a Bill was framed in full consultation with me, and proposed by the Government of Bombay to the Government of India for adoption. The Government of India have, I am glad to say, entirely accepted, in their executive capacity, the main principles and policy of this Bill, which are also, I believe, in conformity with the views of the Secretary of State. The two Bills for which leave has been already granted need not now, therefore, be proceeded with, and it remains for me to ask of this Council leave to introduce the new Bill, reserving all detailed explanations for the occasion of its introduction."

The motion was put and agreed to.

Abstract of the Proceedings of the Council of the Governor General of India, assembled for the purpose of making Laws and Regulations under the provisions of the Act of Parliament 24 & 25 Vic., cap. 67.

The Council met at Government House on Thursday the 17th July 1879.

PRESENT:

His Excellency the Viceroy and Governor General of India, G.M.S.I., *presiding.*
His Honour the Lieutenant-Governor of the Panjáb, C.S.I.
His Excellency the Commander-in-Chief, G.C.B.
The Hon'ble Sir A. J. Arbuthnot, K.C.S.I.
Colonel the Hon'ble Sir Andrew Clarke, R.E., K.C.M.G., C.B., C.I.E.
The Hon'ble Sir John Strachey, G.C.S.I.
General the Hon'ble Sir E. B. Johnson, R.A., K.C.B.
The Hon'ble Whitley Stokes, C.S.I.
The Hon'ble Rivers Thompson, C.S.I.
The Hon'ble F. R. Cockerell.
The Hon'ble Sayyad Ahmad Khán Bahádur, C.S.I.
The Hon'ble T. C. Hope, C.S.I.
The Hon'ble B. W. Colvin.

DEKKHAN AGRICULTURISTS RELIEF BILL.

The Hon'ble Mr. Hope introduced the Bill for the relief of indebted agriculturists in the Deccan. He said:—

" In availing myself of the leave granted me at the meeting of the Council on the 5th ultimo to introduce a measure designed to afford relief to the indebted population of our Deccan districts, I fear it is indispensable that I should tax the patience of my hearers by treating the subject at considerable length. A careful analysis of the condition of the ryots, and an investigation of the cause of that condition, seem to be a preliminary indispensable to a just appraisement of each of the numerous provisions comprised in the contemplated legislation.

"The 'Deccan riots' began in May 1875. They extended to thirty-three villages in the districts of Poona and Ahmednagar, and many more were threatened; but order was restored within a month's time. Symptoms of the bad terms subsisting between the ryot and the money-lender had not been wanting in past years. Whenever, as from time to time happened, the turbulent and predatory aboriginal hillmen—Bhíls, Rámusís or Kolís —rose, they made money-lenders their victims, partly from personal motives, and partly to propitiate the population generally. Not a year passed without isolated murders by exasperated debtors. But in 1875 the uneasiness became general in the Deccan. An individual case set fire to the long-laid train. The villagers began by combining to refuse supplies, water and service to the moneylenders, but soon proceeded to actual outrage. The singular character of the proceedings proclaimed at once their cause and their importance. Setting aside isolated cases of personal violence and plunder, the movement was simply an organized, and temperately but determinedly conducted, effort, directed to the definite object of obtaining and destroying the bonds, decrees and account-books of the money-lenders. No persons except the latter were molested. The mobs were composed of respectable members of the community, not *bádmashes*, and were often led or encouraged by the headmen of the village. On attaining their object they dispersed as rapidly and quietly as they had come together. The eventual cessation of the riots was due, not merely to the prompt action of the police and the military, but to the assurances of the civil authorities that complaints should be enquired into and proved grievances redressed. The latter pledge it remains for this Council to redeem.

"The riots have been followed by investigations in various forms. A Special Commission, in the first place, was without delay appointed by the Bombay Government. It was composed of two European officers, Messrs. Richey and Lyon, of the Revenue and Judicial branches of the service, Mr. Shambuprasád, a distinguished Native administrator, and a civilian from the North-Western Provinces (first Mr. Auckland Colvin, now employed in Egypt, and afterwards Mr. Carpenter). Their report, in five volumes and above 1,500 pages, is a very able survey of the difficulty in all its aspects. Besides this the riots gave a special direction in Bombay to the enquiries into the working of the Civil Courts then going on throughout India in connection with the amended Civil Procedure Code under the consideration of this Council, which eventually became law as Act X of 1877; and a judicial officer, Mr. William Wedderburn, was deputed to report on the subject. Further, other circumstances led in 1878 to the condition of the peasantry in the four districts of the Deccan being subjected to a close investigation, in which the most experienced officers of the Bombay Presidency took part, and which is summed up in a Minute by Sir Richard Temple, dated October 29th, 1878. The Famine Commission also this year obtained a good deal of valuable evidence, to which they have been so good as to allow me free access. Finally, the question has been very ably and instructively discussed by the Press, both in India and in England. It would be impossible for me, on an occasion like the present, to summarize all these enquiries, or to state separately the opinions of all the principal authorities. I can only lay before the Council what seem to myself, by the light of this mass of evidence and of my own knowledge and general experience, to be the condition of the people in the disturbed area and the causes which have operated to produce it, and then explain the measures by which the Executive Government propose that the relief should be afforded.

II.

"The Central Deccan, which is the locality principally distressed, though unfortunately not the only one, and to which the present Bill is intended to apply, consists of four 'districts' or executive collector's charges, namely, Poona, Ahmednagar, Sholápur, and Sátára. The three first-named became British territory in A.D. 1819-21, but Sátára not till A.D. 1849. Their area is 21,000 square miles, and their population three-and-a-half millions; that is to say, the population of Scotland, located in two-thirds of its space. Mountains and forests occupy much of the country, so that the actually cultivated area gives about six acres per head of the agricultural population. The State is the landlord; the tenure *ryotwári* on the Bombay system of permanent occupancy, with revision of assessment every thirty years. The peasant-proprietors themselves cultivate about three-fourths of their land, and sublet the remainder. The assessment or rent they pay to the Government is at average rates of from seven annas ($10\frac{1}{2}d.$) to twelve annas (1s. 6d.) per acre, which is equivalent on fairly good land to from an eighth to a sixteenth of the gross produce, and on the poor soils to much less.

"The proportion and extent of indebtedness are not easy to ascertain. In one batch of twelve villages tested by the Commission of 1875, one-third of the peasant-proprietors were found to be very heavily embarrassed; and of these, two-thirds were petty land-holders, paying assessments of only twenty rupees (£2) per annum and under. Their debts came to eighteen times the average assessment, and two-thirds of this were secured by mortgage of the land. In another batch of seventeen villages in Ahmednagar, forty-three per cent. of the proprietors were deeply in debt, the debts averaging fifteen times the assessment, but reaching forty-five times in individual cases. Only one-third of the debts appeared to be secured by mortgage, but one-eighth of the land had already been actually transferred to the money-lenders; and with regard to much of the remainder, the ryots were virtually mere tenants-at-will of their creditors. The Collector was of opinion that, throughout the whole district, three-fifths of the people were so involved that, in ordinary course, it was impossible for them ever to get free. Upon this and much other evidence I must confess myself unable to share optimist views of the condition of the people. Supposing only one-third of the proprietors to be irretrievably involved, is a ruined, despairing and embittered population of above a million souls beneath special consideration? The proportion seems to me, however, to have been nearer one-half than one-third, and to be, moreover, constantly increasing. Finally, it must not be forgotten that the statistics of the Commission, which I have been quoting, are now four years old. Since then the terrible famine of 1876-77 and the subsequent indifferent seasons have passed over the land, and cannot but have left deep traces behind. True, as it is, that the peasant-proprietary struggled nobly and long to maintain themselves and their dependents without State relief; and vast as was the amount of accumulated savings, in gold and silver ornaments and the like, which they were found to possess, we must not forget that those savings were revealed by their passage to the mint, and that their dissipation must have left at the mercy of the money-lender thousands who were never so before. We may admire the honest pride and fortitude which the peasantry, as a body, displayed throughout their long-protracted trial; but we cannot ignore the obvious effects on their condition.

"Granted, however, that a large proportion of the population are deeply involved, we may well enquire whether such a condition is abnormal. It has been said, and in one sense with truth, that 'poverty and debt were the familiar heritage of the ryots before the advent of the British rule.' Our records of the country when first acquired tell of indebtedness extending largely among the population. The ryots, it is said, 'though usually frugal and provident,' were in many cases 'living in dependence on the sowkár (or money-lender), delivering to him their produce and drawing upon him for necessaries;' and this condition is mainly attributed to the Marátha system of levying heavy contributions from bankers, to whom the revenues of villages were assigned in repayment, and of collecting the State dues generally through the agency of such capitalists, who recovered in kind what they paid in cash. Indebtedness thus arising mainly form a vicious system of collecting the land-revenue paid by all, necessarily extended to a large proportion of the population. But the amount of individual debt appears to have usually been moderate—necessarily so, it may be added, because the security and means of recovery were small, since land was not sold for debts, and little or no assistance in recovering them was given by the State. Very much the same condition of affairs is shown by ample testimony to exist now, to a greater or less degree, in the Native States of India. I have myself noted it in those of Western India, with many of which I have had considerable official experience. The reply to our enquiry, then, is that, as compared with former times and with Native States, indebtedness now in the Deccan extends to smaller numbers, but is heavier in individual incidence, followed by consequences infinitely more serious, and decidedly abnormal.

"Some may feel inclined to question whether, after all, there is any real harm in the present state of things. The institution of private property in land is essential, it will be said, to the well-being and progress of every civilized community, to the encouragement of industry and the accumulation of capital. But it is indispensable that such property should be in the hands of those who by their capital, intelligence and industry are qualified to turn it to the best account. If this condition be not fulfilled, but the land be held by a class who, through their ignorance, improvidence, and want of energy, have burdened their heritage with debt which can never be repaid, and thus have deprived themselves of all incentive to labour and all interest in its results, then the only remedy is to promote rather than to obstruct a gradual restoration of healthier conditions of society by the bankruptcy and eviction of the incapable. True as such principles undoubtedly are in modern European populations, considerable caution is necessary in applying them to the ill-studied and little-understood problems of Oriental life. Assuming hastily a similarity of premises, we are apt to jump to familiar conclusions, and to inaugurate action wholly inapplicable and pernicious. Much of the difficulty in the present instance arises from such inconsiderable interference in the past. When we overturn by an Act of the Legislature institutions which popular consent has maintained for above a score of centuries, we sometimes forget that we are not the bearers of a political revelation from Heaven.

"In the present instance there seem grave reasons for doubting whether the premises upon which a policy of *laissez faire* is based are sound. If the present condition of the Deccan ryots is caused by inherent moral and physical defects, unfitting them for peasant-proprietorship, if they encumber the land to the exclusion of a class of intelligent, enterprising and energetic capitalists, and if the land is such that capital in large single sums can alone effect its improvement, then, indeed, we must perhaps sit down and sit out the process of gradual transfer of the rights of property from the one class to the other, merely softening, if need be, the fall of the sufferers. But consideration will show that no such circumstances exist in the Deccan. The Marátha kunbi is not the defective and useless creature postulated. No such material composed the armies of Sivaji and his successors, which defeated the Mogals, overran half India, and founded an empire of which the remnants still flourish around us. As a soldier the Marátha in olden days was as enterprising as he was hardy, equally able to 'bide a buffet' and to strike a blow. At present he furnishes material perhaps second to none in India for the purposes of modern war. All representations of him as thriftless, enervated and puny are incorrect. As a peasant-proprietor he is no unfavourable specimen of the class. Mr. Chaplin and our other early authorities give him credit for many sterling qualities. He is still represented by the Commission as 'a simple, well-disposed peasant, contented with the scantiest clothing and hardest fare,' not without 'masculine qualities' and 'a stubborn endurance,' though still mostly uneducated, and consequently without a broad range of intelligence. Of course improvidence and slovenly cultivation may be detected in individuals or particular localities. But we must not expect too much. Under British rule the kunbi has undoubtedly progressed as adverse circumstances allowed. He works his fields to the best of his lights, and in the dry season travels far in search of day-labour, or with his cart on hire. During the late famine he displayed resources equally creditable to his thrift and his good-feeling. His embarrassed condition seems to be rather his misfortune than his fault, induced by the calamities of the last century, the obligation of ancestral debt, the burden of the land-revenue demand—formerly in amount and latterly in imposition—and the facilities for extortion conferred by our laws upon his creditors.

"On the other hand, those into whose hands the land is now observed to be passing are not yearning for it in order to improve it by their intelligence, enterprise and capital. With solitary exceptions, the transferees are the professional money-lenders, who have no wish even to hold the status of landed proprietors, much less to invest their capital in comparatively unprofitable agricultural experiments. Often, too, are they aliens, who return home after time. So far from eagerly getting the land formally transferred to their own names, they show general reluctance to do so. They prefer to keep the ryot on his land, and extract all they can from him: the punctual discharge of their advances is the last thing they desire. As Mr. Auckland Colvin says,—

'the position is that of a man recorded as occupier of his holding, and responsible for the payment of revenue assessed on it, but virtually reduced by pressure of debt to a tenant-at-will, holding at a rack-rent from, and sweated by, his Marwari creditor. It is in that creditor's power to eject him any day by putting in force any one of the decrees he has against him; and if allowed to hold on, it is only on condition of paying over to his creditor all the produce of his land not absolutely necessary for next year's seed-grain or for the support of life. * * He has nothing to hope for, but lives in daily fear of the final catastrophe. Under a so-called ryotwari settlement it is gradually coming to this, that the ryot is the tenant, and the Marwari is the proprietor. * * The proprietor is irresponsible; the tenant unprotected. It promises to become, not a ryotwari, but a Marwari settlement.'

Such conditions deprive the transfer of land from distressed to monied classes of all the glamour with which political economy would surround it. They show that the noble gift of property in land, made by the British Government to the peasantry for their sole benefit, is passing, contrary to their intentions and in frustration of their objects, to a class unfitted to possess it. As observed as early as 1852 by Sir George Wingate, the great author of the gift,—

'it was never contemplated that the measures intended to secure these benefits for the class of landholders should transfer their dearest rights and the possessions that had descended to them from their forefathers to a class of usurious money-lenders, and degrade the former to the position of labourers or of tenants cultivating their former lands at the will of the latter.'

In short, the second of the premises on which a policy of *laissez faire* would rest is as unsound as the first. In the words of Mr. Pedder, a gentleman who has long made a special study of this subject, and whose talents have lately led to his transfer from the Bombay Civil Service to a high position at the India Office,—

'it cannot be too clearly understood that only in the dream of a visionary will the English agricultural system of large landlords, capitalist farmers of large farms, and peasant-labourers for wage, ever be substituted for the *petite culture* of India. Happen what will, each ryot will till his petty holding; but he may be, as we have made him in Bombay, its proprietor; he may be, as in the North-West, a member of a proprietary cultivating community; he may be, as in Rajpootana, the customary tenant of an hereditary lord; or he may be, as I fear he is becoming, the prædial serf of a money-lender.'

"Only one of the three premises mentioned above remains— that the land is such that capital in large single sums can alone effect its improvement. That is exactly what it is not. There are indeed certain localities, limited in number, where irrigation projects may alter the character of the produce and counteract seasons of drought. But these are far too extensive for individual enterprise. They must be undertaken by joint stock companies or Government, and the latter has them in hand. But the great proportion of the cultivated area is such that the most it is capable of, can be made out of it either by more careful tillage and economy of stable manure, or by petty improvements, such as, for instance, digging a well, banking-up a stream or watershed at certain seasons, making a supply-channel from a neighbouring canal or river, or altering the level or inclination of a field—by action, in short, of exactly the kind which the peasant-proprietor, standing on his own land, fully realizing its capabilities, and feeling pride and pleasure as well as utility in developing them to meet the growing needs of himself and his children, is at once the most competent and the most likely to apply. That he has so improved his estate since it came into his hands when he could, despite all the adverse circumstances by which he has been met, is proved by the increase in wells and the reclamation of unassessed waste within holdings during the last thirty years. Whether he shall pursue these inclinations freely, or continue, as at present, thwarted and checkmated at every turn, it now mainly rests with us to decide.

" To the question, therefore, whether there is, after all, much harm in the present state of things, we must, perforce, answer that the harm is of the greatest. To a peasantry, such as I have described, expropriation means discouragement, despair and exasperation. To the money-lending class it means the acquisition of what they are unfitted to use and do not particularly desire to have, of what yields them at best a precarious profit, not exceeding that which reasonable rates of interest, combined with easy recovery, would produce, but wrung forth with trouble, anxiety, expense, popular execration, and even personal danger. To society it means the discouragement of labour in extracting wealth from the soil, the application of capital in disadvantageous and comparatively unproductive channels, and the fomentation of disorder and outrage. As reported to the Bombay Government in 1858 by Mr. J. D. Inverarity, the Revenue Commissioner,—

'the question is one of vital importance both to Government and the people. Even the passive society of the East cannot bear so great a burden without making from time to time convulsive efforts to shake it off. These efforts must increase in frequency and strength, unless the legislature seriously takes up the evil and applies the knife to it.'

III.

" Assuming, then, that indebtedness to an unusual and extreme extent is the condition of a large proportion of the people in the British Deccan, we must enter into a critical examination of its probable causes before we can hope to apply an effective remedy. These causes are numerous, and complicated both in themselves and in their action and reaction upon each other. They may be conveniently classed as 'normal' and 'special.'

" The normal causes are those which may be found at work, more or less, at all times, and some in all parts of India, others only in certain localities. First of these stands *poverty*. It is obvious that where there is a peasant-proprietary, though the stimulus to individual exertion is considerable, and in India the Hindú joint-family system tends to prevent minute subdivision, the individual capital cannot be great, and misfortunes comparatively small will throw even a thrifty and industrious person into the hands of the money-lender for temporary loans. Besides this, the kunbi of our Deccan labours under the special disadvantage of a soil mostly indifferent, and a rainfall so precarious, that he hardly gets a full crop once in three years. Finally, the obligation to pay a father's debts, laid by Hindú law upon a son without any equitable restrictions, imposes a burden oppressive at all times, and too often aggravated by fraud in the creditor and ignorance in the debtor. The Commission, in fact, go so far as to term ancestral debt the 'chief cause' of the ryots' embarrassments. Next to poverty comes *ignorance*, which renders the unlettered peasant unable to read, and often to understand, the documents and accounts in which he is vitally concerned, or to state and substantiate in a Civil Court a good defence when he has one, and thus makes him a tempting subject for every kind of roguery. *Social observances*, such as marriage, birth and funeral expenses, also swell the roll of obligations; but being connected with religion they are to a great extent unavoidable. If occasionally excessive in prosperity, they are reduced in bad times. The Commission consider that in amount they are generally not larger than the ryot's income, if otherwise only fairly taxed, would justify, and that undue prominence has been given to them as a cause of his ruin. *Improvidence* must be admitted to contribute its share to the catastrophe; but it consists, as the Commission remark, 'rather in the short-sighted improvidence of an ignorant class, ready to relieve present necessity by discounting future income on any terms, and unable to realize the consequences of obligations foolishly contracted, than in an extravagant expenditure and misapplication of income.' To this may be added an honest and confiding, rather than vigilant, temperament. A soil yielding but one crop, and therefore the whole year's income at one period, a climate so capricious as to preclude at seed-time any safe estimate of what the harvest, if there be one, will be worth, and prices varying above cent per cent., as they twice have done in this century, might well derange the calculations, and produce the bankruptcy, even of sober men of business.

"Besides these normal causes conducive to indebtedness, there exists a long array of special ones, some general in their operation, others peculiar to the Bombay Presidency or the Deccan alone. These I propose to notice in four groups—namely, those increasing credit, diminishing ability to repay, proceeding from the revenue system, and comprised in the term 'arming of the money-lender.'

"*Increased credit* obviously flowed primarily from our establishment of a settled government, and the consequent immunity of the ryot from being plundered and murdered by hostile armies, or drawn from his fields, perhaps killed in battle, on his own side, as also from the grosser forms of private crime. A like effect followed our land-settlements. The meaning of the phrase 'land-revenue' varies greatly in different parts of India. In Bombay the State is the landlord, entitled to the entire rent—that is, to the whole net produce or surplus after deducting the cost of cultivation and of the subsistence of the peasant and his family. The State has no intermediary or landlord to think of, to whom a certain proportion of the rent must be left. It may relinquish to the peasant-cultivator as much or as little of the rent as it chooses. The Native governments preceding us relinquished but little, and the cultivator was rack-rented. Hence, even a small debt pressed heavily, and complaints of indebtedness were general when we acquired the country. Gradually we reduced our land-revenue demands, producing immediate relief and recovery of agriculture, until by the revenue survey system, founded by Goldsmid and Wingate in 1838-40, and gradually extended throughout the Presidency, we levy, says Mr. Pedder, only one-half, *at most*, of the net produce or rent, thus leaving the cultivator a liberal margin upon which to borrow and repay. But we went further than this. Under the Native government a cultivator could not, according to custom, be ejected as long as he paid the revenue demand; but that demand was so high that his right of occupancy was worth little or nothing, and was, besides, mostly not recognized as saleable. The land was not his to sell, being deemed the property of the State. Under our settlement, however, 'this right of conditional occupancy' (to quote Bombay Act I of 1865) 'is declared to be a saleable and transferable property.' Though the land is still termed 'Government land,' the occupant has acquired a tenant-right far wider than that of Ireland, and has virtually become proprietor, while the Government retains only a rent charge, variable once in thirty years, within certain prescribed limits. The right of property thus granted acquired simultaneously a considerable value through the reduction of the revenue demand and its invariability for thirty years. The gift, intended to enrich the ryot, increased his credit along with his means, thus exposing him to the loss, not only of the extra share of net produce bestowed, but of the land from which a livelihood had hitherto been secure.

"Fast upon these additions to solvency and credit came days of brilliant but ephemeral prosperity. Commencing with 1850, railways, roads, bridges and other public works poured millions into labourers' hands, while a series of good seasons gave the best encouragement to agriculture, and brought almost every available acre under the plough. Then came the American war, raising to almost fabulous rates the prices of cotton and other produce. These circumstances had a double effect: many ryots paid off, or greatly reduced, their debts: many more, both of these and others increased their expenses, and some even borrowed largely, upon the strength of increased incomes which they supposed would last for ever: all learned a higher standard of comfort and new wants, which they could not relinquish with readiness equal to the subsequent rapid contraction of their means. A further expansion of the ryot's credit was induced by greater facility in obtaining loans, owing to two reasons. The arming of the money-lender, to which I shall presently allude, rendered frauds and legal recovery of advances easier. Also, the general prosperity increased the capital of money-lenders for investment and the number of persons competing in the business. Money was lent recklessly on unsound credit; money was lent designedly to secure the unwary ryot as a bond-slave for ever.

"*Diminished ability to repay* arose partly from greater pressure on the land by the population, which had grown 45 per cent. in the thirty years ending with 1875. The proportion of 167 souls per square mile becomes extremely heavy after making allowance for mountains, forests, &c., and for the defects of the cultivable soil and the climate. But even the cultivable area cannot be, on an average, as productive as in former days. When only a half of it was cultivated, the best soils were chosen, fallows were readily allowed; the waste land and forests supported cattle freely; the stable manure was sufficient. Now all is reversed. The waste land has disappeared; the cattle and manure are insufficient in proportion; the jungles have become reserved forests; the poor soils reduce the average; and the general result is a lower yield per head for subsistence or repayment of debt. Again, the ryot's solvency was reduced by a great fall in prices after the close of the American war. Between 1836 and 1866 prices rose from fifty-six to eighteen *seers* per rupee: between 1866 and 1874 they fell again to fifty *seers*. With the various causes of low prices; with questions such as those of the effect of levying revenue in money instead of in kind; of the sufficiency of the circulating medium, or of the action of the so-called 'Indian tribute,' I am not now concerned; for our present purpose, to note the fact of the fall is sufficient. A series of bad seasons has, likewise, supervened. Finally, the effect of an absence of stimulus to exertion in lessening ability to repay must not be overlooked. Where the ryot is hopelessly involved, and all produce goes to the creditor, a bare subsistence being given back, what inducement can there be to add to the latter's gains? The ryot pays off less; his debt on paper increases, and what more? He thinks it 'as well to be hung for a sheep as for a lamb.'

"*To our revenue system* must in candour be ascribed some share in the indebtedness of the ryot. Time would fail me were I to attempt to enter here into the elaborate question of the pressure of the land-revenue demand, nor does my subject require that I should do so. The Commission's report and the other enquiries to which I have referred contain the fullest information on the subject. Suffice it to say that it is amply proved that the riots had no immediate connection with the revision of assessment, which was neither imposed nor contemplated in many of the localities where they occurred. Still less can the general indebtedness of the ryot be ascribed to the weight of the assessment, whether unrevised or revised, since the proportion of the net produce taken is low in itself; very low for a *landlord* to take; far lower than that prevailing in 'alienated' British villages and adjacent foreign States. I am here of course speaking broadly, irrespective of individual instances of over-assessment, which in so vast an undertaking may not improbably have occurred. But it seems likely that indebtedness arising mainly from other causes, normal or special, may have been aggravated by our rigid system. If any considerable increase at a revision were gradually worked up to in the course of two to five years, the ryot would have time to re-adjust his expenses to his means instead of being taken by surprise, and perhaps driven to the money-lender. Again, if the recovery of instalments were more coincident with the time when the ryot realizes on his produce, instead of falling sometimes too early and sometimes too late, and so the land-revenue were more in practice (what it is in law) a first charge on the latter, much temporary borrowing, fraud in crediting produce, and eventual Government process for recovery, might be avoided. Some debt, too, may be caused by the fear of eviction—a mode of recovering the revenue for which a substitute is much needed. Moreover, though the system of taking revenue in kind, besides involving the injustice of assessment on the gross produce, instead of the net, is so open to fraud, when adopted on a large scale, as to be impracticable, its object might be attained, in localities subject to drought, by such suspension of the revenue demand as to spread over three or four years, according to the seasons, the aggregate amount to be recovered in that period. Finally, in times of famine, suspension of demand might be systematically granted, as of late it has been by Sir Richard Temple, and even total remission, which is not inconsistent with the Bombay settlements.

And, above all, whatever relief is deemed reasonable should be granted in time.

" *The arming of the money-lender* is a general term which I shall apply to the process of increasing in numberless ways the legal power of creditor over debtor, which has been synonymous with the elaboration of our Indian law procedure. In our early judicial dealings with our newly-acquired possessions in the Bombay Presidency we combined as far as possible the Native model in form with European common sense and equity in practice ; but gradually the system was made more regular and rigid. Mountstuart Elphinstone's Code of 1827, however, still contained much of the old leaven, such as Arbitration Courts, usury law, and a long limitation for suits. Only gradually did creditors perceive and work up to the advantages the law had given them. At first the debtors complained of usurious interest only. From 1843 to 1850 the Court's influence became rapidly more apparent. Attachments, and the extortion of new bonds with a premium for forbearance, increased. From 1850 to 1858 credit and frauds much expanded. Numerous public officers pointed out the mischief which was going on ; none foresaw more clearly than Sir George Wingate how the benefit of his settlement was being turned into wrong channels, or pleaded more earnestly, though in vain, for prompt and effective remedies. While affairs were in this state, the legislature stepped in to aggravate the evil. In 1859 the period of limitation for suits was reduced, and the first Civil Procedure Code was passed, followed by the Stamp Act in 1860.

" The condition then consummated, which has lasted with but slight variation for about twenty years, may be thus briefly summarized as it appears in the Deccan. The procedure is highly elaborate and technical ; the penalties for contravention of it severe, and litigation dangerous without the guidance of a pleader, whose services are costly and interests often at variance with those of his client. The procedure is the same for a debt of Rs. 5 and Rs. 5,000, except in the rare instances where Small Cause Courts are established. Stamp and Court expenses have nearly doubled. Arbitration has been gradually shouldered out, partly by the superior prestige of the Courts, partly by the stamp-duties, partly by its disadvantages for the money-lender. Suits may be heard *ex parte* in the absence of the defendant, and are found to be so, in the four Deccan districts, in above half of the cases. Great weight is attached by the Courts to bonds, and they are, therefore, largely, almost exclusively, depended on. However fraudulent, extortionate or in excess of consideration a bond may be, the burden of proof lies on the debtor, and in practice his defence is generally hopeless. Payments on a decree made by the debtor out of Court were (till

1877) ignored, and were, therefore, obtained, wherever possible, by the fraudulent creditor. The reduction of the limitation period for bonded debts from twelve to six and in some cases three years, and for simple money debts from six to three years, respectively, has subjected the debtor to compound interest, frequent suits, extra costs and a vast increase of his liabilities. The power of obtaining arrest and imprisonment gives the creditor the means of extorting almost any terms for his forbearance in exercising it. Of all the weapons he has obtained, this has been proved to be the most misused. The power of sale in execution extended, till 1877, to *everything* the debtor possessed: since then certain bare necessaries have alone been exempted. Land remains saleable, whether ancestral or acquired, subject to certain provisions for saving it analogous to an *elegit*, which have hitherto proved inoperative, but are now being amended. Of all sales it is a characteristic that the property, through technical difficulties, constantly goes for a mere song, and the creditor is the purchaser. Decrees were, till 1877, interminable, and the Commission found numbers to be of twenty years' standing. Now they may be executed for twelve years. A sub-judge mentions one executed *nine* times. If the persecuted debtor turned towards the law of insolvency, he, till quite recently, found it little more than a name. Until actually arrested or in jail, he could not resort to it at all; and whether, after doing so, he escaped its pitfalls and two years' imprisonment or not, his subsequently acquired property and earnings were liable (unless his debt was under Rs. 100 and the Judge chose to discharge him) until the last pice due, with interest, had been repaid. Finally, the increase of work entailed delay, with loss of time and money, in the disposal of cases; while financial reasons led to reduction in the numbers of the Courts, and consequently to their greater remoteness from the ryot's home. And all this is the more important, in that a vast increase of litigation has followed the new law, so that in 1876 there were 37,128 suits, and in 1878 (after the famine) 27,577, disposed of in our four districts alone.

" The tendency of the change of relations thus gradually brought about by the law will be seen to have been all one way— in favour of the party possessing the most intelligence and money. Even of old, the superiority of the money-lender over the ryot was considerable, though the former had little power of compulsion; but by the law this superiority has been infinitely increased. The likening of the contest between them to one 'between a child and a giant' is no figure of speech; yet the law presumes them both to be equal! That the superiority is fully and **often** fraudulently availed of, is proved by the vast increase of litigation just mentioned; by the evidence of judicial and revenue officers and of numberless debtors; by the scrutiny of accounts by the Commission, and by the use, in 1874, of some 150,000 warrants as threats only. The general result is that through these undue powers the ryot is enslaved by a vast amount of debt, which has been much enhanced by our legal system, and in part was never incurred by him at all. In concluding this sketch it seems scarcely necessary for me to add that the law, and not the judges, are to blame. Some of the most valuable proofs of the defects of the former are derived from judicial officers, Native as well as European; and I fully agree with Mr. Auckland Colvin that it is 'very much to the credit of the subordinate judicial administration that it has expressed itself so clearly as to the position which it is compelled to occupy.'

IV.

"Having thus enumerated the various causes of the ryot's indebtedness, I will briefly classify them according to the possibility or expediency of remedial measures. As causes regarding which little or no special action is practicable we may put down all normal ones. Ignorance, improvidence and extravagant ceremonial or social expenditure can never be eradicated from the world, either in the Deccan or elsewhere; though time, experience and education may reduce their strength. An agricultural population everywhere is comparatively ignorant; they are found so even in England under a compulsory educational system, much more in India, where compulsion cannot be thought of. But village-schools are exceptionally numerous and efficient in the Bombay Presidency; cultivators' children form 21 per cent. of the pupils, and we may hope for gradual improvement in this respect. Comparative poverty must continue the lot of a peasant-proprietary whose soil is poor and climate capricious. Periodical absorption of savings by famine can, at least, be only diminished in degree by palliatives of partial applicability, such as forest conservancy, railways and irrigation, which, under Sir Richard Temple's vigorous administration, are being promoted as rapidly as means allow. Prices must take their course.

"As causes regarding which interference is undesirable may be mentioned the increased credit due to orderly government, property in land and competition of money-lenders, and the lessened ability to repay arising from the diminution of waste land for fallows and grazing by the extension of cultivation and forest reserves. The raising of the land-assessment to the level of Native States in order to stimulate exertion, and the lowering of it so as to pay private debts at the expense of the community in general, are equally out of the question.

"Respecting the remaining causes, action, either executive or legislative, seems open to us. *Executively*, some little might probably be done to relieve pressure of population by favouring emigration to other districts. Then, though the idea of Government agricultural banks appears to me to be unsound in theory and unworkable in practice, the opening of local loans in small amounts, as in France, might offer to bankers an alternative for indiscriminate lending on usury, and to cultivators an investment preferable to ornaments. The system of advances by Government for land-improvement, also, might be simplified. Again, relief might be afforded by modifying, in the directions I have already indicated, the mode in which our land-revenue demand is imposed and levied. Stamp and process fees and batta seem also capable of revision. Finally, there are exchange and cognate financial questions. But I must not dilate upon these executive remedies, which are beyond the sphere of this Council. I have touched on them merely in order to show that I am not so simple as to suppose that all the ryot's difficulties will be removed by the passing of the Bill before us. *Legislatively*, what we can do, what is proved by overwhelming evidence to be the thing required, what we undoubtedly ought to do, promptly and effectively, is to restore, as far as may be, the rude balance between debtor and creditor which has been disturbed by our own legal institutions. We may take back many of the weapons inconsiderately placed in the money-lender's hand and shown to have been misused; we may check the undue credit arising from unjustifiable facilities for recovery; we may increase ability to repay by removing discouragements to industry; we may obey the long-neglected proverbial mandate to hear both parties; we may substitute for the blind and ruthless operation of legal machinery the intelligent dispensation of justice between man and man.

V.

"As introductory to a fuller definition of the principles upon which our proposed measure should rest and to a detailed explanation of the Bill itself, it may be instructive to survey, briefly, the relations of debtor and creditor as they were found on the introduction of British rule and as they may now be seen subsisting in some of the best administered Native States. For the former period I can quote no better sketch than that given in the despatch of the Secretary of State, dated December 26th, 1878, which has recently become public:—

'Under Native Governments it seems no assistance was, ordinarily, afforded by the State to a creditor for the recovery of his debts. No Court of Justice was open to him, and he was left to his own devices to extort what was due, Government winking at very forcible measures that were occasionally employed. The result was not so bad as might have been expected. It speaks well for the national character that contracts were rarely repudiated. And the Commissioners observe that in these proceedings honesty was the best policy for the ryot and caution was a necessity to the money-lender.'

"In order to state correctly the present practice in Native States I have made special enquiries in four cases. As to Hyderabad, His Excellency Sir Salar Jung has favoured me, through the Resident, Sir Richard Meade, with a valuable memorandum and summary of regulations. From Bhávnagar, a large State in Káthiáwár, which was, till lately, under joint-administrators, English and Native, during the minority of the Thákur, and of which a graphic account by Sir David Wedderburn appeared last year in the *Fortnightly Review*, I obtained a note through Mr. Percival. The system in Morvi, another Káthiáwár State, is described in communications from the administrator, Mr. Shambuprasád, who was a member of the Deccan Riots Commission. About Baroda full information is forthcoming in the administration reports of Sir T. Madava Ráo and the letters of some private Native friends I have there. In all these States civil suits for debt are comparatively rare. The limitation period, where there is any definitely laid down, is twelve and six years. The Hindú rule of *dam-dupat*, or disallowance of interest at any time in excess of the principal, is observed in Baroda, Bhávnagar, and Morvi. In Hyderabad, usurious interest is summarily cut down to a reasonable rate. Imprisonment for debt is not allowed in Morvi, nor, apparently, in Bhávnagar. In Baroda it is forbidden altogether during the cultivating seasons, and very sparingly used at other times. In Hyderabad it is reserved for cases of contumacy and fraud. As to the sale of a ryot's land and house for debt, both are exempt in Bhávnagar, and the former (if not both) in Morvi. In Hyderabad the sale of either is said to be resorted to in extreme cases only. In Baroda only such portion is saleable as may be in excess of what is indispensable for the residence and support of the ryot and his family, and sales are not favoured by the Courts. The sale of moveables is also under characteristic restrictions. In Baroda the ryot's implements and cattle necessary for cultivation, cooking utensils and clothes indispensable for daily use, 'the ornaments which a married woman must have on her person as long as her husband is alive' (even if not her's, but her husband's), and two months' corn for the ryot and his family are all exempt. In Bhávnagar only agricultural stock and implements in excess of what is necessary for cultivation, as also the produce, may be sold; and in Morvi the rule seems much the same. In Hyderabad the reservations embrace cattle and implements necessary for agriculture, seed-grain for the next season, grain for subsistence for six months, and necessary apparel and cooking utensils. In all the States the fixing of instalments is common, and, whatever may be the standard rules promulgated through a desire to imitate our judicial institutions and to obtain credit for well-organized government, a summary inquiry into the facts of the case, with scrutiny of accounts, and a more or less rough-and-ready adaptation of the creditor's demands to the debtor's means, appear to be the practice. This practice, being supported by popular opinion, is probably less affected in individual cases by corruption, partiality or oppression than might on general grounds be expected. Having held for many years intimate relations, official and otherwise, with Native States, which in Bombay form one-third of the Presidency, I can say with confidence that, making due allowance for the growing mischievous tendency to copy the British system blindly, the picture just presented is, on the whole, fairly typical of them all.

"This picture may, at first sight, seem to exhibit conditions under which either the ryot can get no credit or the moneylender no returns. As a matter of fact, however, neither result occurs, because all the parties concerned—debtors, creditors, and rulers—thoroughly understand the limits to their several actions which are essential to their several ends. No doubt the ryot has in many cases a hand-to-mouth sort of existence; but even this is endurable, combined with immunity from eviction. I have come upon a passage in Sir T. Madava Ráo's Administration Report of the Baroda State for 1875-76 so ably describing the position, that I must ask leave to quote it at length:—

'Sales must not be made so rigorous as to crush or impair industrial energy or to induce its emigration. The Civil Courts have to be specially careful in regard to the last-mentioned point, which mainly concerns the ryots. These have frequent dealings with the sowkárs, whose exacting tendencies are well known. The Civil Court should take up such a position between the ryot and the sowkár as freely to allow benefits to pass, but effectually to arrest mutual injuries. The ryot here can never, as a rule, altogether dispense with the services of the sowkár; for the seasons are not so regular nor are the means of irrigation so extensive as to ensure equability or constancy of production. Again, the land-tax is in most cases fixed, and absorbs a considerable proportion of the produce; and, again, the prices of produce fluctuate, changing the incidence of the tax on the produce from year to year. In other words, while the outturn of the land is necessarily varying, the ryot has to pay a fixed and considerable tax, which must come from the land. In other words, again, the exchequer has to draw a constant and continuous stream out of a fitful supply. The sowkár by his interposition meets the mechanical necessity of the problem. He is the receiver of the fitful supply, and enables the ryot to pay the sarkár equably. He often performs another useful function, namely, he enables the ryot also to draw from the fitful supply an equable subsistence for himself and family. It is thus to him that both sarkár and ryot are indebted for equalizing to each their annual receipts from a fluctuating source. He, therefore, fulfils very beneficial duties, and deserves to be conserved as an almost indispensable part of the rural organization. At the same time, we are bound to see that he does not override the interests of the ryots. Let the Civil Courts enable the saukár to recover his just claims from the ryots. But the Courts should not permit the sowkár to press the ryots to the point of crushing. This point should be well defined and ever kept in view. No process of the Courts should, without the concurrence of the revenue-officers of the sarkár, deprive the ryot of his land, of his agricultural cattle and implements to the extent necessary for the cultivation of that land, of his cottage, and of food and raiment according to the necessity of himself and family. These should be left to the ryot, and, as a general rule, placed beyond the grasp of the sowkár. It should be understood that the first demand on the produce of the land is that on account of the sarkár tax; the next is that on account of the subsistence of the ryot and his family; and the last is that on account of the debt due to the sowkár. The surplus which may be forthcoming in good seasons after meeting the first two demands may be made available to the sowkár for the recovery of his advances made to or for the ryot in bad seasons. This being understood the sowkár will easily limit his advances to the prospects of such recurring surplus, and will not go beyond. This principle of adjustment may be expected to work well and to the advantage of all the parties concerned, provided that the land-tax is not so excessive as to trench upon the subsistence of the ryot and the remuneration of the sowkár in an average year. As a rule, the principle is not novel in Native States, and has been long in operation, more or less. Our new Civil Courts should recognize and respect it, and by no means set it aside. After what I have stated, I need hardly say that our Courts should not imprison the ryot on account of debts due to the sowkár and consign industrious hands to idleness, unless where the debtor may be fairly presumed to possess the means of payment and to withhold payment from a refractory spirit.'

The *Quarterly Review*, in an able and interesting sketch of the Deccan published last April, further truly describes the useful functions of the money-lender in relation to both the State and Society:—

'The village-banker is essential to the social system of the country. At once the purchaser of rural produce and the local agent of the central mercantile firms, alike the village shopkeeper and money-lender, he enables the peasantry to derive full benefit from a good season, and to moderate the recurring disasters of drought and flood. Without his aid the rent would not be realized. His functions in normal times are most important, but in the abnormal times of famine they are indispensable. Then the banker and shopkeeper is stimulated to double activity in both capacities. He advances from his stores food, seed, stock, and even money to the peasantry, who can offer nothing but their credit in return. By relieving the better classes of the community he lessens the pressure on the public purse. But he does more than this.* * * Experience has proved the advantage of leaving the transport and distribution of food-supplies to private trade. * * It is the sowkár who spans the gulf which separates want from plenty, and fulfils the functions of distribution which no State agency can perform.'

" The problem before us is how to keep the money-lender in his place, to encourage and support him in all useful functions, but to restrain him, as he is restrained in Native States, from becoming the enemy and oppressor of the poor? The leading principles of our new measure, then, should be to give both sides fair play, instead of setting the two classes by the ears; to diminish the risks of fraud in borrowing and extortion in repaying; to diminish the risks of loss in lending and excessive delay in recovery; to obliterate any stigma resting on our judicial institutions. We must foster due credit, check that which is undue, and allow free scope to all civilizing processes and healthy relations between capital and labour. We must hold the royt responsible in our Courts for what he has really borrowed, not for what he has not, and make him repay by his own exertions all that he reasonably can repay, not set him free, by sudden, one-sided or 'heroic' remedies, to enter on a fresh career of indebtedness. In short, we must see the parties as they really are, in a condition of Oriental, not of European, civilization, and deal with them by the Indian experience of success in past generations and failure in the present, rather than by the intrusion *per saltum* of alien institutions which are in their own land the result of centuries of experience under totally different conditions.

"I will now endeavour to set forth, as clearly and fully as time and the occasion permit, the principal provisions of the Bill I am introducing, premising that, as the latter is intended to supplement, modify and dovetail into the Civil Procedure Code, and it, therefore, in some parts presents to the unskilled reader a confused and imperfect aspect, I shall discard its arrangement, and endeavour to express in plain English the effect which its provisions (coupled with the Code) are intended to produce.

"The first object aimed at is to establish precautions against fraud by either debtor or creditor in their original transactions with each other, and so keep them on good terms and out of Court as far as possible. The Commission thus enumerate the chief frauds which are practised:—

> **By** creditors: (1) forging bonds; (2) withholding the consideration mentioned in bond; (3) obtaining new bonds in satisfaction of old bonds and of decrees, and nevertheless enforcing the latter; (4) not giving credit for payments; (5) refusing to explain or wrongly representing their accounts to debtors.
>
> By debtors: (6) retending in evidence false receipts and false evidence of alleged payments; (7) pleading that bonds are false when they are really genuine.

"Chapter VIII of the Bill is intended to meet the first three and the last mentioned kinds of fraud. It provides that every instrument to which an agriculturist is a party shall be written by or under the superintendence of a village-registrar, executed in his presence, and attested by him; that the registrar shall give a copy of it to the party not entitled to the original, and shall both endorse on the original whether transfer of consideration took place before him or not, and mark for future identification any instrument which such original supersedes. The reasonableness of such a measure is evidenced by the provisions for notaries in France and most other European countries, and by the penalty in England on unauthorized persons practising as conveyancers. Instruments not so executed will be invalid. By these means every ryot should at least know what he signs, and both parties should receive due protection. Chapter IX. directed against the remaining three kinds of fraud, provides, under a penalty, for the grant to ryot on demand of written receipts, annual statements of their account, and pass-books, and for the latter being written up from time to time and attested by the money-lender. These two chapters are based on recommendations of the Commission. Certain provisions of both of them may to some eyes appear too minute to be satisfactorily workable. But due allowance must be made for the existence of a ryotwárí settlement; for the detailed regulations which the position of Government as a landlord necessitates, and for the intimate personal relations with the people resulting from residence of revenue-officers (who will supervise the working of these chapters) in camp for six or seven months of every year. For instance, the granting of receipts for revenue payments and furnishing every ryot with a copy of his account have in Bombay been provided for by law since the commencement of British rule, and the calling ryots in person by thousands and testing the pass-books or receipts given to them by the Government books is there one of the most ordinary and useful duties of an assistant or deputy collector.

"The next step contemplated is that, whenever serious misunderstanding unfortunately arises between money-lender and ryot, either party should be able to resort to a friendly non-judicial authority bound to use his best offices to reconcile the two, and that no litigation should be commenced without a certificate from the conciliator (as the authority constituted by chapter VI will be termed) that his endeavours in this behalf have failed. Such Courts of Conciliation were advocated by Sir John Strachey just twenty years ago, and by Mr. Cust in 1870 in the *Calcutta Review*. On the present occasion their success in France was brought forward last year by Sir Erskine Perry in some Notes which have been published in India; and the subject is suggested for consideration in the Secretary of State's despatch already referred to. For details of the French system, derived from personal observation during a residence in France, I am much indebted to Mr. Fitzpatrick, the Secretary to the Government of India in the Legislative Department. The proposed conciliators will so far differ from the French *Juges de Paix*, that they will not have, in addition to conciliatory functions, a petty judicial jurisdiction (up to 100 francs= Rs. 50), nor will they be able to compel the attendance of the defendant before them; but they will, in consequence, be unable to exercise undue pressure, which in India might perhaps under some circumstances be apprehended.

" Closely connected with the subject of conciliation is that of Panchâyats, or arbitration by non-official persons or bodies, such as the Poona Arbitration Court, and of incorporating such arbitration, with more or less assistance and control, into our judicial system. The question is a difficult one in some aspects. All that I am now able to say is that it is under careful consideration, and that any provisions which may be decided on can be inserted hereafter in the Bill when passing through the Select Committee of this Council.

" Supposing that, notwithstanding all the preceding precautions, the dispute unfortunately develops into litigation, the Bill next endeavours to place the Courts of law within easier distance from the homes of the people, and to make them more absolute, less technical, less dilatory and less expensive. I may here mention that, out of 4,650 villages in our four districts, only 29 per cent. are now within ten miles of their Courts; 35 per cent. are from ten to twenty miles off; 24 per cent. from twenty to thirty miles; and 12 per cent. between thirty and sixty miles—distances which, in the absence of railways, represent a considerable inconvenience and loss of time to those obliged to attend. In pursuance of the objects just named, chapter V empowers the Local Government to appoint any Patel of a village whom it deems competent to be village-munsif for his own village, or, if desired, for other villages also within a radius of two miles. The munsif's jurisdiction will be limited to suits for money not exceeding ten rupees, and will generally follow the model of the Madras village-munsif's system, constituted under Madras Regulation IV of 1816, except that the munsif will not have, as there, a further jurisdiction, by consent of parties, extending up to Rs. 100. The munsif's decision will be final, except in case of corruption, gross partiality or misconduct proved before the Special Judge, to whom I will presently refer. This Madras system is well worthy of attention. It is a remarkable fact that these munsifs dispose of nearly one-fourth of the whole civil litigation of the Presidency. In other words, some 45,000 suits, for which the people in Bombay might be dragged to our regular Courts, with all their attendant delay, cost and harshness, are in Madras quietly disposed of at the people's own homes without ony one of these evils. Nearly the whole of these suits are for sums not exceeding Rs. 20, and nearly half for Rs. 5 and under; but the returns do not show how many of them are for Rs. 10 and under and, therefore, tried without the consent of both parties. It has been surmised that many of the disputes here dignified by the name of 'suits' are so petty that in Bombay they are never brought to a regular Court at all; but the general statistics do not bear this out, as in the Bombay Mofussil in 1877 there are 144,412 suits to a population of $15\frac{1}{2}$ millions, while in Madras there were only 190,290 to above 31 millions. Again, I understand from Mr. Carmichael, Member of Council at Madras, who has kindly given me much information, that the bulk of them are not between usurers and ryots. But the fact remains that a very inferior agency can dispose successfully, without appeal, of suits not lower in value, though differing somewhat in nature, from those with which we have to deal. Although, however village-munsifs may thus be a fairly efficient institution in Madras, where they are a survival of ancient times, and where society is still in a comparatively simple state, it would be impossible at the present day to constitute them by law throughout all villages or village-circles in our Deccan districts. The people are now too independent, too active-minded, too irreverent to accept implicitly the decision of village seniors as such, or, as a Native newspaper puts it, 'in the present times of freedom and liberty, when even children do not obey their parents, the village headmen have no authority and influence.' Even if we in Bombay could successfully impose on our hardworked and ill-paid Patels this, to them, novel function, there is the further difficulty in their case that the bulk of our petty suits are brought by money-lenders, with whom the Patel would too often be, by want of education or by absolute interest, unqualified to cope. Our advanced conditions postulate a more skilled judicature, better judges, and, consequently, fewer of them ; and these the Government must in the main provide. At the same time there can be no harm in taking advantage of the present opportunity to empower the Government to invest with petty jurisdiction up to Rs. 10 any village Patels whom it may here and there find to be qualified by education and character. We may hope that the number of such will gradually increase.

"Next above these new Munsif's Courts come the existing Courts of subordinate Judges, who are all trained officers, divided into two classes, with proportionate powers, and receiving salaries of from Rs. 200 to Rs. 800 per mensem. These Courts it is proposed to strengthen in two ways. Their number will be increased from 24 to 36, thus diminishing their local jurisdictions, and the distances to them from the people's homes; but this, being an executive measure, needs not to be provided for in the Bill. Their powers will, moreover, be considerably increased. By chapter II of the Bill all subordinate Judges in the four districts will be invested with what are termed Small-Cause-Court powers but enlarged so as to include mortgage-cases of the class in which agriculturists are so commonly involved. And by chapter IV they will all receive jurisdiction in insolvency. The question of how far the summary jurisdiction, not open to appeal, which the Small-Cause-Court model implies, might safely be entrusted to the two classes of subordinate Judge has received careful consideration in connection with the opinion of the Secretary of State in paragraph 33 of the despatch: 'I am inclined to think that the principle of summary jurisdiction without appeal might be conferred experimentally on all civil Judges in the Deccan with great benefit.' It is considered that such jurisdiction may be conferred on the first class subordinate Judges up to the full limit allowed in the Mofussil Small-Cause-Courts Act, namely, Rs. 500 (£40), and on the second class subordinate Judges up to Rs. 100 (£8) absolutely, and up to Rs. 500 by consent of the parties (on the analogy of the higher jurisdiction of village-munsifs in Madras). But three special safeguards are proposed in chapter VII. *Firstly, inspection.*—A special Judge will be appointed to inspect, supervise and control the proceedings of the subordinate Judges, munsifs and conciliators under the Act in all the four districts, and see its new principles and policy effectively carried out. The special Judge will be aided, in each pair of the four districts, by a special assistant Judge or subordinate Judge, who will during the greater part of the year be engaged in travelling about, inspecting and supervising all subordinate Courts. In Bombay the Collector and his assistants similarly move about, inspecting and controlling the revenue and magisterial administration, mixing with the people, and, in particular, examining the civil work done by mámlatdárs. Long experience has proved that the system produces excellent results. *Secondly, revision.*—The power of revision vested in the High Court by section 622 of the Code of Civil Procedure is extended, on the analogy of section 295 of that Code, to the special Judge, who will be enabled to call for and examine the record of any case and correct failures of justice, as also similarly to deal with cases called for and referred to him by his assistants just mentioned. The powers of the High Court under the same section will remain intact. *Thirdly, sitting 'in banco.'*—The special Judge and the assistants with his authorization are enabled to stay the proceedings in any case pending in a subordinate Court, and to sit with the Judge as a Bench to try it. The power of withdrawing a case and trying it himself, or transferring it to another Court, which the district Judge possesses under section 25 of the Code of Civil Procedure, will also be exercised by the special Judge, and by his assistants with his authorization. These provisions will enable important cases to be tried by superior officers or a Bench, and promote that exercise by such officers of their personal example and that enlargement of their practical experience which are thought so desirable by the Secretary of State.

"In concluding this part of the subject I should explain that the amended jurisdiction will, for convenience sake, supersede altogether that under the Mofussil Small-Cause-Courts Act, and thus litigants who are not agriculturists will in money cases obtain throughout the four districts the special advantages designed for the latter. Also, no special provision is made for subordinate Judges moving about and sitting at different places, because they can be required to do so under the existing law.

"The procedure followed by the Courts under their new jurisdiction will be pretty nearly that of Small-Cause-Courts, which again differs but little, except as to recording evidence at length, from that of the Code of Civil Procedure. One exception, however, is so important as to require special mention. The Commission pointed out that the proportion of cases decided in Bombay *ex parte*, or in the absence of the defendant, vastly exceeded that in any other part of India. In the four districts the proportion ranged in 1876 from 60 to 74 per cent., and last year from 57 to 66 per cent. This has been ascribed to a variety of causes, of which the chief probably are ignorance of the ryot that he has a defence, want of means to pay a pleader, conviction that the Court, for want of time or other reasons, will not go into the merits of his case or look behind the bond, fear of irritating his creditor by a defence or fraudulent non-service of summons. The various provisions of the present Bill, however, completely alter the position. The obligation laid on the Court of going into the whole merits of the case, and behind the bond if necessary, to which I shall presently allude, will remove the first three of the above causes of backwardness on the ryot's part, and will probably lead to his more frequent voluntary appearance. But that obligation can scarcely ever be successfully performed in his absence and without his help; and it is, therefore, considered indispensable to make it incumbent on the Court ordinarily to exercise in all cases of a defendant's non-appearance the power of compelling him to attend now vested in it by the Code for exceptional use. Compulsory attendance will meet the other two causes of absence above mentioned. Any hardship which it might be supposed to involve will be more than balanced by the consequent better hearing of the case, and will, moreover, be much lessened by the proposed bringing of the Court nearer to the debtor's home.

"Closely connected with the question of procedure is that of how far effect should be given to the suggestion of the Secretary of State that possibly it would be desirable to exclude professional pleaders from the 'Courts with summary jurisdiction and without appeal up to a limited amount' which he desires. Upon this point we have two precedents. The French Code excludes all skilled advocacy from the Courts of the *Juges de Paix*, whether in conciliation or trial of suits, in the following most stringent terms :—

'Aucuns avoués, greffiers, huissiers et ci-devant hommes de loi ou procureurs ne pourront representer les parties aux bureaux de paix.'

The Madras Regulation for village-munsifs excludes professionals, but allows the deputation of a relative, servant or dependent—so that, for instance, a sowkár could send his *gumáshta*, and a ryot could send or bring with him a clever son or nephew educated in a Government school. It may be true that where a case, involving even a moderate amount, is intricate, owing to mortgages or other exceptional circumstances, a competent pleader may be of much use both to the parties and the Court. On the other hand, it must be admitted that a pleader is a weapon at the command of the rich alone (one subordinate Judge even states that a pleader who often took ryot's cases would lose his best customers); that in simple suits a pleader can often add nothing of value to what is in evidence, but only wastes time and introduces confusion; and that the presence of pleaders predisposes some judges to decide on what counsel put before them instead of going independently into the merits. Upon a balance of such considerations the draft Bill follows the Madras law in excluding pleaders, but admitting non-professionals, in all cases before a village-munsif or conciliator. It also attempts to check the unnecessary employment of pleaders in higher Courts, by excluding pleaders' fees from the costs awarded in cases before a Subordinate Judge not exceeding Rs. 100, unless the Court certifies that professional assistance was necessary to the proper conduct of the case. The appointment of a pleader by the Court in cases where the debtor needs counsel, but cannot obtain it, is also provided for. This has been suggested in several quarters, and seems reasonable.

"I must here venture to express my regret that a material simplification of the civil procedure with a view to saving delay and expense has not been found to be feasible. I see from official returns that in the Bombay Presidency in 1877 the average duration of uncontested suits was 132 days, and of contested suits 272. It is no doubt true that the intricacy of a suit has no necessary connection with the amount in issue, and that a mortgage for Rs. 50 may present the same features as one for Rs. 5,000; and it may be argued with much show of reason that a Procedure Code should provide for all possible circumstances, and be of general application. At the same time, looking to the fact that, out of about fourteen hundred thousand civil suits of all kinds disposed of annually by the Courts of all grades in British India, some twelve hundred thousand, or 85 per cent., are for sums under Rs. 100 (£8), and six hundred and thirty thousand, or 44 per cent., for sums less than Rs. 20, I cannot but feel, and I think the people feel too, that our Civil Procedure Code, with its six hundred and fifty sections and all that they involve, is in minor cases a burden almost too heavy to be borne. I trust the day may come when not only Deccan ryots but all India will obtain some relief in this respect.

"Having thus noticed the proposed reorganization of the Courts, I proceed to explain some important changes contemplated in the substantive law which they administer. These group themselves round two main heads,—the definition of a debtor's liability, and the mode and extent of its enforcement.

"A Court proceeding to determine the amount of a debtor's liability is met *in limine* (in our four districts at any rate) by the undeniable fact that, as Mr. Pedder expresses it, 'the passing of a bond by a Native of India is often of no more value as proof of a debt he thereby acknowledges than the confession by a man under torture of the crime he is charged with.' The Commission urge two points,—that the money-lenders have learned, through our system, to use and rely upon bonds almost exclusively, and that their bonds are mostly no correct representation of actual transactions. In close connection with this difficulty about bonds is that of usurious and of compound interest whether only levied in the account, or also provided for in the bond. That the money-lenders do obtain bonds on false pretences; enter in them sums larger than agreed upon; deduct extortionate premiums; give no receipts for payments and then deny them; credit produce at fraudulent prices; retain liquidated bonds and sue on them; use threats and warrants of imprisonment to extort fresh bonds for sums not advanced; charge interest unstipulated for, over-calculated, or in contravention of Hindú law, and commit a score of other rogueries—these are facts proved by evidence so overwhelming that I scarcely know whose to quote out of the five volumes composing the Report of the Commission. Hence arises the question whether, as the Secretary of State expresses it, 'the Courts should be obliged to enter into the merits of every money-claim, whether secured by bond or not, and should award only such sums, whether for principal or interest, as they deemed just, and should in no case give compound interest, or a larger amount of interest than the principal sum.'

"The answer in the affirmative has been maintained, in various quarters of not inconsiderable authority, to be in accordance with sound general principles of equity. Sir Arthur Hobhouse, in a note on the execution-sale of land dated April 28th, 1874, when alluding to some remarks by 'a man like Sir John Strachey, who treats the subject with equal sobriety and ability,' continues :—

'From my point of view, I say that, if what he has said, or the major part of it, be now true, it can only be met by a large increase of correctional power over contracts to be vested in judicial tribunals and strengthened by a usury law. In our own country the Courts of Equity invented laws for the protection, not only of persons of weak character and immature age, but of expectant heirs, of reversioners—in fact, of all persons placed under temptation to make improvident bargains. When they came across the usury laws, they made them subject to the more sweeping law created by themselves, and moulded them so as to produce fairly reasonable, though not very legal, results. They laid hold of mortgages under which the mortgagee became absolute owner if the debt were not paid by a certain day, and declared that the parties did not mean what they had said, but that notwithstanding the absolute forfeiture, there remained an equity of redemption in the mortgagor. * * * I do believe that sensible Judges, armed with a large power of moulding improvident bargains, and strengthened by a usury law in the background, may administer more than a trifling palliative.'

Sir George Wingate wrote thus in 1852 :—

'It remains to be shown how it is that the creditor in our Provinces has acquired a degree of power over his debtor which is wholly unknown in Native States. This power, it is clear to me, has been conferred by our laws, which enable the creditor to obtain a decree against a debtor for whatever may be written in his bond, and enforcement of that decree by the attachment and sale of whatever property, moveable or immoveable, his debtor may possess or acquire. * * * The first remedy I have to suggest is as follows. * * The enactment of a law to permit the Court to decree in all cases, on equitable considerations, whatever rate of interest it may deem proper, but that in no case shall the total amount of interest exceed the principal ; and that the Court shall also in all cases be at liberty to fix the amount of the principal on equitable considerations with reference to the amount which it may consider to have been actually received by the debtor, and irrespective of the sum entered in the bond or acknowledgment of the debt.'

Mr. Pedder says :—

'A bond should not be considered sufficient proof of a debt unless its antecedents will bear the light, and show that the consideration for which it was passed was a fair as well as an actual one. * * * *

'It appears to me that some limitation of the rate of interest and some restriction on grossly unfair stipulations in contracts, as contrary to justice and public policy, are practicable and expedient.'

From 'The Land and the Law,' a well-known pamphlet by the Hon'ble Mr. Justice West, of the Bombay High Court, I take the following excerpts :—

'If, on the one hand, therefore, the State must needs lend its aid to the creditor as an essential condition of material progress, it must, on the other hand, assign bounds and conditions to this trial without which it will probably become an instrument of social and political mischief. Particular classes in England supposed to be specially subject to imposition or unfair usage—as seamen and minors—are protected against disadvantageous bargains. The truth is recognized and acted on that there is no real equality, even of the roughest kind, between them and their employers. Still less can such an equality be assumed with safety in a community split up into sections, divided by the impassable barriers of caste and hereditary occupations. The extremes of astuteness and gullibility are thus fostered and brought into contact. * * * At an earlier stage, borrowing at interest in England, as elsewhere, was generally an appeal of helplessness to avarice * * *
There are few who will deny that the India we have to deal with is much more like that earlier England than the England of to-day *
* * In the case of all obligations for a principal of not more than Rs. 500, the Courts should have full power to treat any interest in excess of nine per cent. as simply penal, and to cut it down to such rate as should, under the circumstances, seem just.
* * Compound interest should be disallowed, consistent as it is with sound-commercial principles, in order to make it a disadvantage to creditors to leave obligations unsettled until the debtors are involved beyond redemption.'

"But upon this subject not only opinion but precedent are forthcoming. Of the manner in which our Government, a few years ago, deemed it necessary to protect the ryot we have a striking instance in a clause (still unrepealed) of the Bombay Regulation V of 1827. It runs thus :—

'*Clause* 2.—And in the case of a cultivator of the soil, sued upon a written acknowledgment executed at a place which was not at the time of such execution under British jurisdiction, if the circumstances are such as to convince the Court that the creditor might reasonably be expected to possess other proof of the amount besides such written acknowledgment (the consideration received for the same being contested), then the said writing shall not be held conclusive as to the amount, whether the defendant prove a deficiency in the consideration or not, but the Court shall pass a decree for only such amount as the claimant may otherwise prove to be due.'

The law which preceded it, Regulation I of 1823, was even more explicit:

'*Section* 36.—Whenever a cultivator of the soil is sued upon an acknowledgment in writing executed by him before the territory where it was executed came into the possession of the British Government, it shall be competent for him to plead that he did not receive a full consideration for the same, whereupon the plaintiff shall be required to prove his debt in the same manner as if no acknowledgment had been executed; and such sum only as in the circumstances of the case is just and equitable shall be allowed in the decree.'

The wisdom of our early legislators in thus dealing with the facts around them was greater than their foresight, which led them to hope that with the planting of the British flag and the establishment of 'a regular system for administering justice' the causes would pass away by which 'cultivators were easily induced to grant written obligations for larger sums than were due.'

"What the Bombay Government of Sir Richard Temple have from the first substantially advocated, and what we really need, is something approaching to a restoration of this early law, together with power to cut down unreasonable interest. The Court should set itself to do substantial justice in every case which came before it, instead of being satisfied with the letter of a bond or the bald assertions of either party, and it should of its own motion make such enquiry as it found necessary to this end. On the one hand, a simple denial of consideration should not throw the burden of proof on the plaintiff, but, on the other, if the circumstances were such that he ought to have clear accounts and evidence and he failed to produce them voluntarily or on the Court's requisition, the Court would draw its own conclusions against him accordingly. If he did not come into Court with clean hands, he would be entitled to little consideration. The Court should not go farther in any case or against either side than sufficed to get at the truth of the matter, and to give an equitable decision. There appears no reason to fear that such an exercise of its discretion by the Court would be either unfair to the creditor or demoralizing to the debtor. The objections to usury laws are well known and so cogent that only special circumstances can justify special legislation. Even a maximum legal rate of interest, however, had this advantage that, as Mr. West says, "it set up a standard, and gave fixity to men's vague ideas of what might reasonably be asked for the use of money in those numerous cases in which the loan partook but slightly of the character of a true mercantile transaction." Where the rate of interest is regulated by the ordinary laws of supply and demand, interference is indefensible, unless, as in the case of interest after decree, the security be changed. But where, as Sir John Strachey has said, 'the conditions depend more upon the degree of simplicity in the borrower and of rapacity in the lender than on anything else,' no such respect need be paid to them—the less so that with Hindus we have the support of the law of *dám-dupat*, and that the security will be greatly increased by the provisions for recovery to be mentioned shortly. It has been urged, and with some truth, that there is nothing in the present law to prevent such enquiry and doing of substantial justice; that certain rulings of the Bombay and other High Courts are suggestive of this course and support *dám-dupat*, and that the provisions of the Contract Act as to undue influence are very wide. But, however this may be, the practice of the lower Courts is usually different, and there are good reasons to fear that, unless their duty in this respect be clearly expressed in the law, ignorance of rulings, press of work, indolence or a desire to get through cases rapidly will, as hitherto, tend to prevent its performance. It may be pointed out, finally, that Lord Cranbrook, besides confirming the sanction given by Lord Salisbury to the introduction of the Bombay draft Bill containing provisions on the principle above referred to, appears to look with approval on ' extending the powers of Judges to modify the contracts entered into between man and man.' In accordance with this view the first four sections of chapter III have been framed, and will apply to all determination of the debts of agriculturists which may take place under the Act. The history and merits of disputed or doubtful cases will be enquired into, and an account will be taken in a certain way if the Court considers the agreement not fair and equitable. Whether these sections express intelligibly, or will secure effectively, the action needed, seems doubtful; but they can perhaps be improved in select committee. Regarding this safeguard and those of registration and accounts already explained, 1 should perhaps observe that any ingenious person can imagine methods by which debtor and creditor in collusion may evade them. But the same may be said of many other most beneficial enactments. We can only help those who will help themselves; and I believe a large proportion of our Deccan peasantry will take heart of grace to do so.

"A second important question affecting the determination of the amount of the debtor's liability is that of the period of limitation. The old law of Bombay (Regulation V, 1827, sections 3 and 4) fixed twelve years in the case of debts supported by a bond, and six years in the case of debts not so supported, as the periods within which civil suits for recovery must be brought respectively. By Act XIV of 1859 these periods were reduced to six and three years respectively, with the further restriction that a debt supported by written contract was to come under the three years' period, unless it was registered. This is the present law, Acts IX of 1871 and XV of 1877 having made no material change. There is an almost universal consensus of opinion that, as the Commission say, 'the reduction in the periods of limitation has been the cause of considerable hardship to the debtor.' Under the old law, the debtor was rarely sued or called upon to renew the bond till near the expiration of the twelve years, and then he was, at most, sued under the provision of *dám-dupat* for twice the principal sum lent. But under the law since 1859 the creditor is forced within every three years either to sue the debtor, or to obtain from him a fresh bond for principal and any accumulated interest. In practice, he does so nearly every two years, in order to make sure of not missing the period through any accident or default. To show the difference between the two laws: Rupees 100 at 9 per cent. become Rs. 208 in 12 years; but if the bond be renewed triennially, the amount is raised to Rs. 260. At the higher rates, which are but too common, the effect is more startling. Rupees 100 at 25 per cent. become Rs. 400 in twelve years; but renewals every two years produce a total of Rs. 1,139! That these results are actually enforced in practice is amply proved by the evidence taken by the Commission, from which Mr. Pedder (in an interesting article in *The Nineteenth Century* for September 1877) gives a few illustrations. In short, the debtor thus suffers the cost of writing and stamping a new bond; is charged compound interest instead of simple; often has to bear the expenses of a suit, and, finally, is frequently obliged also to submit to a large nominal increase of the principal, as the price of the creditor's forbearing to sell him entirely up, or to have him arrested and imprisoned. It is perhaps unnecessary for me to quote numerous authorities at length to prove these general results. The collective opinion of the Commission has been stated. Mr. Auckland Colvin summarizes the evils, and favours a change. Mr. Shambuprasád has treated the subject with much minuteness, and strongly urges the restoration of the old Bombay law. Revenue and judicial officers, both Native and European, take the same view in their letters to the Commission. Mr. Pedder has been quoted already. Mr. Wedderburn, in a report specially called for by the Bombay Government, advocates a twelve and six years' limit; and it has, I observe, been adopted as desirable at a public meeting of the inhabitants of Poona held not long ago. The Collector of Poona gave evidence to the same effect before the Famine Commission.

"The only plea which has, as far as I am aware, been advanced in favour of the three years' period is that it obliges the making up of accounts at short intervals, thus enabling the ryot to know how he stands, and preventing his being deeply involved without his knowledge. This objection had, undoubtedly, very considerable weight at the time it was made. Whether the benefit of a short account, thus secured by a three-years' limitation, outweighed the evils of a new bond, compound interest, &c., which it entailed, is a point upon which there may well be difference of opinion. But the whole aspect of the question seems to be changed by the provisions in chapter IX of the Bill regarding receipts and statements of account. Taken in connection with section 17, which enables any agriculturist to sue for an account, and to get a declaration of the amount really due to him under all the new and searching provisions of the Act, it would appear that the object of short accounts will now be attained, and perhaps more efficiently than it ever could have been by the indirect expedient of a limitation-law. Under these circumstances it is proposed to restore, by section 72, the old Bombay law.

" I now proceed to the second head—the mode and extent of enforcement of equitably determined liability. In the execution of a decree by sale of moveables, the necessary wearing apparel of the judgment-debtor and his wife and children, his implements of husbandry, and such cattle as the Court may deem necessary to enable him to earn his livelihood as an agriculturist, are now protected by the amended Code of 1877, so it has not been thought necessary to go further. As to execution against the person by arrest and imprisonment, I rejoice to state that it is now considered expedient to abolish it altogether. Imprisonment will still be inflicted as a punishment for fraud detected on insolvency; but that is a totally different thing. The maintenance of imprisonment for debt, as found in the Indian law, is equally indefensible in principle and in practice. As to principle, the Deccan Riots Commission make clear that point, utilizing the opinions of John Stuart Mill. Their appendices teem with evidence in detail as to the extortion and wrong of which the warrant of arrest becomes in practice the engine. Unacknowledged payments, fresh bonds for sums unadvanced, life-long slavery and even female dishonour may all be obtained—the first three constantly, by the mere production of the warrant of arrest without enforcement. They say, for instance, that in 1874 'it would seem probable that somewhere about 150,000 warrants had been used as threats only.' The outcry against imprisonment from officers well qualified to judge of it has been uniform and persistent. Its abolition is unanimously recommended by the Deccan Riots Commission. Mr. Pedder and Miss Nightingale have in *The Nineteenth Century* brought the evils it causes prominently before the British public. Sir Erskine

Perry gives its abolition his 'unqualified approval' in a note dated December 1st, 1877. Judicial officers and pleaders take the same view as the Executive. Were it even defensible in theory, which we have seen that it is not, the abuses to which, in a country like Western India at least, it is proved to lead in practice, afford sufficient ground for its condemnation in the districts to which the Bill is to apply. The case has already been once laid, though less perfectly and authoritatively than at present, before the Governor General's Council in the debates on the Civil Procedure Bill. The representations I then made had the warm concurrence of Sir Edward Bayley and the learned Advocate General for Bengal (Mr. Paul). The discussions in select committee as well as in Council showed that the objections to the measure related less to its principle than to the other arrangements such as an effective insolvency-law and a speedy recovery of *bonâ fide* debts, by which it ought to be accompanied. These the Select Committee and the Council could not see their way to, owing to the insufficiency of the judicial machinery in the Mofussil; and the matter may be held to have been deferred rather than negatived. But the present Bill provides all these necessary accompaniments for the districts to which it is to apply. Imprisonment was, at best, a barbarous device to meet the case of a debtor's concealing his property or refusing to give it up. Under the draft Bill, it will be quite unnecessary for these purposes and reserved for cases of flagrant fraud or dishonesty in insolvents. In this altered position I trust that no hesitation will now be felt by the Council in abolishing a system which has been proved to be grossly abused as an engine of extortion, and is in opposition to the legislation of the civilized world.

"The case of execution of a decree by sale of immoveable property remains for notice. The problem of whether such sales should be enforced—one of the most difficult by which Indian administration is beset—is entirely the creation of British rule. Although the later Hindú law permitted the sale of land ' on proof of necessity ' and Muhammadan law placed no bar to it whatever, the general feeling of the country against alienation of ancestral lands, coupled with trifling value of the right of occupancy and the political objections to expropriation felt under a Native Government, to which I have already alluded in my sketch of the system of Native States, appear to have co-operated to prevent sales to any noticeable extent. But under our judicial system 'the sale of land registered in the Collector's books is' (as observed by Lord Stanley in a despatch of January 25th, 1859) ' the most ready way of enforcing a judgment: it gives the least trouble to both the creditor and the Court, and holds out every inducement to both to resort to that mode of satisfying the decree in preference to any other, even in the most trifling cases.' The Code provides, indeed, an alternative to sale of the nature of an *elegit*, or temporary alienation, by allowing the land to be placed under the management of the Collector for a term of years, not exceeding twenty, whenever there is reason to believe that the liability can be thereby cleared off. But the sections enacted in 1859 were not efficient for the purpose in view, and therefore little acted on. Those substituted in 1877 accidentally became almost unintelligible, and we are now amending them. Practically, therefore, sale has hitherto stood in the Code unfettered. The extent to which this judicial system has been allowed to play, varies remarkably in different parts of India. In Lower Bengal a zamíndári and certain subordinate tenures are freely saleable, but the tenure of an occupancy ryot is not ; and the local legislature are just now considering whether transfer shall be allowed, provided the purchaser be a brother-ryot and not a money-lender. Saleability in execution will, of course, follow power to transfer. In the Panjáb hereditary or joint acquired land cannot be sold in execution without the sanction of the Chief Court, or other land without that of the Commissioner. In the Central Provinces and Oudh, ancestral property cannot be so sold without the sanction of the Chief Commissioner, or self-acquired property without that of the Commissioner. In Ajmer all sale is absolutely prohibited. In the North-Western Provinces, Madras, and Bombay, sales are unrestricted. The position of the question, as I have just described it, is generally admitted to be unsatisfactory. In a correspondence originated by the despatch of Lord Stanley already quoted, carried on through the last twenty years, and now here embodied in some four hundred pages of print, the question of a remedy has been discussed by the most able administrators throughout India. The alternatives of making land by law absolutely unsaleable for debt ; of enabling proprietors to make it so by voluntary trusts or entails ; of limiting sale (as in some Native States) to any surplus unnecessary for the subsistence of the proprietor and his family ; of replacing sale in execution by usufructuary mortgages for the debtor's life or a maximum term of years ; of restricting sales to specifically pledged land ; and of confining the power of sale to the chief Court of a district—all these have found powerful and zealous advocates. In favour of restriction generally it is urged that to a community whom a variety of circumstances combine to constrain or tempt into debt, the addition of the land to the security they can offer is no advantage whatever, but the reverse. It merely amounts to a permission to live on capital, instead of living on income, anticipated perhaps, but still only income. The process of living on capital is but a short one, all the world over. Abolish the whole land-revenue to-morrow, and the process would merely be somewhat prolonged. The inevitable end must come at last, but its concomitants of eviction and penury will, where the evil is widespread, lead to large charitable relief in famine—perhaps eventually to a poor-law—and are also, in parts of India at least, politically dangerous. But the conclusion of this Council when passing the Civil Procedure Code, as explained most fully by Sir Arthur Hobhouse in a remarkable speech on March 28th, 1877, was that, though special measures might be admissible in particular localities, the plan of temporary alienation through the Collector for a term of years, whenever the property would be ultimately saved thereby, being in accordance with the past course of legislation regarding land in England and not inequitable, deserved a fair trial; and that, before going further, an attempt should be made to give life to the intentions of the legislators of 1859, which have to a great extent failed of effect.

"My object in this statement of the position of the land question, which I fear may be deemed a digression, is to account for the absence in the Bill of any attempt at a final comprehensive settlement of it, and at the same time to show the connection and admissibility of the two limited measures which are proposed. Section 23 exempts the land of agriculturists from attachment and sale, unless it has been specifically pledged. The equity of thus restricting a creditor's security has able champions in the general correspondence already referred to. But in Bombay the question is mainly one of fact, whether the existing debt can be held to have been, on the whole, contracted in view of the security of unpledged land. Keeping in mind the large proportion of such debt which the Commission found to be ancestral, the recent date (1865) of the legalization of transfers of occupancy, the known reluctance of the ryots to pledge their land, and other considerations, the first local authorities have decided that it cannot. I must confess to some misgivings as to how the exemption may work in practice. The money-lender may everywhere make the execution of a bond, laying on the land all his existing unsecured advances, an indispensable condition of further accommodation. At the same time, the exemption rests as to the past upon a perfectly intelligible and reasonable basis, while as to the future, the proposed village-registration will at least ensure that every ryot when he pledges his land shall understand what he is doing, and insolvency will open to him a loophole of escape when unreasonably pressed by an extortionate creditor, if he prefers that alternative. The second measure, also contained in section 23, is the grant of power to the Court, when passing a decree or subsequently, to direct the Collector to pay off the amount by managing for not more than seven years any land not specifically pledged, after deducting a modicum sufficient for the support of the debtor and those of his family dependent on him. This course, which is only a new application of the principle of temporary alienation, will add greatly to the creditor's security, while diminishing the worry and expense to both himself and the debtor; but I reserve further exposition for the Insolvency-chapter, where analogous provisions occur.

"While thus contemplating the continued recovery of debts from moveables and land, however, policy no less than justice demands that the last refuge of an effective insolvency-law should be provided for the debtor. Such a law is really the bottom of the whole matter. Compared with what we mean to compel a man to *pay*, the question of what we shall hold him to owe sinks into insignificance. The need for it has been generally admitted for a long series of years, and has led to various legislative efforts and measures. Sir George Wingate in 1852 advocated strongly 'the enactment of a simple and equitable insolvent-law to enable a debtor hopelessly involved to free himself from all his liabilities within a limited period'; and so recently as December 23rd, 1877, he wrote thus: 'Of all the remedies proposed, I estimate the Insolvency Act as of the highest importance, and as likely to prove the most efficacious.' Sir Bartle Frere in 1853, when Commissioner in Sind, issued Rules which worked well, but were superseded in 1861 by the Code of Civil Procedure. Mr. William Frere, Member of Council at Bombay, introduced into the Legislative Council there in 1863 a Bill based on these Rules and the Insolvent Act of the Presidency-town (11 & 12 Vic., cap. 21), but applicable to the whole Presidency. It was carefully matured in select committee, but was eventually withdrawn in 1867 for a variety of reasons, of which the expediency of awaiting the result of contemplated legislation in England was one of the chief. Sir James Stephen in 1870 introduced into the Legislative Council of the Governor General an Insolvency Bill applicable to all India. It was taken almost entirely from the English Bankruptcy Act of 1869 and on circulation to the Local Governments was generally held to be too complicated and unsuited to the circumstances of the Indian Mofussil. In 1872 Mr. (now the Hon'ble Justice) West, Judge of the Sadr Court in Sind, proposed a Bill with the essential features of the original Rules of that Province; but the matter was not proceeded with. The measure generally is also advocated in his well-known pamphlet 'The Land and the Law.' In 1872, also, the Panjáb made a material step in advance in the Laws Act then passed.

"Upon the acknowledged harshness of the Indian law of insolvency as it stood up to 1877 I need not enlarge. The new

Code of that year, together with the amending Bill, which will, I hope, be passed at our next sitting, have so far relaxed it, that a debtor arrested or imprisoned, or whose property has been attached, may by application obtain a general inquiry into his affairs, a declaration of insolvency, and a release if in jail (with immunity from subsequent arrest for the scheduled debts) on *bond fide* surrender of all his property. A judgment-creditor also may apply for such declaration. A final discharge may also be granted by the Court at its discretion where the debts do not exceed Rs. 200, and is in any case acquired on payment of one-third of the scheduled debts, if the assets do not produce more, or after the lapse of twelve years. The law is still, however, most defective. Application may not be made by a debtor until process has issued against him; arrest is retained and imprisonment, though for a shorter period; *all* property, except the moveables exempt from sale in execution, must be surrendered; the debtor may be summarily imprisoned for a year, ' at the instance of any creditor,' for concealment or bad faith, while no such penalty awaits the creditor; and in some cases the debtor's future earnings will be unreasonably burdened, while in others the creditor will not get what might fairly be recovered for him. Finally, the whole becomes a farce through the restriction that the Court may not grant a declaration unless it ' is satisfied ' that the debtor ' has not, knowing himself to be unable to pay his debts in full, recklessly contracted debts,' as if persons able to pay in full were the usual customers of the moneylender!

" The fact is that insolvency-law for the Indian Mofussil made an altogether false start. In England, fraud by the debtor is the chief danger, and even the legislation of 1869 has failed through his ingenuity; in India fraud by the creditor has almost solely to be guarded against. In England, insolvency is presumably a man's fault; in India it is presumably only his misfortune. In England, embarrassment ordinarily arises from gross extravagance or reckless trading; in India, one or more bad seasons, the loss of a bullock or two, or the religious necessity of marrying a child, are its most frequent origin: extortion and fraud by creditors help its onward course. Yet in England, insolvency has hitherto been treated more leniently than in India. Misfortune has here been made a crime, for which even life-long slavery might not atone. Surely, we must divest ourselves of much confusion of ideas. Whether a man *is* insolvent or not, is a mere question of fact, quite unconnected with the enquiry how he came to be so. How much he *can* repay, without being made a useless or dangerous member of society, is a mere matter of calculation, into which the moral aspects of his past conduct cannot enter. To such enquiries ideas of revenge and punishment are altogether irrelevant. Imprisonment is only appropriate for concealment, contumacy and other forms of fraud. To declare an agriculturist insolvent when he is so; to set a reasonable time before him during which he shall work himself free and reserve the means therefor; and eventually to start him afresh with the lesson of experience, seem more sensible than to lock him up for a time while his family are starving, and then turn him adrift a beggar. To the creditor certainly the former course will be the more profitable, as also to Society.

"In accordance with these principles, the Bill, in the first place, provides (section 20) for the numberless petty cases in which the means of the debtor, the claims against him and his partial or total inability to satisfy them come before the Court in the course of the suit or application for execution. Where this is so, it is far shorter, simpler and less troublesome to all parties to empower the Court at once to settle the matter than to let it go on through the perfectly useless, but costly and vexatious, forms of taking out execution and applying for declaration of insolvency. Where the case is quite simple, the Court will, therefore, release the debtor from any balance which it is satisfied he cannot pay. When there are several creditors or other complications, and the amount exceeds Rs. 50, it may at once direct the taking of insolvency-proceedings. Again, where such proceedings are instituted, either so or on the application of either debtor or creditor, ascertained insolvency will be at once admitted, and the Court will proceed to turn the available assets to the best advantage. To avoid the frequently ruinous loss through selling moveables by auction, the Court may hand over articles at a valuation made by assessors. As to immoveable property, any portion specifically pledged for a scheduled debt may be let rent-free for a premium for a term not exceeding twenty years, instead of being sold, if the debt can thereby be cleared off. Portions unpledged may be handed over for a term not exceeding seven years to the Collector, who will assign to the insolvent sufficient to maintain himself and those of his family dependent on him and lease the remainder for the benefit of the creditors. In practice the lessee will probably sometimes be a creditor, but more often the insolvent himself under due security. If the debts cannot be fully paid off by these measures, the insolvent will be discharged from the balance. The proposal which has been made that the fixed period should be subject to the life of the insolvent has been rejected as too unfavourable to the creditor. The limit of seven years has been fixed after careful consideration of the various proposals relating to temporary alienation contained in the land-sale correspondence already spoken of. If a man's debts are so heavy that he cannot clear them off in this time, it is better that he should get a discharge for the balance, than that he should drag on as a slave without hope of freedom or stimulus to exertion.

VII.

" Reviewing the Bill broadly, it may fairly be said to secure, to an extent not hitherto attempted, (1) precautions against fraud by either debtor or creditor in their original transactions with each other; (2) interposition of friendly conciliation between disputants previous to litigation; (3) approximation of the Courts to the homes of the people; (4) some small simplification of procedure and diminution of the expense and technicalities arising from legal practitioners; (5) equitable jurisdiction to reduce all exorbitant, fictitious and fraudulent claims; (6) finality of judicial decisions, subject to adequate safeguards; (7) prompt and unfailing enforcement, through the Collector when necessary, of all adjudicated claims of reasonable amount; (8) discharge of the debtor from such claims, or balance of them, as, after all reasonable enforcement for a long period, could not be fully realized except by demoralization or life-long bondage.

"Such a result, while falling not short in favour of either debtor or creditor of what is fairly commensurate with the nature of the case, the analogy of law in other countries, the rules of pecuniary need and supply, and the strictest equity, goes no farther in reform than the political necessity of a prompt and effective remedy for the social disorders of the Deccan appears imperatively to demand.

"If I am asked what I think will probably be the effects of the measure and how far I expect it to be successful, I must reply that, although I cannot undertake to answer for all the detailed provisions of a Bill which is the outcome of revision at more hands and authorities than one, I think that it cannot but be most beneficial, and that it will to a great extent meet the needs of the Deccan, provided it be supplemented by executive action in the directions already indicated. Of course, no one expects from it the abolition of indebtedness for all time. The ryots are 'depressed and crushed by a variety of concurrent causes.' With only one class of these, though perhaps the largest, does the Bill profess to deal, but in a way which may reasonably be rewarded with success. At least, it gives effective help to every ryot who is disposed to help himself. The reorganization of the Courts is favourable to all parties. The relations of debtor and creditor are adjusted on fundamental principles, equitable as between the two, and essential to the cohesion of society. A man should pay what he really owes, and no more; but his creditor should not be allowed to use the State for the purpose of beggaring and enslaving him. On the other hand, we cannot justly and reasonably legislate for the summary relief of the debtor from unjust and extortionate claims, unless we also give to the creditor full and effective aid in obtaining all that is fairly due to him and reasonably recoverable. A creditor's difficulties when he has got his decree should be reduced to a minimum. If we make the decree a just one, it should be effectively enforceable. Without ample provision on this principle, the destruction of the ryot's credit or his bondage to secret and extortionate agreements must ensue, and all our well-intentioned interference will do harm instead of good. With such provision the measure will not injure the ryot's legitimate credit, but improve it. Against all prognostications to the contrary I set the actual facts observable in Native States. The ryots there get all the credit that is good for them. I have no faith in the virtues of unlimited 'tick.' Borrowing, and lending with a view to securing permanent enslavement, will no doubt be checked; and so much the better. *Bonâ fide* debts should be more easily recovered, and more reasonable interest would thus be profitable. Finally, a legitimate mode, more practicable than any yet suggested, will be provided for gradually clearing off the mass of existing debt which now weighs upon the people and stops all improvement; while the great institution of a peasant-proprietary, which is at once essentially Indian and considered in Europe the best form of tenure for a free people, will not be destroyed.

"In conclusion, I have only to urge upon the Council that, while the deliberation and care with which this question has been brought to maturity are a sufficient guarantee for the suitability of the Bill now introduced, the period which has elapsed since the ryots first expressed discontent by outrage, the famine which has intervened, and the continued evidences of popular distress, render it desirable that the measure should be passed into law at the earliest practicable date."

The Hon'ble Mr. Hope moved that the Bill be referred to a Select Committee consisting of the Hon'ble Sir A. J. Arbuthnot, the Hon'ble Sir J. Strachey, the Hon'ble Messrs. Stokes and Thompson, the Hon'ble Sayyad Ahmad Khán, the Hon'ble Mr. Colvin and the Mover.

The Hon'ble Sayyad Ahmad Khán said:—"Before the Bill goes to the Select Committee I wish, with Your Excellency's permission, to make a few observations with regard to the principles upon which the proposed legislation is based. These observations I have handed to my friend Mr. Fitzpatrick, who, with Your Excellency's permission, will read them to the Council."

Mr. Fitzpatrick then read the Hon'ble Member's remarks as follows :—

" My Lord,—I agree with the Hon'ble Member in his motion that the Bill should be referred to a Select Committee. But before the Bill goes to the Committee I wish, with Your Excellency's permission, to make a few observations with regard to the principles upon which the proposed legislation is based.

" It may be accepted as an indisputable principle that special laws should only be introduced to meet special cases. The disturbances in the Deccan which has given rise to this Bill revealed the existence of considerable distress among the agricultural classes. The causes appear to have been the following. Owing to the large exportation of cotton during the American war, the prices both of that article and of all agricultural produce greatly increased. This increase led to an increase in the expenditure and in the credit of agriculturists. It also appeared to justify an increase in the Government revenue, which was accordingly imposed in some of the districts, and, as it appears, unequally. When the demand for Indian cotton fell off, the prices of all agricultural produce fell ; and the fund out of which the agriculturists had to meet the increased revenue, and the debts which they had contracted, became insufficient for that purpose. Credit could no longer be procured ; and the ryots, whether instigated by disloyal persons or of their own motion, commenced to attack and plunder the houses of money-lenders, and especially of the class of Márwáris, who, being strangers, were particularly obnoxious to them. It does not appear from the evidence of the rioters taken by the Commission that these men complained of the action of the Civil Courts. Many of them asserted that they were not in debt, and others that they had not been sued for their debts ; but, seeing that the object of the rioters was not only plunder but the recovery of bonds, it seems manifest that there had been a refusal of credit, and, in all probability, threats of proceedings in Court for the recovery of outstanding debts. It also appears that, by reason of a scanty and uncertain rainfall, the productive powers of the districts are usually uncertain, and have for some years been abnormally small.

" My Lord, no doubt a case has been made out for the application of special measures of relief, and I fully admit that that relief should take the form of a law providing facilities for the release of debtors from debts which they can have no hope of discharging, and which, while they remain subject to them, deprive them of the ordinary motives for exertion—the attainment of something more than bare livelihood.

"But, My Lord, while it is desirable to give greater facilities to the ryots of the Deccan, whose ruin has been accomplished by unforeseen circumstances, to free themselves from debts which paralyse their industry, care must be taken that the remedies are such as will not deter the people from having recourse to them, nor impair the credit which is ordinarily given to agriculturists, and without which they would be unable to meet the demand for revenue, or to sustain themselves from harvest to harvest.

"The requirements of the present Bill as to registration appear to me so onerous, that they will operate to deter persons from committing their transactions to writing. Registration affords a very doubtful proof of the payment of money. It is a common experience in this country that money paid in the presence of the registration-officer is in part or wholly returned when the parties leave the presence of the registrar. It is rarely denied that a transaction has taken place; but if a dispute arises, it is as to the amount received.

"The portion of the Bill which relates to conciliation also deserves serious consideration. The Bill provides for the appointment of conciliators, who having invited the parties to attend, are to use their best endeavours to induce them to agree to an amicable settlement. Now, the matter on which the parties are supposed to be at variance is not a mere dispute arising out of domestic or friendly relations, in which the impartiality of a stranger or the influence of a neighbour can be hopefully introduced, to persuade the parties to make mutual concessions; and, therefore, I am not hopeful that this provision will be of practical use. No doubt, a revenue-officer or a police-officer could bring influences to bear on creditors which would induce them altogether to forego their claims; but I need hardly express my conviction that the Government of India would altogether discountenance the exercise of any such influence; and I have no doubt the Council, in order to avoid even the apprehension of its exercise, will see fit to introduce a provision in the Bill prohibiting the appointment as conciliator of any officer exercising revenue or police functions.

"On the other hand, the attendance before the conciliator will put the parties to considerable inconvenience. The conciliator can only 'invite' them to attend; and if the defendant does not attend the conciliator may adjourn the case for an indefinite time and as often as he pleases. A claimant may have to waste any number of days to obtain relief in the most trifling case; and there is no provision to secure him compensation.

"My Lord, in my judgment there is more reason to expect that a creditor will abate his claims when the parties are brought face to face in a public Court of Justice than at a private sitting held by a conciliator; but if it is resolved that an experiment be made, at least provisions should be introduced to secure the appointment of conciliators to whom all parties can resort with equal confidence, and to restrict adjournments.

"My Lord, I now come to the provisions relating to the procedure in the civil Courts; and before I offer any remarks upon them, I must defend my countrymen from some imputations which have been, I think, unfairly cast on them and received as true without sufficient enquiry. It is said they are prone to litigation. In those provinces in which I have acquired experience I have found no facts to warrant this conclusion. Looking to the numbers of the population and their innumerable transactions resulting in credit, the number of suits for the recovery of debt will compare not unfavourably with the statistics of any other civilized country. Creditors rarely sue their debtors unless a dispute has arisen, or unless they desire, by obtaining a decree, to secure an advantage over other creditors. Nor is it true, as has been frequently asserted, that the village money-lender generally desires to acquire the land of his debtor. He looks for the return of his money principally to the crop raised by the labour of his debtor, and takes a mortgage to prevent the debtor's making away with the crop or defeating his claim in favour of another money-lender. In the hands of the money-lender, who cannot himself cultivate, the land is worth only the rent a tenant could give for it.

"Again, in the large majority of cases the claims brought are just, and the defendants do not seek to evade them by unjust defences. I do not mean to say that there are not in this country, as elsewhere, extortionate usurers and persons who advance false claims in Courts of Justice, and also debtors who have recourse to fraud to defeat just claims; but I believe—and I have seen no proof to the contrary—that the civil Courts have in the ordinary course of their procedure, not failed in this country more than elsewhere to detect fraud and defeat its intended consequences. In fact, our acquaintance with such frauds is derived chiefly from the investigations of Courts of civil justice.

"I would also observe that in this country, where opportunities for small investments rarely present themselves except in the shape of loans on the security of land, there is a large number of persons who are not professional money-lenders, but who invest their savings in such securities, and almost universally charge no higher interest than the usual rate in the market. The first devi-

B 862—24

ation from the ordinary procedure which I find in the Bill is the compulsory enforcement of the attendance of the defendant. My Lord, if I am right in supposing that in the majority of cases the claim is just, it follows that in the majority of cases in which the defendant does not appear, it is because he knows the complaint is just, and does not desire to lose the labour of several days, possibly at a critical season for his crop, and incur the expense of going to and from, and attending the Court. It would perhaps be sufficient to require the Court to exercise the power, it already possesses, of enforcing the attendance of the defendant only in those cases in which, on looking into the account, it sees reason to believe the claim is fraudulent or extortionate. The rule prescribed in the Bill appears to me calculated to injure rather than benefit the majority of defendants.

" The provisions of the Bill which direct the Court to go into the history of the case from the commencement of the transactions, I think, also require modification. They may involve an inquiry imposing on a Court many days' labour, and affording it no certain conclusions. It is scarcely reasonable to expect either of the parties to produce reliable evidence of petty money-transactions extending over a number of years and commencing, it may be, a quarter of a century ago, especially seeing that the limitation-law has encouraged them to believe that such evidence would not be required of them. I, therefore, think some definite and not too remote period should be prescribed for such enquiries. So also a definite limit of time should be prescribed for re-opening statements and settlements of accounts. Some debts which will come before the Courts will be the result of transactions commenced and settled before the lifetime of either party to the suit. The consequence of imposing on the Courts a duty they cannot possibly discharge would be to encourage them to evade it.

" My Lord, I think it right to point out that the provisions of section 12, requiring the Court to search for a defence ' on the ground of fraud, mistake, accident, undue influence' (whatever that expression may mean) ' or otherwise,' are calculated to encourage defendants to set up false defences and to support them with false evidence ; and for this reason they call for very serious consideration. Nor can I give my consent to the provisions of section 15, forcing an arbitration on parties, whether they consent to it or not. Competent and impartial arbitrators are rarely to be found in villages ; and it is one of the acknowledged privileges of British citizenship that for the vindication of right recourse may be had to Judges of whose competency and impartiality their selection by the State is a guarantee.

"My Lord, I am also unable to agree with the principle upon which section 16 of the Bill is based. The provisions of that section appear to me to be contrary to Hindú law as administered on this side of India and to general equity. If a Hindú dies leaving assets, then *whoever* takes his assets, in whatever degree he may be related to the deceased, and even if he be a stranger, is liable to satisfy the debts of the deceased to the extent of the assets, and, where such debts bear interest, with interest. This rule is common to the English and Muhammadan as well as to the Hindú law. The Hindú law does, indeed, impose a moral obligation on the descendants of a deceased person to pay his debts, and, when the descendants are related to the deceased in the first degree, with interest; but this obligation, which has not the force of law, is not enforced by the Courts on this side of India, and ought, I think, in no case to be enforced to the injury of *bonâ fide* creditors of the descendants of the deceased.

"In section 20, which provides that a debtor, owing less than fifty rupees, who is unable wholly to pay the debt should be discharged on payment of a portion, it appears to me necessary to specify what portion he is to pay—whether it be so much as he is able or a percentage: but this point will, no doubt, receive the attention of the Committee.

"The provisions of the Bill tending to prevent the employment of vakíls appear to me to be of very doubtful expediency. Having exercised judicial functions for many years I am bound to say the Courts receive considerable assistance from vakils, and that the more ignorant the suitor is, the less probability is there he will be able to explain his case in the confusion he experiences in a Court of Justice as well as he can to his adviser outside the Court. I would prefer to see provision made for the employment of Government pleaders to appear on behalf of debtors in all cases, rather than discountenance the employment of pleaders at all.

"With regard to appeals, which are entirely prohibited in the Bill, I admit that they entail evils, in that they prolong litigation and increase expense; but it seems to me better to experience these evils than the greater evil of imperfect justice. Cases triable by the Courts of Small Causes ordinarily present very simple issues, and do not call for the intervention of a superior Court; but questions relating to land are far more complicated, and involve frequently questions on which the law is not well settled. I can see no reason why appeals should in these cases be refused in the Deccan when they are allowed elsewhere. Revision is, at the best, an imperfect substitute for the right of appeal.

"For similar reasons I considered the expediency of introducing special rules of limitation, proposed in the Bill, open to serious doubt. If it is desirable in the interest of the debtor to extend the period of limitation for the recovery of debts, the benefit should be given to agriculturists everywhere, and, indeed, to debtors of all classes.

"The provisions of the amended Code of Civil Procedure relating to insolvency will afford sensible relief—and relief that was needed—to agricultural and other debtors in all parts of the country. The insolvency provisions in the present Bill go beyond the general law. I am not prepared to dissent from them on that account; for the circumstances have been shown to justify special remedies. But the provision respecting the delivery of property in lieu of cash is anomalous. It will not, I think, be acceptable to either party, nor does it appear called for.

"With regard to section 35 of the Bill, I have only to observe that I can see no reason why a fraudulent insolvent in the Deccan should be exposed to less penalties than a fraudulent debtor elsewhere.

"My Lord, there is one more point to which I wish to invite the Council's attention. Admitting, as I do, that the exigencies of the case require special legislation, I entertain a serious doubt whether the rules framed in the Bill should be enacted more than as a temporary measure. Perhaps, the requirements of the case would be sufficiently met if the operation of the proposed law is limited to a certain number of years. Some of the most important provisions of the Bill relating to interest strongly resemble the laws against usury which for many years were prevalent in this country. I had some share in administering them. They were found ineffective; they encouraged fraud; they operated as a hardship upon the borrower; and as such were repealed both in England and in this country. The revival of any rules of law which limit the rate of interest or empower Courts to interfere in the terms of private contract, cannot be regarded by me as other than a retrograde step—a step which, if justified by extreme emergency, should, at any rate, not be allowed permanently to affect the law, even in a small portion of the country.

"My Lord, I have ventured to offer these criticisms, not in any way pledging myself to oppose any of the provisions of the Bill, in whatever shape they may eventually come before the Council, but with a view to invite the attention of the Select Committee, before which the Bill will be laid, to those provisions of which the expediency appears to me to be doubtful. So far as the Bill tends to relieve the Deccan ryots from their present embarrassments it will have my cordial support. The acerbity of feeling occasioned to creditors by the discharge of their debtors will be sensibly mitigated if the just ascertainment of their claims be secured to them. But should the provisions of the Bill go to deprive them of this privilege, and so far as such provisions tend to hinder the ordinary transactions of the people and render the recovery of debts incurred hereafter uncertain, I should be reluctant to support it.

"My Lord, I should indeed be grieved if, from what I have said, it should be understood I am not cognizant of the difficulties and hardships under which the agricultural classes of India labour. I have for many years felt a deep sympathy with the ryot, and should look upon it as a great piece of good fortune to take part in the passing of any measures which would relieve him from the miseries which indebtedness brings upon him. But at the same time I am convinced that no law can be framed which will do away with the necessity of borrowing, or, so long as the recovery of loans is uncertain and fraught with difficulty, put a stop to exorbitant rates of interest. An experience of thirty-five years, during which I had the honour of serving as a judicial officer of the Government, induces me to say that all rules which aim at regulating the rate of interest on private loans or which place difficulties in the way of their recovery, far from relieving, are injurious to the borrower, whose necessities compel him to evade the law by secret and collusive agreements of which the terms are more onerous because they cannot be enforced. The condition of the Indian ryots not only in the Deccan, but in other parts of India, fully deserves consideration at the hands of the Government: perhaps in their pecuniary difficulties may be traced some of the causes which make famine so severe and oft-recurring a calamity. The question is undoubtedly momentous; and Your Excellency's administration is to be congratulated upon having undertaken its solution. But, My Lord, the solution, in my humble opinion, lies not in conferring anomalous privileges of protection against the demands of the money-lender, not in placing difficulties in the way of borrowing money, not in making the recovery of judgment-debts dilatory or uncertain—but in providing the agriculturists of India with facilities for borrowing money on moderate interest, and in making the recovery of such loans speedy and certain."

The Hon'ble Mr. Cockerell said that, whilst he readily admitted that a case had been made out for the application of some remedy, through special legislation, for the evil shown to exist in the heretofore subsisting relations between the agriculturists and the money-lenders in the Deccan districts, he thought the Bill before the Council aimed at a much greater interference with those relations, and a more extensive variation of the ordinary law of the country than was necessary or justifiable ; and he felt bound to record his dissent to those provisions of the Bill which in his opinion came within this designation. He considered the sections relating to the establishment of village Courts for the trial of petty cases and a system of village registration of contracts between the agriculturists and the money-lending classes, as well as the enforcement of the delivery of receipts and statements of account, as likely to prove efficacious in the removal of many of the evils now complained of. He would not object to the enactment of the conciliatory clauses of the Bill by way of experiment, though he apprehended that their effect for good or for evil would depend entirely on the character of the agency selected for the discharge of the functions of a conciliator.

If the powers conferred by the Bill were to be vested in officers trained in that school of thought which had devised some of the provisions of the Bill to which he would advert presently, the results to be anticipated could be hardly otherwise than unsatisfactory; they might be exceedingly mischievous.

The proposed abolition of imprisonment for debt had his concurrence as a measure which, if found to work satisfactorily in a limited area, might be advantageously extended at some future period to all India ; and he was free to admit also that the proposed alteration of the law of limitation in regard to the recovery of debts (though personally he had doubts as to its advantage) had for its recommendation the support of the most competent authorities on such a question. He would have had no great objection to the disallowance of appeals if the unqualified power of revision to be substituted therefor were vested in the ordinary superior Courts ; but he distrusted the action of a special revising agency, such as was to be created under the Bill, which might be constituted so as to operate as a mere machine for carrying out the ruling policy of the day towards the classes affected by the proposed legislation.

He thought that the provisions of section twenty, which gave a discretionary power to the Court to absolve any debtor, after a partial satisfaction of a decree or claim, from his remaining liability to his creditor without any of the safeguards which belonged to the ordinary insolvency procedure, were unjust to the creditor, and wholly uncalled-for in the circumstances of the case.

His greatest objection, however, was to the provisions of chapter IV of the Bill, which contained a special insolvency procedure for the benefit of the indebted agriculturist. In the first place, it was proposed in section twenty-seven to virtually declare that no amount of falsehood or dishonesty on the part of the ryot-debtor should deprive him of the advantages of an adjudication of bankruptcy if, as a matter of fact, he was found to be in insolvent circumstances. He would ask what tenable ground there could be for enacting that misrepresentation and fraud on the part of a Deccan agriculturist should not be attended with the same disabling and punitory consequences which would be the result of such conduct on the part of any other person. The Hon'ble Mover of the Bill had argued that, for an insolvency procedure to be efficient, the only question to be considered was whether a person seeking its benefits was in insolvent circumstances, and that, if he was, he was entitled to obtain the relief sought for; he (Mr. Cockerell) regarded such an argument as wholly fallacious; an insolvency law was intended for the relief of honest debtors; hence, when it appeared on the face of a case that a person applying for a declaration of insolvency had been guilty of misrepresentation and dishonesty in regard to the matter of his application, he was most justly and properly thereby debarred from obtaining benefits and privileges to which from the nature of the case he was not entitled.

The next provision on which he had to comment, was contained in section thirty.

That provision was no less remarkable for its excessive unfairness than for the originality of its conception. After the moveable property of an insolvent had passed into the hands of a Receiver, the Court was to be allowed to interfere for the purpose of prohibiting its sale, and to force its acceptance on an unwilling creditor, at a valuation made under no sort of responsibility, and consequently wholly unreliable, in liquidation or part liquidation of his claim against the insolvent.

The property so thrust upon the creditor might be wholly unacceptable quite apart from any question of a fair valuation; it might be a village pig, and the unfortunate creditor might have a conscientious objection to have anything to do with the unclean animal! It might be said, perhaps, that he was putting an extreme case; but it was a case that might well occur under the operation of the proposed section.

The provisions in section thirty-four of the Bill, which was designed to give an absolute release from all further liability for existing debt to an insolvent debtor whose available assets had been distributed amongst his creditors, had been conceived in the same spirit, *i.e.*, it was intended thereby to make a special concession to the insolvent agriculturist at the expense of his creditors which nothing in the circumstances of the case in any way justified, and this moreover, at a time when, through the passing of the Bill for amending the Code of Civil Procedure, the general law of the country would be made as favourable to the insolvent-debtor in this direction as was reasonable, having regard to the just claims of the creditor to impartial consideration. The Hon'ble Mover had said in the course of his remarks that a man *ought* to pay what was *justly* due from him, but no more. He (Mr. Cockerell) did not understand how the proposed enactment of section thirty-four of the Bill could be reconciled with that sentiment ; for the effect of the general provisions of this Bill, if passed into law, would be so to scrutinize and cut down the money-lender's claims against the agriculturist that the residuum found to be due from him must surely come within the category of just debts, and leave the insolvent-debtor with no title to obtain any greater immunity from liability to meet them than was enjoyed by other insolvent-debtors throughout the Empire.

He now came to the provisions which in his judgment evinced, perhaps, the greatest disregard of all equitable principles ; he referred to section thirty-five which limited the power of Subordinate Judges to inflict punishment for offences under section 359 of the Civil Procedure Code to a sentence of three months' imprisonment in certain cases and one month in others—the punishment allowed in such cases by the said Code extending to one year's imprisonment. This section was so worded as to make it appear at first sight that the provision just described was a mere matter of jurisdiction ; but then, even in that view, there would appear to be something anomalous in curtailing the jurisdiction which would be exercised by Subordinate Judges vested with the powers of Insolvent Courts outside of the Deccan in the case of the Judges upon whom as regards other matters unusually large powers were to be conferred by this Bill. But when section twenty-five, which required all insolvency cases to be disposed of by these Subordinate Judges exclusively, came to be considered in connection with this section (thirty-five), it was clearly the intention of the framer of the Bill to reduce the maximum penalty which could be imposed for offences under section 359 of the Code from one year to three months' imprisonment in some cases and only one month's imprisonment in others. Now, he (Mr. Cockerell) entirely concurred in what had fallen from the last speaker on the subject of this provision of the Bill, and he would ask why the punishment to be awarded for rascality of the kind dealt with in section 359 of the Code should be appraised by a different standard when the acts evincing such rascality were committed by indebted agriculturists ? He (Mr. Cockerell) could not too strongly deprecate such class-distinction in the punishment of criminal offences as was contemplated by this section of the Bill.

The provisions of this chapter (IV) on which he had been commenting were mildly described in the Statement of Objects and Reasons as constituting a " procedure more liberal to the debtor than that of the Civil Code"; and the Hon'ble Member in charge of the Bill had endeavoured in his remarks to defend them as quite consistent with the exigencies of the case. The Hon'ble Member's explanation had in no degree shaken his (Mr. Cockerell's) conviction as to the monstrously inequitable character of these provisions, which he would describe as marked by a degree of partiality and one-sidedness which he believed to be without precedent in the annals of Indian legislation. He wished to be understood, however, in these remarks as not opposing the motion for the reference of the Bill to a Select Committee; but he had thought it right to state his views thus plainly in the hope that the provisions of the Bill on which he had specially commented would undergo such pruning and purging by the Select Committee to which it would be referred that the Indian Statute-book would not be tarnished by the admission to its pages of enactments conceived in a spirit diametrically opposed to that sense of fairness and strict impartiality in dealing with the interests of all parties affected by it which had heretofore characterized the legislation of this Empire.

His Honour the Lieutenant-Governor said he did not wish to criticize in detail any of the provisions of this Bill, but he thought that the circumstances which had led to its being introduced were of such general prevalence throughout India that the mode in which they were to be treated in the Deccan might possibly form a precedent for their treatment in other parts of the country. He was not acquainted with the state of the revenue administration in Bombay, but he knew in the Panjáb there were many agriculturists and land-proprietors whose condition was very much the same as that described in the speech of the Hon'ble Member who introduced the Bill; there were parts of the country in the Panjáb, as doubtless there were in every Presidency, where the rainfall was uncertain and the crops precarious; yet in all those districts the Government had introduced its revenue system, which obliged the peasant-proprietor who had engaged for the revenue to pay a fixed sum at fixed times as Government revenue, and the Government had imposed the most stringent conditions with regard to the realization of its own demands. It seemed to him that too little attention had been paid to this cause, which must in a great degree have contributed, if it did not entirely originate, the difficulties of the Deccan ryots in the part of the country to which this Bill was to be made applicable. The peasant-proprietor who had become indebted to a banker was still obliged to satisfy the Government demand in cash : to procure that cash he had again to resort to the money-lender, and, as the Government demand came upon him at the usual season of the year with regular recurrence, he was obliged to resort again and again to the money-lender in order to procure the cash wherewith to meet it. The Government in this Bill proposed to take very stringent measures to protect the ryot from the demands of the money-lender ; but the provisions of the Revenue-law for the realization of the Government demand had apparently been in no way altered. Every one knew the great stringency of those regulations, and it seemed to him unreasonable that, while we upheld them for the realization of our own revenue, we should make such alterations in the ordinary law in regard to private contracts. He thought it would have been more satisfactory if, before introducing this Bill, we had been told what measures the Bombay Government proposed to take in order to lighten the burden which the payment of the Government revenue demand imposed upon the peasant proprietor. He thought it desirable that, at the same time as measures of relief were afforded to the ryot from his private creditor, the Government, which appeared as a public creditor of the ryot, should also take measures to in some way lighten the pressure of his own demand—not perhaps by reduction of assessment, but by taking that assessment in some other way which would not impose upon the ryot the burden of meeting all the risks of a scanty rainfall and a precarious crop, but would leave those risks on the Government itself, and relieve the peasant-proprietor, who had shown himself unfit to meet them. He thought there was considerable danger in altering the ordinary law of contract in the manner now proposed in this Bill in the case of agriculturists, unless Government itself took measures to relieve the burden which it had itself imposed upon them.

The Hon'ble Mr. Stokes said :—"I shall vote for referring this Bill to a Select Committee, and I do not intend, either now or hereafter, to oppose it, so far as it carries out the express orders of the Secretary of State, that is to say, so far as it requires the Courts to enter into the merits of all money-claims by sowkárs against Deccan ryots, and forbids them to compel a ryot to pay a sowkár compound interest, or an amount of interest exceeding the principal sum lent ; so far as it provides that the principle of the Presidency-towns Insolvent Act (11 & 12 Vic., c. 21) shall be extended to the Deccan ryots ; that their land shall not be sold in execution, unless specially pledged by a bond duly registered ; that the number of Courts with small-cause jurisdiction shall be increased, so that there shall be at least one within reach of every ryot's home ; and that Courts of Conciliation shall be established.

"Those instructions have been accepted by the Government of India in its executive capacity, and I am not now going to raise any question as to the necessity or propriety of such acceptance. I may, however, remark that the Bill, so far as it requires the Courts to enter into the merits of money-claims, is simply declaratory of the existing law : so far as it provides a special law of insolvency, it is, to my mind, rendered unnecessary by the great extension which the Select Committee on the Bill to amend the Code of Civil Procedure has recently given to chapter XX of the Code—an extension of which the Secretary of State was not, and is not, fully aware ; and, so far as it provides for multiplying Courts with small-cause jurisdiction, all that is really needed may be done by executive orders under section 3 of Act XI of 1865 and section 28 of Act XIV of 1869.

"The remarks with which I shall venture to trouble the Council have reference merely to the additions which the Bombay Government and the Hon'ble Mover have thought fit to make to the simple scheme recommended by the Secretary of State. It seems to me that, in framing a measure of which the policy is, to say the least, questionable, we should not go an inch beyond the instructions which the Indian Executive is bound to obey ; and that we should all, whether we are ordinary Members or Additional Members of this Council, regard with the utmost jealousy accretions as to which the authors of the Bill have wilfully abstained from consulting the Bombay High Court Judges and other persons of judicial experience.

"The first of these accretions to which I shall call your attention is section 73 :—

'No appeal shall lie from any decision or order in any suit or proceeding before a Subordinate Judge under this Act.'

"The effect of this section, coupled with section 3, will probably be the reverse of what is intended. It shuts out from appeal the decisions in almost all mortgage-suits. The object of doing so is, of course, to relieve indebted ryots from expense and prolonged litigation. But, first, I am informed by Mr. Justice West that in the Bombay Presidency the Courts of first instance, in dealing with these suits, usually apply the harsh letter of the law in favour of the creditor. Relief is got from the Higher Courts, in which modifications favourable to the ryot are much more frequent than those in favour of the sowkár. And, secondly, the useful power which the Appellate Court now possesses under section 551 of the Code of Civil Procedure of confirming the decision of the Lower Court without sending or serving notice has in most cases rendered the cost of an appeal quite insignificant. The result of this part of the Bill will, therefore, be, on the whole, to place the indebted ryot in a worse pecuniary position than he is in at present. As to cutting off all appeals in order to shorten litigation, the remedy will be worse than the disease. Let us remember that, in the absence of an Appellate Court, the Judges of first instance will have no one (as Bentham says) 'to stand in awe of.' The errors arising from corruption, incapacity, laziness, precipitation, ignorance and love of arbitrary power, which are certain to be committed in these difficult land-suits, especially where the Judges are inexperienced and unaided by a Bar, will remain uncorrected and cause hardship and discontent. The barring of an appeal in cases of the small-cause type (suits for debts, damages or moveables not exceeding Rs. 500 in amount or value) may be justified, because, as a rule, those cases are simple and easy, and practically it is better, on the whole, for the community that in such cases the decision should be rapid than that it should be careful and correct. But mortgage-cases sometimes involve the investigation of difficult questions as to title, priorities, marshalling securities, contribution and rights of maintenance, and always the taking of complicated accounts. A Judge who does all this rapidly will simply scamp his work; and the power of calling for and revising his imperfect records will, as I shall show, be a very inadequate substitute for an appeal—a remedy which, wherever wrong has been done, the appellant's interest urges him to apply.

"The effect of abolishing appeals should also be considered in connection with the rule as to *res judicata* (Code of Civil Procedure, section 13). It seems to me that great hardship may sometimes be caused by regarding (as we must, if the Bill is passed in its present form) the uncontrolled judgments of these subordinate Courts as conclusive on questions of title to land. We may, of course, insert a clause declaring that, for the purpose of section 13 of the Code, no Court trying a suit under this Bill shall be deemed, as regards the title to immoveable property in respect of which the suit is brought, a Court of competent jurisdiction. But, then, suitors would be exposed to the harassment of repeated litigation, which the rule as to *res judicata* has been framed to prevent.

"The power given by section 54 to the Special Judge to call for and examine the records of suits tried by Subordinate Judges is intended as a substitute for appeals. But, first, the records of cases tried by second class Subordinate Judges at Rs. 150 a month will, it is safe to say, generally be defective; and the Bill (section 11) expressly provides that in the bulk of cases (those of which the subject-matter does not exceed Rs. 10 in amount or value) there need not be even a memorandum of the evidence.

Under the Bill, therefore, the revising Judge will constantly have to exercise his jurisdiction on imperfect materials.

"Secondly, the revising Judge, no matter how carefully he is selected and how highly he is paid, will be greatly inferior in learning, ability and experience to the Judges of the High Court, who now form the ultimate Court of appeal in the Presidency. The result will be that rights will be established all over the Deccan founded on the Judge's crotchets and erroneous ideas of law, and the greatest confusion and hardship will result when these rights are upset (as they are sure, at last, to be) by the High Court or the Judicial Committee of the Privy Council.

"Thirdly, those records, if, as I suppose, they resemble the Bengáli nathis, will be masses of ill-written documents in a Native character and language which, it is safe to say, no revising Judge will have time or skill to decipher and translate. The business of revision will, therefore, practically be placed in the hands of the shirastedárs, who are notoriously open to the sowkárs' bribes; and here, again, the Bill will work to the injury rather than the benefit of the ryot.

"Another mode in which it seems to me certain that the provisions of the Bill will be used to injure the ryots is suggested by sections 45 and 46. Those sections provide that when the parties to a case before a conciliator (who is intended to represent in India the French *Juge de Paix*) come to an agreement finally disposing of the matter, the agreement shall be reduced to writing and signed, and that the conciliator shall forward the same in original to the Court of the Subordinate Judge of lowest grade having jurisdiction in the place where the agriculturist who is a party thereto resides. The Bill then proceeds thus :—

'The Court which receives the agreement shall order it to be filed ; *and it shall then take effect as if it were a decree of the said Court passed on the day on which it is ordered to be filed, and from which no appeal lies.*'

"It requires no power of divination to say how this provision will work. The sowkár will say to the ryots, who, we are told, is generally weak and apathetic : 'I will lend you the Rs. 50 for which you ask ; you need not give me a mortgage, and you will thus not have to pay the sarkár anything for stamps or registration-fees. We can arrange the matter thus. I shall apply to the conciliator 'to effect an amicable settlement' between us, and you will come with me before him and agree to pay me Rs. 100 three months hence.' The wretched ryot will have to do so, and the sowkár, chuckling at the ease with which he twists a foolish law to his own advantage, will see the agreement taking effect as if it were a decree 'from which no appeal lies.'

"Chapter VIII, which requires all money-obligations executed by ryots to be written by or before village registrars, also seems to me a specimen of blundering benevolence. The chief result of this well-meant attempt to ensure the authenticity of documents will, I am certain, be to discourage the use of written agreements and to force *oral* contracts on persons who would otherwise have expressed themselves in writing. I need hardly say that this is impolitic and contrary to one of the wisest aims of our recent legislation. If the scheme succeeds, it will also add greatly to the cost of all loans, such cost falling finally on the ryots, who cannot pay their revenue without occasionally borrowing. But wherever sowkárs are concerned the scheme is, I think, pretty sure to fail. The sowkár will give up mortgages and written instruments altogether. He will say to the ryot: 'I will lend you money at 60 per cent. ; but, mind, if you do not repay me on the day fixed, I shall never lend to you again, nor will any of my brother-sowkárs.' The ryot will borrow on the terms proposed, and his last state will be worse than his first.

"Section 69 declares that, in awarding costs in suits before Subordinate Judges in which the subject-matter does not exceed Rs. 100 in amount or value, nothing shall be allowed, unless the Court is of opinion that professional assistance was necessary. This, I fear, will practically exclude pleaders from appearing in most of the difficult mortgage-cases cognizable by Subordinate Judges. Now, on this point I have only to say that the experience of India and of every other country in the world proves that an honest, learned and independent Bar is of the greatest advantage to the Judge in the trial of complicated cases. And if the Bombay pleaders are, as a rule, honest, learned and independent (as to which, not having the needful local knowledge, I offer no opinion), the exclusion of them will be a public calamity as well as an unmerited slur on an honourable profession. It may be true that some of them are dishonest and ignorant; but the arbitrary exclusion of the whole body from their proper functions will deprive the peccant members of all chance of improvement, render them discontented and dangerous, and compel them to earn their livelihood by all kinds of dishonourable practices. To draw the line at Rs. 100 or any other amount is absurd ; for the difficulty of a mortgage-case does not vary directly as the amount involved. To give the Subordinate Judge power (as is done by section 69) to refuse any pleader's fees will obviously tend to excite suspicions of favouritism whenever the Judge grants those fees, and to destroy that independence of the Bar which, for the sake of the Bench as well as the suitors, a wise Government ought to encourage. Lastly, if, as is probably the case, the legal profession in the Bombay

Presidency is as influential as it is elsewhere, to make this powerful body of men bitterly hostile to the Bill seems to me the most certain mode of ensuring the failure of the experiment which it has been framed to try.

" The provisions which I have hitherto noticed are, in my opinion, unwise; but those to which I shall now ask the attention of the Council are grossly unjust and (if I may use the expression in India) unconstitutional. Both section 20 and section 49 are retrospective in their operation. They relate to decrees passed *before* the proposed Act will come into force, and the former section at least seriously interferes with the vested rights of the holders of such decrees. Section 20, paragraph 1, runs as follows :—

'When a decree has been passed, *whether before or after this Act comes into force*, under which any sum less than fifty rupees is recoverable from an agriculturist, the Court may, whether in the course of execution of the said decree or otherwise, if it is satisfied that there is no other claim against him, and that he is unable to pay the whole of such sum, direct the payment of *a portion of the same, and grant him a discharge from such* [sic] *balance.*'

Under this section, therefore, if a man (whether he be a sowkár or not) has before the first of October 1879 obtained a decree against a ryot for Rs. 49, the Court, if it is satisfied that there is no other claim against the ryot, that he is unable to pay more than Rs. 48, but that he is quite able to pay that amount, may direct him to pay only *one* anna, and grant him a discharge from the balance. Surely such a provision was never before proposed for the consideration of a Legislature ! Section 49 declares that no application for execution of a decree passed before the proposed Act comes into force ' to which any agriculturist residing within any local limits for which a conciliator has been appointed is a party ' shall be entertained by any civil Court unless the decree-holder produces a certificate under section 48. When the judgment-debtor refuses (as he often will) to appear before the conciliator, the decree-holder cannot execute his decree until the expiration of that incalculable space of time which the Bill describes as ' such period as the conciliator thinks reasonable.' Section 30 is also retrospective. It runs as follows :—

'Whenever any moveable property of an insolvent is liable to be sold by a receiver under section 356 of the said Code, the Court may direct that it shall not be so sold, and may, after recording the opinions of two Assessors appointed by the Court in this behalf, determine the value of such property, and direct the receiver to transfer it to any of the scheduled creditors who may be entitled to receive in the distribution under the said section 356 an amount equal to or greater than the value so determined ; *and such creditor shall accept such property in full or partial liquidation (as the case may be) of the amount to which he is so entitled.*'

A creditor who before the first of October 1879 has contracted to be paid in money may be compelled, under this wonderful section, to receive payment of his debt in old brass pots, or worn-out bullocks, or village-pigs, or anything else which he does not want and which he may be unable to sell. I believe that the Hon'ble Mover is the sole author of this section—at least I can find nothing about it in the letter from the Bombay Government. Remedial statutes may be retrospective when they only go to confirm rights already existing and add to the means of enforcing existing obligations. But sections like these, that disturb absolute vested rights against which there is no equity, are founded on unconstitutional principles, and I, for one, will never be a party to passing them into law."

The Hon'ble Sir Alexander Arbuthnot said :—" At this late hour I will detain the Council by a very few remarks. This Bill, which has been placed in charge of the Hon'ble Mr. Hope by the Executive Government in consideration of his experience in the districts now in question and of the attention which he has given to the subject, is in a great measure based on a draft Bill which was sent up to the Government of India by the Bombay Government, and in the preparation of which Mr. Hope's aid and advice were made available. I have no doubt that, if the Bill had emanated entirely from the Executive Government of India, it would have assumed in some matters of detail a very different shape. There are several provisions in the Bill with which I, for one, am unable to agree; but, as regards the general scope of the Bill, apart from those particular provisions, I feel bound to say that I consider that a sufficient case has been made out for special legislation, and that I approve of certain leading principles which the Bill embodies. On the other hand, I think that there is great force in many of the remarks which my hon'ble colleague Mr. Stokes has made regarding the section which bars appeals in cases of claims founded on mortgages. I personally entertain very little doubt that, when the Bill has undergone that examination and sifting which it will undergo at the hands of the High Court of Bombay and of other judicial authorities, and when it has been examined and revised by the Select Committee, that section will, if it does not entirely disappear, be very materially modified. In all that Mr. Stokes has said on the subject of those provisions of the Bill which provide for supervision and inspection in lieu of appeals I entirely concur. I may also say that I agree with my hon'ble colleague Mr. Cockerell in thinking that several of the insolvency provisions are exceedingly questionable. My impression is that it will be found that the insolvency law which we hope to see enacted in the course of a few days in the Bill amending the Code of Civil

Procedure will be found sufficient for the particular districts which are dealt with in the project of law now before us, as well as for the rest of India. However, I think it was only right that, looking to the circumstances under which the Bill has been framed, we should send it forth for criticism and examination, not exactly in the shape in which we, looking at the question from our point of view and not from the local point of view, might be disposed to regard it, but that we should pay very great deference to the suggestions made by the local Government, and afford every opportunity for those suggestions being examined and criticised in the Presidency to which the Bill refers.

"There are one or two points in connection with the address which was delivered by the Mover of the Bill on which I should wish to say a few words. The full and exhaustive and, I am bound to say, very interesting and suggestive address to which we have listened this morning shows that the Hon'ble Member has exhausted every source of information which was available to him. It shows that he has carefully studied the Report of the Commission which has led to this project of law, and the correspondence which during a long series of years has passed on the particular subject to which this project of law refers, and on other subjects cognate to it. Naturally, in the Hon'ble Member's address a great deal was taken from the Report of the Deccan Riots Commission. From that report he was able to adduce a great deal of evidence in support of the views which he individually entertains. But it struck me that on one or two points on which, as I read the Report of the Deccan Riots Commission, the opinions expressed by the members of that Commission seemed to differ from those entertained by the Hon'ble Member, he failed to give us the benefit of the observations which are to be found in the Commission's Report.

"I do not think that the tone in which the Hon'ble Member expressed himself with regard to the character of the sowkárs in the Deccan districts is by any means fully supported by the text of the Commission's Report. The Hon'ble Member used the expression 'usurious money-lenders.' He said many other things which, as his address was read rapidly, I cannot repeat *verbatim*, but which gave me the impression that he regards the money-lenders of the Deccan districts as a class, with scarcely an exception, of usurious and rapacious men—a class of men who make enormous and extravagant profits at the expense of the ignorant ryot, and a class against whom it is desirable that the Government should direct very stringent legislation.

"Now, it seems to me that this is not the view held by the members of the Commission. On the contrary, I find it expressly stated, in the 85th paragraph of their report, that 'on the whole there is no reason to believe that the sowkárs dealing with the agricultural classes make higher profits than are warranted by the nature of their business, which is always precarious and unpopular—occasionally, as we have seen, dangerous.' There are other passages in the report on which I cannot lay my hand at this moment which convey to my mind a similar impression; and I think it would be wrong that this Bill should go forth to the public or to the people of the districts which it will affect with the impression that the Government of India entertain in regard to this particular class of the community—a class more or less intelligent, which is really very useful, and the existence of which in the circumstances of the country is an absolute necessity—views such as those which appear to be entertained by the Mover of the Bill. I have no doubt that among this class, as among other classes of money-lenders in other parts of the world, there are many black sheep, and that here, as elsewhere, there are instances of gross extortion and rapacity; but I do not for a moment believe that the case is nearly so bad—that the class, as a class, is so extortionate and such a curse to society—as might be inferred from some of the expressions used in the Hon'ble Member's address; such expressions, for instance, as that 'money is lent designedly to render the ryot a bond slave'; or that 'fraud by the creditor is, in India, the only thing to be guarded against.'

"On another point it appears to me that the remarks of the Hon'ble Member are not borne out by the Report of the Deccan Riots Commission. I refer to the alleged technicality of the procedure of our Courts. Nor do I think that those remarks are borne out by the actual facts of the case.

"In the 116th paragraph of the Report of the Commission I find it stated that 'upon these and similar statements the first remark we have to make is that it is a mistake to suppose that Courts in India are bound only to administer law in the strict sense in which the term is here used. They are distinctly Courts 'of equity and good conscience' as well as of law. Secondly, it is certain that the laws of this country, as, for instance, the Contract Act, the Evidence Act and the Civil Procedure Code, are as little open to the charge of technicality as any laws can possibly be.'

"I listened with great attention and with great interest to the speech of our hon'ble colleague Sayyad Ahmad Khán, the Native Member of this Council, and the only Native Member present. One of the observations made by him which particularly struck me, was that in which he expressed his opinion as to the expediency of prohibiting in this Bill the appointment of revenue or police-officers as conciliators. I agree in every word which the Hon'ble Member said on this point; and I trust that in this respect the Bill will be amended by the Select Committee. On the other hand, I do not agree in all that the Hon'ble Member said in regard to the Limitation-law. The alteration of the Limitation-law for these districts, and I should think for the country generally, in the direction in which it is proposed to alter it in this Bill seems to me to rest on very substantial grounds.

" There was one remark made by my hon'ble colleague Mr. Stokes at the commencement of his speech in regard to the scope of the Bill, with reference to the instructions which we have received from the Secretary of State, with which, if I understood him correctly, I am unable to concur. I do not conceive that this Government is either positively bound to enact every provision which was recommended in the despatch of the Secretary of State, or that it is debarred from going beyond those provisions, if, on full consideration, it appears to us that the main object which the Secretary of State had in view will be advanced by our enacting additional provisions which were not contemplated by him. Everything that the Secretary of State has written on the subject of this Bill, as well as on all other subjects, whether relating to executive or legislative matters, is entitled to the most careful and respectful attention of the Council of the Governor General. But it does not appear to me that in such a case as this, or indeed in any case, the Government of India is precluded from deviating from the letter of those instructions; or, at all events, from urging their reconsideration, if such a course should be deemed necessary. I conceive that it is quite open to us, if any of the provisions recommended by the Secretary of State to be inserted in a project of law appear to us to be either inexpedient or impracticable or inadequate, to make such alterations or additions as we deem to be required.

" It only remains for me to advert to the remarks made by His Honour the Lieutenant-Governor—remarks for which I think the Government and this Council are very much indebted to His Honour—because it is very desirable that it should be known to the public generally, and to the community which will be affected by this Bill, that the question raised by the Lieutenant-Governor has not been overlooked by the Government of India; that, on the contrary, the view which is entertained by the Government of India on that particular question is, I may say, entirely in accordance with the opinion expressed by Mr. Egerton. With the permission of your Lordship I will read the concluding paragraph of the letter which was addressed to the Government of Bombay previous to the preparation of the draft Bill, which, as I have said, formed the basis of the Bill now before the Council. After making various observations, which form the subject of fifteen paragraphs of the letter, in regard to the general scope and tenor of the projected legislation, the Government of India expressed themselves as follows on the particular point to which the Lieutenant-Governor alluded :—

'There is one point, however, which, although it may positively not involve legislation, appears to the Governor General in Council to demand further consideration from the Bombay Government, namely, *the possibility of adapting the assessment of the land-revenue to the variations in the season.* This question is discussed in paragraph 10 of the Bombay Government letter of the 6th April, 1877. The Governor General in Council fully agrees in the view that, in ordinary cases and where the land-revenue is moderate, it would not be good, either for the ryots or for the public treasury, that the land-revenue demand should fluctuate. But the system which is best for districts enjoying an ordinary regular rainfall may not be the best for the arid tract of the Central Deccan, where (it is said that) a good rainfall comes only once in three years. In view of the very great fall of prices and the vicissitudes of season in the Deccan during the last few years, it would be desirable that the present Government of Bombay should consider whether the recent (1873-75) revisions of the revenue have given sufficient relief from an assessment which was based, in part, on an unduly high estimate of the normal value of field produce in the Deccan. And, further, the Governor General in Council would wish the Government of Bombay to consider whether in these four districts, or in parts of them, it would not be wise to have *a varying scale of revenue* demand to be applied in unfavourable seasons, whereby the normal assessment might be reduced by a certain percentage over an entire district, or division of a district, in the event of a failure of rain or other cause of serious damage to the crops.'

" These instructions expressly refer only to the four districts included in the scope of this Bill; but I quite agree with His Honour the Lieutenant-Governor that they are instructions which are probably very applicable to many other districts, not only in Bombay but in other Provinces in other parts of the Empire. And I may mention that at this moment, and for some time past, the expediency of applying such a system to another district in another part of India—I refer to the district of Jhánsi—is, and has been, under the consideration of the Executive Government."

His Excellency the President here adjourned the debate to the following day, and the remainder of the business was proceeded with.

Abstract of the Proceedings of the Council of the Governor General of India, assembled for the purpose of making Laws and Regulations under the provisions of the Act of Parliament 24 & 25 *Vic., cap.* 67.

The Council assembled at Government House on Friday the 18th July 1879.

PRESENT:

His Excellency the Viceroy and Governor General of India, G.M.S.I., *presiding*.
His Honour the Lieutenant-Governor of the Panjáb, C.S.I.
His Excellency the Commander-in-Chief, G.C.B.
The Hon'ble Sir A. J. Arbuthnot, K.C.S.I.
Colonel the Hon'ble Sir Andrew Clarke, R.E., K.C.M.G., C.B., C.I.E.
The Hon'ble Sir John Strachey, G.C.S.I.
General the Hon'ble Sir E. B. Johnson, R.A., K.C.B.
The Hon'ble Whitley Stokes, C.S.I.
The Hon'ble Rivers Thompson, C.S.I.
The Hon'ble F. R. Cockerell.
The Hon'ble Sayyad Ahmad Khán Bahádur, C.S.I.
The Hon'ble T. C. Hope, C.S.I.
The Hon'ble B. W. Colvin.

DEKKHAN AGRICULTURISTS RELIEF BILL.

The adjourned debate on the Bill was resumed this day.

The Hon'ble Mr. Rivers Thompson said:— "My Lord, in the very few remarks which I wish to offer on the resumption of this important debate, I have no desire to question the propriety of the free and impartial criticisms which have passed upon many details of the Bill before the Council, but would prefer to confine myself to the general aspects of the measure; because I think, from the tendency of many of the observations which we heard yesterday it would seem as if we were losing sight of the main principles which we wish to maintain, and of the causes which have led to the interference of the Government in a matter which, if special reasons did not exist, it would have been right to leave to the ordinary laws and procedure of our Civil Courts. For my own part, I take no exception to the severity of those criticisms; for I think when a case of such grave and far-reaching importance, and one which has occupied the attention of Government for many years, comes before the Legislature of the Supreme Government, it is necessary and desirable, and not incompatible with an earnest desire for an effective solution of long-standing and serious difficulties, that there should be the most unqualified freedom of debate. I think it right to express this opinion very decidedly, because, obviously, we are not dealing with a sudden emergency of the immediate past, nor with a question in which unanimity of opinion has always existed as to the relief to be afforded, but one the magnitude of which has claimed the close attention of successive administrators in the single Presidency affected by the Bill, and for the remedy of which innumerable proposals have been put forward by the most experienced officers upon whom it has devolved to consider the matter. In confirmation of this view I would refer the Council to the single page at the beginning of the second volume of the Commission's Report, from which it will be seen this complicated question of the Deccan ryot's indebtedness and troubles has since 1843-44 been continuously before the Local Government; and in the *précis* of correspondence on the remedial measures from time to time under notice, we find the recommendations of the Bombay Government in 1844; suggestions by the Chief Justice in 1863; proposals by Captain Wingate in 1852; by Mr. Fraser Tytler in 1859; by the Hon'ble Mr. West's pamphlet in 1872, and by Mr. Pedder's report about the same year. Even of these it is said that the summary covers but a fractional part of the recommendations with which the Bombay records abound.

"With such facts before us it is inconceivable, in the first place, that any single measure, and that referring chiefly to the procedure of the Courts, should provide the complete cure of evils of such great intensity and arising from such a vast variety and combination of causes; and, secondly, it is impossible that, constituted as this Council is and representing the different experiences of different parts of the Indian Empire, even that single measure, framed on exceptional lines for a special object and to be tentatively applied, should not elicit a diversity of opinion on many of its details. For myself, therefore, I may say that, while I listened with the greatest interest to the speeches of Hon'ble Members objecting to detached provisions of the Bill, and value their contributions so far as they demand a careful scrutiny of the impugned sections, I maintain still the necessity which is imposed upon us as the Government of the country to support the leading principles on which the Hon'ble Member in charge of the Bill would propose to legislate. At this stage—the second reading, if I may so call it of the Bill—it would have been open to any member, as I understand the rules, to attack the principles of the measure and to oppose its reference to a Select Committee. I am glad that no such course has been taken. It seems to me that, having regard to the time and labour which preceded its introduction—to the urgent request of the Local Government for such a law—and to the correspondence which has passed with the Secretary of State, it would have been unreasonable to have done so. And if in some of its features it still appears open to objection, I would remind the Council that the Bill has still to go to the Bombay Government for reconsideration, with a request that it may be submitted to the learned Judges of the High Court of that Presidency, and that, when their views upon the measure have been received (and I have no doubt their attention will be directed to all the points of difference which this debate has brought out), it has afterwards to undergo a detailed revision by the Select Committee here. There is thus ample security that no hurried or imperfect project of law will issue from this Council.

"I take it that the general view in which we may regard the position of the question so far as this Bill is concerned, is that, upon the evidence adduced by the Commission, which gives no uncertain sound in the matter, the districts of the Deccan, with an impoverished and ignorant population, are suffering from our having imported into them laws and institutions suited only to an advanced and educated community; and that, where the people are not educated and not prepared for an elaborate and technical procedure in the administration of the law, we are bound to introduce for their benefit some simpler form for the adjustment of their numerous disputes. I share in no way the sentiments expressed by the Hon'ble Member from Bombay as to the character and effect of the regular civil code procedure upon the country. Though I did not remember his exact words, and am unable at this moment to refer to his speech, I think I am not incorrect in stating that he looks upon the 650 sections of the Civil Procedure Code as a burden too heavy to be borne by India, and as a curse from which it should be relieved. It requires no words from me to rebut such radical sentiments; but, if the Hon'ble Member considers that his present scheme of procedure in civil actions between creditors and debtors is a model for general imitation, or is capable of extension to all classes of the people and to all parts of the country, I am sure not only that he will be disappointed in his expectations, but that most people will rejoice at his disappointment. On the exceptional grounds that we are in the presence of a great calamity, I am prepared to support this Bill. That calamity in the Deccan is due in part to the caprices of climate and to the natural evils to which all Indian agriculture is exposed, and which no Government action could prevent or anticipate. But, so far as it is in our power to help, by the establishment of special Courts, by an increase in the number of the Judges, and by the substitution of less complex rules and laws of procedure, in the settlement of difficulties for which, in an embittered social condition especially, our present law is unsuited or inadequate, I have accepted this measure as a tentative proposal for the relief of the emergency. In that character I am ready to support it as desirable for the present need; and in that character I am prepared to favour any reasonable amendments when they come before us for later consideration.

" At the same time, My Lord, I think we must all feel that, however necessary and urgent this present measure of legislative reform is, it is but a small instalment of the remedies which the disorder demands. We have to deal with a case of poverty, ignorance and indebtedness among the people prevalent in these districts for a long series of years, dating, I believe in some parts, to a period antecedent to our advent as rulers; and a heavy responsibility rests upon the Local Government to meet the claims of the case by liberal administrative arrangements. The country possibly needs the introduction of a system of canal irrigation, and it certainly will not suffer by the extension of its schools and the improvement of those which are already in existence. I hope the attention of His Excellency the Governor of Bombay will be attracted also to the remarks of my hon'ble friend the Lieutenant-Governor of the Panjáb as to inflexible terms under which the Government revenue is realized; and, though the difficulties of that problem are great in the presence of what I believe to be generally a light assessment, the attempt to solve that problem and the caution necessary at the revision of settlements in the matter of the enhancement of the land-revenue will receive, I am satisfied, the consideration which the great importance of the subject demands at the hands of the Bombay Government."

The Hon'ble Sir John Strachey said :—" I hope I shall not detain the Council for any length of time to-day, but I do not ike to remain altogether silent when a subject of such importance is under discussion. The subject, although, no doubt, it now comes before the Council in an extreme and aggravated shape, is one which has occupied the minds of Indian statesmen for a very long time past.

" I myself have repeatedly had to take part in discussions which have virtually been identical with those in which we are now engaged, and my hon'ble friend Mr. Hope did me the honour to quote opinions which I expressed some twenty years ago. Consequently, whatever may be the value of my ' prophetic strain ' in judging what the effect of this measure may be, I may, at any rate, claim the qualification of ' old experience.'

"I may say, in the first place, that I think the Government and the public are greatly indebted to Mr. Hope for the able and interesting account which he gave to us yesterday of the unfortunate condition of these districts of the Deccan and for the Bill which the Bombay Government has prepared in communication with him; and I think that we are the more indebted to Mr. Hope for the great care that he has given to this question; and this Bill is the more important because, unfortunately, a great deal that has been said is true, not only of the Deccan, but of many other parts of India also. I think my hon'ble friend Mr. Colvin could tell us very nearly as lamentable a story about the state of Jhánsi as Mr. Hope has told us regarding the Deccan; and I am afraid others could tell us equally lamentable stories about some other parts of India. These of course are, nevertheless, extreme and exceptional cases; for, taking India as a whole, it is, beyond a doubt, a happy and a prosperous country. Nevertheless, much that we have been told of the state of the Deccan is more or less true of the peasantry in some other provinces, and, therefore, although the problems now before us possess special local urgency, they have also a more general interest, and I think there can be no doubt that the success or failure of the experiment which we are now about to try may have results which will extend far beyond the limits of the Deccan.

"My Lord, I do not propose to criticise any of the details of this Bill, and there is a good deal in it which I, for my part, do not feel competent to criticise; for there is much in it which requires local knowledge without the possession of which no useful opinion can, in my opinion, be given. While the Government of India is entirely responsible for the general principles on which this Bill is based, and while the Executive Government has been unanimous in accepting those principles which have been most fully and most carefully considered, the Bill is in its details essentially a local Bill; and, in judging of these details I think that local opinion must to a very great extent guide us. The discussion of yesterday shows, as my hon'ble friend Mr. Thompson has justly observed, that in regard to the details of the Bill there will be a very great diversity of opinion; but I agree with Mr. Thompson in the satisfaction he expressed that nothing that was said yesterday, so far as I can judge, touches really the main principles on which the Bill is based. The matters referred to yesterday are, after all, all, or nearly all, matters of detail, which, until they are fought out and decided in the ordinary way by a majority of this Council, we must be content to differ about.

"No one has denied the necessity for special legislation to meet the great evils which have been described. We desire to give to every man the means of cheap and speedy justice near his own home : and cheap and speedy justice means the simplest possible procedure of the Courts, and we desire that these Courts should be Courts of equity in the broadest sense, doing simple justice between man and man, and creditor and debtor alike. We desire also, further, that every effort should be made to bring about amicable agreements without imposing upon debtors and creditors the necessity of going into Court at all by the establishment, in some form or other, of Courts of Conciliation.

" Speaking of justice to creditors, I may say that I think that justice has hardly been done to Mr. Hope by some of the remarks which have been made in criticism of his speech of yesterday.

" I do not understand that Mr. Hope made any such general attack upon the creditors as has been attributed to him. I understood him to recognize in the clearest way that the money-lender is an essential element in the agricultural system of the Deccan and of India; and he quite admitted that protection and security for the creditors were as necessary as protection for the debtors.

" It would be a great misfortune and mistake if people were to suppose that the Government approved the idea of a crusade against the money-lenders. Money-lenders are obviously as necessary to the Indian agriculturist as the seed which he sows, or as the rain which falls from heaven to water his fields. Agriculture without them would probably be impossible ; but, while I believe this of the money-lenders, and have no doubt it is quite true that vast numbers of them—I hope I may say the great majority of them—are honest and honourable men, it seems to me that it is impossible to ignore the vast amount of evidence which exists in proof that there are still very many of them who deserve a different character, and that this section of the money-lending class is so numerous that it has become absolutely necessary to give to the debtor some better protection against it than is now available. In regard to these questions between creditor and debtor there have always been two great parties ; and it is inevitable that the old discussions on this subject should again be entered into in regard to the Bill now before the Council. With reference to this question I should like, with your Excellency's permission, to read to the Council a passage from the admirable speech made by Sir Arthur Hobhouse on the 28th March 1877 on the Code of Civil Procedure. It appears to me entirely applicable to the present case, and I think that it serves excellently to illustrate the principles upon which we are now proposing to legislate. Sir Arthur Hobhouse said :—

' I will try to show what seem to me to be the broad differences of opinion between the opposing parties.

' I may be wrong, and I hardly suppose that our opponents will accept my view of what is necessary to make their position a sound one; but it seems to me that they cannot support their objections without first making good two propositions. The first of these is that, when a man has made a contract with another man, he is entitled to call upon the supreme forces of society to step in and enforce his contract in every jot and tittle, and that without allowing to society any moderating influence over the contract, unless, perhaps, it can be shown to be grounded in fraud. The second proposition is that a contract by A to pay B a hundred rupees is a contract by A to strip himself of every shred of property that he possesses in order to make good that hundred rupees.

'Now, both these propositions seem to be exaggerations of principles which, if stated with their due qualifications, most people will be ready to accept. Of the first proposition, I should say that is a most sound and important principle that people should be held to the substantial performance of their contracts. But I should add that, if the rigid and extreme performance of contracts is found to produce misery and disorder, then society, which is called in to enforce these contracts, should exercise some moderating influence over them, and that such a duty is the more imperative in proportion to the helplessness of the debtor class. Of the second proposition I should say that a contract to pay a sum of money seems to me quite a different thing from a contract that the borrower shall strip himself of all the property that he has for the support of himself and his family in order to pay that money. It may be argued that, in order to enforce a contract to pay money, it is the duty of society to step in and strip the borrower naked. But I do not see how it is even arguable that, if such a process takes place, the creditor does not get something outside the terms of his contract. If he does, terms may be reasonably imposed upon him in return, such as are found necessary for the peace and welfare of society.

' How far society should step in and insist upon some moderation as the price of its assistance, is a question of detail which has to be solved in every age and in every country. But it seems to me that all laws intended for the protection of debtors on terms short of the payment of the whole debt —laws of bankruptcy, laws for the exemption of property from execution— are founded on the view I take of the duties and interests of society.'

"The principle thus laid down by Sir Arthur Hobhouse is, I think, the basis of our proposed legislation now. Those 'duties and interests of society' of which Sir Arthur Hobhouse spoke require most urgently that we should interfere in the districts of the Deccan between creditors and debtors. We shall hurt no honest, honourable and reasonable creditors ; and, if this legislation and other measures of relief should be successful, and happier times should come round, I for my part shall not think it a matter of regret if the dishonest and rapacious money-lender finds no means to recover his ill-gotten gains, and if, after all the claims of justice to all parties have been met, he is left to lament, like Sganarelle,—

" tout le monde est content ; il n'y a que moi seul de malheureux. Mes gages, mes gages, mes gages !'

" There is only one other point to which I wish to refer. I entirely agree with my hon'ble friends the Lieutenant-Governor and Mr. Thompson with regard to the extreme importance of sparing no administrative efforts to improve the revenue system in such a way that the pressure of the Government demand upon the land may be lightened. This problem has to be solved not only in Bombay but throughout nearly the whole of India.

" There can be no doubt that the demand of the Government is almost everywhere moderate. Mr. Hope has assured us that in the districts of the Deccan in particular there can be no doubt of its moderation.

" In other parts of India with which I myself am acquainted, I know that the same is true, and that our revenue demand is far lighter than that ever imposed by any Native ruler. Nevertheless, it is equally true that this demand upon the land falls not infrequently in bad seasons with extreme severity. It is not that the assessment is too heavy, but that the procedure under which it is levied is too rigid. I cannot doubt that means will be found—although they unfortunately have not been found up to the present time—to combine complete and proper security for the recovery of the Government demand upon the land with some greater leniency to the peasant-proprietors, who, from no fault of their own, but from misfortune of season, cannot meet their engagements to the State. Bombay has now for its Governor a great administrator : if he can initiate measures in the direction to which I have now been referring, he will do a greater service to the country than any which this Council can accomplish by this Bill."

The Hon'ble Mr. Hope said :—" I am glad to find that the main principles of the Bill, which have, as I was already aware, the approval of the Executive Government, are also, I think I may venture to say, accepted by this Council, and that my task is confined to replying upon what are, by comparison, matters of detail.

" In the first place, it was suggested by the Hon'ble the Law Member that chapter XX of the Civil Procedure Code, as amended in the Bill presented yesterday, would meet all the wants of our Deccan districts in respect of insolvency. But I must altogether demur to accepting it as sufficient or suitable for that purpose. The objections to the law, even when amended by the Bill, which I stated yesterday need not be repeated ; but I may add to them that the provision for granting a discharge when an insolvent has paid one-third of the scheduled debts, which has been imported from the Presidency Insolvency Act, seems to me false in principle, and likely to work unreasonably in practice, sometimes giving the creditor less than might be recovered for him, and sometimes pressing harshly on the debtor. It has, moreover, been discarded from bankruptcy legislation in England. I admit that by the Bill in question an advance has been made; but an advance somewhat haphazard, tentative and restricted by the difficulty as to insufficiency of Courts, &c., which, as I said yesterday, has hitherto prevented this Council from going even so far as is now ventured on. Finally, one thing which that amended chapter does *not* do is, singularly enough, the very thing which has been represented in the official correspondence, and is indicated in the Secretary of State's despatch, as urgently required—namely, the allowing a debtor to apply for declaration of insolvency, though no process has issued against him.

"Another remark of the Hon'ble Law Member was that it would be sufficient, as to jurisdiction of the Courts, if Small-Cause-Court powers were conferred on all of them. But it seems to me that the only course open to us consistent with common sense is that the Courts should have power to deal with all the sorts of cases in which ryots are ordinarily involved. That such cases must very frequently comprise mortgages, is clear from the fact ascertained by the Commission, as I said yesterday, that in the villages in Poona tested by them two-thirds of the indebted ryots' land was mortgaged. To provide Courts professing to deal with ryots' difficulties, but unable to touch, perhaps, one-half of the cases in which ryots are concerned, would be a half-measure, from which no good results could be expected.

"The next question raised is that of appeals, for which the Hon'ble Law Member considers the revision provided for by the Bill an inadequate substitute. Here I may point out that the Bill goes farther in caution than even the suggestions of the Secretary of State. His Lordship says, in the quotation which I read yesterday: 'I am inclined to think that summary jurisdiction without appeal might be conferred experimentally on all Civil Judges in the Deccan with great benefit.' But the Bill provides the safeguard of a thorough supervision. It is a misapprehension to suppose, as I understood the Hon'ble Mr. Cockerell to do, that the supervising agency will be a special one. It will be merely a strengthening of the regular staff for the purpose of thoroughly carrying out section 9 of the Bombay Civil Courts Act (XIV of 1869), which runs thus :—

'The District Judge shall have general control over all the Civil Courts and their establishments within the district, and it shall be his duty to inspect, or to cause one of his assistants to inspect, the proceedings of all the Courts subordinate to him, and to give such directions,' &c.

" The officers appointed will be members of the regular judicial department subordinate to the High Court: they will work the law subject to its general control: the Local Government will have no special jurisdiction over them, and will be unable to make them, as the Hon'ble Member apprehends, a machine for carrying out the policy of the day.

" As to the merits of allowing appeals, compared with a system of revision, I would point out that by the former from three to four per cent. of the cases tried are brought before the Courts, while by the latter the proportion is probably not less than from fifty to sixty per cent. Moreover, the cases which come up in appeal are often not those which deserve to come. Many a man who has a good case cannot afford to appeal: many a man with money needlessly drags his opponent through all the Appellate Courts. As an illustration of the persistency of monied litigants, I may mention that I have heard that Sir Barnes Peacock, with reference to the petty appeals, about Rs. 5 sometimes, by which the High Court was troubled, remarked that it would be more economical for Government to pay the amount of the appeals than to keep up Judges and establishments to hear them. Again, the Hon'ble Law Member has said, as an objection to revision, that the record called for will be inaccurate, incomplete and in the vernacular. As to inaccuracy and incompleteness, the objection, if good at all, applies just as much to appeals as to revision. As to the third point, I feel it my duty to repudiate, on behalf of the Bombay Civil Service, of which I have the honour to be a member, the suggestion that they are unable to deal with cases in the vernacular. Again, the Subordinate Judges will not be inexperienced, as the Hon'ble Member supposes. It is true that twelve new men will be appointed; but they will be added, as stated in the official letter from Bombay, to the list of Subordinate Judges for the whole Presidency: and I cannot doubt that the Executive Government will place men of experience, drawn from other districts, in charge of the newly-opened Courts.

" In favour of the retention of appeals, much stress has been laid on the mortgage cases, which are said to be intricate, involving difficult questions of account. But this is a misapprehension. Mortgage-cases in which ryots are concerned are not necessarily intricate, and do not involve more accounts than simple money-cases. This can easily be seen by reference to the actual cases of ryots of which a large number are given in full detail in the Appendices to the Commission's Report. If a ryot owes money, there is an account of it—possibly long and intricate; but it is no more so when he happens to have pledged his land as security for the debt than when he has not. Mortgage-cases are usually only difficult if they happen to involve questions of priorities and the like, or there are several creditors."

The Hon'ble Sir Alexander Arbuthnot enquired whether there might not be questions of title.

The Hon'ble Mr. Hope replied :—"Under the Bombay revenue system the name of the owner of every field is entered in the Government books. It would only be in most rare instances that the man whose name appeared was not the real owner; and so questions of title are not likely to give trouble.

"I may mention to the Council," the Hon'ble Mr. Hope continued, "that, as regards this question of appeals, contrasted with revision, I happen to have had a very considerable experience—if not actually in civil cases, still in criminal ones, which for this purpose come to the same thing. I was once for a long time Magistrate and Collector of a district so large that appeals lay to me from the decisions of twenty-nine Subordinate Magistrates; and the cases they tried, which came up to me, and of which it was my duty regularly to examine a large proportion, sometimes reached five hundred in the month. My experience was that all the serious abuses and irregularities came to light in the examination and revision: scarcely anything ever came out in appeal. After all, however, the would-be appellant is deprived of nothing by the proposed substitution of inspection and revision; for he can draw attention to his case by petition, and practically get it dealt with just as he can now. If, as the Hon'ble Law Member says, Appellate Courts are less harsh than the Courts of first instance, there is nothing to prevent the revising Judge from showing leniency too: if Appellate Courts often confirm decisions on mere perusal of the record, his inspection may have the same effect.

"The Hon'ble Law Member has next expressed his fears that section 46, about agreements before conciliators, and also the registration-provisions, may be defeated by collusion and fraud. As to agreements, of which he seems to think their having the force of a decree the objectionable feature, I would point out that the case is analogous to that of awards filed under section 525 of the Civil Procedure Code, which have the force of a decree too. The objections, if there be any, to the one must apply equally to the other. As to both the agreements and the registration, I would repeat my observation of yesterday, that the same objection as to being open to fraud may be made to many other good laws. The Registration Act may, as the Hon'ble Sayyad Ahmad has said, be easily defeated by one party to a deed returning to the other at home the consideration which they have paid and received before the registrar. The stamp-laws are constantly evaded by the re-use of spoiled stamps, &c., and the coinage-laws do not prevent the circulation of false money. Yet we do not think it necessary on this account to abolish registration stamps and our coinage. The Bill will help those who help themselves: if any persons prefer collusive evasion of it, they will suffer accordingly, and rightly so.

"I will now notice the objections of the Hon'ble Law Member and Mr. Cockerell to certain details of the Insolvency chapter. First, as to the power given to the Court to admit as an insolvent a person found to be so, and to give him a discharge, both Hon'ble Members seem to me to be, if I may say so in all courtesy, still under that confusion of ideas between the fact of insolvency and the conduct of the insolvent which I referred to in my speech of yesterday. If a man is really insolvent it is perfectly futile to call him anything else. If a man cannot pay more than one anna—to take the Hon'ble Law Member's illustration,—the Court may *now*, under section 358 of the Code, let him off the whole balance, so that the Bill makes no change of principle whatever. Secondly, it is complained that section 20 is retrospective. But so is the present law; and so will be the new Civil Procedure Bill, which I hope we shall pass at our next sitting. If a man, the day after that Bill is passed, applies and is declared an insolvent, all the old decrees against him may be wiped out when he has paid only one-third of their amount, and after twelve years, whether he has paid even that much or not. Thirdly, as to imprisonment and the Hon'ble Mr. Cockerell's objections to the reduction, by section 35 of the Bill, of the power of Subordinate Judges under section 359 of the Code to imprison debtors up to one year for fraud, I have as great a hatred of 'proved rascality' as any one else. But I consider the power given by the Code a most arbitrary and oppressive one. So far from the rascality being really 'proved,' the Judge is practically allowed simply to say, at the end of the proceedings—'I think the insolvent's conduct very disreputable: he is no doubt a rascal'; and thereupon, without any specific charge, or hearing him in his defence, or even recording a judgment, to send him off to jail for a twelvemonth. In the Bill this power is, in the case of Subordinate Judges, reduced nearer to what officers of their rank and emoluments would exercise if they were Magistrates. It is essential to note, however, that the Court has always the alternative, under section 359, of sending the insolvent to a Magistrate. Before him, and not in any Civil Court, all serious rascality ought to be dealt with; and I hope it will be.

"To sec. 30 exception has been taken by the Hon'ble Sayyad Ahmad, Mr. Cockerell and the Law Member. The latter, after expressing his objections, concluded with some warmth by affirming his belief that I was the 'sole author' of the section, and giving as his reason for this belief that he 'did not remember anything about it in the Bombay letter.' If he attributes to me everything which is not mentioned in that letter, I presume that, by parity of reasoning, he acquits me of responsibility for everything he does not like which is, and I feel grateful for the relief accordingly. I must, however, protest against any such attempt to individualise the authorship of any particular parts of the Bill. The Hon'ble Member is well aware that the measure now before us is no private Bill; that it emanated from the Bombay Government; that, after modifications thought suitable, it is presented to this Council by the order, sanction and authority of the Government of India, and that I am officially charged with the duty of doing justice to it, irrespective of my personal convictions. I think the Hon'ble Member would have shown more generosity if he had abstained from the remark he has made, and if he had evinced some sympathy for, and desire to render less onerous, the difficult and delicate task I have to perform, instead of endeavouring to fix on me personally the odium of what he seems to consider one of the most obnoxious features of the Bill.

" Turning from this personal question—on which I entered with reluctance, and only from a sense of what was due to myself and to the Government—to the subject-matter of section 30, I find that making over moveable property at a valuation to a creditor is considered unfair ; and the Hon'ble Mr. Cockerell has enforced his objections by an illustration about a pig. Now it so happens that this provision is a very old and well-established one in English law, in execution of writs of *elegit*, which is thus described in a well-known text-book :—

'The sheriff is bound upon receipt of the *elegit* to empannel a jury, who are to enquire of all the goods and chattels of the debtor and appraise the same, and also to enquire as to his lands and tenements and their value. After inquisition had, the sheriff delivers to the execution-creditor all the goods and chattels of the debtor (except his oxen and beasts of the plough) at the value set upon them by the jury ; if they be insufficient, he delivers also execution of the lands, and he then returns the writ', &c.

" Between this English law and our Bill, however, there is this essential difference, that, whereas by the latter it is optional with the Court to use the power regarding any particular articles of property, or not at all, by the latter the action of the sheriff is unavoidable and compulsory. Whenever the Hon'ble Law Member returns, as in due time I hope he will, in health and honour to his native land, he will be liable, in the event of his having to resort to legal proceedings to recover money due to him, to have forced on him, at a valuation fixed by a jury, his debtor's goods and chattels—pig and all!

"With regard to the Hon'ble Sir Alexander Arbuthnot's remarks, I am glad to thank him for the kindly expressions of appreciation which fell from him, and to add my satisfaction that he found in my speech nothing to comment on more serious than what seemed to him the one-sidedness of my description of the money-lender. But I have every confidence that, when he is able to study my remarks in print at leisure, he will agree that I have done the money-lender full justice. It is no doubt difficult to catch the general scope, or even the exact words, of a long and rapidly-spoken address. Thus, the phrase 'usurious money-lender' which he ascribes to me I believe I did not employ. As to extravagant profits, I have nowhere attributed them to money-lenders. On the contrary, the very passage which he has read from paragraph 85 of the Commission's Report was the germ of my remark, that in the land money-lenders acquired 'what yields them at best a precarious profit, not exceeding that which reasonable rates of interest, combined with easy recovery, would produce, but wrung forth with trouble, anxiety, expense, popular execration, and even personal danger.' Nor did I say that in India fraud by the creditor was 'the only thing' to be guarded against. I said it had 'almost solely' to be so. Speaking as I did, in broad terms and of the Mofussil, what I said seems correct; and it is borne out by a recent remark of the Hon'ble Sir Charles Turner's, that even in the town of Madras the bulk of insolvents were not traders, but part of the general population. So far from keeping frauds by debtors in the background, however, I enumerated them specially, and explained the provisions of chapters VIII and IX for counteracting them. Finally, nothing could be more complete than the terms in which I have acknowledged the usefulness and necessity of the sowkár, and the propriety of giving him all fair help. In this respect the Hon'ble Sir John Strachey has done me no less than justice ; and I have, as I said, every confidence that the Hon'ble Sir Alexander Arbuthnot will eventually do the same. These remarks will, perhaps, be a sufficient reply to what the Hon'ble Mr. Rivers Thompson said on the same subject.

"In conclusion, I have only a few words to add on what fell from His Honour the Lieutenant-Governor of the Panjáb. I fully recognize, as he does, the gravity of the subject, and the possibility of this Bill being followed by similar legislation, or demands for it, in respect of other parts of India. But the circumstances of the different provinces of India are so diverse that I hold, and have held in other cases before this Council, that they need separate treatment. This Bill will, therefore, furnish to them, at most, an analogy and not a precedent. It is expressly a local Bill, and has been so deliberately made so, that a power of extension to other parts of the Bombay Presidency, which was in the draft, has been cut out. The subject of the other remedies of executive application has, as the Hon'ble Sir Alexander Arbuthnot has shown, been brought to the notice of the Executive Government. What I would, therefore, earnestly deprecate is, first, any hampering of the progress of the Bill by consideration of other parts of India ; secondly, any delay of it while executive remedies, which are a separate affair, are being matured ; and, lastly, any serious mutilation of it by the Select Committee or the Council. It should be remembered that the Bill is essentially local in character, and the outcome of careful consideration by those who are best acquainted with local circumstances, and the best judges of popular feeling and the probable result of what they recommend. The Bill has only come to this Council by accident, so to speak, through the local legislature not having power to pass such parts of it as affect the Civil Procedure Code. It should, therefore, be taken as a whole. Its main principles are already accepted by the Executive Government and, I think I may add, by this Council. If it be altered, cut down and emasculated in detail, it will end in *fiasco*, for which there will be no satisfaction to the Local Government in the reflection that it is not responsible."

His Excellency the President said :—" I do not think it consistent with the importance I personally attach, and which, I may add, the Government collectively attaches, to the subject of the motion now before us that my own vote upon this motion should be an altogether silent one. But the Bill introduced yesterday by the Hon'ble Mr. Hope has already been the subject of such prolonged and exhaustive comment, and also of such copious explanation by the Hon'ble Member himself, that I think I can promise that my own remarks upon it will not be very lengthy. I am the better able to make this promise because, in the observations made at the commencement of the discussion this morning by my hon'ble colleague Mr. Rivers Thompson, and at the close of the discussion yesterday by my hon'ble colleague Sir Alexander Arbuthnot, those Hon'ble Members largely anticipated what I should otherwise have wished to say myself on behalf of the Government as regards the various points to which they alluded. I think, however, that I gathered from the remarks of my hon'ble colleague Sir Alexander Arbuthnot that some words which had previously fallen from my hon'ble colleague Mr. Stokes had conveyed to his mind (and possibly, therefore, they may have conveyed it to the minds of other Hon'ble Members) an impression that the Member of this Government who is specially concerned in the conduct of its legislative business had characterized the vote he was about to give as a vote given in more or less reluctant compliance with instructions from the Secretary of State to the support of a measure which he generally deprecated. Now, I am bound to say that this was not the impression conveyed to my own mind by the remarks of my hon'ble colleague on the left (Mr. Stokes). I was listening, as I always do listen, with great attention and interest to his remarks ; and the impression they conveyed to my mind was essentially different from that which appeared reflected in the remarks of my hon'ble colleague on the right (Sir Alexander Arbuthnot). Had it been otherwise, I should not have failed to interrupt my hon'ble friend Mr. Stokes in order to afford him that opportunity, of which he is now deprived by our rules, of clearing his language from a construction entirely inconsistent with his position as a Member of this Government. But, whilst I am persuaded that the remarks of my hon'ble colleague were not quite accurately caught on this side of the table, I am grateful to my hon'ble friend Sir Alexander Arbuthnot for having promptly repudiated on behalf of the Government a position which I feel sure no member of it would be less willing to accept than my hon'ble friend Mr. Stokes. What I understood that Hon'ble Member to say, and what I believe he really did say (he will correct me if I misrepresent him), was simply this. He said that, whilst approving the purpose, and supporting the essential principles, of this measure, he found in it, as at present drafted, certain provisions which he could not reconcile himself to acquiesce in—*firstly*, because he regarded those provisions as unconstitutional; and, *secondly*, because he did not regard them as in any wise essential to the recognized purpose of the Bill. And then, in support of the view thus expressed by him, he went on to point out that those provisions had not been suggested, or even considered, by the Secretary of State, in concert with whom the essential principles of the Bill had been laid down by the Government of India. Well, whatever view be taken of those particular provisions,—and on such a subject the opinion of my hon'ble friend carries a weight of a legal authority which is entitled to the greatest respect—I must venture to say that the statement thus made by him appears to me perfectly consistent with the position and sentiments of the Government of India in reference to this measure, to which we, one and all of us, attach the greatest importance, and which we, one and all of us, are most earnestly desirous to carry into law without any avoidable delay. But it is precisely for this very reason—that is to say, because the measure now before us is a measure in which the Government is earnestly interested ; a measure in which our responsibility is largely concerned, and because, moreover, it is necessarily, and properly, of a more or less experimental and tentative character—

that it seems to me undesirable, even if it were practically possible, that on the part of its warmest well-wishers there should be at the present stage of it complete unanimity of opinion upon every one of its seventy-seven clauses. For my own part I am persuaded that nothing but great advantage can accrue from the fullest consideration of all points in connection with any portion of this Bill upon which differences of opinion have been entertained or expressed ; and I sincerely trust they will receive such consideration from the local and legal authorities, as well as from the Select Committee to which the Bill is about to be referred. The Government of India has not committed, in an equal degree, to every single detail of every single clause of this elaborate measure the maintenance of those important principles which we regard as absolutely essential to its efficiency. But on those principles the mind of the Government is unanimous, and we are fully resolved to maintain and enforce them.

" I should like for a moment to refer to the genesis—if I may so call it—of this measure. As pointed out just now by my hon'ble colleague Sir John Strachey, the distressed condition of the peasantry in many parts of the Deccan is a matter which has been long—perhaps too long—under the anxious consideration of the Government of India. It has been the subject of profuse correspondence and protracted inquiry ; and from all that correspondence and inquiry we were at length led to one very clear, definite and settled conclusion. That conclusion was that the case we have to deal with here is a special case, absolutely requiring special legislation. In that conclusion we have had the concurrence, support and approval of the Secretary of State ; and, having come to that conclusion, and at the same time most fully recognizing all the risks inseparable from special legislation of this kind, we deemed that our best security for the preparation of a thoroughly practical measure would be to obtain as speedily as possible the fullest available special knowledge and local experience on the subject of it. Well, it was with this object, and in this belief, that the Hon'ble Mr. Hope, who had given to this question long and special study, was deputed by the Government of India to proceed to Bombay, and there, in concert with the Bombay Government, and in personal conference with the Governor, whom my hon'ble colleague has justly called a most able and experienced administrator, to frame the measures which, at our request, he yesterday laid before this Council. Of course the measure thus framed naturally contains various clauses which have not been devised by the Government of India, and on which I do not think the Government of India is at present in a position to express any decisive opinion. Our position in regard to all these clauses is a very obvious one.

We deem it due to the Local Government, which is so especially and directly interested in the effects of this measure, and due also to its experienced coadjutor in preparing the measure, that no clause devised by them, whatever opinion may at present be entertained in regard to it, shall be altered or withdrawn, disturbed or modified, without the amplest and most searching examination during those preparatory stages through which the Bill has still to pass. But the Bill, as it now stands in its present form, satisfactorily embodies certain great principles on which the opinion of the Government is unanimous—principles which we believe to be essential to the efficiency of the measure. Those principles it is our intention to uphold intact; and on those principles the Government of India is not prepared to entertain any compromise at any stage of the Bill. The principles I refer to have been practically indicated in the course of our discussions, and they may, I think, be briefly enumerated under seven main heads. There is, in the *first* place, that power which was referred to yesterday—the power to go behind the bond; *secondly,* the necessity for simplifying the procedure; *thirdly,* the augmentation of the number of tribunals; *fourthly,* village registration, to which we attach great importance; *fifthly,* the establishment of Courts of Conciliation; *sixthly,* the extension of the period of limitation; and *seventhly,* the abolition of imprisonment for debt.

"All these principles are principles on which the Government of India has, after lengthened deliberation, come to a definite and final conclusion; and I certainly think that the Hon'ble Member who introduced this Bill was fully entitled to observe, as he did, that the general suitableness of the Bill is amply guaranteed by the lengthened deliberation with which it has been brought on to maturity. For my own part, I am of opinion that this measure has not come before us a day too soon; and I entirely agree with the Hon'ble Mr. Hope in thinking that, for the reasons stated by him, the passage of this measure into law at the earliest possible moment is a matter of supreme importance.

"The Hon'ble Member reminded us that it now rests with this Council to redeem the pledges given four years ago for the redress of grievances which have been thoroughly investigated and amply proved—grievances which are, indeed, too notorious to be disputed. But I think he might have gone even further, and taken deserved credit to himself for the fact that the measure now before the Council really represents the first serious effort to deal practically and directly with the deplorable state of things urged on the attention of the Legislature no less than twenty years ago by the Local Government. In 1858 Lord Elphinstone, who was then Governor of Bombay, passed in Council a Resolution which is very brief, and which, with the permission of the Council, I should like to read. It is as follows :—

'His Lordship in Council entertains no doubt of the fact that the labouring classes of the Native community suffer enormous injustice from the want of protection by law from the extortionate practices of money-lenders. He believes that our civil courts have become hateful to the masses of our Indian subjects from being made the instruments of the almost incredible rapacity of usurious capitalists. Nothing can be more calculated to give rise to widespread discontent and disaffection to the British Government than the practical working of the present law. The attention of the Legislative Council on the subject should be requested, and copy of the Revenue Commissioner's letter forwarded for their consideration.'

"I think there can be no doubt that the state of things that Resolution describes has since then gone on growing from bad to worse; and, so far as I am aware, up to the present moment there has really been no practical effort made to deal directly with it. The Code of Civil Procedure has been completed; the Usury Law has been revoked; but these measures have not been taken with special reference to the condition of the rural population in the Deccan: and I do not think it can be asserted by anybody that the condition of the peasantry of that part of India has been appreciably affected by those measures. For my own part, I must say that I regret that the effort now being made has been so long deferred. I regret the circumstances in which this measure has been introduced. I do so because I cannot but fear that in those circumstances there is much that may not impossibly expose the motives of the Government in the eyes of ill-disposed or superficial observers to misconstruction. That part of India for which we are now legislating has again been afflicted with social disturbances. I think it not improbable that many persons will be disposed to attribute the source of those disturbances to the still unremedied condition of the indebted ryot. As a matter of fact, that supposition would be erroneous. There is no evidence in support of it; and there is much evidence to the contrary which points to a very different cause of these troubles. I have lately received several communications from the Government of Bombay on the recent disturbances and dacoities in the Deccan; and this is what His Excellency writes :—

'There is no sign of agrarian connexion in this case—that is, the landholding community had nothing to do with it. This disposes of the idea that indebtedness of ryots is at the bottom after to them'.

"I have no doubt that Sir Richard Temple, who is in the best position to do so, has arrived at a sound conclusion on that point. But I would ask the Council—is it not obvious that—if in any part of India the actual cultivators of the soil see not only the proceeds of their labour, but actually their personal freedom, passing from them into the hands of a class whom, rightly or wrongly, they regard as the authors of their ruin, and under the operation of laws which, rightly or wrongly, they regard as the engines of it—the bitterness of sentiment, the sense of hopelessness and irremediable wrong, engendered by such a state of things must be a chronic incentive, if not to social disturbances of this kind, at least to personal crime? Allusion has been frequently made in the course of this discussion to the report of the Deccan Riots Commission; and that report abounds in evidence that this is actually the case. I select a single instance furnished by the First Assistant Collector of Ahmednagar. He writes :—

'Another sad case occurred at Visápur, táluka Tásgaon. One Appa Rowji owed money on a bond to Hirachand Guzar. Hirachand threatened to sell him up, but promised not to do so if Appa Rowji would get one Appa Malli to go bail for him. Appa Malli was accordingly induced to befriend Appa Rowji, and passed a bond for Rs. 200 to the Guzar, giving as security for payment his house and land. The agreement was that Appa Rowji should at the same time give to Appa Malli a bond of Rs. 400 with his land as security. Other money was owing by Appa Rowji to Appa Malli, which made the whole amount up to Rs. 400. This bond, however, was never forthcoming. Time after time Appa Malli was put off. Meanwhile, the Guzar lost no time in enforcing the bond for Rs. 200 which Appa Malli had so weakly executed. His house and lands were seized after all due proceedings in the civil Court; and, to add insult to injury, the latter were given to Appa Rowji to cultivate. Accordingly, Appa Malli, despairing of obtaining redress by the ordinary course of law against his more crafty opponent, waylaid Hirachand Guzar and murdered him in open daylight, and in the presence of several witnesses. He confessed everything, and courted the fullest inquiry into his money transactions. Appa Malli has been hanged as a matter of course. Such executions, however, would appear to have little effect in deterring others placed in similar circumstances from committing similar crimes. Nor, on the other hand, do the Guzars appear to grow a whit less grasping through fear of meeting a violent death at the hands of maddened debtors. The motive in all these cases is the same; and in all these appears an utter recklessness which is deplorable in the extreme. Careless and untutored, the ryots learn by bitter experience that they have little chance of obtaining redress in the civil Courts against the more cunning sowkárs. Brooding over their wrongs, real or fancied, makes them desperate; and in an evil hour, without fear for the present or hope for the future, they turn upon their oppressors. It is certainly the case that in our Courts, as at present constituted, the poor and ignorant have no chance against the wealthy and clever.'

" I do not wish to multiply illustrations of this kind, which might be very easily done; nor do I desire to dwell on this particular one. Nothing could be further from my own wishes, or more contrary to my own views, than to lend countenance to a popular cry, which in so far as it is general I believe to be unjust against that much-abused, but most important and useful, class of middle-men on whose co-operation the agricultural industry of this country is entirely dependent. I should be very sorry if anything said in the course of this discussion appeared to give on the part of the Government countenance to such a cry. I do not, of course, suppose for a moment that the sowkár and the baniyá are, as a class, invariably animated by the highest moral sentiments, but I do not believe that, in the exercise of their calling, they show a greater indifference to honesty than any other class exposed to similar temptations and difficulties. My hon'ble colleague truly pointed out yesterday that there is ample evidence in the report of this Commission that the source of their profits are extremely precarious as well as unpopular. Nor is there any evidence that those profits, as a rule, are unfair. The creditor is, no less than the debtor, entitled to the protection of the law in the maintenance of his honest interests; and any legislation unduly directed against the small capitalist to the unfair advantage of the debtor might very possibly paralyse the whole agricultural industry of this country by shaking to its foundation the system of credit upon which its operations are conducted. But, in saying this, I think it obvious that what is good for the honest debtor is also good for the honest creditor. It cannot be to the interests of the sowkár that the ryot, who is his partner in the operations of agricultural industry, should be systematically pauperised and embittered against him. It cannot be for the interest of the community itself that the relations between these two classes should be such as to provoke feelings of animosity, often breaking out into crime, upon either one side or the other; and I think it cannot be doubted that, in that part of the Deccan for which we are now legislating, the relations between the sowkár and the ryot have been brought by a variety of causes into a condition which no legislator could have ever contemplated, and which must withdraw popular confidence and esteem from any law which artificially tends to perpetuate it. The Hon'ble Member who introduced this Bill referred to Mr. Pedder; and I think no one will dispute that of this state of things there is no more competent observer than Mr. Pedder. Mr. Pedder sketched, not long ago, in the pages of a London periodical a very graphic picture of this state of things drawn from the life; and, so far as I am aware, I do not think the truth of that picture has ever been challenged. But I can say that in the truth of such a picture I find the amplest justification for the special and exceptional legislation embodied in this Bill. This is how Mr. Pedder describes the career of a Deccan ryot who has once fallen into debt :—

'The indebted peasant executes a bond, bearing high interest and burdened with onerous conditions. For a couple of years he is not pressed; but when the period of limitation is drawing near, he is told that his payments cover only what he has had in necessaries, and that the sum borrowed, with interest, is still due. He pays something and executes a fresh bond on still more onerous terms for the balance, with a premium for renewal. Then he pays all he can; yet, at the end of the next period of limitation, finds that the debt has increased. Perhaps the process of execution of fresh bonds is repeated again and again; but at last the sowkár deems it desirable to bring a suit. In nine cases out of ten it is decided *ex parte*, because the people say it is useless to appear in Court unless they can deny execution of the bond sued for, or without the aid of a pleader, whom they have not the means to pay. The creditor then partially executes the decree by sale of the cattle, household utensils and other personal property of the debtor, and holds over him the threat of imprisonment in satisfaction of the balance. Even female honour is sometimes the price of forbearance. * * * * Thenceforward, lending the peasant on exorbitant terms the seed and cattle absolutely necessary for cultivation, he takes all the produce of the land, except the barest subsistence of the nominal owner and his family. * * * * But sometimes the creditor sells the land of the debtor in execution, and usually buys it in at a price very far below its value, leaving the balance of the decree unsatisfied, since no peasant dares to bid against a powerful sowkár, and it would be thought unbusiness-like in another sowkár to do so. Then the best that can happen to the unfortunate yeoman is to remain as a tenant-at-will at an exorbitant rack-rent on the land he once owned. * * * * If the creditor does not allow this, the peasant flies the country, and tries to begin life again in some distant locality. * * * * Even there, unless he takes refuge in foreign territory, the arm of the law reaches the judgment-debtor as soon as he has got together a little property. * * * * As soon as the colonists, who are assisted with advances by Government, have acquired any property, it is seized in execution of decrees for old debts. * * * * There is, however, a depth lower than penury or exile. Sometimes the wretched debtor executes an agreement which almost avowedly makes him the bond-slave of his creditor.'

" Well, then, that is the state of things for the remedy of which this Bill has been introduced. My hon'ble friend, the Lieutenant-Governor, pointed out to us yesterday what I am afraid is only too true, that this state of things exists, not indeed in the same degree of intensity, yet more or less potentially as it were, throughout the greater part of India, where a comparatively slight aggravation of existing circumstances might not impossibly produce results scarcely less distressing than those which it is our present object to mitigate in some parts of the Deccan. In view of this fact, His Honour observed that the condition of the Indian peasant could only be partially improved by the measure we are now taking for his protection from the exorbitance of claims upon the part of the money-lender, unless we simultaneously relieve him from the unvarying pressure of claims on the part of the State itself, by relaxing the rigidity of our land-revenue system. Well, I do not feel in a position to enter into that question, which is a very large and very important one. I may say at once that the Government is certainly not indifferent to any of the considerations which suggested the remarks of my hon'ble friend. It was mentioned yesterday by my hon'ble colleague Sir Alexander Arbuthnot that this question has been urged by us on the attention of the Government of Bombay in special reference to those districts of the Deccan for which we are now legislating, and that it has engaged our own attention in reference to other parts of India. I may add that this question, in all its aspects and bearings, was some time ago commended by the Government of India to the special attention of the Famine Commission, from whose report I anticipate much practical aid in the further consideration of it. The indifference of the Government to this aspect of the question must not, therefore, be assumed from the absence of all allusion to it in the terms of the present measure. I am personally disposed to believe that the rigidity of our present land system might in various directions be relaxed with great benefit to the cultivator, unaccompanied by any serious inconvenience to the State. But, were I now to indicate my own views on this important question, I feel that any expression of them would be necessarily crude and premature, inviting discussion on a subject which is not at present under the consideration of this Council. All that I am concerned to point out is that alterations in the *modus operandi* of our land-revenue system, whether as regards the collection assessment of revenue, can be effected without legislation; and that, therefore, the provisions of the Bill now before us are properly confined to those remedial measures which absolutely require not only legislation, but legislation of a special and somewhat novel character. The Bill in this respect embodies certain definite conclusions at which the Government has arrived, and represents our settled determination to carry those conclusions into effect. It is essentially a local Bill and is a Bill of a tentative character. If the measure works well, it may be cautiously extended. If it works badly, it can be promptly modified; and, as regards these minor features of it on which differences of opinion still exist, and will, doubtless, continue to exist, I do not think they can be satisfactorily removed or reconciled by any other authority less conclusive than that of experience. It is for this reason that I sincerely hope the measure now before us may be passed into law before the close of the present year."

The motion was put and agreed to.

The Hon'ble Mr. Hope moved that the Bill be published in the *Bombay Government Gazette*, in English and in such other languages as the Local Government might think fit.

The motion was put and agreed to.

THE DECCAN AGRICULTURISTS RELIEF BILL, 1879.

(Introduced into the Council of the Governor General by the Honourable Mr. Hope on the 5th June 1879.)

CONTENTS.

PREAMBLE.

CHAPTER I.
PRELIMINARY.

SECTIONS.
1. Short title.
   Local extent and commencement.
2. Interpretation-clause.

CHAPTER II.
OF THE HEARING IN CERTAIN SUITS BY SUBORDINATE JUDGES.

3. Application of this chapter.
4. Certain suits to be instituted in Courts of first class Subordinate Judges.
5. Subordinate Judges not to act as Judges of Small Cause Courts.
6. Jurisdiction of Subordinate Judge and Small Cause Court.
7. Summons to be for final disposal of suit.
8. Service of summons.
9. No suit to be heard *ex parte*.
10. Written statements.
11. Record of evidence.

CHAPTER III.
OF SUITS AND OTHER PROCEEDINGS TO WHICH AGRICULTURISTS ARE PARTIES.

12. History of transactions with agriculturist debtors to be investigated.
13. Mode of taking account.
14. Interest to be allowed.
15. Reference to arbitration in certain cases.
16. In the case of ancestral debts, interest to be disallowed or limited.
17. Agriculturist debtors may sue for accounts.
    Amount of debts in such cases to be determined according to foregoing provisions.
18. Decree may provide for payment by instalments.
    Execution of decrees under this section.
19. Payment into court in cases under section 17.

20. Power to discharge judgment-debtor.
    Power to direct institution of insolvency proceedings.
21. Power to fix instalments in execution.
22. Arrest and imprisonment for debt abolished.
23. Land exempted from attachment and sale unless specifically pledged.
24. Ancestral debt.

CHAPTER IV.
Of Insolvency.

25. Subordinate Judges to have jurisdiction in agriculturists' cases.
26. Agriculturist may apply for adjudication in cases not provided for by Code.
27. Modification of section 351 of the Code.
28. Receiver.
29. Proof of debts.
30. Power to make over moveable property to creditor at valuation.
31. Immoveable property not to vest in receiver, but may be managed for benefit of creditors.
32. Secured debts.
33. Insolvent incompetent to sell, &c., property dealt with under sections 31 and 32.
34. Scheduled debts discharged.
35. Limitation to powers of Subordinate Judges under section 359 of the Code.

CHAPTER V.
Of Village-Munsifs.

36. Appointment of Village-Munsifs.
37. Suits triable by them.
    Jurisdiction of other Courts excluded.
    Proviso.
38. Special Judge's power of revision.
39. Power of Local Government to make rules.

CHAPTER VI.
Of Conciliation.

40. Appointment of Conciliators.
41. Matters which may be brought before Conciliator.
42. Procedure thereupon.
    Day for attendance may from time to time be postponed.

43. When all parties appear, Conciliator to endeavour to reconcile them.
44. Conciliator to hear statement of witnesses, &c.
45. Any agreement arrived at to be reduced to writing.
46. Procedure when agreement finally disposes of case.
47. Procedure where agreement is for reference to arbitration.
48. Certificate to be given to applicant if conciliation fails.
49. Suit, &c., not to be entertained by Civil Court unless such certificate is produced.
50. Local Government to frame rules.

CHAPTER VII.
Superintendence and Revision.
51. Special Judge.
52. District Judge may withdraw case from Subordinate Judge, or sit with Subordinate Judge as a Bench for trial of any case.
53. Appointment of Assistant or Subordinate Judge to aid Special Judge.
54. Of revision.

CHAPTER VIII.
Registration by Village-Registrars.
55. Appointment of Village-Registrars.
56. Instruments executed by agriculturist not to be deemed valid unless executed before a Village-Registrar.
57. Such instruments to be written by or under the superintendence of a Village-Registrar and executed in his presence.
    Attestation of such instruments.
58. Registration of instruments by Village-Registrars.
59. Consideration to be fully stated in every instrument executed before a Village-Registrar.
60. Registration under this Act to be deemed equivalent to registration under the Indian Registration Act, 1877.
61. Village-Registrars to be subordinate to the Inspector General of Registration.
62. Exemption of instruments to which Government or any officer of Government is a party.
63. Power of Local Government to make rules.

CHAPTER IX.
Of Receipts and Statements of Account.
64. Agriculturists to be entitled to written receipts,
65. and annual statements of account;
66. and to have his account made up from time to time in a pass-book.
67. Penalty for contravention of sections 64 to 66.

CHAPTER X.
LEGAL PRACTITIONERS.

68. Pleaders, &c., excluded in certain cases.
69. Pleader's fees.
70. Power of Court to appoint pleader for agriculturist.

CHAPTER XI.
MISCELLANEOUS.

71. Mortgages, &c., to be valid only when written and registered.
72. Limitation.
73. No appeal in cases tried under this Act by Subordinate Judges.
74. Decision as to whether person is or is not agriculturist final.
75. Civil Procedure Code to apply in Subordinate Judge's Courts.
76. Additional power to make rules.
77. Rules to be published.

For the Relief of Indebted Agriculturists in certain parts for the Deccan.

WHEREAS it is expedient to relieve the agricultural classes in certain parts of the Deccan from indebtedness; It is hereby enacted as follows :—

Preamble.

CHAPTER I.
PRELIMINARY.

Short title.

1. This Act may be cited as "The Deccan Agriculturists Relief Act, 1879" :—

Local extent and commencement.

It extends only to the districts of Poona, Sátára, Sholápur and Ahmednagar, and it shall come into force on the first day of October 1879.

Interpretation-clause.

2. In this Act, unless there is something repugnant in the subject or context,—

" agriculturist."

(1) " agriculturist " means a person who earns his livelihood wholly or principally by agriculture;

" money."

(2) " money " includes grain and any other agricultural produce:

" special judge."

(3) " special judge " means the officer appointed under section fifty-one.

CHAPTER II.

OF THE HEARING OF CERTAIN SUITS BY SUBORDINATE JUDGES.

Application of this chapter.
3. The provisions of this chapter shall apply to—

(*a*) suits for an account instituted on or after the first day of October 1879, by an agriculturist in the Court of a Subordinate Judge under the provisions hereinafter contained, and

(*b*) suits of the descriptions next hereinafter mentioned and instituted on or after the same date—

(1) when such suits are heard by Subordinate Judges of the first class and the subject-matter thereof does not exceed in amount or value five hundred rupees, or

(2) when such suits are heard by Subordinate Judges of the second class and the subject-matter thereof does not exceed in amount or value five hundred rupees, or

(3) when such suits are heard by Subordinate Judges of the second class and the subject-matter thereof exceeds one hundred rupees, but does not exceed five hundred rupees in amount or value, and the parties agree that such provisions shall apply.

The descriptions of suits referred to in clause (*b*) are the following (namely):—

suits of the nature cognizable by Courts of Small Causes, and

suits between mortgagors, being agriculturists, and mortgagees for the foreclosure or redemption of the mortgage, for the enforcement of the mortgage lien or for the possession of the property mortgaged.

Certain suits to be instituted in Courts of first class Subordinate Judges.
4. Where a Subordinate Judge of the first class and a Subordinate Judge of the second class have jurisdiction in the same local area, every suit referred to in section 3, clause (*b*), to be instituted in such local area shall, if the amount or value of the subject-matter of such suit exceeds one hundred rupees and does not exceed five hundred rupees, be instituted in the Court of the Subordinate Judge of the first class.

Subordinate Judges not to act as Judges of Small Cause Courts.
5. Notwithstanding anything contained in the Bombay Civil Courts Act, 1869, section 28, no Subordinate Judge shall, while this Act continues in force, be invested with the jurisdiction of a Judge of a Court of Small Causes; and any such jurisdiction heretofore conferred on any Subordinate Judge shall be deemed, except as regards suits instituted before the said first day of October 1879, to have been withdrawn.

6. The Local Government may from time to time by notification in the local Gazette direct that any class of suits which a Subordinate Judge would be precluded from hearing by section twelve of Act XI of 1865 *(to consolidate and amend the law relating to Courts of Small Causes beyond the local limits of the ordinary original civil jurisdiction of the High Court of Judicature)* shall be heard and determined by him and not otherwise, and may by a like notification cancel any such direction.

Jurisdiction of Subordinate Judge and Small Cause Court.

7. In every case in which it seems to the Court possible to dispose of a suit at the first hearing, the summons shall be for the final disposal of the suit.

Summons to be for final disposal of suit.

8. If the officer employed to serve a summons on a defendant cannot find such defendant and there is no agent empowered to accept the service of the summons in his behalf, nor any person on whom the service can be made, the serving-officer may, instead of proceeding in manner prescribed by section 80 of the Code of Civil Procedure, leave such summons for service with the Patel of the defendant's village.

Service of summons.

A Patel with whom a summons is left under this section shall, if he within one week from the date on which the summons is so left finds the defendant in the village, serve such summons on the defendant in manner prescribed by section 79 of the said Code, endorse the same or cause the same to be endorsed in manner prescribed by section 81 of the said Code, sign such endorsement and return the summons by post or otherwise to the Court.

An endorsement made on a summons under this section shall be *primâ facie* proof of the facts stated therein, and the Court shall take judicial notice of the signature thereto.

9. No suit shall be heard *ex parte*, unless the Court, for reasons to be recorded in writing, thinks that it ought to be so heard.

No suit to be heard ex parte.

In any suit which the Code of Civil Procedure directs to be heard *ex parte*, but which the Court does not think ought to be so heard, the Court shall adjourn the hearing and take steps to secure the attendance of the defendant by the issue of a fresh summons or of a warrant of arrest.

10. In suits of the nature cognizable by Courts of Small Causes no party shall be entitled to file a written statement without the permission of the Court.

Written statements.

11. When the subject-matter of any suit does not exceed ten rupees in amount or value, it shall not be necessary to take down the evidence or make a memorandum thereof in manner provided by the Code of Civil Procedure; but in cases where the evidence is not so taken down and no memorandum is so made, the substance of the evidence shall be stated in the judgment.

Record of evidence.

CHAPTER III.

OF SUITS AND OTHER PROCEEDINGS TO WHICH AGRICULTURISTS ARE PARTIES.

12. When any suit is brought for the recovery of money alleged to be due on account of money lent or advanced to, or paid for, the defendant, or as the price of goods sold or on an account stated, or on a written or unwritten engagement for the payment of money, or for the foreclosure of a mortgage, or for the possession of mortgaged property, and the defendant or any one of the defendants, not being merely a surety of the actual debtor, is an agriculturist,

History of transactions with agriculturist debtors to be investigated.

and when any suit is brought for the redemption of a mortgage and the plaintiff or any one of the plaintiffs is an agriculturist,

the Court shall, if the amount of the creditor's claim is disputed, enquire into the history and merits of the case, from the commencement of the transactions between the parties out of which the suit has arisen, first, with a view of ascertaining whether there is any defence to the suit on the ground of fraud, mistake, accident, undue influence or otherwise; and secondly, with a view (if necessary) to taking an account between the parties in manner hereinafter provided.

When the amount of the claim is admitted, and the Court sees no reason to doubt the truth of such admission, the Court shall not be bound so to enquire, but may do so if it thinks fit.

When the Court sees reason to doubt the truth of such admission, it shall be bound to enquire as aforesaid.

Nothing herein contained shall affect the right of the parties to require that any matter in difference between them be referred to arbitration.

13. When the Court enquires into the history and merits of a case under section twelve, it shall, if it considers any agreement between the parties as to interest or the profits of mortgaged property or

Mode of taking account.

determining in any way the manner of taking the account fair and equitable, give effect to such agreement and take the account on the footing thereof; but, if it does not consider such agreement fair and equitable, it shall, notwithstanding the same,

and notwithstanding any statement or settlement of account or any contract purporting to close previous dealings and create a new obligation,

determine the amount due according to the following rules (that is to say) :—

(*a*) separate accounts of principal and interest shall be taken :

(*b*) in the account of principal there shall be debited to the debtor only such money as may from time to time have been actually received by him or on his account from the creditor :

(*c*) in the account of interest there shall be debited to the debtor monthly simple interest on the balance of principal for the time being outstanding at the rate allowed by the Court as hereinafter provided :

(*d*) all payments by or on account of the debtor, and all profits or advantages of every description received by the creditor in the course of the transactions, shall be credited, first, on account of interest; and when any payment is more than sufficient to discharge the balance of interest due at the time it is made, the residue of such payment shall be credited to the debtor in the account of principal :

(*e*) the accounts of principal and interest shall be made up to the date of suit, and the aggregate of the balances (if any) of both such accounts against the debtor on that date shall be deemed to be the amount due, except when the balance of the interest account exceeds that of the principal account, in which case double the latter balance shall be deemed to be the amount due.

14. The interest to be awarded in taking an account according to the rules set forth in section thirteen shall be—

Interest to be allowed.

(*a*) the rate, if any, agreed upon between the parties, unless such rate is deemed by the Court to be unreasonable ; or

(*b*) if such rate is deemed by the Court unreasonable, or if no rate was agreed upon, such rate as the Court deems reasonable :

Provided that, in any case in which the parties have agreed that the profits of mortgaged property shall be taken by the mortgagee in lieu of interest and such agreement has been set aside under section thirteen, the rate of interest to be allowed shall be nine per cent. per annum.

15. Instead of enquiring into the history and merits of a case under section twelve, or if upon so enquiring the Court is unable to satisfy itself as to the amount which should be allowed on account of principal or interest or both, the Court may, of its own motion, direct that the question be referred to arbitration.

Reference to arbitration in certain cases.

If the parties are willing to nominate arbitrators, the arbitrators shall be nominated by them in such manner as may be agreed upon between them: if the parties are unwilling to nominate arbitrators or cannot agree in respect of such nomination, the Court shall appoint any three persons it thinks fit:

Provided that if both parties reside in the same village, town or city, and, in the opinion of the Court, three fit persons can be found among the residents of such village, town or city, it shall appoint residents of such village, town or city.

The provisions of sections 508 to 522 (both inclusive) of the Code of Civil Procedure shall apply to every reference to arbitration under this section.

16. If the debt, or any portion thereof, was not contracted by the person from whom the creditor seeks to obtain recovery, but by such person's father or other ancestor, the said person shall be called upon to state whether he is willing to accept the full responsibility for such debt or for such portion thereof;

In the case of ancestral debts interest to be disallowed or limited.

and, if he accepts such responsibility, shall be held liable for the full amount payable on account of such debt, or of such portion thereof subject to the other provisions of this Act, or of any law for the time being in force relating to ancestral debts;

but if he declines to accept such responsibility, he shall not be held liable for more than the principal amount of such debt, or of such portion thereof, with interest up to the date of the death of the person who incurred such debt, or of such portion thereof, if such person was related to him in the first degree, and otherwise only for the principal amount of such debt or of such portion thereof.

17. Any agriculturist may sue for an account of monies lent or advanced to or paid for him by a creditor or due by him to such creditor as the price of goods sold or on a written or unwritten engagement for the payment of money and of

Agriculturist debtors may sue for accounts.

monies paid by him to such creditor, and for a decree declaring the amount, if any, still payable by him to such creditor.

Amount of debts in such cases to be determined according to foregoing provisions.

When any such suit is brought, the amount payable by the plaintiff shall be determined under the same rules as would be applicable if the creditor had himself sued for recovery of the debt.

Decree may provide for payment by instalments.

18. A decree passed under section seventeen may, besides declaring the amount due, direct that such amount shall be paid by instalments, with or without interest; and, when any such decree so directs, the plaintiff may pay the amount of such decree, or the amount of each instalment fixed by such decree, as it falls due, into court, in default whereof execution of the decree may be enforced by the defendant in the same manner as if he had obtained the decree in a suit to recover the debt.

Execution of decrees under this section.

Payment into court in cases under section 17.

19. The plaintiff in any suit instituted under section seventeen may at any stage of such suit deposit in court such sum of money as he considers a satisfaction in full of the defendant's claim against him.

Notice of the deposit shall be given by the Court to the defendant, and the amount of the deposit shall (unless the Court otherwise directs) be paid to the defendant on his application.

No interest shall be allowed to the defendant on any sum so deposited from the date of the receipt of such notice, whether the sum deposited be in full of the claim or fall short thereof.

Power to discharge judgment-debtor.

20. When a decree has been passed, whether before or after this Act comes into force, under which any sum less than fifty rupees is recoverable from an agriculturist, the Court may, whether in the course of execution of the said decree or otherwise, if it is satisfied that there is no other claim against him and that he is unable to pay the whole of such sum, direct the payment of a portion of the same, and grant him a discharge from the balance.

Power to direct institution of insolvency proceedings.

When the sum payable under the decree amounts to fifty rupees or upwards, or when there are other claims against the debtor, the Court may direct proceedings to be taken with respect to him as nearly as may be as if he had applied to be declared an insolvent under the provisions hereinafter contained.

21. **Power to fix instalments in execution.** The Court may at any time direct that the amount of any decree against an agriculturist or the portion of the same which it directs under section twenty to be paid, shall be paid by instalments with or without interest.

22. **Arrest and imprisonment for debt abolished.** Except as provided in the Code of Civil Procedure, section 359, no agriculturist shall be arrested or imprisoned on account of debt.

23. **Land exempted from attachment and sale unless specifically pledged.** No agriculturist's land shall be attached or sold in execution of any decree or order unless it has been specifically pledged as security for the repayment of the debt to which such decree or order relates, and the mortgage lien still subsists.

But the Court may, when passing a decree or at any subsequent time, direct the Collector to take possession, for any period not exceeding seven years, of any land of an agriculturist judgment-debtor to the possession of which such judgment-debtor is entitled, and which, in the opinon of the Collector, is not required for the support of such judgment-debtor and the members of his family dependent on him, and deal with the same for the benefit of the decree-holder in the manner provided by section thirty-one.

24. **Ancestral debt.** If, upon application being made for the execution of a decree for the payment of money against an agriculturist, it appears that the person against whom execution is sought is not the person made liable by the decree for the amount thereof, but the heir of such person, the amount recoverable under the decree shall be limited in accordance with the provisions of section sixteen.

CHAPTER IV.
Of Insolvency.

25. **Subordinate Judges to have jurisdiction in agriculturists' cases.** Every Subordinate Judge shall have the powers conferred by sections 344 to 359 (both inclusive) of the Code of Civil Proceedure, as modified by the provisions next hereinafter contained, for the purpose of dealing with applications under the Code of Civil Procedure or under this Act to have agriculturists residing within the local limits of his jurisdiction declared insolvent and proceedings taken under orders passed by him under the second clause of section twenty, and no such application or proceeding shall be dealt with by any other Court.

26. Any agriculturist who is in debt to the amount of fifty rupees or upwards and who resides within the said districts may apply to any Subordinate Judge within the local limits of whose jurisdiction he resides to be declared an insolvent, though he has not been arrested or imprisoned, and though no order of attachment has issued against his property in execution of decree.

Agriculturist may apply for adjudication in cases not provided for by Code.

27. Notwithstanding anything contained in section 351 of the Code of Civil Procedure, the Court shall declare an agriculturist an insolvent if it is satisfied that he is in insolvent circumstances, and that the application to have him declared an insolvent has been properly made under section 344 of the said Code or section twenty-six of this Act.

Modification of section 351 of the Code.

28. No person other than the Názir of the Court shall be appointed as receiver, and no receiver shall be entitled to commission.

Receiver.

29. In determining under section 352 of the said Code the amount of any claim of the nature referred to in section twelve of this Act due by an insolvent agriculturist, the Court shall proceed in the manner prescribed by sections twelve to sixteen of this Act, both inclusive.

Proof of debts.

30. Whenever any moveable property of an insolvent is liable to be sold by a receiver under section 356 of the said Code, the Court may direct that it shall not be so sold, and may, after recording the opinions of two Assessors appointed by the Court in this behalf, determine the value of such property and direct the receiver to transfer it to any of the scheduled creditors who may be entitled to receive in the distribution under the said section 356 an amount equal to or greater than the value so determined; and such creditor shall accept such property in full or partial liquidation (as the case may be) of the amount to which he is so entitled.

Power to make over moveable property to creditor at valuation.

31. No immoveable property of the insolvent shall vest in the receiver; but the Court may direct the Collector to take into his possession, for any period not exceeding seven years from the date on which the receiver has been appointed, any such property to the possession of which the insolvent is entitled, and which, in the opinion of the Collector, is not required

Immoveable property not to vest in receiver,

but may be managed for benefit of creditors.

for the support of the insolvent and the members of his family dependent on him, and, subject to any rules the Local Government may from time to time make in this behalf, to manage the same for the benefit of the creditors, by letting it on lease or otherwise:

Provided that if the insolvent or his heir at any time pays into court the balance of the scheduled debts then unpaid, he shall, subject to any rights created in favour of other persons by the Collector, be entitled to recover possession of such property.

32. When any scheduled debt is secured by a mortgage of any portion of the insolvent's immoveable property, the Court may direct the Collector, if he can obtain a premium equal to the amount of such debt by letting such property rent-free for a term not exceeding twenty years to let such property, and if he cannot so obtain such premium, to sell such property by public auction or otherwise as he thinks fit.

Secured debts.

Where property is let under this section, the premium shall be applied to the payment of the debt.

When property is sold under the section, the sale-proceeds shall be applied, first, to the payment of the debt; and the balance, if any, shall be paid to the receiver.

33. So long as any management under section thirty-one or letting under section thirty-two continues, the insolvent and his representative in interest shall be incompetent to mortgage, charge, lease or alienate the property or any part thereof.

Insolvent incompetent to sell, &c., property dealt with under sections 31 and 32.

34. When the balance available for distribution among the scheduled creditors under section 356 of the said Code has been distributed, the claims of such creditors shall be deemed to have been discharged, except as regards the right to share in the profits of any property managed by the Collector under section thirty-one.

Scheduled debts discharged.

35. No Subordinate Judge exercising the powers conferred by section twenty-five, if he is a Subordinate Judge of the first class, shall sentence any person under section 359 of the said Code to imprisonment for a term longer than three months, or if he is a Subordinate Judge of the second class, shall so sentence any person for a term longer than one month.

Limitation to powers of Subordinate Judges under section 359 of the Code.

CHAPTER V.
OF VILLAGE-MUNSIFS.

Appointment of Village-Munsifs.

36. The Local Government may from time to time appoint any Patel of a village to be a Village-Munsif for such village or for such village and for any other villages the sites of which are situate not more than two miles from the site of such village, and may cancel any such appointment.

Suits triable by them.

37. Every Village-Munsif so appointed shall take cognizance of suits for money lent, or advanced to, or paid for, the defendant, or due as the price of goods sold or on an account stated, or on a written or unwritten engagement for the payment of money when the amount or value of the claim does not exceed ten rupees, and all the defendants at the time of the commencement of the suit actually and voluntarily reside or carry on business or personally work for gain within the local area for which such Village-Munsif is appointed.

Jurisdiction of other Courts excluded.

A suit cognizable by a Village-Munsif shall not be heard by any other Court:

Proviso.

Provided that the Special Judge may from time to time transfer any suit instituted before a Village-Munsif to any other Civil Court in the district for trial:

Provided also that no Village-Munsif shall try any suit in which he is a party or is personally interested, or shall adjudicate upon any proceeding connected with or arising out of such suit.

Special Judge's power of revision.

38. The Special Judge may on a petition being presented within thirty days from the date of any decree or order of a Village-Munsif by any party deeming himself aggrieved by such decree or order, set aside such decree or order on the ground of corruption, gross partiality or misconduct of the Village-Munsif.

Except as herein provided and as provided in section 622 of the Code of Civil Procedure, every decree and order of a Village-Munsif shall be final.

Power of Local Government to make rules.

39. The Local Government may from time to time, by notification in the local Gazette, make rules for regulating the procedure of Village-Munsifs and for conferring on them any of the powers for the trial of suits or the execution of decrees exercised by a Civil Court under the Code of Civil Procedure or any other enactment for the time being in force.

CHAPTER VI.

OF CONCILIATION.

Appointment of Conciliators.
40. The Local Government may from time to time appoint any person to be a Conciliator and cancel any such appointment.

Every Conciliator so appointed shall exercise his functions under this Act in respect of matters affecting agricultrists residing within such local limits as the Local Government may from time to time determine.

Matters which may be brought before Conciliator.
41. When any dispute arises as to, or there is a prospect of litigation regarding, any matter within the cognizance of a Civil Court between two or more parties, one of whom is an agriculturist residing within any local limits for which a Conciliator has been appointed, any of such parties may apply to such Conciliator to effect an amicable settlement between them.

Procedure thereupon.
42. If the application be made by one of the parties only, the Conciliator shall take down, or cause to be taken down, in writing a general statement of the applicant's case, and shall thereupon, by summons or by such other means as he deems fit, invite the person against whom such application is made to attend before him upon a day to be fixed for this purpose, and shall direct the applicant also to be present on such day.

Day for attendance may from time to time be postponed.
If the said person fails to appear on the day first fixed, the Conciliator may, if he thinks fit, from time to time extend the period for his appearance.

When all parties appear, Conciliator to endeavour to reconcile them.
43. Whenever all the parties are present, the Conciliator shall call upon each in turn to explain his case regarding the matter in question, and shall use his best endeavours to induce them to agree to an amicable settlement or to submit such matter to arbitration.

Conciliator to hear statements of witnesses, &c.
44. The Conciliator shall hear the statement of any witness and peruse any book of account or other document produced by the parties, and if any party or witness consents in writing to affirm any statement upon oath or solemn affirmation in any form not repugnant to justice or decency and not purporting to effect any third person, shall arrange for such oath or solemn affirmation being duly taken in the presence of all the parties.

45. If on the day on which the case is first heard by the Conciliator or on any subsequent day to which he may adjourn the hearing, the parties come to any agreement, either finally disposing of the matter or for referring it to arbitration, such agreement shall be forthwith reduced to writing, and shall be read and explained to the parties, and shall be signed or otherwise attested by the Conciliator and the parties or other representatives respectively.

Any agreement arrived at to be reduced to writing.

46. When the agreement is one finally disposing of the matter, the Conciliator shall forward the same in original to the Court of the Subordinate Judge of lowest grade having jurisdiction in the place where the agriculturists who is a party thereto resides.

Procedure where agreement finally disposes of case.

The Court which receives the agreement shall order it to be filed; and it shall then take effect as if it were a decree of the said Court passed on the day on which it is ordered to be filed and from which no appeal lies.

47. When the agreement is one for referring the matter to arbitration, the Conciliator shall forward it to the Court having jurisdiction in the matter, and such Court shall cause it to be filed and proceed thereon in manner provided by section 523 and 524 of the Code of Civil Procedure.

Procedure where agreement is for reference to arbitration.

48. If the person against whom any application is made before the Conciliator cannot be found, or if he refuses or neglects, after such period as the Conciliator thinks reasonable has been allowed for his appearance, to appear before the Conciliator, or if he appears but the attempt to reconcile the parties or to induce them to resort to arbitration fails, the Conciliator shall, on demand, give to the applicant, or when there are several applicants to each applicant, a certificate under his signature to that effect.

Certificate to be given to applicant if conciliation fails.

49. No suit and no application for execution of a decree passed before the date on which this Act comes into force to which any agriculturist residing within any local limits for which a Conciliator has been appointed is a party shall be entertained by any Civil Court, unless the plaintiff or decree-holder produces a certificate as aforesaid.

Suit, &c., not to be entertained by Civil Court unless such certificate is produced.

Local Government to frame rules. 50. The Local Government may form time to time make rules—

(a) regulating the proceedings of Conciliators in matters not provided for by this Act;

(b) fixing the charges to be made by Conciliators for any thing done by them under this Act; and

(c) determining what record and accounts shall be kept by Conciliators and what returns shall be framed and furnished by them.

CHAPTER VII.

SUPERINTENDENCE AND REVISION.

Special Judge. 51. The Local Government shall appoint an officer, as Special Judge, to inspect, supervise and control the proceedings of all Subordinate Judges, Village-Munsifs and Conciliators under this Act, and to discharge in respect of such proceedings before Subordinate Judges all the functions of the District Court.

The officer so appointed shall not, without the previous sanction of the Government of India, discharge any public function except those which he is required by this Act to discharge.

If any conflict of authority arises between the Special Judge and the District Judge in regard to any matter, the High Court shall pass such order thereon consistent with this Act as it thinks fit.

52. The Special Judge may—

District Judge may withdraw case from Subordinate Judge, (a) transfer to his own file, and himself as if he were a Subordinate Judge dispose of any suit or other matter pending before the Court of any Subordinate Judge; or

or sit with Subordinate Judge as a Bench for trial of any case. (b) stay the proceedings in any such suit or matter, and sit together with such Judge as a Bench to dispose of such suit or matter in accordance with the provisions of this chapter.

If the members of any Bench sitting under this section differ in opinion, the opinion of the Special Judge shall prevail.

Appointment of Assistant or Subordinate Judge to aid Special Judge. 53. The Local Government may appoint any Assistant or Subordinate Judge to inspect and supervise, subject to the control of the Special Judge, the proceedings of all Subordinate Judges, Village-Munsifs and Conciliators under this Act in one or more districts.

Any Assistant or Subordinate Judge so appointed may in the districts for which he so appointed, if the Special Judge so directs, exercise the powers of the Special Judge under section fifty-two of this Act, and transfer any suit under section 25 of the Code of Civil Procedure.

54. The Special Judge may call for and examine the record of any suit or other matter tried by a Subordinate Judge for the purpose of satisfying himself of the legality or propriety of any decree or order passed, and as to the regularity of the proceedings, and may pass such order thereon as he thinks fit : and any Assistant Judge or Subordinate Judge appointed by the Local Government under section fifty-three may similarly in the districts for which he is appointed call for and examine the record of any such case, and, if he see cause therefor, may refer the same, with his remarks, for the orders of the Special Judge :

Of revision.

Provided that no decision or order shall be reversed or altered for any error or defect, or otherwise, unless a failure of justice appears to have taken place.

CHAPTER VIII.

REGISTRATION BY VILLAGE-REGISTRARS.

55. The Local Government may—

(*a*) appoint such persons as it thinks fit, whether public officers or not, to be Village-Registrars, for such local areas as it may from time to time prescribe;

Appointment of Village-Registrars.

(*b*) direct that the Village-Registrar for any local area may discharge the functions of a Village-Registrar for any other local areas concurrently with the Village-Registrars of such other local areas ; and

(*c*) delegate to any person by name or in virtue of his office the powers conferred on it by this section.

56. No instrument purporting to create, modify, transfer or evidence an obligation for the payment of money or a charge upon any property executed after the passing of this Act by an agriculturist residing in any local area for which a Village-Registrar has been appointed shall be admitted in evidence for any purpose by any person having by law or consent of parties authority to receive evidence, or shall be

Instruments executed by agriculturist not to be deemed valid unless executed before a Village-Registrar.

acted upon by any such person or by any public officer, unless such instrument is written by, or under the superintendence of, and is attested by a Village-Registrar :

Provided that nothing herein contained shall prevent the admission of any instrument in evidence in any criminal proceeding.

57. When any persons, one or more of whom is an agriculturist, desire to execute any such instrument, they shall present themselves before the Village-Registrar appointed by the Local Government for the area in which the said agriculturist or any one of the said agriculturists resides and such Registrar, after satisfying himself in such manner as he deems fit as to the identity of the parties, and receiving from them the fee (if any) prescribed by the Local Government and the stamp (if any) which may be necessary, shall write the instrument, or cause the same to be written under his superintendence, and require the parties to execute it in his presence.

Such instruments to be written by or under the superintendence of a Village-Registrar and executed in his presence.

Every instrument so written and executed shall be attested by the Village-Registrar, and also, if any of the parties thereto is unable to read and write, by two respectable witnesses.

Attestation of such instruments.

58. Every Village-Registrar shall keep a register of instruments executed before him in such form as shall from time to time be prescribed by the Inspector General of Registration under section sixty-one of this Act.

Registration of instruments by Village-Registrars.

As soon as any instrument has been completely executed before a Village-Registrar, he shall make or cause a copy of it to be made in his register, and shall deliver the original instrument to the party entitled to the custody of the same, and a certified copy thereof to the other party, or to each of the other parties, if there be more than one.

Previous to delivery, the original instrument and each such copy shall be endorsed under the Village-Registrar's signature with the date of registration, the name and residence of the Village-Registrar and the volume and page of the register in which the instrument has been registered

59. In every instrument written by or under the superintendence of the Village-Registrar, the amount and nature of the consideration, if any, shall be fully stated.

Consideration to be fully stated in every instrument executed before a Village-Registrar.

The Village-Registrar shall also endorse upon the instrument a note, under his signature, recording whether or not the transfer of the consideration stated therein, or of any part thereof, took place in his presence.

If the instrument is to be executed in supersession, or partly in supersession, of a previous instrument, such instrument shall be produced before the Village-Registrar and shall be fully described in the instrument to be executed, and shall be marked by the Village-Registrar under his signature for identification.

60. Every instrument executed and registered in accordance with the foregoing provisions shall be deemed to have been duly registered under the provisions of the Indian Registration Act, 1877 ; and no instrument which ought to have been executed before a Village-Registrar, but has been otherwise executed, shall be registered by any officer acting under the said Act, or in any public office, or shall be authenticated by any public officer.

Registration under this Act to be deemed equivalent to registration under the Indian Registration Act, 1877.

61. The said Inspector General shall exercise, by himself and his subordinates a general superintendence over all Village-Registrars, and shall have power from time to time to make rules consistent with this Act for regulating their proceedings and for providing for the custody of their records.

Village-Registrars to be subordinate to the Inspector General of Registration.

62. Nothing in this Act shall be deemed to require any instrument to which the Government or any officer of Government in his official capacity is a party to be executed before a Village-Registrar.

Exemption of instruments to which Government or any officer of Government is a party.

63. The Local Government may from time to time make rules regulating the appointment, suspension, dimissal and remuneration of Village-Registrars, and prescribing the fees to be levied by them.

Power of Local Government to make rules.

CHAPTER IX.

OF RECEIPTS AND STATEMENTS OF ACCOUNT.

64. Every agriculturist who makes any payment of money in liquidation of a debt shall be entitled to receive at the time of such payment a written receipt from the person to whom such payment is made.

Agriculturists to be entitled to written receipts.

If such payment is made under any instrument executed before a Village-Registrar, the receipt shall, if the agriculturist so require, be endorsed on the copy of the instrument furnished to him under section fifty-eight.

65. Any agriculturist by whom any money is due under any instrument shall be entitled to receive from the person claiming under such instrument, within one month after the date on which by local custom annual accounts are balanced, a statement of his account up to that date.

and to annual statements of account;

The Local Government may, by notification in the local Gazette, declare what date shall in any district or portion of a district be taken to be the date on which annual accounts are balanced for the purpose of this section.

66. Any agriculturist in whose name an account is kept by any trader or money-lender shall be entitled to receive from such trader or money-lender, on demand, a pass-book, and to require from time to time that his account up to date be written therein and attested by the signature or mark of the said trader or money-lender.

and to have his account made up from time to time in a pass-book.

An entry so made in any such pass-book of any payment made to the trader or money-lender shall be deemed to be equivalent for the purposes of section sixty-four to the grant of a receipt for the amount so entered.

67. Any person who, in contravention of section sixty-four, sixty-five or sixty-six, refuses or neglects to give a receipt or a statement of account or a pass-book, or to write, or cause to be written, any account or any part of an account in a pass-book, or to attest the same when so written, shall be punished for each such offence, with fine which may extend to one hundred rupees.

Penalty for contravention of sections 64 to 66.

CHAPTER X.

LEGAL PRACTITIONERS.

68. No pleader, vakíl, mukhtár, and no advocate or attorney of a High Court, shall be permitted to appear on behalf of any party to a case before a Village-Munsif or a Conciliator:

Pleaders, &c., excluded in certain cases,

Provided that any party to any such case may be permitted, on reasonable cause being shown to the satisfaction of the Conciliator or Munsif, to employ any relative, servant or dependent, who is not, and has not previously been, a pleader, or a mukhtár or vakíl to appear either conjointly with or in lieu of such party.

When a relative, servant or dependent appears in lieu of a party, he shall be furnished by him with a power of attorney defining the extent to which he is empowered to act.

69. In awarding costs to any party in any suit or proceeding before a Subordinate Judge under this Act in which the subject-matter does not exceed one hundred rupees in amount or value, nothing shall be allowed on account of the fees of any pleader, vakíl, mukhtár, or of any advocate or attorney of a High Court, unless the Court, for reasons to be recorded by it in writing, thinks that professional assistance was necessary to the proper conduct of such party's case.

Pleaders' fees.

70. When in any suit or proceeding before a Subordinate Judge under this Act to which an agriculturist is a party, any pleader, vakil or mukhtár, or any advocate or attorney of a High Court, appears on behalf of any party opposed to such agriculturist, the Subordinate Judge, if he is of opinion that such agriculturist has not the means of obtaining proper professional assistance, may, with the consent of such agriculturist, direct the Government pleader or some other competent person (who is willing so to do) to appear on his behalf.

Power of Court to appoint pleader for agriculturist.

CHAPTER XI.
Miscellaneous.

71. No mortgage, lien or charge of or upon any immoveable property belonging to an agriculturist shall be valid unless it is created by an instrument in writing signed by the person creating such mortgage, lien or charge.

Mortgages, &c., to be valid only when written and registered.

72. In any suit against an agriculturist under this Act for the recovery of money, the following periods of limitation shall be deemed to be substituted for those prescribed in the second column of the second schedule annexed to the Indian Limitation Act, 1877 (that is to say) :—

Limitation.

(a) when such suit is based on a written instrument registered under this Act or any other law in force at the date of the execution of such instrument,—twelve years ;

(b) in any other case,—six years :

Provided that nothing herein contained shall revive the right to bring any suit which would have been barred by limitation if it had been instituted immediately before the passing of this Act.

No appeal in cases tried under this Act by Subordinate Judges.

73. No appeal shall lie from any decision or order in any suit or proceeding before a Subordinate Judge under this Act.

Decision as to whether person is or is not agriculturist final.

74. The decision of any Court of first instance that any person is or is not an agriculturist shall be final.

Civil Procedure Code to apply in Subordinate Judges' Courts.

75. Except in so far as it is inconsistent with this Act, the Code of Civil Procedure shall apply in all suits and proceedings before Subordinate Judges.

Additional power to make rules.

76. The Local Government may from time to time make all such rules as it may deem necessary for carrying out the provisions of this Act.

Rules to be published.

77. All rules made by the Local Government under this Act shall be published in the local official Gazette, and shall thereupon, in so far as they are consistent with this Act, have the force of law.

STATEMENT OF OBJECTS AND REASONS.

1. The inquiries made into the causes of the riots which occurred in the Deccan districts in 1875 and the discussions which have since taken place show that the difficulties under which the agriculturists in those districts labour are due, in a great measure, to the unsatisfactory nature of the relations at present subsisting between them and the money-lending classes.

2. In order to put those relations on a better footing, it is deemed necessary—

first, to provide some safeguards against the money-lenders committing frauds in their accounts and obtaining from ignorant peasants bonds for larger amounts than are actually paid to or due from them;

secondly, to arrange disputes by conciliation as far possible; to increase the number of Courts, and to simplify and cheapen the administration of justice, and thus to afford facilities to the agriculturist to defend any suits that may be brought against him;

thirdly, to insist that in suits against agriculturists the Court shall in certain cases of its own motion investigate the entire history of the transactions between the parties, and do substantial justice between them ;

fourthly, to restrict the sale of the ryot's land in execution of decree, and to provide an insolvency-procedure more liberal to the debtor than that of the Code of Civil Procedure.

The present Bill has been drafted with a view to securing these objects, in so far as they can be secured by legislation. It extends only to the four districts in which the agricultural distress has been most felt.

3. An attempt has been made to secure the first object by sections 55 to 63, providing for the appointment of village-registrars before whom every written obligation for the payment of money by an agriculturist must be registered ; by sections 64 to 67, requiring money-lenders to give receipts to agriculturists for all payments made by them, to render accounts, and to furnish a pass-book in which the agriculturist's account will be periodically written up ; and by section 71, which invalidates all mortgages created by an agriculturist otherwise than by a written instrument.

4. With a view to the second of the proposed objects, the Bill provides in sections 40 to 50 for the establishment of a system of conciliation under which it is hoped a large number of disputes will be settled out of court ; and in sections 36 to 39 for the appointment of village munsifs, like those in the Madras Presidency, to dispose of petty cases. A further addition to the machinery for the disposal of suits will be made by an increase of the number of Subordinate Judges ; but, as this is a matter which it is competent to the Local Government to deal with under the existing law, no reference to it will be found in the Bill.

5. As regards procedure, it is proposed, with a view to a more rapid despatch of business and to diminishing the cost of litigation, to simplify the record in certain respects (sections 10 and 11) ; to discourage the employment of pleaders in petty suits (section 69) ; and to substitute for the present system of appeals a very strict and searching supervision (sections 51 to 54).

6. Sections 12 to 16 provide in certain cases for a thorough investigation into the history of the transaction between the parties (the third of the four objects mentioned above). They prescribe the system in which the ryot's account is to be made up in cases where the Court finds it necessary to set aside oppressive or inequitable arrangements between the parties, and they guard especially against exorbitant demands for interest.

7. The presence of the defendant being essential for the thorough investigation proposed, and the ryots being, through various difficulties, apt to leave their suits undefended, it has been provided (in section 9) that except for special reasons, no suit shall be decided *ex parte*, but that the Court shall compel the defendant to appear.

8. The last of the four objects proposed will be found provided for by sections 25 and 33, which enact that land shall not be sold to pay the debt of the owner except where it has been specifically pledged, but admit of its profits being made available to the creditor for a term of years, and by the sections relating to insolvency.

9. The chief points in which the provisions of the insolvency-chapter differ from those of the Code are that they allow an agriculturist to apply to be adjudicated an insolvent, though no process in execution has been issued against him; that they entitle him to an adjudication in all cases in which, as a matter of fact, he may be insolvent, leaving any misconduct on his part to be punished under the Code of Civil Procedure; and that they similarly entitle him in all cases to a complete discharge from debts which, after all reasonable enforcement, he is unable fully to pay.

10. This insolvency procedure is further supplemented by section 20, which gives the Court a summary power in petty cases to discharge a judgment-debtor who is clearly insolvent, and by section 22, which abolishes imprisonment for debt.

11. The only other provisions of the Bill which appear to call for special notice are section 70, which empowers the Court to direct the Government pleader to appear on behalf of a ryot when he is unable to engage the services of a professional advocate and the opposite side is represented by a pleader, and section 72, which extends the period of limitation in suits for debt instituted against agriculturists. This latter provision has been introduced into the Bill, as there appears to be a pretty general consensus of opinion to the effect that the difficulties of the ryot are much aggravated by the present law of limitation, which compels the money-lender at very short intervals to sue him or take a fresh bond, either of which steps commonly entails a considerable addition to the debt.

SIMLA,
The 7th July 1879.

(Signed) T. C. HOPE.

No. 780.

To

THE CHIEF SECRETARY TO THE
GOVERNMENT OF BOMBAY.

Simla, the 26th July 1879.

SIR,

I am directed to forward herewith thirty copies of the Bill for the relief of indebted agriculturists in certain parts of the Deccan (with its statement of objects and reasons), introduced into the Legislative Council of His Excellency the Governor General by the Honourable Mr. Hope, together with the papers noted in the margin, and to request that the opinions of the Government of Bombay, the Honourable the Judges of the High Court, and such of the local officers not exceeding six in number, as the Government of Bombay think fit to consult thereon, may be forwarded to me, for submission to the Select Committee to which the Bill has been referred, before the 15th of September.

1. From the Honourable T. C. Hope, C.S.I., dated 26th April 1879, and enclosures.
2. Explanatory note by ditto, dated 8th May 1879.
3. Further note by ditto, dated 29th May 1879.
4. Statement by ditto regarding the trial of civil suits in the disturbed districts of the Bombay Presidency.
5. Ditto showing the business of the Civil Appellate Courts in the disturbed districts for the Bombay Presidency.
6. Ditto of the Poona Arbitration Court, 1876-79.
7. Abstracts of Proceedings of the Council of the Governor General, dated the 17th and 18th July 1879.

2. I am also to request that the Bill and statement of objects and reasons may be published in the *Bombay Government Gazette* in English and in such other languages as His Excellency in Council may deem proper, and that the dates of such publication may be communicated in your reply.

3. It will be seen from the report of the debate in Council on the 17th and 18th instant that, while the principles of the Bill are accepted, there has been some difference of opinion on certain points of detail. The authorities consulted will doubtless give these points their best consideration; but to some of them, as well

as to one or two additional points which have not formed the subject of discussion in the Legislative Council, I am to invite special attention.

4. In the first place, there is the question as to the extent to which the present right of appeal should be curtailed. This question has been left by paragraphs 31 to 34 of the Secretary of State's despatch of the 26th of December last completely in the discretion of the Supreme Government and the Government of Bombay, and there has been some difference of opinion on it here.

5. The Bill as it now stands has, in accordance with the views of the Government of Bombay, been so drawn as to exclude appeals in all those classes of cases to which it applies; and the machinery provided for conducting the system of revision which is to take the place of appeal has been strengthened by the addition of a Special Judge, who is to devote himself exclusively to superintending and controlling the working of the Act.

5. The Governor General in Council is of opinion that, looking to the arduous nature of the duties which the Act imposes on the Subordinate Judges and the large discretion it confers on them, the appointment of a special officer of this sort, who would ordinarily be chosen from the more experienced District Judges, is essential to the proper working of the system proposed; but the Governor in Council will observe that it has been questioned here whether any system of revision, even if worked under the control of the ablest Judge that could be chosen, would in the case of all the suits dealt with by the Bill be an adequate substitute for the present system of appeals. It has been argued that, at all events in mortgage suits, the right of appeal should be maintained, and the Government of India have determined to treat the question, in so far as lies in them, as an open one pending the receipt of your reply to this letter.

6. The provisions of the Bill to which I am next to invite attention are those contained in section 13, regulating the mode in which the account is to be taken in cases where it is found necessary to set aside an inequitable agreement into which an agriculturist has been inveigled. The corresponding provisions contained in the Bill submitted with your No. 2056, dated 18th April last, were found on examination to be on more points than one susceptible of various constructions. An attempt has been made in section 13 of the present Bill to express what it is believed was intended, and it is for the Government of Bombay to say whether that attempt has been successful, or, if not, what modifications in the wording of the section are required.

7. In connection with section 13 of the Bill I am to invite attention to sections 16 and 24, which go to relieve an heir from a portion of his ancestor's debt, though he may have inherited from that ancestor property sufficient to pay such debt. Similar provisions were contained in the Bill submitted with your predecessor's No. 308, dated 19th January 1878; and as the subject was one which the Bombay Legislature was competent to deal with, the letter from the Revenue, Agriculture and Commerce Department, No. 404, dated 1st July 1878, left it to be dealt with by that Legislature; but I am to say that, now that the question has come to be dealt with here and has been considered further and in more detail, the Governor General in Council is unable to see any ground on which such provisions can be supported.

The Governor General in Council cannot understand why when the ancestor's debt has under the ample powers contained in sections 12 to 15 of the Bill been fully inquired into and reduced to its just limits, the heir should not be bound to pay it to the extent of the property he has inherited. The obligation binding him to do so is, as observed by the Hon'ble Sayyad Ahmad in his speech, a matter of natural equity common to the English, Hindú and Muhammadan legal systems. Moreover, it is an obligation with the force of which the people of this country are perhaps more strongly impressed than those of any other country, and the sense of which, as observed in your predecessor's letter of the 6th April 1877, is " one of the best traits in their character."

8. For these reasons the Governor General in Council would be disposed to omit altogether the sections of the Bill referred to, and he is the more disposed to do so as he gathers from your predecessor's letter just cited that the Deccan Riots Commission and the Government of Bombay in the year 1877 were opposed to any attempt to afford relief in this way.

The sections have been allowed to stand pending your reply to this letter; but I am to beg that, if the Governor in Council proposes to advocate their retention, you will submit for the consideration of the Select Committee a redraft of them providing in more detail for the various cases that may present themselves— cases, *e.g.*, where the debt is secured by a mortgage, cases in which the ancestor's account has been for some time dealt with as incorporated in the heirs, cases where the heir has given a fresh bond, and so on.

9. In the chapter relating to village munsifs it will be seen that the main lines of the Madras system have been to some extent restored. It appears to the Governor General in Council that it is of the essence of that system that the qualification for the office

of munsif should be based, not on literary attainments, but on social status and local influence; that accordingly the appointments should, as in Madras, be restricted to village headmen; and that, as these must in many instances be illiterate persons whose judgments could not be expected to stand the tests applied by our Courts of revision, their decrees must, as in Madras, be made final, except when they are impugned on the ground of corruption or partiality.

If, unhappily, it should appear that the number of village headmen in the Deccan districts who can be trusted to decide petty suits without any regular check in the way of appeal or revision is inconsiderable, the proper conclusion seems to be that the village munsif system is scarcely suited to those districts, and it may be a question whether the provisions relating to it should not be altogether omitted from the Bill.

10. In connection with chapter VIII, relating to registration, it has been suggested that the persons available in the Deccan for the post of village registrar are not always to be trusted. I am directed to mention this; but the point, I am to add, is one upon which the Government of Bombay are most competent to form an opinion.

11. The portions of the Bill relating to the procedure in civil suits and to insolvency were, in the draft submitted with your No. 2056, dated 18th April 1879, so drawn as in the opinion of the Governor General in Council to lead to an impression that the deviation from the ordinary law involved in them was more extensive than it in fact was. In the Bill as now drafted the safer and simpler course, as it appears to the Governor General in Council, has been taken of providing directly only for the particular points on which a deviation from the ordinary law seems unavoidable, and then enacting that as to the rest the ordinary law shall apply. It is hoped that, in effecting this alteration in the form of the Bill, no special provision has been omitted to which the Government of Bombay attach any considerable importance; but however this may be, it should be borne in mind that even in their present shape the portions of the Bill now referred to have met with considerable opposition here, and that, if any further deviations from the ordinary law are introduced, they will prove so many additional obstructions to the progress of the Bill through its remaining stages.

12. Regarding the exclusion of pleaders (as provided for in the Bill submitted by you) in suits not exceeding one hundred rupees in value or amount, there has been much discussion here; and the course adopted in section 69 of the present Bill, of

empowering the Courts to refuse costs, has, I am to say, been adopted with a view to a compromise between conflicting opinions.

13. The only other matters to which I am to refer in connection with the Bill are the suggestions contained in Mr. Hope's note of the 29th of May last. The first of these suggestions—that as to the extension of the period of limitation in debt cases—is supported by a considerable body of authority; the arguments on which it is based appear to the Governor General in Council to be sound; and the Government of Bombay, though not supporting it themselves, have expressed no strong opinion against it. It has accordingly been provisionally adopted in the Bill.

14. Mr. Hope's other suggestion, that the Arbitration Courts which have established themselves at Poona and elsewhere should be recognized and have a certain status and position in our judicial system accorded to them and that a mode of reviewing their decisions should be provided, is one which involves not only the general questions as to the desirability of setting up a body of standing arbitrators and as to the propriety of allowing awards to be revised on their merits, but also the question as to the expediency of recognizing in the manner proposed the particular bodies referred to. These are questions on which the Governor General in Council deems it undesirable to come to any conclusion pending the receipt of your reply, especially as it appears that the Government of Bombay had provisions identical with those now proposed submitted to them for their consideration in Mr. Hope's draft Bill, and, for some reason not stated in the correspondence, did not think fit to adopt them. For this reason no provision regarding Arbitration Courts has been made in the present Bill.

15. I am, in conclusion, to invite attention to the question referred to in the last paragraph of the letter from the Home Department, No. 222, dated 26th February 1879, as to the possibility of making improvements in the revenue system now prevailing in the Deccan districts—a question which you will observe was discussed by several Hon'ble Members in the recent debate. That question, however, should be kept separate from those connected with the present Bill, and any communication you may have to make on it should be addressed to the Secretary for the Home, Revenue and Agricultural Department.

I have, &c.,

(Signed)   D. FITZPATRICK,
Secretary to the Government of India.

No. 4495 of 1879.

REVENUE DEPARTMENT.

Bombay Castle, 27th August 1879.

To

D. FITZPATRICK, Esq.,
Secretary to the Government of India,
Legislative Department,
Simla.

SIR,

I am directed to acknowledge the receipt of your letter No. 780, dated July 26th, 1879, wherewith you forwarded thirty copies of the Bill for the relief of indebted agriculturists in certain portions of the Deccan and other papers, and conveyed the request of His Excellency the Governor General in Council that the opinions of this Government, of the Honourable the Judges of the High Court, and of selected local officers, not exceeding six, may be recorded and forwarded to you for submission to the Select Committee, to which the Bill has been referred, before the 15th of September.

2. I am to inform you that the views of the Hon'ble the Judges and of six officers whom this Government has thought fit to consult, will be forwarded to you as soon as their reports are received, and that it has been desired in all cases that these reports may be sent in on or before the 1st of September. In the meantime His Excellency the Governor in Council desires me to communicate, without any delay, the opinions of the Government of Bombay upon the Bill.

3. The first point to which special attention is invited by your letter, is the question to what extent the right of appeal should be curtailed? You observe that this question has been left by the Secretary of State's despatch of December 26 completely in the discretion of the Supreme Government and the Government of Bombay; that the Bill, as it now stands, has been drawn in accordance with the views of this Government so as to exclude appeals in all those classes of cases to which it applies, but that the machinery for the system of revision, which is to take the place of appeal, has

been strengthened by the addition of a special Judge. I am to say that His Excellency the Governor in Council is of opinion that no alteration should be made in the Bill as it now stands. He considers that though in some instances advantage may follow on the hearing of a case by an Appellate Court, yet advantage is not likely to result in so large a number of cases as to outweigh the disadvantage of allowing an appeal in all cases; that no distinction need be recognized between appeals in mortgage cases and appeals in simple money claims; and that where errors have to be corrected, relief can be afforded on a petition for revision as well as on a regular appeal. The cost of the special Judge and his establishment will have to be met from the Provincial Revenues in addition to the charges previously contemplated, and this Government are prepared to accept this liability in order that the machinery for revision may be as complete as possible.

Sections 12 to 16.

4. Adverting next to para. 6 of your letter, the Governor in Council regrets that he is wholly unable to accept the provisions of sections 12 and 13 of the Bill framed by the Government of India as a sufficient or satisfactory substitute for those of sections 3, 33, 34 and 36 (Proviso) of the draft Bill submitted by this Government. His Excellency the Governor General in Council is aware, from the previous correspondence, that the remedies contemplated in these sections are regarded by this Government as considerably the most important of all those which it is intended that the proposed enactment shall provide for. These remedies have been on several occasions described as those which will enable the Courts to "go behind the bond." This expression, however, only partially describes the specific objects which this Government has had in view, which may be stated as follows: (viz.):

(1). To compel the Courts, in every case of a claim against an agriculturist for debt, to inquire into the transactions out of which such claim has arisen from their very commencement;

(2). To require the Courts—independently of all bonds or other documents purporting to contain an admission, by the agriculturist, of his liability for a definite amount— to ascertain the actual amount of money lent to, or due by him;

(3). To authorize the Courts, in the case of doubt arising as to the real nature or extent of the transactions between the parties, to fix the amount to be paid by the agriculturist on account of principal with reference to such considerations as the respective means and positions of the parties, the circumstances under which the money was borrowed, and such like;

(4). To enable the Courts, of their own motion, to refer the question of the sum to be allowed on account of principal to arbitration whenever they might think fit;

(5). To throw the burden of proof in all such cases, notwithstanding any such admission as above mentioned, unreservedly on the creditor;

(6). To require the Courts in every case to consider the equity of the interest charged and to allow only what is equitable;

(7). To make it illegal to award compound interest;

(8). To refuse to allow the creditor to receive, in the aggregate, an amount of interest exceeding the amount of the principal debt;

(9). To limit the liability of agriculturists for ancestral debt.

5. Each of these points was provided for in the draft Bills which have been submitted by this Government to the Government of India; and, as pointed out in para. 15 of my letter No. 654, dated 18th April 1879, an endeavour was made, in the final draft therewith submitted, to mould the sections dealing with them in such a shape as to render them less open to the objections which were entertained to them by the Government of India in their original form. If, therefore, the sections which have been substituted by the Government of India for those proposed by this Government had substantially preserved the principles which this Government had sought to embody in its proposals, the Governor in Council would not have demurred to the particular form in which His Excellency the Governor General in Council might think it expedient to give effect to those principles. But sections 12 and 13 of the Government of India's Bill entirely ignore the 3rd and 5th, and do not by any means completely secure the 1st, 2nd, 7th and 8th of the above-mentioned objects.

6. The Governor in Council is not in possession of the arguments which have led the Government of India to omit from their Bill the highly important provisions of the Bill of this Government under the heads (3) and (5) above set forth. Those under head (3) were contained in section 34 of the Bombay Bill, which purported, where the nature and extent of the transactions between plaintiff and defendant are left in doubt by the direct evidence

procurable, to permit the Judge to attach weight to certain equitable considerations as relevant facts. The points for consideration named were the means and position of the parties at the time, the state of the borrower's credit, the circumstances under which the loan was incurred, and the probable requirements of the borrower under those circumstances. I am desired to say that the Governor in Council continues to be of opinion that these considerations are often an essential element of the history and merits of the case into which the Court cannot without disadvantage neglect to inquire. When due regard is paid to the superior intelligence of the creditor class, to the confusion and obscurity which is often designedly thrown over the history of the transactions, and to the frequent extravagance and unreasonableness of the obligations into which the debtor is decoyed, a relaxation of the rigour of existing practice as to the admission of evidence, which may at first view appear of doubtful expediency, is invested with signal advantage by the special circumstances under which jurisdiction will be exercised by virtue of this Act. For the Subordinate Judges, holding their Courts among the homes of the parties, will have at command the completest knowledge of the suitors, their habits, possessions and necessities, wherefrom they may draw conclusions of substantial truth and equity in cases wherein creditors, for the embarrassment of the Court and the confusion of the debtor, have thought fit to substitute a veil of chicanery for the plain and honest exposition of their claims, and thus to baffle the Judge in his attempt to explore to the fountain head the history of the transactions between the money-lender and his client. The admission of such considerations in aid of more direct evidence is familiar to the people of this country in the settlement of their debts, and has not been discarded by the Courts of Native States. The Governor in Council has not failed to observe that, by section 13 of the Bill, the Court is empowered to refer either the whole enquiry into the history and merits of the case, or the amount to be paid as principal or interest or both, to arbitrators nominated by the parties or the Court. It is readily granted that a reference to arbitration may be authorized with advantage, and may frequently be resorted to with success, but it is not considered by this Government that this expedient will compensate for the omission of the authority conveyed to the Court itself by the 34th section of the Bombay Draft Bill, and His Excellency in Council trusts that, on further consideration of the special character of the jurisdiction contemplated, the Government of India will be pleased to restore that section to the Bill before the Council.

7. The modification of the ordinary rules as to the burden of proof in suits between money-lenders and ryots (which is the

point named in clause 5 of my 4th paragraph) is a matter closely connected with the same subject. The views of this Government on this point have been fully explained in the former correspondence; but I am directed again to call attention to the following passages from the Minute recorded by His Excellency the Governor under date the 30th August 1878, in which all the Members of this Government fully concurred:—

"13. The gist of the matter, then, is this. The Deccan ryots were sued, still are sued, and will always be sued—unless there be fresh legislation—on bonds which are, in many instances, utterly unjust, though they may have been executed in due form. I mean by 'unjust,' repugnant to the sense of natural justice as between man and man, that moral sense which is present in the minds of all men whether educated or uneducated. The harassment therefrom arising drove these ryots in 1875 to commit agrarian outrages. A special Commission showed after elaborate inquiry that the essential injustice of the majority of the bonds was the root of the mischief. It is clear that this injustice would be demonstrated by any judicial inquiry which might be had regarding the origin, progress and circumstances of the debts. The existing law provides for judgment being given on the bonds only; that much is certain. Whether it provides for the Court by its own inquiries going behind the bond is, as we submit, uncertain. The Government of India seems to consider that it does so provide, while apparently admitting that the provision is indirect rather than direct, and must be gathered from scattered rulings and clauses, rather than learnt from positively clear enactment. We submit with deference that the uncertainty is such that the Courts practically do not go, can hardly be expected to go, and for the most part are sure not to go, behind the bond. Therefore, we urge that there ought to be direct and positive legislation, without which the existing evils must be perpetuated."

"16. I must next advert to the apprehension apparently felt by the Government of India lest we should by our point (*a*) (causing the Court to go behind the bond) unduly throw upon the plaintiff the burden of proof in cases where no defence is attempted.

"17. At present the indebted ryots seldom set up any defence to these claims. They see the futility of disputing the bonds in Court, whatever they may think of the injustice. Indeed, they have no chance whatever before the law of setting up any defence which the Courts could be expected to act upon. But, if our point (*a*) be passed into law, they would set up defences fast enough, and this, too, with some chance of equitable success. In this event it is manifestly just and reasonable that the burden of proof should fall upon the plaintiffs. But in the absence of defence in cases of this sort it seems to me but right that the plaintiff should have to satisfy the Court that the bond is a just one. I am unable to follow the reasoning (as above quoted) to the effect that to cast on the plaintiff the burden of proving receipt of the consideration, and the absence of fraud,—would afford opportunities of evasion to dishonest debtors, and might thus be an incentive to reckless borrowing. Here we have educated, skilful and wealthy creditors bringing claims against uneducated, unskilful and poor debtors. Is it unfair to cast upon such creditors the burden of proving such claims to be just, even if undefended ? On the contrary, does not fairness demand that such burden should be cast upon them ? In fact, too, these ryot debtors are not, for the most part, evasive or dishonest debtors; they generally pay all, and much more than all, they really owe ! It is this notorious circumstance which underlies the whole argument. The feeling of despair of ever getting out of the money-lenders' books makes them reckless in going on borrowing, and borrowing destroys all hope of independence. Our provisions will not be incentives to reckless borrowing, but will have the very reverse effect."

8. I am to repeat the unalterable conviction of this Government, that unless provision is made in the Bill for throwing the burden of proof in all cases between money-lenders and ryots unreservedly upon the former, and for effectually barring the operation, in such cases, of clause 1, section 9 of Bombay Regulation V of 1827, which requires the defendant to show that the amount stated in a written acknowledgment of debt was not received by him, the enactment which the Government of India propose to pass will be deprived of all virtue and efficacy, and will entirely fail in affording the relief which it is designed to afford to an ignorant, illiterate, but, generally speaking, honest peasantry.

9. I am next to advert, in detail, to the provisions of sections 12 and 13 of the Government of India's Bill, which are as follows :—

    (A). That if the amount of the creditor's claim is disputed, or if it is admitted, but the Court sees reason to doubt the truth of the admission, the Court shall be bound to inquire into the history and merits of the case from the commencement;

(B). That if the claim is admitted, and the Court sees no reason to doubt the truth of such admission, it may make such inquiry, but shall not be bound to do so;

(C). That the object of the inquiry shall be, *first*, to ascertain if there is any equitable defence to the suit, and, *second*, to take an account, if necessary, in the following manner:—

(D). That the account shall be taken on the footing of any agreement between the parties as to (*a*) interest, or (*b*) the profits of mortgaged property, or (*c*) the way of taking the account, if such agreement appears to the Court fair and equitable; but

(E). That if not, the Court may set aside such agreement and any statement or settlement of account, or any renewed bond, and determine the amount due:

> (*a*) by taking separate accounts of principal and interest;
>
> (*b*) by allowing as principal only the sums actually received by the debtor;
>
> (*c*) by allowing simple interest only on the balance of principal from time to time outstanding;
>
> (*d*) by crediting all payments, &c., as far as they go, in settlement of interest due at the time they are made, and the balance in reduction of capital, and
>
> (*e*) by disallowing any balance of interest due at the date of suit in excess of the balance of principal due at such date.

10. With reference to (A) and (B) the Governor in Council desires me to observe that the provision in the Bill which expressly authorizes the Court to inquire into a claim after the amount of it has been admitted by the defendant, appears to be, on the face of it, inequitable. The course suggested by this Government is, it is thought, a much preferable one, viz., to require the Court to hold an inquiry into the history and merits of every case, and to leave it to treat the admission, if any, of the defendants as evidence, and, unless there be good cause for not doing so, to act upon it as it would in a suit between any other parties.

11. With reference to (D) I am to remark that section 13 of the Bill is open to the objection that it provides for the account being taken in the manner therein described, only when there has been an agreement between the parties, and such agreement is

thought by the Court not to be fair and equitable in respect of any of the three specified matters, although agreements may be the reverse of fair and equitable in many other respects than those indicated. The benefits of the section are thus limited to a portion only of the cases to which they ought, it is thought, to be extended. Moreover, the section in question is open to the further objections that a Subordinate Judge who is inclined to be indolent may at any time save himself the trouble of all further inquiry by saying that he thinks an agreement fair and equitable; and that when an agreement is held by the Court, whether *bonâ fide* or not, to be fair and equitable, the agreement will have to be carried out to the letter, even if it contemplates the award of compound interest and the payment of interest in contravention of the rule of *dám-dupat*, which with respect to Hindús is now in this Presidency recognized as an established rule of law applicable to all contracts. Section 13 of the Government of India's Bill thus fails to fulfil the objects of this Government set forth above in clauses (7) and (8) of my 4th paragraph, viz., that it shall be illegal to allow compound interest or interest exceeeding the principal in any case.

12. With regard to the subject of interest, I am also to ask attention to the fact that the effect of (E) (*e*) will be merely to prevent interest being awarded in the decree in excess of the amount of the balance of principal due at the date of the suit, quite irrespective of any payments of interest that may have been previously made to the creditor. The proposal which has been made by this Government is, however, that the amount of interest received by the creditor shall not exceed, *in the aggregate*, the amount of the principal debt (*vide* clause (8), para. 4). This, looking to the relative positions of money-lenders and ryots and to the admitted necessity for protecting the latter from exorbitant claims, is thought to be a reasonable provision, and the Governor in Council would be unwilling to acquiesce in its omission.

13. With reference to (E), (*b*) and (*d*), which relate to the ascertainment of the amounts actually lent to the debtor, and of the sums from time to time received from him by the creditor, the Governor in Council cannot anticipate that these proposed rules for taking an account will effect any appreciable good, unless the omitted provisions as to the method of ascertaining, in cases of doubt, the amount to be allowed as principal, and as to the burden of proof, are incorporated with them.

14. Upon the whole, after the most careful consideration the Governor in Council regrets that he is unable to accept sections 12 and 13 of the Government of India's Bill as at all equivalent to the sections of the draft Bill submitted by him for which they

have been substituted. The changes which have been made have so completely emasculated the proposals of this Government, so deprived them of all virtue and vigour, that it would, in the opinion of the Governor in Council, be better that the contemplated legislation should be deferred, or not proceeded with at all, than that the Bill should pass into law, containing, in respect of the most important of all the remedies which it is intended to supply, such impotent and inadequate provisions as those of its present sections 12 and 13.

15. With reference to paragraphs 7 and 8 of your letter which deal with sections 16 and 24 of the Bill, I am to mention that the object of those sections was to render it no longer worth the while of a money-lender to lend his money to an agriculturist for the purpose of realizing, by means of the interest he may be able from time to time to exact, an annuity payable by the debtor from generation to generation, and without any intention of ever getting the capital repaid. The operation of the sections was thus intended to be quite independent of the general law, which limits the liability of heirs for ancestral debts to the extent of the assets which they may inherit. But as the proposed provisions appear not to be approved by His Excellency the Governor General in Council, and the need for them will be, to a great extent, obviated by the portions of the Bill relating to insolvency and to the inquiry into claims, if such inquiry is conducted subject to the rules proposed by this Government, I am to say that the Governor in Council will have no objection to the sections in question being omitted.

16. I am to observe that new provisions have been added to sections 23, 31 and 32 for the management of the debtor's land or immoveable property by the Collector. His Excellency in Council, after considering these additions to the Bill, has no general objection to make to their introduction. Again, with reference to section 30, His Excellency the Governor in Council has perused the remarks made in Council on the transfer of moveable property to the creditors, and is of opinion that this section should be retained.

17. I am to say with reference to section 35, which limits sentences of imprisonment under section 359 of the Civil Procedure Code, that His Excellency the Governor in Council, after giving consideration to the comments made on this section of the Bill in the Council of the Governor General, does not desire to press the introduction of the proposed reduction in favour of agriculturists of the terms of imprisonment prescribed in the Code, and is also opinion that sentences passed under section 359 of the Code, by Subordinate Judges exercising powers under the proposed Act, should be subject to appeal.

18. I am next to remark on section 36 relating to village munsifs, regarding which you observe that the main lines of the Madras system have been to some extent restored. It has consequently been provided in the Bill that patels only are to be eligible for the office of village munsif; and you remark that if the number of village headmen who are competent to decide petty suits without the check of appeal or revision is found to be small, the proper conclusion seems to be that the village munsif system is scarcely suited to the districts of the Deccan. On this subject I am directed to say that although the intelligence of the patels is unquestionably low, and will not be sensibly improved until the younger generation, now for the most part being educated in the Government schools, replaces the present patels in office, yet there are not only some patels who are already fit for the duties of village munsif, but there are, in addition, respectable residents of various classes whom His Excellency in Council would much regret to see excluded from the field of selection. He is, therefore, of opinion that the restriction to patels of villages should be enlarged, and that the description of the persons whom the local Government may appoint to be village munsifs should include village headmen, inámdárs, village or district hereditary officers, and other persons whom this Government may deem possessed of sufficient social *status* and local influence.

19. No restriction has been proposed in the selection of persons for the function of conciliator; but, with reference to the remarks of the Hon'ble Sayyad Ahmad in the Council, I am directed to say that it is not desirable to exclude from the office of conciliator all revenue officers, some of whom are capable of exerting a very intelligent and beneficial influence in that capacity.

20. In reply to your remarks (paragraph 10) on the subject of the persons available in the Deccan for the post of village registrar, I am to say that the kulkarnis, to whom it is proposed to commit the registration, are, in the opinion of this Government, men of much capacity for public business, and that there is no objection to entrust to them the duties to be performed by the registrars under chapter VIII.

21. Regarding the subject of procedure, I am to say that the proposed new provision in section 4, that suits for amounts between Rs. 100 and Rs. 500 shall be instituted in the Court of a 1st Class Subordinate Judge, appears to the Governor in Council open to objection if, as is presumed, it is intended thereby that all such suits which arise in an entire district shall be instituted in the Court of the 1st Class Subordinate Judge of that district. In the four districts, to which the Bill will extend, there are but three 1st

Class Subordinate Judges. They hold their Courts, respectively, at Poona, Sátára and Ahmednagar, exercising, in accordance with sections 24 and 25 of the Bombay Civil Courts Act, both a local jurisdiction in two or three tálukas and a special jurisdiction in all cases exceeding Rs. 5,000 in value, which arise " within the local jurisdictions of the Courts in the district presided over by Subordinate Judges of the 2nd Class." If, therefore, section 4 of the Bill becomes law, the suits described in section 3, of which the subject-matter is valued at between Rs. 100 and Rs. 500, will in the Sátára and Ahmednagar Districts have to be instituted at Sátára and Ahmednagar respectively, and in the Poona and Sholápur Districts at Poona—Sholápur being counted, for the purposes of civil-judicial administration, a division of the Poona District merely.

22. The result would thus be to entirely frustrate, so far as regards the suits in question, one of the principal objects which Government have in view in the remedial measures about to be adopted, viz., to bring the Courts as near as possible to the homes of the suitors. I am to say that the Governor in Council would not willingly assent to any provision which would have this effect; and that he deems it preferable that the provisions of chapter II of the Bill should be inapplicable to the suits in question when they arise within the local jurisdiction of a 2nd Class Subordinate Judge. This is what was contemplated in the draft Bill submitted by this Government; but the Governor in Council entirely approves the amendment introduced in clause (3) of section 3 of the Government of India's Bill, which will allow 2nd Class Subordinate Judges to try such suits, subject to the provisions of chapter II with the consent of the parties.

23. The provisions of section 8 of the Bill are also new. The Governor in Council doubts whether it is expedient to entrust patels with the duty which it is here proposed to impose upon them, and would prefer that the service of summonses should be left to be mode in the manner at present prescribed in the Civil Procedure Code.

Section 69.

24. With reference to paragraph 12 of your letter, I am desired to state that this Government fear that the compromise which has been adopted with respect to section 69 of the Bill will render the provision for the exclusion of pleaders in cases before Subordinate Judges altogether futile. The amount to be allowed in the costs of a suit on account of the fees of pleaders is fixed by law (Act I of 1846, section 7; Regulation II of 1827, section 52 and Appendix L), and in the case of suits for not more than Rs. 2,000 it amounts to 3 per cent. only of the value of the suit. The amount

of the fee at stake in any case contemplated by section 69 of the Bill could thus never exceed Rs. 3, and it is obvious that the possible loss of so small an amount as this will not deter either suitors from engaging or pleaders from giving professional assistance. The latter will, of course, depend, as they do now, for the most part upon the remuneration privately agreed upon, and, when possible, will take care to be paid beforehand. The Governor in Council trusts, therefore, that it will be found practicable to restore substantially the provisions of section 70 of the draft Bill submitted by him in respect of the exclusion of legal practitioners from cases tried by Subordinate Judges; but I am to add that, if such concession would tend to remove the objections of the opponents of those provisions, he would not object to their being limited in their operation to district pleaders, so as not to affect pleaders or advocates or attorneys of the High Court.

25. In section 72 of the Bill provision has been introduced for the extension of limitation in debt cases. This Government have on a previous occasion expressed the opinion that it is better not to alter the general law, unless a necessity for it is proved, and on this ground did not press the alteration of the law of limitation. As, however, there is undoubtedly a strong body of public opinion in favour of a return to the old periods of limitation, and as the agriculturist is now enabled by other provisions of the Act to obtain an account from his creditor at any time, this Government do not desire to raise any strong objection to the introduction of section 72. But His Excellency the Governor in person is still of opinion that a law which has operated generally in a beneficial manner should not be lightly departed from. He is aware that the reduction of the limitation periods has, in some sense, acted severely on the agriculturists of the Deccan; but with the removal of all future possibility of hardship by the provisions of the measure for their relief which is now before the Council, the arguments in favour of the shorter periods here also recover their force, and he is unable, therefore, to advocate any change in a law which was enacted after the fullest deliberation and with the most enlightened motives.

* * * * * *

27. With regard to your concluding paragraph, in which you invite attention to the remarks made in the letter of the Government of India, Home Department, No. 222, dated February 26, 1879, on the possibility of improving the revenue system in force in the Deccan districts, and to the observations made on this subject by several Hon'ble Members of the Council in the recent debate, I am directed to say that this Government have not ceased to pay close attention to the aspects and effect of the

Bombay system of land-revenue collection in these districts at the present time, and that I shall be instructed hereafter to make to the Secretary to the Government of India for the Home, Revenue and Agricultural Department any communication on the subject which may appear to His Excellency the Governor in Council to be required.

I have the honour to be, &c.,

(Signed)   J. B. PEILE,
Acting Chief Secretary to Government.

Report of the Select Committee on the Bill for the relief of Indebted Agriculturists in certain parts of the Deccan.

WE, the undersigned Members of the Select Committee, to which the Bill for the relief of indebted agriculturists in certain parts of the Deccan was referred, have the honour to that report we have considered the Bill and the papers noted in the margin.

From Pandit Eshwant Sridhar, Poona, dated 17th August 1879 [Printed paper No. 1].
Notes by Mr. Ganesh Wassudeo Joshi, Joint Secretary, Poona Arbitration Court, dated 9th August 1879 [Printed paper No. 2].
From Acting Chief Secretary to Government, Bombay, No. 4495, dated 27th August 1879 [Printed paper No. 3].
Note by Mr. Ganesh Wassudeo Joshi, Joint Secretary, Poona Arbitration Court, dated 25th August 1879 [Printed paper No. 4].
Observations by the Hon'ble R. West, dated 10th September 1879 [Printed paper No. 5].
Abstract of letter of Bombay Government, No. 4495, dated 27th August 1879 [Printed paper No. 6].
From Acting Chief Secretary to Government, Bombay, No. 4787, dated 8th September 1879, and enclosures [Printed papers No. 7].
„ Ditto ditto No. 4774, dated 8th September 1879, and enclosures [Printed papers No. 8].
„ Ditto ditto No. 4838, dated 11th September 1879, and enclosures [Printed papers No. 9].
„ Mr. Shivram Hari Sathé, Secretary, Poona Sarwajanak Sabhá, No. 89, dated 6th September 1879, and enclosures [Printed papers No. 10].
„ Acting Chief Secretary to Government, Bombay, No. 5088, dated 22nd September 1879, and enclosures [Printed papers No. 11.]

2. We have not been so fortunate as to agree among ourselves on all the points presented for our consideration; but we do not deem it necessary to refer in the body of this report to such differences of opinion as have arisen. The most convenient course, we think, will be to treat the conclusions of the majority as the conclusions of the Committee, leaving individual members to record separate dissents upon such points as they think fit.

We shall refer to such of the amendments made by us as seem to us to call for special notice in the order of the sections of the Bill as introduced.

3. Section 8, providing for the service of summons by patels, which was inserted on a suggestion made here at the time the Bill was prepared, has been struck out, as it has not met with the approval of the Government of Bombay.

4. Section 9, empowering the Courts, instead of hearing the case *ex parte*, to issue a warrant for the apprehension of a defendant who does not appear and requiring them to adopt this procedure as the general rule, has given rise to some difference of opinion. On the one hand, it has been urged that the habits which the ryots of the Deccan have fallen into of allowing suits instituted against them to go undefended, has contributed in no small degree to produce the evils which this Bill is intended to remedy. On the other, the obvious hardship of forcibly dragging a man away from his home and his cultivation, perhaps at a season when every day is of importance to him, merely with a view to compelling him to appear in a suit to which he has no defence, has been much dwelt on by Mr. Justice West, Mr. Naylor and others.

After weighing the arguments on both sides, we have come to the conclusion that those which may be urged against the introduction of this novel and very stringent rule preponderate; and we are confirmed in this conclusion when we remember that under section 12 of the Bill the Court is bound to make an investigation into the history of the case, even though it is not defended, and that, if it is necessary for the proper conduct of such investigation to have the defendant in Court, the Civil Procedure Code gives power to summon him as a witness.

5. In order to prevent the provisions of chapter III of the Bill being evaded, as it has been pointed out to us they might be, by entering into contracts with the agriculturists of the four districts to which the Bill extends at places beyond the limits of those districts, we have introduced a section in the beginning of chapter III requiring suits against such agriculturists to be brought where the defendants reside.

6. The next provisions of the Bill calling for notice are those contained in sections 12 to 15, commonly described as the sections requiring the Court " to go behind the bond," and they are by far the most important we have had to consider.

Section 12 is in the main merely introductory to those that follow. It provides that, when the amount of a claim is disputed, the Court shall inquire into the history and merits of the case, partly with a view to ascertaining whether there is any defence to the suit on the ground of fraud, &c., and partly with a view to taking the account between the parties according to the rules laid down in the following sections; but that, when the amount of the claim is admitted, the Court shall not be bound to institute such inquiry, unless it sees reason to doubt the truth of the admission.

7. The Government of Bombay object to the latter portion of the rule. We have felt some doubt as to the precise grounds of their objection as set forth in paragraph 10 of their letter of the 27th August; but we understand that their view is that it is necessary to institute the inquiry in *every* case, even though the defendant may admit the claim, and there may be no reason to doubt the truth of his admission.

We are not prepared to go quite this length. There must, it appears to us, be some cases in which it will be clear enough for all practical purposes that the admission of a defendant is true and reasonable—cases, for example, in which, though the defendant is an agriculturist within the meaning of the Bill, he is a man of some little education and as well able to keep an account of his transactions and understand his position as the plaintiff. In such cases, we think, we should be inflicting an unnecessary hardship on both parties and wasting the time of the Court by insisting on an inquiry which, even where both parties were agreed, would, if the Judge were to be put in possession of the whole history of the case, often be lengthy and troublesome. We have, however, introduced an amendment which we believe will, in practice, secure all that the Government of Bombay desire by providing in section 12 that, in cases where the defendant admits the claim, the Court shall nevertheless inquire into the history of the case, unless, for reasons to be recorded by it in writing, it believes that the admission is true and is made by the debtor with a full knowledge of his legal rights as against the creditor. The result of this amendment will be that it will no longer be possible for an indolent Judge, as it would be under the Bill as introduced, to shirk the labour of the inquiry by saying that he sees no reason to doubt the truth of the admission. The inquiry must be made, unless the Judge is prepared to give some specific reason for accepting the admission— some such reason, *e.g.*, as might be given in a case of the description just referred to.

8. Section 13, which lays down the mode in which, after the inquiry prescribed by section 12 has been made, the account between

the parties should be taken, has been recast in order to bring it as nearly as possible into accordance with the views of the Government of Bombay.

As it originally stood it provided that, if the Court found that there was any agreement between the parties as to the mode of taking the account, and considered such agreement fair and equitable, the account should be taken in accordance with such agreement; but that otherwise the account should be taken according to certain rules, the principal of which were—

first, that compound interest should not be allowed in any shape or under any circumstances;

secondly, that all profits and advantages received by the plaintiff in connection with the transaction should be brought to credit at a value to be determined by the Court; and

thirdly, that the Hindú rule of *dám-dupat*, by which the sum recovered on account of interest shall not exceed the sum recovered *on the same occasion* on account of principal, should be observed in all cases without reference to the religion of the parties.

9. The Government of Bombay desire to have the two first of these rules applied absolutely and in all cases without any regard to the agreement between the parties, even where such agreement may, under the circumstances, be a fair and equitable one.

The third rule they desire to have similarly applied, but with a modification in favour of the debtor of so extensive a nature as to make it in form and in substance a completely new rule.

In short, the Bill, as it at present stands, goes far in the direction of setting aside contracts which under the law hitherto in force have been held good. The Government of Bombay desire to make it go much further.

10. The question is accordingly one of those of degree, of more or less, on which opinions will necessarily differ.

On the one side it is urged that it is necessary, on political grounds, to adopt strong and unusual measures in favour of the ryots in order to prevent irritation and discontent.

On the other it is urged that, in so far as the question can be considered to have assumed a political aspect, we must be careful lest by going too far in our efforts to allay the discontent of one class we excite the disaffection of the other.

11. Turning from the political to the economical aspect of the question, we have; on the one hand, the very obvious arguments as to the desirability of providing for the ryots some

means of escape from their present thraldom and of giving them a fresh start on something like a solvent footing ; on the other, we have been much pressed with the argument that by going too far in subverting contracts we may destroy the credit of the ryots, and thus in the long run both aggravate their pecuniary difficulties and place the Government revenue in jeopardy.

12. Amid these conflicting considerations we have, we need hardly say, desired to be guided, as far as possible, by the view of the Government of Bombay. There is indeed much in the Bill as now settled by us which, if it were not for the deference we feel for the strongly expressed opinion of that Government, we should propose to alter. But we cannot altogether devolve upon others, whatever our respect for their views may be, the duty of forming an opinion on the important questions submitted to us.

Looking at the matter in this way, and having given it our most anxious consideration, we find ourselves in a position to recommend that the views of the Government of Bombay be adopted fully in regard to one of the three rules above referred to, and partially in regard to the other two.

13. To begin with the rule as to crediting profits irrespective of any agreement which may have been made regarding them, we think that that rule may, without any great danger of injustice, be made, as the Government of Bombay wish it to be, applicable to all cases.

It is true that, in the case of a usufructuary mortgage, it sets aside agreements which have hitherto not only been enforced when expressly entered into by the parties, but which the law in Bombay (Bombay Regulation V of 1827, section 15) presumes, in the absence of any express agreement, to be implied : we mean agreements to the effect that the profits of the mortgaged property shall be taken by the mortgagee without account in lieu of interest. But such agreements when made between the parties to a mortgage, whether expressly or by tacit reference to the Regulation just mentioned, usually proceed on the calculation that the profits of the property will be equivalent to reasonable interest on the loan; and there can accordingly be no great hardship in providing that the approximate estimate of the profits made by the parties shall be set aside and an actual account taken, reasonable interest being at the same time allowed to the mortgagee.

14. In regard to the matter of compound interest, we are unable to adopt in their entirety the proposals of the Government of Bombay. We have no doubt that, in a very large proportion of the cases that will come before the Courts under this Bill, it will be found that the debt has been unduly swollen by frequent rests

and consolidations of interest with principal; but it seems to us that there must be some cases in which a consolidation of interest with principal, or perhaps a novation, as a lawyer would term it, of the entire transaction, has taken place under such circumstances that the refusal to recognize it would work a gross injustice. This being so, we deem it impossible to lay down any absolutely hard-and-fast rule on the point; but in order to bring the Bill in this particular, as nearly as we can venture to do, into conformity with the views of the Government of Bombay, we have, following a course similar to that which we have adopted in regard to section 12, provided that compound interest shall be disallowed, unless the Court, *for reasons to be recorded by it in writing*, is of opinion that it is fair and equitable to allow it. We may add that we feel confident that the law as thus amended will fully secure the object which we understand the Government of Bombay to have in view.

15. As regards the Hindú rule of *dám-dupát*, it has, at the desire of the Government of Bombay, been extended to the whole agriculturist population of the four districts, without reference to creed or sect. We now propose, in further compliance with the views of that Government, to make it an absolute rule overriding all contracts between the parties; but it is in our opinion quite impossible to adopt the extensive modification of the rule, or, speaking more properly, the completely new rule which is now proposed. That new rule, which would provide that the total amount claimable *from first to last* on account of interest shall in no case exceed the principal, has not, like the rule of *dám-dupat*, the authority of Native law or ancient custom to support it. It rests on no principle that we have been able to discern; and from the tenth paragraph of a letter from the Government of Bombay, No. 4579, dated 5th September 1878, which has been laid before us by the Secretary, it would appear that it was introduced merely in order to provide an additional mode of reducing the claims of sowkárs. We would further observe that no attempt has been made, as far as appears, to estimate its effect upon existing claims; but we gather from the papers before us and the report of the Deccan Riots Commission that in the case of a very large proportion of those claims interest in excess of principal has already been paid; and wherever this is so, the result of the rule would be that, when the claim had been cut down in the various modes required by the very stringent provisions of section 13, it would be necessary again to reduce it by one-half. It appears to us impossible to enact arbitrarily a new rule of this description.

16. We have next to refer to a section which appeared in the drafts submitted by the Government of Bombay in January 1878:

and in April last, but which was omitted from the Bill as prepared here, and for the re-introduction of which the Bombay Government now strongly press.

The section in question, as it appeared in the Bill submitted in January 1878, provided that where the nature or extent of the transactions between the parties was doubtful the Court should determine the "amount of money lent *upon an equitable estimate* with reference" to such considerations as the means and position of the parties, the state of the borrower's credit at the time, the occasion on which the money was advanced, the needs of the borrowers, &c. Mr. Naylor, the Legal Remembrancer to the Government of Bombay, in the able paper submitted by him, seems still to press for the introduction of the section in this form. He considers it to be one of the two essential points of the proposed measure that the Courts should be empowered, when "the evidence is doubtful, to determine the amount payable *upon equitable considerations.*"

Now, it is common enough to speak of adjusting *rights* on equitable grounds; but we are altogether at a loss to understand what is meant by deciding *a pure question of fact* "upon an equitable estimate" or "upon equitable considerations."

We apprehend, however, that if we adopted the section in this its original form, as Mr. Naylor would apparently have us do, it would probably be construed by the lower Courts as an instruction to them in default of satisfactory proof to make a guess at the amount of the loan, and in making such guess to have a special regard to circumstances which would, as a rule, tell in favour of the debtor.

17. In the Bill submitted in April last, this section appeared in a new shape, namely, as a provision simply to the effect that the circumstances above referred to, namely, the means of the parties, &c., should, upon any question arising as to the extent of a transaction, be relevant facts; and it is apparently in this shape that the Government of Bombay now advocate its re-introduction. In pressing us to re-introduce it, however, they are apparently influenced by what appears to us to be a misapprehension as to the existing state of the law. They speak of it as "a relaxation of the rigour of the existing practice as to the admission of evidence." This, as it appears to us, it would not be. We are clearly of opinion that the facts referred to, though their weight in evidence would, as a rule, be small, would be relevant facts within the meaning of the Evidence Act, and that accordingly the proposed section would be simply nugatory, that is to say, without any legal operation.

We are by no means sure, however, that if it became law it would not indirectly work mischief. We are inclined to think that an enactment expressly requiring the facts referred to to be treated as relevant facts would lead the Courts to attach an artificial weight to them over and above the weight which naturally belongs to them; and we are strengthened in this opinion when we see the extraordinary importance which the Government of Bombay and some of the local authorities appear to attach to the proposed section,—an importance which could scarcely be attributed to it if the facts to which it refers were to be estimated at their natural value.

The great anxiety shown by the Government of Bombay for the re-introduction of this section must be our excuse for stating at such length our reasons for rejecting it.

18. Sections 16 and 24, which go to relieve an heir from a portion of his ancestor's debt, though he may have inherited from that ancestor property sufficient to pay that debt, have been struck out.

The Government of Bombay do not appear to attach much importance to them, the Judges of the High Court have objected to them, and it is hard to see why, when the ancestor's debt has under the ample powers contained in sections 12 to 15 of the Bill been fully inquired into and reduced to its just limits, the heir should not be bound to pay it to the extent of the property he has inherited. The obligation binding him to do so is, as observed by the Hon'ble Sayyad Ahmad in his speech when the Bill was introduced, a matter of natural equity common to the English, Hindú and Muhammadan legal systems. Moreover, it is an obligation with the force of which the people of this country are perhaps more strongly impressed than those of any other country, and the sense of which, as observed in a letter from the Government of Bombay of the 6th April 1877, is one of the best traits in their character.

19. Section 30 of the Bill, which empowers the Insolvency Court, instead of selling the moveable property of an insolvent, to insist on one of his creditors accepting it at a valuation in payment or part payment of his claim, has given rise to much discussion. On the one hand, the danger of property being sold at a great loss when put up to public auction has been much dwelt upon; on the other, the hardship of forcing upon a creditor an article for which he may have no use for himself, and which *ex hypothesi* it is not easy to sell, has been urged especially by Mr. Justice West. On the whole, it appears to us that the arguments against this section preponderate over those in its favour, and we have accordingly struck it out.

20. We have, in accordance with the views of the Government of Bombay, removed the restriction in section 36 of the Bill under which no one but a patel could be appointed to the office of village-munsif. Under the section as now amended any person possessing local influence may be appointed.

21. Section 35, limiting the power of the Subordinate Judges to commit fraudulent insolvents to jail under section 359 of the Code of Civil Procedure, has been omitted, and a section providing for an appeal from the orders of Subordinate Judges in such cases substituted for it, at the instance of the Government of Bombay.

22. We have deemed it necessary to guard against the dangers adverted to by the Hon'ble Sayyad Ahmad in his speech, by the introduction of words in section 40, excluding revenue and police officers from the office of conciliator.

We have further, in order to furnish a simple and inoffensive means of getting rid of a conciliator who proves unfit for the position, added a clause in the same section providing that conciliators shall vacate their office at the end of three years, but shall be re-eligible.

23. In section 49 we have, adopting the view of the High Court and the Legal Remembrancer, struck out the words which made the conciliation system applicable to proceedings in execution of decrees passed before the new law comes into force as well as to suits.

We find it difficult to understand why this system should be applied to decrees passed before this Bill becomes law and not to those passed after, unless upon the assumption that the decrees already passed were unfair to the judgment-debtors, and that some pressure should be brought to bear to induce the holders of such decrees to forego some portion of what they are entitled to claim under them. We can give no countenance to any such assumption. The Courts will no doubt, if this Bill becomes law, proceed in future on principles more favourable to the debtor than those on which they have been hitherto proceeding; but when a man has obtained a decree from our Courts in accordance with the law for the time being in force, we cannot think it right to enact that his decree should be placed on the same footing as an unproved claim. If the judgment-debtor requires time to pay, the Bill gives the fullest power to the Courts to allow time. If he is altogether unable to pay, the Insolvency Courts are open to him; but we cannot admit that under any circumstances the rights of the decree-holder under his decree should be brought in question.

24. The question whether appeals should be allowed in any cases tried under chapter II of the Bill or whether we should trust entirely to the powers of superintendence and revision conferred by chapter VII has given rise to much discussion. It is not so important as might at first sight appear, inasmuch as there can be little doubt that, if the right of appeal were withheld, petitions for revision would take the place of petitions of appeal, and then the chief difference would be that an application for revision not being, like the presentation of an appeal, a matter of right, might be more summarily dealt with by the superior Court. Having considered all that has been said on both sides, we have come to the conclusion that in mortgage cases, in which questions of difficulty and importance are likely to arise, an appeal should be allowed, and we have amended the Bill accordingly.

25. If an appeal is to be allowed in these cases, which form a very large class, and the most important class, of cases to be heard under the Bill, we think that the Special Judge, who was to have been appointed to strengthen and superintend the staff of officers employed in the work of revision, will no longer be required, and we have accordingly omitted all reference to him, and transferred his duties to the District Judges.

26. We have omitted section 69, which empowered the Subordinate Judge to refuse in petty cases to allow any costs between parties on account of pleader's fees; as it has been argued, and we think with great force, that, owing to the smallness of the fees in such cases, it would rarely effect the object desired, namely, that of deterring parties from employing pleaders; and further that, in so far as it had any effect, it would tend to render the pleaders subservient to the Judges.

27. We have been urged to introduce in the place of this section the provision of the draft Bill submitted by the Government of Bombay, which would have, as a rule, excluded pleaders in these cases altogether; but we deem it undesirable to do so.

We believe that well-qualified pleaders are a material aid to the Judge in dealing with a case of any complication or difficulty, and there is nothing in the letters from the Government of Bombay to lead us to suppose that the pleaders practising in the Deccan Courts are not well qualified. If the view of those who urge us to adopt this novel provision is that in suits under Rs. 100 in value the aid of pleaders cannot be required, we think it is a mistaken view, inasmuch as the difficulty of a case does not depend on the amount at issue; and as for any notion that the ryots would be placed on something more like a footing of equal advantage with the sowkárs by the exclusion of pleaders, we are of opinion that it would be directly the reverse, inasmuch as the sowkár, having ordinarily a good deal of business in Court, would be able to employ as his servant, and send to Court on his behalf, some man who, though not a professional legal practitioner, would have a considerable knowledge of law and of the ways of the Court, whereas the ryot would have to appear in person and depend upon himself.

On the whole, we are convinced that it will be best not to interfere with the existing law on this particular point.

28. The only other amendment made by us which calls for special notice in this report is the insertion of section 71 of the Bill as now amended, requiring all mortgages below Rs. 100 in value executed before the Bill becomes law to be registered within one year. This section has been inserted at the instance of the Government of Bombay and of some of the other authorities consulted, and it appears to us to be necessary in order to guard against documents being forged with dates prior to the passing of the Bill with a view to evading the provisions of the chapter on village registration.

29. The Bill has been published in English in the *Bombay Government Gazette* of the 24th and 31st July and 7th August last, and in Maráthi in the same Gazette of the 9th instant. Some of the amendments we have made are doubtless of importance; but, looking to the urgency of the measure and the very full discussion it has already undergone, we think no further publication is necessary, and we recommend that the Bill as now amended be passed.

(Signed)   A. J. ARBUTHNOT.
,,   WHITLEY STOKES.
,,   RIVERS THOMPSON.*
,,   SAYYAD AHMAD.
,,   B. W. COLVIN.

The 10*th October* 1879.

* I CANNOT accept the conclusions arrived at by the majority of the Committee on several paragraphs of this report. In exceptional legislation of this kind applicable to a limited tract of country which has for years been subject to great distress from various causes, I am of opinion that the fullest freedom should be given to the Local Government as to the agency it should employ for carrying out the purposes of the Bill, and I would not impose

any restrictions upon that freedom as advocated in the first clause of paragraph 22 of the report. I think, too, under the special circumstances of the case, and when the primary object in view is to bring about, not so much by the technical procedure of Civil Courts as by conciliation between the parties, the adjustment of long-standing disputes, the rejection of the proposal to have a Special Judge to supervise all the proceedings under the Act is a mistake. As the Bombay Government were prepared to meet the expenses of such an arrangement, I would retain it, and would prefer that such officer should be vested with general powers of revision, and that the provision for appeals and the intervention of pleaders in any class of suits up to Rs. 100 should be given up.

There are some minor points (section 30, sale of moveables, and section 49, conciliation on old decrees) in which I differed from the majority of the Committee; but as I shall have an opportunity of stating the reasons of my dissent when the report comes up for consideration in Council, I need say nothing further on those points at present.

(Signed) RIVERS THOMPSON.

The 13*th October* 1879.

I REGRET that I am unable to sign this report even *pro formâ*. It contains some inaccuracies; the Bill it supports overrules, even in many matters of secondary importance, the opinions of the Local Government and other authorities in the best position to judge rightly; and its fourth, sixteenth, seventeenth, nineteenth and twenty-second to twenty-seventh paragraphs in particular seem to me to support by insufficient arguments conclusions fatal in the aggregate to the success of the measure.

(Signed) T. C. HOPE.

The 14*th October* 1879.

Abstract of the Proceedings of the Council of the Governor General of India, assembled for the purpose of making Laws and Regulations under the provisions of the Act of Parliament 24 & 25 Vic., Cap. 67.

The Council met at Government House on Friday the 24th October 1879.

PRESENT:

His Excellency the Viceroy and Governor General of India, G.M.S.I., *presiding.*
His Honour the Lieutenant-Governor of the Panjáb, K.C.S.I., C.I.E.
His Excellency the Commander-in-Chief, G.C.B., G.C.S.I., C.I.E.
The Hon'ble Sir A. J. Arbuthnot, K.C.S.I., C.I.E.
Colonel the Hon'ble Sir Andrew Clarke, R.E., K.C.M.G., C.B., C.I.E.
The Hon'ble Sir John Strachey, G.C.S.I., C.I.E.
General the Hon'ble Sir E. B. Johnson, R.A., K.C.B., C.I.E.
The Hon'ble Whitley Stokes, C.S.I., C.I.E.
The Hon'ble Rivers Thompson, C.S.I.
The Hon'ble Mumtáz-ud-Daulah Nawáb Sir Muhammad Faiz Alí Khán Bahádur, K.C.S.I.
The Hon'ble T. H. Thornton, D.C.L., C.S.I.
The Hon'ble T. C. Hope, C.S.I.
The Hon'ble B. W. Colvin.

DEKKHAN AGRICULTURISTS RELIEF BILL.

The Hon'ble Mr. Hope moved that the Report of the Select Committee on the Bill for the relief of Indebted Agriculturists in certain parts of the Deccan be taken into consideration. He said:—

" My Lord, in making this motion it seems convenient to mention that, while the Bill is being considered, I propose to confine my remarks to the subjects of the several amendments which my deference for the views of the Local Government, no less than my personal convictions, oblige me to move in opposition to certain decisions of the Select Committee, passed by a majority which, but for the absence through illness of the Hon'ble Sir John Strachey, would have been a narrow one. I shall reserve, until my motion that the Bill be passed, various explanations and comments of, I hope, an uncontentious character, which may perhaps contribute to a better understanding of the measure by those who will have to work it and by the public."

The Motion was put and agreed to.

The Hon'ble Mr. Hope then moved that in section 10 of the Bill the following words be omitted (namely :) "except suits of the description mentioned in section three, clauses (*y*) and (*z*)." He said :—

"My Lord, in explanation of this motion I may remind the Council that paragraph 33, of the Secretary of State's despatch of the 26th December last contains these words : 'I am inclined to think that the principle of summary jurisdiction without appeal might be conferred experimentally on all Civil Judges in the Deccan with great benefit.' In consequence of this suggestion, the draft Bill submitted by the Bombay Government provided that, within certain pecuniary limits, there should be no appeal from the decisions of the Subordinate Courts in cases, including those relating to mortgages, in which agriculturists were concerned, but that the proceedings of the Courts in such cases should be subject to inspection and revision by special officers under the District Judge. The Government of India in its executive capacity, after carefully considering whether the exclusion of mortgage-cases from appeal was desirable, allowed the Bill to be brought into this Council with the exclusion maintained; but substituted, as a further safeguard, the control of one Special Judge for that of the District Judges of the four districts. At the same time, in a letter dated July 26th, calling for the opinions of the Local Government, the High Court and local officers on the Bill generally, it invited attention to the question as still an open one. The reply of the Bombay Government on it was as follows :—

"'His Excellency in Council is of opinion that no alteration should be made in the Bill as it now stands. He considers that, though in some instances advantage may follow on the hearing of a case by an Appellate Court, yet advantage is not likely to result in so large a number of cases as to outweigh the disadvantage of allowing an appeal in all cases ; that no distinction need be recognized between appeals in mortgage-cases and appeals in simple money claims ; and that, where errors have to be corrected, relief can be afforded on a petition for revision as well as on a regular appeal.'

"The opinion of Mr. Justice Maxwell Melvill on the same point, concurred in by the four other Judges of the Bombay High Court who minuted on the reference, runs thus :—

" 'I think that, if the Subordinate Judges and Special Judge be well selected, the system of revision will be an adequate substitute for the present system of appeals. We have had a long experience of the system of revision in the High Court. In cases in which no appeal lies, applications for the exercise of our extraordinary jurisdiction are very frequent; and, though we are of course more strict in admitting such applications than we should be in admitting appeals, I do not think that any case of special hardship or injustice ever goes unredressed, or at least without an effort to redress it. Probably, in practice, there will not, under the system proposed in the Bill, be any great difference between the procedure in revision and in appeal. That is to say, every party aggrieved by a decision of a Subordinate Judge will apply to the Special Judge to revise the decision; and if the Special Judge does his duty, he will call for the proceedings in every case in which he thinks that injustice may have worked. The system of revision seems certainly most in accordance with the general spirit of the Bill, which is to leave everything as much as possible to the discretion of the Judges. I see no practical advantage, if appeals be allowed, in limiting the right of appeal to mortgage-suits.'

"Notwithstanding this concurrence in opinion of the Local Government and five Judges of the local High Court in favour of the Bill as it stood, the Select Committee, by a majority which, but for the reason I have named, would have been a narrow one, have decided to allow appeals under the ordinary law in these mortgage-cases, and to put in the place of section 73 of the Bill as introduced a new section (10) in the Bill now presented, containing the words which I have just read in my motion. As the matter is one of primary importance, likely vitally to affect the success of the whole measure, I feel bound, as I have said, by my own convictions no less than by the obvious propriety of affording full hearing for the views of the Local Government, to request the Council to reverse this decision.

"I will now endeavour to summarize the case. Against the appeal system the following objections are urged :—

"*First*, that it is a tedious process. This is sufficiently notorious; but, as actual proof is forthcoming, I may mention that the Bombay returns of civil justice for the last five years show the average percentage of appeals pending at the end of the year to be 36 per cent., with a maximum of 44 per cent. Again, the proportion of those so pending which had lasted above four months is 57·6 per cent., with a maximum of 66 per cent. How long above four months some of them had gone on, the present forms of return do not show; but by going back to 1872 we learn that, of the 3,191 appeals pending at the end of that year, 615, or about one-fifth, were two years old, 183 were three years old, while 31 were in the fourth, 8 in the fifth, and 5 in the *sixth*, year of their existence! No wonder that sometimes, as stated in an able report on the judicial administration of Khándesh in 1875, written by the Assistant Judge, Mr. Batty, 'after all the worry and expense of a suit, followed by long-delayed decision in appeal, the judgment-creditor finds he has nothing to attach.' To expose the various causes of these delays is perhaps unnecessary; but one important cause may be mentioned, that appeal may be a double process, first to the District Court, and then on to the High Court. About 13 per cent. of the appeals hitherto heard in a year have been such 'second' appeals; and I fear the proportion will be increased by the lately passed amendment of the Civil Procedure Code.

"*Secondly*, appeal is an expensive process. This is obvious, as the parties have to operate at the District or High Court, far from their homes, and where pleaders of a higher class are indispensable. The mere recognized costs of appeals, such as stamps, process fees, subsistence to witnesses, pleaders' fees, &c., are recorded in 1872 as 13·6 per cent. on the value. The real costs were of course much more, especially for pleaders, who, we are told in the papers before the Council, always exact higher fees than the rate authorized by law.

"*Thirdly*, appeal is a specially uncertain process. Where one Appellate Court sits in appeal upon another, the uncertainty is aggravated; and where this is not so, the natural and proper reluctance of an Appellate Court to interfere with findings on questions of fact, passed in full view of the demeanour of parties and witnesses and in the hearing of the local public, imparts a fictitious and undeserved importance to issues and refinements of law and procedure, upon which opinions may differ greatly. Hence an appeal is too often a gambling or speculative transaction, resulting in the denial of the substantial justice awarded by the Court below. Where, as sometimes happens, the Appellate Court is fond of re-appreciating the evidence and meddling with facts, the uncertainty is of course greater still.

"*Fourthly*, appeal is an unsuitable mode of redress; that is, it on the whole suits those least who most need help. As I said in my speech on July 18th, 'the cases which come up in appeal are often not those which deserve to come. Many a man who has a good case cannot afford to appeal; many a man with money needlessly drags his opponent through all the Appellate Courts.' To appreciate the full meaning of this, it must be remembered that appeals lie not merely on the final decision, but on a whole string, lately much lengthened, of intermediate orders of one kind or another. Appeal, in short, is a luxury within the reach of monied litigants only.

"*Lastly* the process is one of small general application. In 1877 the proportion of appeals to cases disposed of in the whole Bombay Presidency was just 3 per cent. In the four disturbed districts it reached $3\frac{1}{2}$ per cent. in 1876, but fell to $2\frac{1}{2}$ in 1878. But these are appeals in suits of all kinds. If we exclude those as to title, &c., which are known to be numerous, what will be the proportion applicable to our Bill? Yet we are asked by some to believe that by this insignificant check our Courts are kept braced up to high efficiency, and that on its withdrawal they will subside into models of superficiality, incapacity, laziness, precipitation, favouritism, corruption, and I know not what other theoretical attributes of irresponsible power. Nay rather, the truth more probably is that though now, under the existing appeal system, work is so done as to command our confidence, 68 per cent. of decisions appealed against being confirmed, still, as stated by the Bombay Legal Remembrancer, 'Subordinate Judges are left too much to themselves; their work is never sufficiently overhauled and scrutinized; their errors and shortcomings are not pointed out to them,' &c.

"The remarks just made have reference to the appeal system in general. But the majority in the Select Committee only propose that it shall be applied to 'mortgage-cases.' To this I would object that there is no real reason for making a distinction between these cases and others. The theory is that a mortgage-case is something to look very grave about; that it sometimes involves the investigation of difficult questions as to title, priorities, marshalling securities, contribution and rights of maintenance, and always involves the taking of complicated accounts. But the fact is that a mortgage-case, like most other cases, may be easy or may be difficult. Each one of the points named, title, priorities, &c., may present no special feature, and be promptly and safely settled on well-known rules. Questions of title, and curious ones too, sometimes arise about moveable property; and that litigation on them is not inconsiderable may be seen from the statistics of suits arising out of execution of decrees. As to accounts, it may be safely affirmed that they will be found, on an average, to be more complicated in money-suits than in mortgage-suits. An account on a simple money debt, to liquidate which grain, bullocks, cash, personal service, &c., have to be brought to credit under section 13 (*f*) of the Bill, may be complicated indeed. A mortgage account, on the other hand, judging from very full statistics of the mortgages of different kinds customary in the districts of Poona, Násik, Ahmednagar, Sholápur and Kaládgi, which I lately obtained from the Hon'ble Colonel Anderson, Survey Commissioner for Bombay, must usually contain very simple items, even where an agreement to set off profits in lieu of interest has been set aside. This conclusion, that there is no reason for making any distinction as to appeals between mortgage-cases and other cases, is that which we find given in the papers before us by authorities undoubtedly the best acquainted with the subject. The Judge of Ahmednagar says that experience shows that any nominal classification of suit is fallacious as a test of intricacy; and Mr. Justice Maxwell Melvill, with whom his four colleagues concur, says he sees no practical advantage, if appeals are allowed, in limiting them to mortgage-suits.

"I must now say a few words about revision. It appears to be in a very great measure free from the evils which I attribute to the appeal system. As the Special Judge and his two assistants will be moving about their charges for nearly two-thirds of the year, parties will be able to come freely before them at the time most convenient to themselves, while cases which they take up *proprio motu* will of course [be chiefly taken up at once on the spot, after perusal of the record. The saving to parties in time, trouble and expense is obvious; the long purse will have less advantage over the short one, and the temptations to technicality will be dim- nished. But, above all, the percentage of cases which will come under scrutiny—scrutiny of a direct, personal and searching character—will certainly be ten times as large as under the appeal system, and probably more. That Judges who have one-third of their whole work looked into on the spot by picked officers having nothing else to do, will not be more careful in it than Judges who have only one-thirtieth, and that of a tolerably defined special class, brought by haphazard before a distant authority, I am wholly unable to believe.

"Against the substitution of revision for appeal what little has been hitherto advanced has mostly been met. But I must invite attention to the utterly insufficient grounds on which the majority of the Select Committee, in paragraph 24 of the report, attempt to justify the conclusion in favour of appeals at which they have arrived. They merely observe that the question, whether appeals should be allowed in any cases, or whether we should trust entirely to the powers of superintendence and revision,

'is not so important as might at first sight appear, inasmuch as there can be little doubt that, if the right of appeal were withheld, petitions for revision would take the place of petitions of appeal; and then the chief difference would be that an application for revision not being, like the presentation of an appeal, a matter of right, might be more summarily dealt with by the superior Court.'

Here the whole of the objections to the appeal system, as also the far wider controlling influence of the revision system, are simply ignored; and it is assumed that selected officers of the judicial department will take advantage of the almost imperceptible difference of status between appellants and petitioners for revision in order to deal 'summarily,' that is, I suppose, to leave, as Mr. Justice Melvill puts it, cases of special hardship to go unredressed or without an effort to redress them. Such reasons are a virtual surrender of the case.

"In conclusion, I would beg the Council to bear in mind that the revision system secures whatever advantages the appeal system possesses, but removes the disadvantages which that system involves, and has a far wider beneficial influence; that the abolition of appeals, even without the revision safeguard, is thought desirable by the Secretary of State; that there is no real difference between mortgage-cases and other cases, as far as this question is concerned; that the exclusion of appeals in mortgage-cases is emphatically advocated by the Local Government; and, finally, that the five Judges of the High Court have reported officially that revision is an adequate substitute for appeal. In view of these facts I cannot doubt that the Council will decide favourably on the motion I have brought forward."

The Hon'ble Mr. Thornton said :—" I take the opportunity of the consideration of the first of Mr. Hope's amendments to explain the general principle which will regulate my votes this day. The measure we have to consider is, it appears to me, to all intents and purposes a local one, and, but for certain technical objections, might have been dealt with by the local Legislature of Bombay. This consideration should, I think, induce the Council to accord special respect to the views and wishes of the Local Government. But, apart from this, I look upon this measure as an honest and earnest attempt by the Bombay Government to meet and grapple with a local and exceptional difficulty; and I think, therefore, that their proposals should, wherever possible, receive the cordial support of the Members of this Council, even though some of them may not be in strict accordance with our views of what is best.

"I have said that the difficulty to be grappled with is local and exceptional. I say 'local,' because I desire to protest against the notion, which has obtained some currency, that the condition of the Deccan ryot is to be considered as typical of the condition of the peasantry in all parts of India. At any rate, I can assert that is it not typical of the condition of the people of the province over which my hon'ble friend Sir Robert Egerton presides.

"I say also that the difficulty is an exceptional one; for, although some of the causes which have contributed to the depressed condition of the Deccan ryot—such as the burden of ancestral debt, the *crassa ignorantia* of the kunbi, the absence of a law of bankruptcy or provision for winding-up the estates of deceased persons, the rigid system of collecting the full land-revenue in good and bad seasons alike, the distance of Courts of Justice from the homes of the people—were certainly not to be ignored, yet I venture to think the *causa causans* (to borrow an expression from the old logicians) was a sudden and enormous inflation of credit during the American civil war, followed by a terrible contraction of credit. Such an event would bring about in England that state of things known technically as a commercial crisis. It would more or less ruin and demoralize any peasant proprietary in the world; and how much more a simple-minded peasant proprietary in India, where, by laws or custom or from a creditable sense of family honour, it is usual for the son to take upon himself the personal liabilities of his deceased father, even though he may have received no assets from the estate.

"Truly, my Lord, after considering the Report of the Deccan Riots Commission, my ground of astonishment is, not that 66 per cent. of the Deccan ryots should be insolvent, but that 33 per cent. should be in a position to pay their debts!

"But whatever may be the causes of the situation, there it is, and it *must* be dealt with vigorously, thoroughly and practically; and in so dealing with the situation I, for one, am prepared to sacrifice a large amount of theory.

"Keeping, then, the above principle in view, I proceed to the consideration of the first amendment—that is to say, the amendment which provides that *all* cases, including mortgage-cases, coming before the small-debt Courts shall not be liable to appeal. The statistics relating to appeals in the Bombay Presidency which have just been read to us by the Hon'ble Mr. Hope are certainly not encouraging. But I venture to hope that the facts he has quoted, and the deductions he has drawn, are not applicable to other provinces in India; they are most certainly not applicable to the province with which I am connected.

"Our experience in the Panjáb is that the right of appeal is greatly valued by the people, and it would also appear that the right, though freely used, is not abused; for although in the Panjáb justice is comparatively accessible,—there being, as a rule, a Court of Justice within an easy day's walk of a peasant's home—as many as 82 per cent. of appealable cases are unappealed."

His Excellency the President:—"Does the Hon'ble Member mean that in 82 per cent. of the cases in which an appeal lies the decisions are unappealed?"

The Hon'ble Mr. Thornton :—" Yes, my Lord. What I am seeking to show is that, though the right of appeal exists, and is highly valued, and can be easily enforced, it is not abused in the Panjáb.

"But, although our experience of the working of an appellate system is not similar to that of Mr. Hope in the Bombay Presidency, yet, as the Local Government of that Presidency considers that the regular appellate system is objectionable in the case of the smaller class of suits by money-lenders, including mortgage-suits, and prefers to substitute and pay for a somewhat costly system of revision, control and superintendence, which is to all intents and purposes an easy, though somewhat uncertain, system of appeal, I am certainly not prepared to vote against the Hon'ble Member's amendment on this point."

His Honour the Lieutenant-Governor said :—" I have very few words to say upon this amendment. I consider the Bill, as my hon'ble friend Mr. Thornton has remarked, to be a local one, and that it is for technical reasons alone that it comes before this Council. Holding this view, I think that the utmost deference should be paid to the wishes of the Local Government in regard to the details of the measure. The whole chapter in which the section which it is proposed to amend occurs, sets aside many of the existing provisions of the Code of Civil Procedure; and I can see no reason why the appeal, for which revision is substituted in regard to the other classes of cases specified in section 3, should be allowed in mortgage-cases only. I consider that the same procedure should be adopted for all the classes of suits specified, as the Bombay Government desire. In their letter on the case they state distinctly that they do not wish any appeals to be allowed in mortgage or other cases; and it seems to me desirable to follow their wishes."

The Hon'ble Mr. Rivers Thompson said :—" As a member of the Select Committee which very carefully went through all the details of this Bill, and unfortunately a member who was in a minority on this point, I do not like allowing it to pass with a silent vote. The question before the Council, I would remind them, is not whether there should be no supervision at all as regards the proceedings of Courts in any class of cases, but the simple one whether, in dealing with disputes connected with mortgage-suits, the principle to be adopted should be one of appeal from the Subordinate Judge to a superior Court or one of revision by a Special Judge. Now I trust I shall not be out of order if I remark that, with regard to this particular question about appeals, it depends very much upon whether the next amendment which the Hon'ble Member for Bombay will move—that is, with regard to section 54—will be carried or not. It seems to me that the two sections hang or fall together. If, as the Bill now stands, the Special Judge is excluded, I am prepared to say that some system of appeal ought rightly to be admitted with regard to this particular class of cases; but if it is a question whether there shall be appeals, or whether this particular class of cases shall come under the revision of a Special Judge, I am certainly in favour of the amendment proposed by the Hon'ble Member for Bombay, that the latter alternative should be adopted. I would call to the remembrance of the Council that, before even the Bill was introduced, there was a committee of officers who considered very carefully the provisions of the measure, and it was at that time proposed, and adopted almost I believe with unanimity, that, considering the very exceptional and admittedly tentative character of this legislation, it would be very much better that a special officer should be appointed, not only for the duty of revising judicial decisions of inferior Courts, but for the general supervision of all proceedings under the Act.

" I myself fully accepted that proposal; and as the Bill was first drafted, it contained a provision for the appointment of a Special Judge. This arrangement secured, as I have said, the necessary special superintendence required for the work in the four districts to which the Bill was to apply; and that not only as regards any particular class of suits in Court, but for the whole general administration of the law. I still think that this is a necessity under the circumstances in which this measure is introduced into these four districts. They have suffered from longstanding troubles and difficulties arising from causes in a great measure beyond the control of the Government; and in the embittered relations which now exist between debtor and creditor special legislation has been resorted to for the removal of the evil. Now, when the question of appeals came before the Select Committee, while it was accepted, as a rule, that appeals should not be allowed in simple money claims, it was decided that they should be admitted for those two classes of cases that come under clauses (y) and (z) of section 3; and stress was laid by the majority of the Committee on the fact that this class of cases was a very difficult one, and that in consequence of that difficulty Appellate Courts must be provided for securing that no injustice takes place in such litigation. I agree with Mr. Hope in thinking that, considering the class of people for whom we are legislating, and the amount for which the money-value of appeals is fixed in the measure, these mortgage-cases will probably not present greater difficulties than the general class of cases which will come under its provisions; and I am also inclined to say that, whatever these difficulties may be, they will much more advantageously be met by an officer fully vested with the powers of revision, specially selected and reserved for the consideration of these cases, than by the ordinary procedure in civil suits. It seems to me that if a system of appeals is to be allowed, and such appeals are to lie to four different Judges, holding their Courts at different places, at long distances from the homes of the people, the long delay that always arises in the disposal of appeals, and the technicalities of procedure that attend such a course, will be fatal to the success of the Act. I would also point to the fact that, as regards the objection taken as to the difficulties and intricacies of such suits, in section 12 of the Bill as it now stands special provisions are made to enable the Courts to go, as it is called, behind the bond; and that in mortgage-suits also it will be in the power of those Courts to analyze the whole history of the transaction. As the general scope and object of the whole measure is to bring the two parties together, and in their presence to try and get to the foundation and origin of the debt, and the whole proceedings connected with it, the Subordinate Judges will have ample power to go into the entire case, and to arrive at a fair decision upon its merits. With these observations I have only to say that I shall support the Hon'ble Member in his amendment."

The Hon'ble Sir John Strachey said :—"The Hon'ble Mr. Hope, in his opening speech, referred to the fact that, although I was a member of the Select Committee on this Bill, I had unfortunately been unable to attend the meetings of the Committee; otherwise I should certainly not only have expressed in the Committee views in accord with the present amendment, but also with the other amendments of which notice has been given. I should have agreed on every point with him and my hon'ble friend Mr. Thompson. I am strongly opposed to the alteration which the Select Committee has proposed to make in the Bill in regard to the question of appeal; and I think the change, if allowed to stand, will be a most unfortunate one. I do not for a moment deny that it is necessary in a great many cases of importance to allow suitors the right of appeal. Nevertheless, I believe it to be true that among all the causes which have rendered the administration of justice in India slow, expensive and uncertain, the system of appeal has been one of the most serious and the most mischievous. I think it has been clearly shown that nine-tenths of the cases in which it is now proposed to allow appeals, will be of a most simple character, and that there is no more reason for allowing an appeal in them than there is for allowing in the other cases in which an appeal is forbidden by the Bill.

"It seems to me that far greater security for the correction of erroneous decisions, and for ensuring supervision of the Subordinate Courts by competent superior Judges, was afforded by the Bill as it stood before it was altered by the Select Committee.

"As my hon'ble friend Mr. Thompson has just said, the amendment now being considered and the second amendment which refers to the appointment of a Special Judge are closely connected with one another, and they must stand or fall together. As the Bill formerly stood, there was to be a Special Judge, who was to devote his whole time to examining the proceedings of the Subordinate Courts, and to revising their decisions whenever a failure of justice appeared to have taken place. It seems to me that every honest suitor considering himself aggrieved by the decision of the lower Court would have every opportunity, under the system formerly proposed by the Bill, of getting his case re-heard which he could have under the system of appeal. His petition would be called a 'petition for revision' instead of a 'petition of appeal'; but I cannot see that he would be deprived of any single advantage which under the system of appeal he would have. It seems to me that, taking the first and second of these amendments together, it is now proposed to abolish one of the very best and most essential parts of the Bill as it was introduced. It is proposed to substitute for the provisions under which we should have got security for the constant and personal superintendence by a competent officer over al the proceedings of the lower Courts the altogether illusory and imaginary security afforded by extending the power of appeal. The Bill as it originally stood in respect to this matter was, I believe, approved by the majority of this Council. It was strongly approved by the Local Government; and we know now that it was also approved by the five Judges of the Bombay High Court. Under these circumstances, my Lord, I shall vote for the amendment."

The Hon'ble Mr. Stokes said that the effect of the amendment would be to deprive the parties to all suits for foreclosure or redemption of the right of appeal which they now enjoyed, and to substitute for it a system of revision. On the expediency of providing an appeal in cases of this kind he had but little to add to what he had said when the Hon'ble Mr. Hope had introduced the Bill. He had then pointed out that, in the absence of an Appellate Court, the Judges of first instance would have no one to stand in awe of, and that the errors arising from corruption, incapacity, laziness, precipitation, ignorance and love of arbitrary power would remain uncorrected, and cause hardship and discontent. These general remarks did not pretend to be original, but were founded on the writings of the great master in these matters *di color che sanno*—Bentham—and he had heard nothing here to-day, and did not expect to hear anything, that would lead to a different conclusion. But the matter seemed more complicated than he had supposed. It now appeared that these mortgage-suits were of such importance as to demand a special procedure, or, at all events, to be free from a summary procedure, not merely because of their difficulty, of which he would say a few words hereafter, but because they related to land, and because to the natives of India land was of abnormal importance. Having no manufactories, their livelihood depended solely on the cultivation of their fields; and for that reason, as well as for others—as he understood from persons better acquainted with the subject than he could pretend to be—they attached extraordinary value to the right of appeal in all questions relating to land. The question had, therefore, a political as well as a juristic aspect. Furthermore, the suits referred to in the amendment were mortgage-suits; and, as the Bill was now framed, the number of mortgage-suits would be enormously increased. As far as he could make out, with section 22 forbidding attachments or sales of immoveable property not specifically pledged, no sowkár would ever lend money except on the security of land; and, unless the nature of such litigation was different in the Bombay Presidency from what it was elsewhere, no suits could be named in which difficult questions more often arose and which were, therefore, less adapted for a summary procedure. There was always a more or less complicated account to be taken; and questions as to title, priorities, marshalling securities and contribution were certain to arise in almost every case—that is, provided the Judge understood his business, and saw difficulties where they really existed. That Bombay litigation formed no exception to this rule, appears from the able paper of Mr. Naylor, the Bombay Legal Remembrancer, who wrote :—

"Suits between mortgagors and mortgagees generally entail questions of considerable importance and difficulty; and, after having given the matter much consideration, I am unable to concur with those who think that when agriculturists are parties to such suits they should be tried summarily. The intricacy of a suit in no way depends upon the social status or occupation of the parties thereto. It is to the subject-matter of an action that we must look in order to judge whether it is likely to involve complicated issues; and those who are acquainted with the usual range of litigation will unhesitatingly affirm that questions relating to mortgage-claims are amongst those which are most prolific of knotty points and legal difficulties. It makes no difference in this respect whether the value of the matter in dispute be small or great, or whether the parties to the suit belong to one class or another."

It was true that the Hon'ble Mover in his speech on introducing the Bill, and in reply to a question put by the Hon'ble Sir

Alexander Arbuthnot, said that "mortgages are usually only difficult if they happen to involve questions of priorities and the like, or there are several creditors. . . . .
Under the Bombay revenue system the name of the owner of every field is entered in the Government books. It would only be in most rare instances that the man whose name appeared was not the real owner; *and so* questions of title are not likely to give trouble." Mr. Stokes thought the Hon'ble Member in making the latter statement must have overlooked the fact that the Bombay High Court had decided more than once that the Collectors' books were kept for purposes of revenue, and not for purposes of title (10 Bom. 187); and that the fact that a person's name was so entered did not establish his title or defeat that of any other person (10 Bom. 187, 192). As to the disadvantages in civil cases of the system of revision as compared with the system of appeal, he rejoiced to find that the remarks which he had ventured to make upon this subject, drawn as they were from theoretical considerations rather than practical experience in the Mofussil, were now confirmed by three such men as Mr. Naylor, whom he had just quoted, Mr. Wedderburn, District Judge of Ahmednagar, and Mr. Justice West.

Mr. Naylor at page 9 of his paper said :—

"The cases in which it would be justifiable to interfere with a decision of a civil matter, except upon the application of one or other of the parties, must be very few. If the Special Judge revises a decision upon the complaint of one of the parties, he will, in effect, hear an informal appeal. But he will do so subject to the following disadvantages over a regular system of appeal (namely) :—

(1) that there is no limit to the period within which applications for revision may be made or granted, and the parties can, therefore, never be certain that the decision they have obtained is final.

(2) that the application will generally have to be enquired into at a great distance from the homes of the parties, *i. e.*, wherever the Special Judge may happen to be on tour, and on no fixed date, and must, therefore, be disposed of without hearing the parties or anybody in their behalf;

(3) that the parties will have no absolute right to bring their cases before him, and that it will therefore be in his power to refuse applications without any inquiry at all.

"The right of appeal to a fixed Appellate Court within the district itself is, I think, a far preferable remedy to this; and in mortgage-cases it is most undesirable, not to say altogether inequitable, that the people should be deprived of it."

Mr. Naylor did not seem to be quite correct in saying that there was no limit to the period within which applications for revision might be made. The Limitation Act XV of 1877, schedule II, No. 178, fixed a period of three years for this and other applications not expressly provided for. But for three years the parties would never be certain that the decision they had obtained was final; whereas now, when the periods prescribed for presenting appeals under the Code of Civil Procedure (thirty days and ninety days) had lapsed, the decision might practically be regarded as final. As to the disadvantages respectively numbered (2) and (3) he (Mr. Stokes) entirely agreed with Mr. Naylor.

Mr. Wedderburn in the fifth paragraph of his note also said:—

"With regard to the efficacy of revision as a substitute for appeal it appears to me that this method of control is better suited for criminal than for civil business. By examining a criminal return which gives an abstract of the incriminating circumstances, and states the section under which the accused has been convicted and the amount of the punishment, a superior Court can form an opinion as to the general propriety of the orders passed, and by sending for the record can effectually remedy a failure of justice. But the difficulty of carrying out such a duty would be very much greater in civil suits, where the issues are so much more complicated. And I think it would be difficult to devise a form of return which would, within moderate dimensions supply to the Special Judge the information necessary to enable him to carry out the revision described in section 54 of the Bill. It must also be borne in mind that, unless such returns are framed in English,* most European officers would, in making use of them, have to rely on subordinate agency, which would, in great measure, defeat the purpose of the Legislature in appointing a Special Judge to exercise a vigilant personal control. If, on the other hand, the Special Judge does not rely upon civil returns, but modifies the decisions of the Subordinate Judges upon the complaint of the parties, I do not see wherein this method will materially differ from a system of appeal. To disturb the decision of the lower Court on a mere inspection of the record, would be a risky proceeding; and the party to whose detriment the alteration was made would consider himself highly aggrieved if he had no opportunity of being heard in support of the original decree."

* The Subordinate Judges in this district write their judgments mostly in Maráthi.

The Council would perhaps remember that when the Bill was introduced he (Mr. Stokes) had suggested that the revising Judge would have neither time nor skill to decipher and translate the records kept, as they would be in a native language, and that he would therefore have to rely upon some corruptible subordinate, such as the shirastedár. He was glad to find this suggestion fully supported by the District Judge of Ahmednagar. To the same effect was the remark made by Mr. Justice West in what he would take the liberty of calling one of the most interesting and statesmanlike papers ever laid before this Council. "The brief notes of evidence and of the judgment," says Mr. West, "will, it is supposed, be nearly always in English. *It is absolutely necessary that they should be, if there is to be any trustworthy scrutiny of them by the supervising officers."*

But to return to the general question as to the relative advantages of a system of appeal and a system of revision, Mr. Justice West, in the paper he had just quoted, remarked :—

" The power of superintendence and revision is one which in discreet hands may be very usefully exercised ; yet, according to my experience, it bears much more frequently upon matters of form than of substance. If there has been any active departure from the prescribed rules of procedure, the papers recorded will usually indicate the error. Omissions to do this or that thing which ought to have been done are less readily betrayed by the record ; and all signs of any total departure from justice or propriety will be carefully excluded from it. If a Subordinate Judge towards the close of a wearying case refuses to take the evidence of certain witnesses or to accept a well-grounded application for adjournment, there will, as a rule, be nothing on record to show this dereliction of duty. If he cuts short the examination of witnesses whose testimony is received, his notes or the substance of their statements will not afford any evidence of his impatience. A smooth and specious surface presented by the written proceedings is quite consistent with a defective, arbitrary and partial investigation in substance. The parties only, and the people who were present in Court, can say how far the record is an actual representation of what took place. It is the interest of the defeated litigant to point out all errors of the Judge through which, as he thinks, justice has been defeated. It is equally his interest not to indulge in misrepresentations, the discovery of which will cause distrust, and probably the dismissal of his appeal. It is thus, and thus only, that material failures of justice arising from indolence, impatience or caprice will, with any reasonable certainty, be brought to light. The record ought to be kept with such fulness and regularity that, except by a conspiracy between the Judge and his principal subordinates, it should by mere inspection of it afford a corroboration or refutation of most of the imputations which a disappointed suitor is apt, rightly or wrongly, to cast upon the Judge who has decided against him.

" It is true that the same disappointed suitor who, under the ordinary system, may make an appeal may, under the system of revision, present his complaints in the form of a petition for review. Some check on absolutely false statements will be imposed by a rule which shall exact a verification on oath of the matters of fact set forth in the application. But whether its assertions as to a defective examination of the witnesses or a perverted note of their statements are true or not, cannot really be ascertained in case of a denial, by means of the Judge's note, which is itself impugned. It is certain that many false or greatly exaggerated complaints will be made, and, under cover of these, a careless or hasty Judge will enjoy impunity in cases in which he has been really and seriously to blame."

He (Mr. Stokes) felt it his duty to bring these remarks before the Council ; for he had reason to believe that, owing to great press of work, they had not been read by some of the Hon'ble Members. They had, moreover, been made by men who had had very considerable experience in civil judicature—an advantage which, so far as he was aware, the Hon'ble Mover, however distinguished as a Collector and Magistrate, had not enjoyed. Mr. Justice West then proceeded to show that the system of revision would tend to cause deterioration of judicial work:—

<blockquote>
"The brief notes of evidence and of the judgment will, it is supposed, be nearly always in English. It is absolutely necessary that they shoud be, if there is to be any trustworthy scrutiny of them by the supervising officer. But, for the purpose of publicity, of bringing the people in the Court and the Judge into effective and corrective relation, these notes might as well be written in Japanese or Hebrew. It is a rare thing for even one member of the assembly in a Subordinate Court to know English. The Subordinate Judge may take down as much as he likes and in what terms he likes. The reasons he chooses to assign for his decision may be good, bad or indifferent, and no one in Court will be a bit the wiser. If theory and experience both are not entirely at fault, this substantial withdrawal of judicial work from the light of full publicity cannot but be attended with a rapid deterioration of its quality. Few human beings are fit for irresponsibility—natives of India least of all. From a personal examination, some years ago, of a large number of unappealable cases disposed of by Subordinate Judges, I became satisfied that the inherent weakness of the native character (or indeed of human character) showed itself as markedly in judicial proceedings as in any other work. The evidence I found was taken in a much more slovenly manner; the whole business of the Subordinate Judge was performed with far less care and precision than in the cases subject to appeal. And if this was so when the whole record was in the vernacular and open to effective discussion by every one about the Court, how much more may the same laxness be expected to prevail when everything is hidden away in an unknown tongue?"
</blockquote>

Civil Procedure Code, sections 189 to 203.

It was said that the system of appeals led to inordinate delay and expense, to loss of time and to uncertainty, which checked exertion. He (Mr. Stokes) had touched on this matter in the remarks which he made when the Bill was introduced, and was not going to repeat himself; but he would read what Mr. Justice West had written on this matter:—

<blockquote>
"It is said, however, that this system of appeals leads to inordinate delay and expense, to loss of time and an uncertainty which checks exertion. The ryot himself, however, does not, in fact, appeal in more than one in a hundred of the suits of small amount that are brought against him. In cases of larger amount he belongs generally to a class needing no special protection. If he has no means, he may appeal without expense *in formâ pauperis*. If dissatisfied, he may again present his case free of cost to the High Court. His applications are rejected only if it appears that he is in the wrong. If his creditor appeals against an adverse decree, the necessary expense falls on that creditor, at least in the first instance. To be a respondent does not necessarily cost anything: a debtor successful in the Court of first instance is not even called on to appear in the Appellate Court, unless a good *primâ facie* cause appears for reversing the decree in his favour. If
</blockquote>

the decree was absolutely wrong, it will hardly be contended that it ought not to be set right. Such is the degree of uncertainty produced by the right of appeal; and this itself is controlled and restricted by the power of the High Court. It is not for a moment to be compared with the uncertainty in which people would live with respect to any possible claim that might be trumped up against them under the *régime* of ill-informed, poor and practically irresponsible Judges. The loss of time is as nothing to that which will be occasioned by the enforced double appearance in many cases before conciliator and Judge, by the necessity of bringing forward unwilling gratis witnesses and getting a presentable statement of defence driven into a stolid brain by a pleader not allowed himself to plead.

" Considered as a means for ameliorating and elevating the condition of the peasantry, this scheme of imperfect investigation, defective record and casual supervision seems as unpromising as any that could be devised. It has not, I think, emanated, and could not have emanated, from any one really acquainted with the working of the Civil Courts in this country. It meets no actual or even fancied need of the people themselves. They do not complain of the Appellate Courts except as they complain of all Courts which enforce the payment of debts. They have more confidence in the Court of higher than in that of lower rank, and, like the rest of mankind, they are pleased to think that an appeal lies open to them, even if they do not resort to it. What they really complain of about the Courts are the enormous fees, which it is not apparently proposed to reduce; the loss of time in attendance which will be considerably increased; and the improvident sales of their property, which could as well be prevented under the existing organization as under that by which the Legislature is asked to replace it. From 1880 onwards they will have in every case or almost every case to sell their farms outright, where now they would but contract a loan. When a suit is instituted, they will lose their patrimonies more rapidly and irrevocably than ever before. Such 'relief' will to some of their untutored minds be hardly distinguishable from a new form of oppression."

After all, on such a matter the only opinions likely to be of much practical value were those of men familiar with the working of the local Civil Courts: to such familiarity he (Mr. Stokes) could not pretend; and with these remarks on appeal and revision, which he had studiously refrained from making on his own authority, he begged to state that he would oppose the motion.

The Hon'ble Sir Alexander Arbuthnot said :—" My Lord, I intend to vote against the amendment. I had not intended to speak at any length on this question, and the few remarks I proposed to make have been for the most part anticipated by my hon'ble friend Mr. Stokes. But there is one point which has been dwelt on by some of the speakers in favour of the amendment regarding which I should like to say a word. My hon'ble friend Mr. Thornton in his interesting observations, and my hon'ble friend the Lieutenant-Governor and, if I remember right, Mr. Thompson also, dwelt on the importance of our giving the utmost possible support to the views of the Local Goverment in regard to what they described as an essentially local Bill. Now, My Lord, I quite agree with those Hon'ble Members that, in this as in all other matters affecting the local concerns of a particular presidency or province, we should pay the greatest and the most respectful attention to the views and opinions of the Local Government. But it appears to me that this principle may be carried too far. The Government of India exists, both in its executive and its legislative capacity, for the purpose of directing, controlling and laying down the principles upon which this country is to be administered, both executively and legislatively. It is very desirable that, as far as we possibly can, we should abstain from interference with the Local Administrations in matters of detail; but when we come to important questions of principle, when we come to proposals which are in contravention of the principles which have been laid down by the wisest administrators and legislators who have dealt with such matters, whether in our own country or in India, then I think the Government of India are bound to consider carefully whether it is not their duty to interpose. It appears to me that in this particular matter the supporters of the amendment moved by the Hon'ble Member are ignoring the wisdom and the opinions of the most eminent men who have dealt with legislation not only in this country, but in Europe. My hon'ble friend Mr. Stokes quoted the opinion on this particular matter of the great founder of nearly all the law reforms which have taken place in England in the course of the present century—the opinion of Jeremy Bentham. It is often said that Jeremy Bentham was a man of closet—that he was a pure theorist; but somehow or other there are very few of his theories which have not come to be copied, and that have not brought about the most beneficial results. The Mover of the amendment told us that the nominal classification of suits is fallacious as a test of intricacy. Now, it so happens that this particular test is the test which during the last thirty or forty years, since Courts of Small Causes—Courts expressly framed for the purpose of exercising prompt and summary jurisdiction—were founded in England, and since those Courts have been established and extended in this country,—this, I say, has been the test which the wisest men among us, the most learned, the most thoughtful and the most practical of our predecessors have deemed it necessary and found it convenient to adopt. It appears to me that on our part it is not wise to ignore the lessons of experience, the teachings which have been handed down to us by men certainly not less eminent than those who are seated round this table. The Hon'ble Member who has moved the amendment has treated a despatch of the Secretary of State, which was the immediate origin of the preparation of the Bill now before us, as laying down that it was desirable that in regard to all suits in which the Deccan ryots were concerned the right of appeal should be abolished. The despatch to which he has alluded is on some points, and certainly on this point, somewhat vague in its wording. But I must express my conviction that the framer of that despatch had no such intention as that which has been attributed to him. It seems to me that all that the Secretary of State intended was that the system of summary, or what we call small-cause, jurisdiction should be extended in these particular districts of the Deccan more than they have been generally extended in the Mofussil in this country. I do not for a moment believe that it was his design that, in suits of the class of those which not only throughout the Mofussil but in the Presidency-towns it has been necessary to provide for and regulate under the ordinary rules of civil procedure, a new system should be introduced. My hon'ble friend Mr. Stokes, and the experienced officers from whose writings he has largely quoted, have, I think, sufficiently shown that the test which the wisdom of our predecessors, which the experience of the past, have pronounced to be adequate and sufficient, is one which ought not to be departed from on the present occasion; and I think he might have added that, if the objections which have been advanced against the system of appeal by the Mover of the amendment and by his supporters in this Council are really valid objections, they apply to our whole system of judicature throughout India. If it be the fact that the evils which accompany that system are so great as they have been described, then I say that those evils are just as applicable to Bengal, the Panjáb, the North-Western Provinces or Madras as they are to the Deccan districts of Bombay. It appears to me that in arguing in support of their contention my hon'ble colleagues have somewhat overstated their case.

" Then, as it appears to me, there is another objection to the amendment which has been moved with reference to the section now under discussion.

"I quite agree with Sir John Strachey and Mr. Thompson that the question of appeals and the question of a supervising Judge hang together. If a majority of this Council shall this morning decide that the right of appeal in these cases shall be abolished, and shall also decide, as I have no doubt in that case they will, that these suits shall be withdrawn from the cognizance of the established District Judges, and shall be brought under the supervision of a special officer, the result will be that the Subordinate Judges, by whom the suits will be tried, will be serving under two masters. The District Judges before whom appeals from all their decisions will lie in all cases other than those provided for in this Bill, not excluding cases above the value of

Rs. 500 in which agriculturists are concerned, will be deprived of the opportunity of observing the working of the Judges subordinate to them in that which will form a very large portion of their jurisdiction. The Subordinate Judge will be receiving from one master that description of instruction which may be afforded by the exercise of the powers of revision; he will be receiving from another master the instruction which is afforded by the trial of appeals from his decisions. It seems to me that such a system will give rise to a great deal that is unsatisfactory in the practical working of our Courts, and will end in all sorts of complications. Sir John Strachey observed that the honest suitor under a system of revision would have every opportunity of having his appeal heard if he had a real grievance; but he omitted to remark that the application for revision might very often be preferred by dishonest suitors; and in such cases the system, it appears to me, will be open to all the objections which have been advanced against it by Mr. Naylor and by Mr. Justice West. 'Mr. Naylor points out,' as Mr. Stokes has told us, 'what a serious grievance it will be that these suits should be heard in the informal manner in which they may be heard under the Bill as it is proposed to amend it.' Taking the case which I have just suggested—the case of a dishonest suitor who prefers what will really be an appeal to the revising Judge—suppose the revising Judge does not think fit to call upon the opposite party to hear what he has got to say on the other side, then a grievous injustice may be committed. It appears to me that this is a point and an aspect of the question which ought not to be left entirely out of consideration.

"Lastly, I would remark that in depriving the people of these districts of the right of appeal in that class of cases in which it is now given in every district throughout the country —a right which elsewhere it is proposed to maintain—we shall be depriving the people of the Deccan of what to them, as to other natives of India, is a valued and cherished privilege."

His Excellency the Commander-in-Chief said:—" I have no intention of saying a word on this Bill, as I believe I come more strictly under the category of those referred to by my hon'ble friend Mr. Stokes who have not read all the papers. But I have listened with great interest to my hon'ble friend Mr. Thornton's speech; and if anything is clearly stated by him, it is the immense value attached by the ryots of the Panjáb to the privilege of appeal. I must say I was rather astonished at the conclusion arrived at by the Hon'ble Member and the vote which he proposes to give. I assure you that his speech has quite convinced me of the propriety of taking a directly opposite course to that which he himself has taken. I have not altogether omitted reading a portion of the papers concerned and the Bill itself; but it appears to me that, if the Bill is intended for any purpose at all, it is for the relief of the ryot; and it seems to me a very strange method of relieving the ryot that we should at the very first discussion that occurs on the Bill withdraw from him his most valued privilege. I have only to say, my Lord, in conclusion that I shall vote in opposition to the amendment."

The Hon'ble Mr. Hope said:—"My Lord, I trust that the Council will extend to me some sympathy in the difficult task which I am called upon to perform, at a moment's notice, of replying to two such long speeches as those we have just heard, adverse to my amendment, and which go into such an enormous number of petty details; and I must only ask it to accept my assurance, by way of covering any omissions which I may inadvertently make, that there is not a single phrase, or a single allegation, used in either of these two speeches which is not capable of being effectively contradicted.

"In the first place, the Hon'ble the Law Member led off by saying that the objections which he put forward were not original. This I can well believe. He proceeded further to base them upon the authority of Bentham; and the Hon'ble Sir Alexander Arbuthnot also enlarged upon the same and other authority. We were told that we were committing a great crime in ignoring the wisdom of eminent men, who were considered to be the very first authorities not only in Europe, but, in fact, throughout the world. Now, in the first place, I beg to deny the premises. We are not ignoring the authority of Bentham at all; and Bentham is simply a very great name, brought in under perhaps the erroneous impression that it would frighten or persuade somebody. The mention made of Bentham by the Hon'ble the Law Member in his speech on the 18th July was that, 'in the absence of an Appellate Court, the Judges of first instance will have no one (as Bentham says) to "stand in awe" of.' Well, the whole point in this simple question is, whether the Courts will have any one to stand in awe of or not; and, therefore, all that we have got to do, in order to carry out to the full Bentham's theory, and to defer to his authority, is to take care that we keep a proper authority for Courts 'to stand in awe' of. Now, the argument in this matter, which I am glad to see neither of the Hon'ble Members has ventured to allude to, that the system of revision is much wider in its application than the system of appeal, effectively disposes of this question; for it stands to reason, except, perhaps, in the minds of persons of such very uncommon sense that I should be loth to recognize it as sense at all, that Courts which have 30 per cent. of their work carefully looked after by special officers are likely to stand a little more 'in awe' than Courts which have only 3 per cent. of their work looked after. Therefore, I entirely deny that we go against the authority of Bentham or any other of the great experiences which are held up to frighten us."

The Hon'ble Sir Alexander Arbuthnot :—" I should like for a moment to interrupt the Hon'ble Member. I wish to remark that, if the Bill should be left as it is at present framed, there will still be a system of revision under Act XIV of 1869, which I believe is a Bombay Act."

The Hon'ble Mr. Hope :—" I am much obliged for the Hon'ble Member's interruption, which I will make a note of, and deal with in due course. Well, to continue regarding this matter of our old experiences, having answered with reference to Bentham, I may notice that it has been urged that we ought not to abandon a system which has stood a test thirty or forty years old, and that we should not cast aside the experience of the past. To that I reply, that the experience of the past is exactly what brings us to our present position; because the experience of the past has shown us that this system of appeal is *not* efficient, and that the system of non-appeal has been gradually coming round into favour, first of all in England, and now in India, where at last a little ray of light has come to us. In India even, in money cases, within the last thirty years appeals have been cut off in the Small Cause Courts; and in England the system had been much more largely extended. Therefore, the practical experiences of the past are entirely in favour of our measure.

"Next, we were told by the Hon'ble the Law Member that it was not only because mortgage-suits were difficult that he thought they should be subjected to appeal, but because they also related to land, and that land is a very important thing, and a thing to which the people of this country attach an extraordinary value. This is a change of ground from that previously taken up by the Hon'ble Member; but at the same time it is a perfectly fair and reasonable ground to occupy, and I have only to remark with regard to it that the observation seems to me to be totally irrelevant. Nobody ever said that the people do not attach value to the land. The question here really is, whether the cases which relate to land will be a bit less carefully tried under the system proposed than under the system it is proposed to abolish."

The Hon'ble Mr. Stokes :—" The point, I may remark, was that the people attached an extreme value to the right of appeal in suits relating to land."

The Hon'ble Mr. Hope:—" I am much obliged to the Hon'ble Member. Now, to come to the value which people attach to the right of appeal, I cannot but think that His Excellency the Commander-in-Chief—although no doubt he will pardon me if I am in error—may possibly have misunderstood, as I myself did at first, the manner in which the Hon'ble Mr. Thornton expressed his view regarding the appreciation of the people of the Panjáb of the system of appeal. He put it—if I correctly took it down—that of the cases which might be appealed against, 82 per cent. were not appealed against. That statement, inverted, means that the people only appeal in 18 per cent. out of all the cases."

His Excellency the Commander-in-Chief:—" That is exactly the view I took of it and it only shows the appreciation the ryot has of his position in not making futile appeals; and I suppose the Deccan ryot is as sensible a man as the Panjáb ryot."

The Hon'ble Mr. Thornton :—" Perhaps I had better explain that what I wished to say was that, as a matter of experience, in which I think my hon'ble friend the Lieutenant-Governor concurs, the peasant of the Panjáb does, as a matter of fact, attach the greatest importance to the power of appeal, and also that he does not abuse that power. I, therefore, adverted to the statistics to which the Hon'ble Mr. Hope has referred."

His Excellency the Commander-in-Chief wished it to be understood that he had fully and rightly comprehended the remarks of his hon'ble friend Mr. Thornton.

The Hon'ble Mr. Hope:—" I am glad to find that my surmise was incorrect; but as I did not at first fully understand the matter through the way it was put, I thought there might have been a misapprehension. But with regard to this I have only to say that, greatly as I respect the knowledge my hon'ble friend Mr. Thornton possesses of the Panjáb, and fully prepared as I should ordinarily be to accept any inference which he might draw from it, I somewhat hesitate to infer from the simple fact that the people do not appeal in 82 of the cases in which they might do so that they abstain from appealing solely through moderation. I should require a great deal more proof than those statistics afford before I should be inclined to admit that. But I do say that it appears to me that the large proportion of appeals may be very easily accounted for on one of the grounds which he assigns for it, namely, that the Courts are nearer to the homes of the people, which is one of the great things we find the Deccan Courts are not. Whether, if the Deccan Courts were situated as those of the Panjáb are, the people would appeal in the same number of cases I am not prepared to say; but I do not think that any sound generalization can be drawn from one province in India as compared with another, since we find that, with regard to all these provinces, the most essential differences exist between them. As a matter of fact, we find that the people in the Deccan do not appeal in cases above the proportion which I have stated, and that there is an enormous mass of evidence in the Deccan Riots Commission Report all telling us why they do not appeal. It was *not* found there that they do not appeal because they enjoy and value their right of doing so ; but it *was* found that they do not appeal simply because, for the various reasons already stated in my introductory speech on this motion, and which I will not now weary the Council by recapitulating, they find that they *cannot* appeal.

"But even as regards the matter of the people valuing this right, we are told that they do, upon the strength of a statement, if I recollect rightly, of Mr. Justice West.

"Now, I wish, with the permission of the Council, to read to it the statement of an officer—whose name, unfortunately, I am not at liberty to mention—who has not, like some of our critics, never been in the Deccan at all, but who has spent a large portion of his Indian service in Mofussil work of the most arduous and searching character. What he says is this" :—

The Hon'ble Sir Alexander Arbuthnot :—"Has this officer been in the Deccan ?"

The Hon'ble Mr. Hope :—" Yes ; and he was for some time Collector of one of the four districts for which we are at present legislating. He writes :—

"'Another argument is, that "the people" value the power of appeal. If by ",the people" is meant the plaintiff class—the sowkárs—I do not doubt this at all, since the more lengthy, dilatory and costly are legal processes, the greater advantage has the rich and intelligent suitor over a poor and ignorant opponent ; but I deny it altogether as regards the more numerous class of defendants.'

"The Hon'ble the Law Member next said that no suits could be named in which such difficulties occurred as in mortgage-cases ; and that Bombay was no exception Mr. Naylor was called in to prove. Mr. Naylor, so far as I can see, states very little more than, and that not in a very different manner from, that which I stated myself. He says, which is a truism I suppose, that—

'the intricacy of a suit in no way depends upon the social status or occupation of the parties thereto' ;

and he goes on—

"'It is to the subject-matter of an action we must look in order to judge whether it is likely to involve complicated issues ; and those who are acquainted with the usual range of litigation will unhesitatingly affirm that questions relating to mortgage claims are amongst those which are most prolific of knotty points and legal difficulties. It makes no difference in this respect whether the value of the matter in dispute be small or great, or whether the parties to the suit belong to one class or another.'

"In this he furnishes no answer whatever to the statement which I make, that the mortgage-cases may some of them be easy and others difficult. As to looking at the subject-matter, he is at variance with the other judicial officer, Mr. Wedderburn, who tells us that 'experience shows that these tests are fallacious.' There is nothing in this quotation from Mr. Naylor to controvert what I have said, that even these matters of priorities, &c., may not often all be settled on very ordinary rules. In fact, if it was not so, it would not be possible for our Subordinate Judges to deal with them so satisfactorily as we see they do, from the fact that only about 16 per cent. of all their decisions are reversed in appeal.

"The Hon'ble Mr. Stokes next passed a criticism upon an answer which I gave at the time of the introduction of the Bill to a question put by the Hon'ble Sir Alexander Arbuthnot. I was saying that 'mortgage-cases are usually only difficult if they happen to involve questions of priorities and the like, or there are several creditors'; and Sir Alexander Arbuthnot enquired 'whether there might not be questions of title.' I answered that 'under the Bombay revenue system the name of the owner of every field is entered in the Government books. It would only be in most rare instances that the man whose name appeared was not the real owner; and so questions of title are not likely to give trouble.' That is every word of it absolutely correct. The ruling of the Bombay High Court which the Hon'ble the Law Member produces is a ruling perfectly well known to every revenue-officer in the Bombay Presidency. I did not say that the entry of a man's name in the books was absolute evidence of his being an owner of a field. I did say that, owing to the system of so entering names,—and I repeat it now in more detail—in nineteen cases out of twenty it is the man to whom the field really belongs that will get his name entered, and that, therefore, if you take up a name in the books, the chances are that in nineteen cases out of twenty the person is the owner; and therefore, finally, questions of title will give a great deal less trouble where there is this system of entry than they would do if it did not exist. Questions of title are not likely to give special trouble; and I defy any one to contradict the statement."

The Hon'ble Mr. Stokes:—"I wish to explain that the remark of the Hon'ble Mr. Hope was intended to convey the impression that difficult questions as to title could not arise, inasmuch as the Collector's record would serve as evidence of the title."

The Hon'ble Mr. Hope :—"I have only to say that I usually endeavour to speak with great care ; that my words are carefully weighed; that what I have said is exactly what I mean, and that I neither said what the Hon'ble Member attributes to me, nor did I mean to say it. What I did say was that ' questions of title are not likely to give trouble'—and no more they are.

"I must now, before going into one or two matters with which I propose to finish my unavoidably long reply, refer to the remarks of the Hon'ble Sir Alexander Arbuthnot in reply to the observations of the Hon'ble Messrs. Thornton and Thompson and Sir Robert Egerton, who had been urging the necessity of supporting the Local Government. The Hon'ble Sir Alexander Arbuthnot reminded us that it was very well to support the Local Government on matters of detail, but that when we come to matters of great principle we must judge for ourselves, and interpose if necessary. That struck me as a very singular argument, because, if my memory does not deceive me, the hon'ble gentleman is one of those who have been distinguished for arguing hitherto that this question of appeals was a matter of detail, and one which might fairly be left open, and not considered as a matter of principle. In the original consideration of the Bill by the Government of India the question was left open as one of detail ; and in consequence of this, the question of ' appeals *versus* revision' was not mentioned as one of the seven great matters of principle which His Excellency the President enumerated in his concluding speech on the last occasion. It may perhaps be convenient to the Hon'ble Member to argue at one time that a thing is a matter of detail, and at another time that it is a matter of principle ; but I can only say that I cannot follow him to that extent."

The Hon'ble Sir Alexander Arbuthnot :—"I beg to remark that I am not at all conscious of having ever argued that this question of appeal was a matter of detail. I used no argument before to-day on that subject at all in this Council. If my memory serves me rightly as to what passed in the Executive Council, my view was—and it was the view concurred in by the Viceroy—that it was a point that might fairly be treated by the Executive Government as an open question.—Still I regard it as involving an important principle."

The Hon'ble Mr. Hope :—"I do not understand, even with the explanation now given by the Hon'ble Member, how the matter can at one and the same time be so important in principle that it is necessary to overrule the Local Government on it, and yet of such minor importance that it may be left entirely an open question.

"It has next been objected by the Hon'ble Sir Alexander Arbuthnot that I have treated the despatch of the Secretary of State as advocating the abolition of appeal. The Hon'ble Member points out that the words of the despatch are somewhat vague, and that he believes the framer had no intention to extend the system of appeal—if I have not correctly taken down his remarks I hope he will point out my error—that the framer of the despatch had no intention to extend the system of appeal to mortgage-cases. Of course, what may have been in the inner consciousness of the framer of this despatch I am unable to affirm; but, reading the despatch on the broad lines on which it seems to have been drawn, it appears to me perfectly clear that what the Secretary of State did intend was that there should be Courts, without an appeal, for the relief of the Deccan ryot in the mass of those troublesome cases in which he finds himself involved. The Hon'ble the Law Member tells us that the mass of the cases will be mortgage-cases; it, therefore, seems to follow that either we must exclude appeals in mortgage-cases, or, if we admit them, we shall be going directly contrary to the intention of the despatch of the Secretary of State.

"The Hon'ble Sir Alexander Arbuthnot has also remarked that Sir John Strachey and others of us have overstated our case in this matter, because, if this abolition of appeal is necessary in Bombay, then it must be good and necessary for all India. I do not at all follow the inference, for my own part. The Hon'ble Mr. Thornton, for instance, has very strikingly pointed out to us that in one province in India—the Panjáb—appeals in certain cases are largely resorted to, whereas in another province—the Deccan—we find that the people appeal in only 3 per cent. of the cases. There is, therefore, no ground for drawing any such inference as that of the Honourable the Law Member. Whether appeals are good in other provinces or not, is a question not now before us, and on which we must now reserve our opinions until a proper time arrives for forming and expressing them.

"Then, again, it was urged by the Hon'ble Sir Alexander Arbuthnot that the Hon'ble Sir John Strachey had omitted to say that an application for revision might be preferred by a dishonest suitor, and that the revising Judge might not call on the opposite party for a reply; in which case grievous injustice might possibly be done. Now, unless my memory deceives me, we were told by the Hon'ble the Law Member at the time the Bill was introduced that one of the great advantages of the system of appeal was that the Judge could, if he thought fit, dispose of the appeal at once, without calling on the other side for a reply. I confess myself somewhat perplexed whether to follow the pleading of the Hon'ble the Law Member or of the Hon'ble Sir Alexander Arbuthnot. It seems to me that on this particular point they have placed themselves on the horns of a dilemma; and I think I had better leave them there.

"Now, as to the difficulty alluded to by Sir Alexander Arbuthnot, of the Subordinate Judges having to serve two masters, I think that is very greatly exaggerated by Mr. Naylor and others. The only occasion on which the work could possibly overlap is, as Sir Alexander Arbuthnot has very correctly said, when a Subordinate Judge in his capacity of an ordinary Sub-divisional Judge of the district had tried a suit of the value of over Rs. 500 in which an agriculturist was concerned: I admit that under those circumstances the District Judge might take one view of points in chapter III of the Bill and the Special Judge another. If, however, the Hon'ble Sir Alexander Arbuthnot had pointed this out in committee, perhaps there would have been no objection to providing that cases in which agriculturists were parties should come under the control of the Special Judge, even when they exceeded Rs. 500, although I must say that I do not think it necessary. But the main answer to the objection is that cases of this kind are so few that for one case of over Rs. 500 in value there will probably be fifty on the other side; and the rulings of the Special Judge in the larger work will practically prevail.

"The Hon'ble Mr. Stokes told us, in concluding his remarks, that in making them he had studiously abstained from statements on his own authority. I think that, considering the high position the Hon'ble Mr. Stokes holds in this Council, we might have hoped, for our own guidance, that he would have been able to come forward and state to us with some authority his own personal views and opinions, to which no doubt the Council would have deferred as far as possible. I will not pursue that question by noticing the remark he was pleased to make regarding what he considers the absence of judicial experience in myself. I consider that such a remark was uncalled-for, and that I cannot do better than leave it, as a specimen of good taste, upon the records of this Council.

"I regret having to detain the Council by speaking at such length; but, at the same time, I feel it my duty to meet, as far as I am able, the various points brought forward against the proposed amendment; and I must therefore notice very briefly the allusions to the three Bombay officers upon whom, it would appear, the Hon'ble the Law Member relies. Mr. Naylor, first of all, is quoted as showing that the Special Judge in revising the decisions will do so under three disadvantages. The first one out of the three read out by the Hon'ble the Law Member he had himself to confess was partially wrong. Then with regard to the second, that the application would generally have to be inquired into at a distance from the homes of the parties, I can only say that it appears to me a complete misapprehension ; but, as I shall have on the next amendment to say a few words upon that point, I will not detain the Council with it now. Then as to the third, that the parties will have no absolute right to bring their cases before the Special Judge, and he may refuse their applications without any inquiry at all, I have already met that by saying that it was absurd to suppose that a selected officer, such as a Special Judge, would not do careful and equal justice, although there might be an infinitesimal difference of status between appellants and applicants for revision. Again, in connection with Mr. Naylor's remarks, if I correctly took down the Law Member, he said that the system of revision would produce uncertainty in decisions for a period of three years, within which a petition might be brought forward ; whereas under the system of appeal a certain number of days—ninety I think—would render a decision unappealed against final, and dispose of the whole matter.

" Now, in the first place, ninety days would not dispose of the whole matter. In any case where there was a double appeal, and through the delays which I have already pointed out, it might so occur that the whole matter, instead of ending in ninety days, could not be disposed of in less than six years. But, besides that, I should like to ask the Hon'ble Member whether there is any limit to the period of time within which the High Court may exercise its own power of revision under section 622 of the Civil Procedure Code."

The Hon'ble Mr. Stokes :—" There is no limit."

The Hon'ble Mr. Hope :—" I am aware of the fact. Therefore, in this matter the appeals stand upon exactly the same footing as the revision does ; and the agreement that under the appeal system there would be a finality obtained in a short time instead of along one, is not worth the breath expended on it.

" Next as to the observations of Mr. Wedderburn. Mr. Wedderburn, be it remembered, should, in fairness I think, be counted, when he speaks, on our side as well as against it ; for he says 'experience shows that these tests (of making appeal depend on the class of suit) are fallacious.'

"As to revision, Mr. Wedderburn's remarks are evidently based upon a total misapprehension of the sort of revision intended. Mr. Wedderburn writes as if it was intended that the revision should be merely carried on upon returns. I have never said anything which could have given countenance to that supposition. The revision will, as it has been shown, and as the Bombay Government say, be mainly conducted by reading the record. As to that record, and to the remarks of the Hon'ble the Law Member regarding it, in which he considers that he has the support of Mr. Wedderburn, I have only to say, if we are to suppose that the Judge will be unable to deal with these cases because they are written in the vernacular, then it is obvious that the executive officers who conduct the whole administrative work of this great empire are in ninety-nine cases out of a hundred equally unable to dispose of the matters before them. Any person who has had any executive experience— to which perhaps I may pretend—knows that three-fourths or five-sixths, and in some districts ninety-nine-one-hundredths, of his time is taken up in disposing of work in the vernacular. Now, if these officers can do their work in the vernacular efficiently—and I do not think any one doubts that they can so do it—then the Special Judge will be able to do his work too. But if they cannot, then all I can say is, that I am very sorry for British India!

"In conclusion, I have to turn to a subject which I enter upon with great reluctance; and that is a criticism of the Hon'ble Mr. Justice West's paper which is before us. I myself was in hopes that that paper would only have been quoted where it could have been quoted without provoking any adverse criticism; because it seems to me to be somewhat invidious and ungracious to bring into Court the writings of an officer who has kindly volunteered to give us his opinion, to criticize that opinion, and still more to criticize it in a place where he is unable to reply. At the same time, so much has been said in praise of this paper, and so much weight has been attributed to it by the Hon'ble the Law Member, that I cannot but advance upon the task, however distasteful to me.

"I hope I do not imply any disrespect to Mr. West when I say that the paper is a very diffuse and a very involved document. As far as I can make out, and I shall, I hope, do my friend Mr. West no injustice, his argument appears to be this. In the first place, he assumes, the Subordinate Judges to be 'ill-informed,' 'poor,' 'half-educated,' of 'weak moral natures,' if not corrupt, still open to 'influence leading to partiality,' of 'exuberant ingenuity,' 'well crammed with English legal formulas but unimbued with the animating spirit of English institutions,' and hence liable to 'very wild notions,' and subject to fits of 'capricious harshness' and 'ill-judged benevolence.' These are all Mr. West's own phrases. The Subordinate Judges of Bombay will no doubt be extremely interested to hear the opinion held of them by one of their own High Court Judges, and will assume that Mr. West himself will not be disposed to promote them to the post of District Judge, to which they probably hope to attain under the new regulations for admitting Natives to offices held by the Civil Service. In the second place, he assumes that there will be no more than 'casual supervision,' though on what ground does not appear, since the supervising staff will be large, they will spend above half the year in travelling about the districts, supervision will be their sole occupation, the provisions of the Bill as to their powers are stringent, and they will be picked men. From these two premises he makes the deduction that there will be 'imperfect investigation' and 'defective record,' and that the scheme is ' as unpromising as any that could be devised.' Now both of these premises are erroneous. The Subordinate Judges are *not* as black as they are painted ; and I do not think that any elaborate argument from me is necessary to substantiate that. We find that, as a matter of fact, in these appeals nearly 68 per cent. of the decisions of these Subordinate Judges are upheld, and only 16 per cent. are reversed. Therefore, upon what grounds they are held to be so worthless as they are represented, I cannot comprehend. And, as I said before, the second premise is also defective. Still, even if this were not so the deduction which is drawn can only be drawn, firstly, by attributing to all suits, with reference to the record, what can only apply to ten-rupee suits ; and, secondly, by ignoring the fact that many of the remarks made apply just as much, if at all, to the appeal system as to the revision system.

" But even if the two premises were not incorrect, and if the deductions, even supposing the premises correct, were not unsound, Mr. West entirely demolishes his own case by one statement, which will be found in paragraph 31, which is as follows: 'The ryot himself, however, does not, in fact, appeal in more than one in a hundred of the suits of small amount that are brought against him.' Where, then, is the security offered to him ? Where is his alleged appreciation of the appeal system of which we have been told so much ? And why does he not appeal ? Is it because he is always wrong, poor fellow, as the Hon'ble Sayyad Ahmad says ? Is it really true, as Mr. West would have us believe in another place, that in ' nine out of ten of the suits that now come before the Deccan Courts' the ' claim is a just one'? Nay rather he sits quiet in his ignorance, his poverty, his despair of contending successfully with those who are in every way his superiors. Who *do* appeal then ? Those who are always right? Or those who know they are most likely to win ? But the Hon'ble Mr. Stokes would endeavour to persuade us that it is the ryot who is right, and that it is he who gains by the appeal system. All I can say is that, if he gains by it, he abstains from what is to his advantage in a very singular manner."

The Hon'ble Mr. Stokes :—" It is the benefits arising from the existence of the system upon which his appreciation of it depends."

The Hon'ble Mr. Hope :—" Well, I can only say that he shows very great self-denial. But with reference to all this I will only add that, depend upon it, the truth really is that, while the appeal system may sometimes be a remedy for the rich, it is usually nothing but a mockery for the poor. As to Mr. West's paper in general, I must say—and I trust this is the last occasion on which I may be called upon to criticize it—that, while I have read it with pleasure, as one must read everything proceeding from his brilliant and facile pen, I cannot shut my eyes to his obvious tendency to mistake assertion for argument, and to cover fallacy by sarcasm. Opening, as it does, with the vision of 'a kind and impartial authority' sitting up aloft and dealing out to the ryot the 'minimum of land' 'requisite for his decent subsistence,' and at the same time dispensing the rest of his worldly goods to his honest and satisfied creditors ; and closing, as we see it, with a tableau of this same ryot become wealthy—one does not quite know how—with his cheque-book sticking out of his coat-tail pocket (he will have a coat by then), we cannot but look upon it as a pleasing work of fiction, rather than as a serious contribution towards a useful solution of the difficult question we are dealing with. In conclusion, I have only to add that it should be borne in mind that, when the Bill was introduced, the Hon'ble the Law Member found great fault with the Bombay Government for not having, in the first place, consulted the Bombay High Court. The Bombay Government have now consulted the High Court ; and we know what the High Court have said. Why the Hon'ble Member objects to follow the authority which he has invoked, it is difficult to perceive. He has appealed to Cæsar, and Cæsar has decided against him. He has called upon the High Court to curse his enemies ; but it seems to me that they have blessed them altogether."

The Hon'ble Mr. Stokes said that no one who read the opinions of the Bombay Judges between the lines—especially the remarks of Mr. Justice M. Melvill—could fail to see that they were laughing at the whole thing.

The Hon'ble Mr. Hope :—"I have no such powers of penetration as the Hon'ble Member ; but I can see no irony in it, except the irony of fate, which has led to the reference he desired ending in the manner it has done."

His Excellency the President said:—"I have felt in the course of this very protracted discussion that the first and second amendments placed on the notice paper by my hon'ble friend Mr. Hope are virtually and substantially interdependent parts of what for all practical purposes is the same motion, and that it is difficult to consider them with convenience or advantage separately for that reason. But, assuming that the Bill as eventually passed will be so far replaced in harmony with the original intentions and purpose of the framers of it and of the Local Government as not to exclude mortgage-cases from that supervising authority which the Bill provides for all other cases mentioned in it, I must frankly say that, after having read with care the Report of the Select Committee, and after listening with great attention to the remarks of my hon'ble colleagues the Law Member and Sir Alexander Arbuthnot, I have not heard any argument which satisfies my own judgment that there are sufficient grounds for separating mortgage-cases from all the other cases referred to in the clause which the Hon'ble Mr. Hope proposes to amend, and applying specially to those cases the system of procedure which, as I understand, the majority and the minority of the Committee have, both of them, agreed to exclude from all the other cases—a procedure which the Local Government and those who framed the measure regard as absolutely incompatible with the attainment of one of the main objects of the measure, which is to simplify and to cheapen the administration of the law to a helpless and poverty-stricken portion of the population. It appears to me that all the arguments used in favour of admitting appeals in mortgage-cases would equally apply to the extension of appeals to all the other cases referred to in this clause; and as the whole of the Committee have agreed in excluding the right of appeal from these cases, I fail to recognize that any sufficient case has been made out for applying it to mortgage-cases. With reference to the remarks of my hon'ble friend Sir Frederick Haines and my hon'ble friend Mr. Thornton, it appears to me that they wandered a little away from the practical subject we have to deal with. I have no doubt that nobody is in a better position than my hon'ble friend Mr. Thornton to tell us what are the feelings of the peasantry of the Panjáb, and what are the facts of the experience derived from the working of the appeal system in that province. But we are not legislating for the Panjáb; we are legislating for a peasantry of the most poverty-stricken, depressed, and miserable portion of the Deccan, and with the object of ameliorating their condition. The case which we are legislating for, is avowedly an exceptional case; and it is because it is exceptional that we are called upon to legislate for it. I think we must all hope that the condition of the peasantry in the Deccan is not the condition of the peasantry in other parts of India; and that this exceptional and, as we are obliged to acknowledge, discreditable state of things has notoriously grown up unchecked, if not encouraged, by the practical operation in certain localities of our existing Civil Code, and the application of those legal conceptions which govern the procedure and lead to the decrees and judgments of our civil tribunals. That being the case, I must say that my own vote will be given without hesitation in favour of this amendment."

The question being put, the Council divided—

Ayes.	Noes.
The Hon'ble T. C. Hope.	The Hon'ble B. W. Colvin.
The Hon'ble T. H. Thornton.	The Hon'ble Whitley Stokes.
The Hon'ble Faiz Alí Khán.	The Hon'ble Sir Andrew Clarke.
The Hon'ble Rivers Thompson.	The Hon'ble Sir A. J. Arbuthnot.
The Hon'ble Sir E. B. Johnson.	His Excellency the Commander-in-Chief.
The Hon'ble Sir J. Strachey.	
His Honour the Lieutenant-Governor.	
His Excellency the President.	

So the motion was carried.

The Hon'ble Mr. Hope next moved that for section 54 of the Bill the following section be substituted (namely) :—

"54. The Local Government from time to time may, and if the Government of India so direct shall, appoint an officer, as Special Judge, to discharge in the place of the District Judge all the functions of the District Judge under this Act in respect of the proceedings of all Subordinate Judges, Village-Munsifs and Conciliators, and may cancel any such appointment.

Special Judge.

" Such Special Judge shall not, without the previous sanction of the Government of India, discharge any public function except those which he is empowered by this Act to discharge.

" If any conflict of authority arises between the Special Judge and the District Judge, the High Court shall pass such order thereon consistent with this Act as it thinks fit.

" No appeal shall lie from any decree or order passed by the District Judge under this chapter, or by the Special Judge, or by an Assistant or Subordinate Judge appointed under section fifty-two, or by a Bench, in any suit or proceeding under this Act."

He said:—" My Lord, I have already mentioned that the Government of India, while fully approving of the proposal of the Bombay Government to accompany the curtailment of appeals by inspection and revision, thought it desirable to strengthen the staff by a Special Judge.

" 'The Governor General is of opinion,' it was said, 'that, looking to the arduous nature of the duties which the Act imposes on the Subordinate Judges, and the large discretion it confers on them, the appointment of a special officer of this sort, who would ordinarily be chosen from the more experienced District Judges, is essential to the proper working of the system proposed.'

The Local Government readily acceded to this.

" The majority of the Select Committee have now held that their admission of appeals in mortgage-cases, which, they say, 'form a very large class, and the most important class of cases to be heard under the Bill,' renders the Special Judge unnecessary."

The Hon'ble Sir Alexander Arbuthnot:—" If the Hon'ble Member will excuse my interrupting him, I wish to say that, as the first amendment proposed by him has been passed, I for one, and I think also my hon'ble colleagues who voted with me on the first amendment, are not disposed to oppose the second amendment, and therefore I think the time of the Council might be saved by my mentioning this at once."

The Hon'ble Mr. Hope:—" With reference to that, I have only to say that in that case I shall be most happy to save the time of the Council and myself; but as some objections have been made with reference to the question of a Special Judge which I intentionally left unanswered, perhaps I may be allowed to read my remarks on the subject, or, if that is not convenient, perhaps they might be taken as read and placed on record."

The Hon'ble Sir Alexander Arbuthnot:—" Cannot the Hon'ble Member speak on the points on which he wishes to reply? I for my part have the strongest objection to written speeches; and think that written speeches not delivered in Council, but placed on record, are especially open to objection."

The Hon'ble Mr. Hope:—" I quite agree with the Hon'ble Member. For reasons well known to him, however, I have found it necessary to prepare written speeches in this instance."

His Excellency the President said it was desirable to save time, if possible.

The Hon'ble Mr. Hope having then waived his objection, the motion was put and agreed to.

The Hon'ble Mr. Hope then moved that for section 68 of the Bill the following section be substituted (namely) :—

Pleaders, &c., excluded in certain cases.

"68. No pleader, vakíl or mukhtár, and no advocate or attorney of a High Court, shall be permitted to appear on behalf of any party to any case before a Conciliator or a Village-Munsif, or to any case cognizable by a Subordinate Judge under this Act, the subject-matter whereof does not exceed in amount or value one hundred rupees:

"Provided that any party to any such case may be permitted, on reasonable cause being shown to the satisfaction of the Conciliator, Village-Munsif or Subordinate Judge, to employ any relative, servant or dependent who is not, and has not previously been, a pleader, vakíl or mukhtár or an advocate or attorney of a High Court, to appear either conjointly with, or in lieu of such party:

"Provided also that a Subordinate Judge may permit a pleader, vakíl, or mukhtár, or an advocate or attorney of a High Court, to appear before him on behalf of any party to any case of the description aforesaid in which, for reasons to be recorded by him in writing, he deems it desirable that the party should have such assistance.

"When a relative, servant or dependent appears in lieu of a party, he shall be furnished by him with a power-of-attorney defining the extent to which he is empowered to act."

He said :—" My Lord, the whole essential difference between this and the section now in the Bill lies in the third clause. This question of pleaders originated in a suggestion of the Secretary of State in paragraph 31 of his despatch already alluded to, that possibly the exclusion of professional pleaders from the 'Courts with summary jurisdiction and without appeal up to a limited amount,' which he recommended, would be desirable. The Bombay Government's draft Bill accordingly contained a section substantially similar to that which I am now proposing. From Conciliation and Village-Munsifs' Courts the exclusion, following in the case of the latter the Madras law, was absolute; from cases before a Subordinate Judge it only extended up to a limit of Rs. 100, and was subject to a proviso allowing the Court to admit a pleader in any case in which professional assistance seemed to it to be really desirable. This proviso remains as section 69 of the Bill now before us. The limit of Rs. 100 was carefully chosen, in order to check evasion by slight exaggeration of the claim in the petty suits which form the bulk of litigation. The Bill as introduced maintained, as does also the Bill now reported, the exclusion from Conciliation and Village Courts; but, as a sort of compromise between conflicting opinions regarding exclusion from Subordinate Judges' Courts, it adopted the expedient of empowering the Judge to refuse costs, which was said to work well in the Small Cause Courts of the Presidency-towns. To this the Bombay Government emphatically object, in the following terms:—

"'This Government fear that the compromise which has been adopted with respect to section 69 of the Bill will render the provision for the exclusion of pleaders in cases before Subordinate Judges altogether futile. The amount to be allowed in the costs of a suit on account of fees of pleaders is fixed by law (Act I of 1846, section 7; Regulation II of 1827, section 52 and Appendix L); and in the case of suits for not more than Rs. 2,000 it amounts to 3 per cent. only of the value of the suit. The amount of the fee at stake in any case contemplated by section 69 of the Bill could thus never exceed Rs. 3; and it is obvious that the possible loss of so small an amount as this will not deter either suitors from engaging or pleaders from giving professional assistance. The latter will of course depend, as they do now, for the most part upon the remuneration privately agreed upon, and when possible will take care to be paid beforehand. The Governor in Council trusts, therefore, that it will be found practicable substantially to restore the provisions of the draft Bill submitted by him,' &c.

As to the futility of the expedient about costs, all parties seem now agreed, and the Select Committee unanimously struck out the section (69) regarding it. But the majority have gone further, and would get rid of a difficult question by substituting no provision at all, and leaving pleaders to appear in all cases, as at present. Now, I submit that on its merits, no less than in view of the decided opinion of the Bombay Government, the question cannot be thus passed by. As to the remarks in section 27 of the report, they seem to me to be altogether beside the mark. No one has denied, as far as I can see, that 'well qualified pleaders are a material aid to the Judge in dealing with a case of any complication or difficulty,' nor does anybody that I know of allege that 'in suits under Rs. 100 in value the aid of pleaders cannot be required,' or that 'the difficulty of a case' depends ' on the amount at issue.' What *is* affirmed is, that well-qualified pleaders are of little use, that ill-qualified or unprincipled pleaders cause much harm, and that both are a needless expense, in cases which are *not* of complication and difficulty; and that from these alone they should be excluded. This, and no more, is accordingly what my amendment provides for. It may be added that the fees which parties can afford to pay in those petty suits are not, even when they exceed the legalized limits, sufficient to afford a livelihood to the best class of pleaders. As for the idea, to which the remarks also allude, that the sowkár will get behind the exclusion of pleaders by employing as his servant and sending to Court in his behalf 'some man who, though not a professional legal practitioner, would have a considerable knowledge of law and of the ways of the Court,' it seems to me to bear a strong family likeness to certain other devices, more ingenious than practical, by which we have already been told that other provisions of the Bill may be defeated. Page 338 of Appendix C to the Commissioners' Report shows that the largest number of suits filed by one money-lender in a year in a Court taken as a test was 31. It, therefore, certainly would not pay any except the great money-lenders, who, we are told, are the most respectable, and probably would not pay even them, to employ a separate servant of the class indicated solely to carry on suits. It would also be the duty of the Court to put down, by means of the discretion allowed it, any palpable evasions of the spirit of the law, and in doubtful cases to give the defendant, under section 69, proper professional assistance. And, finally, the cases in which the device could be used at all would, by the hypothesis, be only those simple ones in which knowledge of law would give no great advantage.

" But I find in the weight evidently attached by the majority of the Select Committee to 'knowledge of law and of the ways of the Court,' as I did in the remark of the Hon'ble Sayyad Ahmad when the Bill was introduced, that ' the Courts receive considerable assistance from vakíls, and that the more ignorant the suitor is, the less probability is there that he will be able to explain his case in the confusion he experiences in a Court of Justice as well as he can to his adviser outside the Court ' —I find, I say, in both these the traces of false ideas and practices which this Bill, by one of its fundamental provisions, aims at destroying, root and branch. What I refer to is the view of the mere lawyer, that a Court of civil justice should be a place where a man sits on a high seat, in gown and bands, to manufacture decrees out of materials laid before him, rather than the view of the practical statesman, so well set forth by Sir James Stephen, that the Judge should confront the parties, note what they say, see the facts sifted to the bottom, and pass order accordingly.

" To sum up: I am making no attack upon pleaders either in general or in particular. I say nothing whatever as to the character and qualifications of the pleaders to be ordinarily found at Subordinate Judges' Courts. I merely affirm that in all simple cases they should be excluded, because they are a heavy expense to the parties, while the Court can follow the law and ascertain the facts as well, if not better, without them; but that, on the other hand, they should be admitted wherever it is clear that they can really be of use. This is all my amendment provides for. To the objection that to give to Judges a discretionary power of exclusion will lead to subserviency on the one hand and favouritism on the other, and will destroy the independence of the Bar and the efficiency of the Judge, I reply that none of these consequences have followed the discretion, as to the costs of even advocates, which Presidency Small Cause Court Judges have for nearly thirty years enjoyed.

The objection that many pleaders may be driven to seek other employment I meet by saying that, if the profession be weeded of inferior members, so much the better for those really competent and for suitors, as also that, after all, Courts and suitors are not made for pleaders. In conclusion, what I advocate is merely what is the law in France; what is aimed at by the denial of *all* costs in cases up to Rs. 100 in the Presidency-towns; what has not been objected to by the Judges of the Bombay High Court; and what is deemed essential by the Local Government."

The Hon'ble Mr. Thornton said :—" In accordance with the general principle I have already explained, I shall not vote against this amendment; at the same time, while fully sympathizing with the object of the Bombay Government, yet, judging from my own experience, I strongly doubt whether this extensive exclusion of pleaders, vakíls, mukhtárs and others from practising in the Courts will have the effect that is intended. I strongly doubt it; because, although such exclusion might be possible and beneficial in a newly-acquired province, it is questionable whether it can be beneficially introduced in a locality where people have been for years accustomed to the assistance of the legal practitioners. I very much fear the practical result will be that, while the respectable pleaders and mukhtárs will be excluded from the Courts, a class of legal practitioners will continue to practise outside the Courts, and will be all the more unscrupulous for being unrecognized and uncontrolled.

" My opinion on this point, my Lord, is not a mere surmise, but is based upon practical experience at Delhi, where I was district officer many years ago. That district was formerly attached to the North-Western Provinces Government, and the people were accustomed to employing professional agency in Courts of law. When it was transferred to the Panjáb the Panjáb system was introduced, which at that time excluded all legal practitioners from the Courts. It soon, however, became apparent that, although legal practitioners were excluded from the Courts, there sprung up outside the Courts a number of most disreputable and unscrupulous practitioners. The result eventually was that in the year 1866 my respected Chief and lamented friend Sir Donald Macleod—a patriarch and philanthropist to the backbone, that is, a lover of all mankind except lawyers—decided to extend the Pleaders Act to the Panjáb. But, though the results of my own experience are adverse to the proposals of the Bombay Government, it does not follow of a certainty that what happened in the Panjáb will happen in the Deccan; and as the Local Government strongly desires to try this measure, I shall not oppose it."

The Hon'ble Mr. Colvin said :—" As I understand the arguments which have been advanced by my hon'ble friend the Mover; he wishes to exclude pleaders in petty cases, on the ground that, even when well-qualified, they are of no use, and that, if ill-qualified, they may do great harm. Now the first of these two propositions seems to me very questionable. I am not at all disposed to admit that well-qualified pleaders are of no use. On the contrary, I believe that in all cases they are of very great assistance to a Court. It so happens that I have served for some years in a province where no pleaders are, or ever have been, admitted; and I must say that my experience there has not led me to think that the absence of pleaders is an advantage in administering justice. More harm, I believe, results from excluding well-qualified legal practitioners than from admitting them. The apparently simple procedure of leaving parties to conduct their own cases, does not tend to simplify justice, even with a practised Judge. With an inexperienced one it is more likely to pervert it. Ignorant and uneducated litigants are not unlike a pair of the swordsmen that one sees in this country making feints and flourishes in the air before they cross swords. They are slow to commit themselves to statements of fact, which may hereafter prove inconvenient, but are quite ready to be voluble about their adversary's private character and general misdeeds. The Court cannot arrive at the facts if it refuses to listen to any thing that is confused and irrelevant, and is obliged, even in simple cases, to waste much of its time in finding the issues before it can try them. When the points in issue have been ascertained, matters are not much advanced. The parties know very well what they want, but have very confused notions of the way in which it should be proved, and of the evidence which they require. The Judge, if he wishes to do justice, must not only try the suit, but must also in a great measure conduct it on behalf of both parties without losing his impartiality. The labour and responsibility which this throws upon a conscientious Judge is excessive, and with a careless and a lazy one may lead to much injustice.

"The second part of my hon'ble friend's argument is that bad pleaders may do a great deal of harm. I do not deny this; but I doubt whether by excluding pleaders from appearing in Court we shall get rid of any harm which they may be able to do. It is not what unscrupulous pleaders do or say in Court that is usually mischievous, for there they are acting under a sense of responsibility and are subject to control. They can do much more harm out of Court by giving bad advice; and their power to do this will be in no way diminished by prohibiting their appearance in Court.

"A point to be remembered also is that by narrowing the field for legitimate practitioners, more room will be left for a worse class of legal advisers. Litigiousness and chicanery are no monopoly of unscrupulous pleaders. As has been truly said by my hon'ble friend Mr. Thornton, there are always a tribe of petition writers, stamp-sellers and other such hangers-on of the Courts who are ready to take the place of pleaders when pleaders are not forthcoming. These men, if they do not know much of law, often have a pretty good knowledge of the character and habits of the Court officials, and a familiarity with the forms of ordinary procedure which impose upon novices and strangers to litigation. Suitors prefer the advice of these men to none; and very bad advice they often receive. However bad it may be, the givers of it are under no kind of responsibility for what they do. There is no recognized relation between them and the litigants, and they are neither amenable to the opinion of their fellows nor to the executive control of the Court. I think that anything which is likely to throw more business into the hands of such men as these can do nothing but mischief.

"On these grounds alone I should be opposed to the exclusion of pleaders. But I must also say that Mr. Justice West's argument on this subject has made more impression on me than it appears to have produced on the mover. It has been objected to that argument that the sowkár never has a very large stake in a single case, and that it would not be worth his while therefore to employ a special agent. But a sowkár does not lend money to a single individual. He has a number of transactions. It is quite impossible for him whenever he wants to recover money in Court to attend personally on every occasion. He must employ somebody. The Bill allows him to appoint an agent; and naturally he will appoint an agent, if he can procure one, who has some knowledge of the business to be done. Even if the agent has not that knowledge to commence with, the habit of attending the Courts will give him a familiarity with their practice. The ryot, who is often an utter stranger to them, will be at a great disadvantage in contending against such an adversary. My objections to the present amendment are urged as much on behalf of the ryot as of the Court and the pleaders—in fact, more so; and I believe, if this amendment should be carried, that the ryot will be the chief sufferer from its effects."

The Hon'ble Mr. Rivers Thompson said :—" As a member of the Select Committee who voted for some such provisions in the Bill as the amendment now proposed, I am, of course, prepared to support that amendment. My hon'ble friend Mr. Thornton has, contrary, I must say, to his usual practice, spoken in one sense and voted in another. I have no doubt the Council, while it enjoyed his speech, will gratefully accept his vote; but I think he makes one mistake. In speaking generally of the benefits of admitting pleaders and the evil that is done by excluding them, he seems (as also does my hon'ble friend who spoke last) to have argued rather on the supposition that pleaders were absolutely excluded in all cases; but, as far as I understand the amendment, it goes only so far as to extend the exclusion to cases cognizable by a Subordinate Judge, the subject-matter of which does not exceed in amount or value one hundred rupees. Therefore, in all the larger cases, which are of greater importance, there is no prohibition against the admission of pleaders; and, practically, what the amendment will establish is that pleaders shall be excluded from suits up to one hundred rupees, but that beyond that amount they will have a right to appear; and that, even as regards smaller cases, it will always be in the option of the Court, at its own discretion, and for reasons to be recorded in writing, to admit the pleader where it is thought essential that he should appear. The argument, therefore, against the exclusion of pleaders generally has no place in the present discussion; and taking the general object of the proposed measure, namely, to attempt by conciliation to adjust all petty differences I question whether the admission of advocates would be beneficial to either side in such cases. We are passing here legislation which is purely exceptional in its character; and in the interesting speeches which we heard on the first amendment, in which the revered name of Bentham appeared frequently, and the legal acumen of Mr. Justice West and other judicial officers was brought forward, it struck me that, had any of these eminent authorities been present here, they would have been the last persons we should have desired to consult with respect to a measure which is one rather of executive and administrative arrangement than of precise legislative requirement and procedure; and admitting, as I do, the force of the criticisms upon which such great stress has been laid, as to the advantages of a qualified Bar in regularly constituted tribunals, I think we are dealing here with a state of things which requires exceptional treatment, and on which, on the authority of those best able to advise, we are justified in going out of the beaten track. Indeed, I believe, if Jeremy Bentham had been in this room, and had had to discuss any of the sections which form part of this Bill, he would probably not have remained very long amongst us."

The Hon'ble Mr. Stokes said that on the occasion of the introduction of this Bill he had expressed his views with considerable fulness against doing anything calculated to exclude pleaders in assisting Judges in the consideration of the very difficult cases which would come before them under the Bill, even when the value was limited to one hundred rupees. All these mortgage-cases would come before Subordinate Judges; and it seemed to him that the optional power of the Subordinate Judge to refuse to permit pleaders to appear, was calculated to cause great subserviency on the part of the pleaders and a great suspicion of favouritism on the part of the Judge. With reference to that point, although the Hon'ble Mover had very wisely, for his own interests, refrained from a fuller citation of Mr. Justice West's remarks, he (Mr. Stokes) would take the opportunity of reading to the Council another short passage from Mr. West's paper. After pointing out that it had been our long endeavour, now approaching complete success, to supply the Courts with an educated, honest and independent Bar, and that every material proceeding, being taken in public, appealed to the moral and legal consciousness of the assembly, Mr. West proceeded:—

"The sense of responsibility thus engendered in the Subordinate Judges the Bill proposes, as far as possible, to destroy. In the first place, as the great majority of suits are for sums of less than Rs. 100, the Court will not be bound to allow pleaders' fees, and certainly will not allow them, except in special cases and for favoured practitioners. The amount of possible business being thus materially cut down, many pleaders will be forced to seek other employment. At present in many of the Subordinate Courts the three, four or five pleaders who only can gain a livelihood are barely sufficient to secure to all litigants who desire it independent assistance. If the numbers are reduced by lack of employment, as has happened in some cases in Sind, to two, a creditor by retaining both pleaders, or securing them generally to his service, virtually cuts off his adversary from effective professional aid. But what is quite as important is that the pleaders who remain will in practice be entirely dependent on the Subordinate Judge. Any independence of bearing, any troublesome persistence, on the part of a pleader will be subject to punishment by the loss of his livelihood. Thus the salutary constraint of professional opinion will be altogether removed. The Judge's efficiency will sink with his sense of responsibility, with the independence and intelligence of his natural critics and interpreters to the public."

The case of the Presidency Small Cause Courts, which had been referred to by the Hon'ble Mover as justifying the discretionary power of excluding legal practitioners, did not appear to be in point. In the Presidency-towns the Judges of those Courts performed their functions in the midst of a large and independent society. They were controlled by an educated public opinion: they were subject to public criticism. Some of them were barristers themselves; and none of them would for a moment dream of riding roughshod over any barrister or pleader who appeared before him.

The amended section also went beyond what he (Mr. Stokes) understood to be the requirements of the Bombay Government.

It put advocates and attorneys of the High Court on the same level as district pleaders and mukhtárs; but in a letter from the Secretary to the Bombay Government, referring to the provisions of the draft Bill respecting the exclusion of legal practitioners from cases tried by Subordinate Judges, he found the following passage :—

"I am to add that, if such concession would tend to remove the objections of the opponents of those provisions, he [that is, the Governor of Bombay in Council] would not object to their being limited in their operation to district pleaders, *so as not to affect pleaders or advocates or attorneys of the High Court.*"

It was a curious fact that might also be mentioned that the Hon'ble Mover had omitted all mention of this passage in the précis of that letter with which he had favoured the Council, and which had been printed and circulated as a paper relating to the Bill.

The Hon'ble Sir Alexander Arbuthnot said :—"It is perhaps almost useless that I should take up the time of the Council by any remarks on this amendment; for it is already evident what the decision of the Council is going to be. To the very strong, lucid and forcible arguments adduced against the amendment—an amendment, however, which the author of those arguments is prepared to support by his vote—I really have nothing to add that would be worth the attention of the Council. To my mind, those arguments, supported as they are by the arguments advanced by Mr. Colvin and by Mr. Stokes, are perfectly conclusive as to the inexpediency of the amendment now before us. I shall vote against the amendment."

The Hon'ble Mr. Hope said :—"The remarks of my hon'ble friend Mr. Thompson have been so complete and comprehensive with reference to the misconception under which it seemed to him, as to me, that the Hon'ble Messrs. Thornton and Colvin were labouring as regards the entire exclusion of pleaders, that there is very little left for me to say. The paragraph from the letter of Mr. Justice West upon which the Hon'ble Mr. Stokes would rely, has already been answered by anticipation ; and I do not find anything in it which calls for any further explanation. Mr. West states his opinion, and that opinion is, of course, entitled to whatever weight each reader of it may consider it to be worth. As to the control which is supposed to be exercised in Presidency Small Cause Courts by the public, I must confess that, I think, that control is very much exaggerated very frequently, and that all arguments of that kind may to a considerable extent be termed 'clap-trap arguments.' But, as a matter of fact, we happen to know that the arrangement checking employment of pleaders has worked for thirty years with perfect success in these Courts ; and I see no reason why it should have worked otherwise.

"Regarding the charge which the Hon'ble the Law Member has made against me, of having omitted, because I supposed it would suit my purpose, a certain paragraph in a letter of the Bombay Government, I have only to say that my summary is as correct as the allegation regarding it is incorrect. Any person who will read the paragraph dispassionately will see that the Bombay Government are exactly of the opinion that they always were. But they say at the end regarding an admission of only pleaders, advocates or attorneys of the High Court that—

'if such concession would tend to remove the objections of the opponents of those provisions, he would not object to their being limited,' &c.

That is to say, the Government of Bombay offer, as a compromise, a concession which they would not mind making.

"If the Hon'ble the Law Member had expressed any desire in Select Committee to accept that compromise, it might no doubt have been considered. The only objection to inserting such a compromise in the Bill would have been that it is so utterly ridiculous, that I myself should have been ashamed of it. If, as the Hon'ble Member has been telling us, and quoting Mr. Justice West to prove, the business in these Courts is so small that only four or five pleaders can get a livelihood from it, and the tendency of our measure is to reduce this further, then I should like to know where is the business to come from which is going to support advocates and attorneys of the High Court ? It is simply ridiculous to suppose that the attorneys and advocates will go out into the highways and hedges of the districts of the Deccan in order to carry on their business.

"Therefore, whether these words were put in or left out would not make the slightest difference in the section, and being ridiculous, as I take them to be, I think they are better left out."

The question being put, the Council divided—

Ayes.	Noes.
The Hon'ble T. C. Hope.	The Hon'ble B. W. Colvin.
The Hon'ble T. H. Thornton.	The Hon'ble Whitley Stokes.
The Hon'ble Faiz Alí Khán.	The Hon'ble Sir Andrew Clarke.
The Hon'ble Rivers Thompson.	The Hon'ble Sir A. J. Arbuthnot.
The Hon'ble Sir E. B. Johnson.	His Excellency the Commander-in-Chief.
The Hon'ble Sir J. Strachey.	
His Honour the Lieutenant-Governor.	
His Excellency the President.	

So the motion was carried.

The Hon'ble Mr. Hope next moved that in section 39 the following words be substituted for the words "any of such parties" (namely) :—

"or when application for execution of any decree in any suit to which any such agriculturist is a party, and which was passed before the date on which this Act comes into force, is contemplated, any of the parties";

and that in section 47 the following words be inserted after the word "suit" (namely) :—

"and no application for execution of a decree passed before the date on which this Act comes into force."

He said :—" My Lord, the object of this motion is to restore to the Bill the provision for making conciliation precede application for the execution of old decrees, which has been cut out by the majority of the Select Committee. As to its details, I may explain that the words for insertion in section 47 are those which were cut out, but that the alteration in section 39 is new, and intended to meet a mere doubt of drafting, raised by Mr. Naylor, as to whether the section as it stood fully tallied in respect of these old decrees with section 47 of the Bill as introduced.

"The reasons assigned for this excision will be found in paragraph 23 of the report, and are, briefly, that every existing decree must be assumed to be just; that no influence, however mild, can rightly be applied to induce a decree-holder to forego one jot or tittle of his legal rights; and that, if the debtor cannot pay, he may resort to the Insolvency Court.

"I may point out, *in limine*, that the statement that this excision is 'adopting the view of the High Court' would seem to be mistaken. The High Court have evidently not understood what was contemplated, and have supposed that it might be intended that the Civil Court should 'ultimately refuse to execute its own' decree. What Mr. Justice Melvill would have said if the scope and grounds of the measure had been explained to him it is impossible to judge. But the High Court cannot now be fairly quoted in the matter. Such explanation I will endeavour to afford.

" I am content to accept the premise that every existing decree must be assumed to be just; although I might easily impugn it by pointing out that the present Bill, in obliging the Courts in future to go behind the bond, and giving them special powers to reduce claims which they have been in the habit of admitting, proceeds on the very contrary assumption that their decrees made in the past have often been unjust. And I also admit that the debtor *can* obtain full relief from the Insolvency Court. But I maintain that friendly mediation rightly *may*, and under existing circumstances certainly *ought* to be applied to obtain an early settlement of these old decrees. In the first place, we know that these decrees are very commonly for amounts which the debtor may, indeed, have made himself legally liable for, but which the creditor could not have reasonably expected ever to receive. The Deccan Riots Commission and Mr. Auckland Colvin both bring out this fact. Then, again, we know that, owing to frauds in execution, many of these decrees have really been satisfied over and over again. I must trouble the Council to listen to one illustration of the sort of thing which goes on, taken from page 250 of Appendix C to the Commission's Report :—

"'The Subordinate Judge of Rihuri passed a decree for Rs. 19-9, including costs. In execution of the same he issued a warrant to seize property therein detailed and valued at Rs. 160. The judgment-debtor appears to have objected; for the Subordinate Judge sent to Mr. Reid (the Magistrate) a sanction to prosecute him for resisting the attachment. Upon examination of the details of the warrant and comparison with the market prices, Mr. Reid found that, for instance, six candies of bajri were valued at Rs. 51, the market value being Rs. 288, and 8 bullocks were valued at Rs. 32.'

"Thus, if this poor fellow had not had the pluck to stand up in defence of his rights and even to incur criminal proceedings, he would have been simply plundered in the name of the law. This is what may, and does sometimes, happen when the warrant is duly served and returned. But sometimes it is not so. Here is a case which, for brevity's sake, I will partly summarize in my own words from the same source :—

"'Pemraj and Koniram got a decree from the Subordinate Judge at Sangamner for Rs. 7-5-11 against Bhikaji and Ramji. Execution was entrusted to a peon of the Court, who returned the warrant with an endorsement signed by Koniram stating that he did not wish for execution. Ramji petitioned the Court that his grain, cart-wheels, and silver bracelets had been attached and handed over to Pemraj. Some enquiry followed, ending with an order, dated two months after the offence, that as Ramji had not paid the fees, his petition was rejected. The peon died before the District Judge acted in the matter. Pemraj and Koniram were discharged, on accusation of an offence against public justice, by the benefit of a doubt, the Magistrate making damaging remarks. Ramji *never got back his property*, and it is believed that Pemraj has some of it yet.'

That this case is no isolated one we may infer from the fact that, according to the latest returns available, 139,285 warrants were in one year returned unexecuted as the result of 185,293 applications for execution—that is, 75 per cent. !

"Another mode in which these decrees are engines of oppression is through the fraudulent attachment of property of third parties. The civil returns for 1872 (the latest extant with these details) show that out of 4,224 suits arising from execution of decrees, 60 per cent. were decided in favour of third parties. In other words, 2,529 innocent persons were found by the Courts to have been put to the worry and expense of a civil suit in order to defend their property from falsely-alleged liability! The costs of execution, too, are enormous, being shown by the same returns to be about $22\frac{1}{2}$ per cent. on the amount recovered. What with frauds, costs, &c., some decrees are a standing property to the holder; and Mr. Auckland Colvin gives instances furnished by Subordinate Judges where, after *nine* executions, the original sum due was unabated, or even increased! Finally, the Commission ascertained that in eight tálukás only, out of the thirty-six which the four disturbed districts contain, about 3,000 decrees, of above seven years' standing and of $3\frac{1}{2}$ lakhs of rupees in value, were unsatisfied.

"The Local Government are surely right in recognizing the necessity, on political no less than moral grounds, of healing this festering sore, of drying up this source of fraud and oppression on the one side, and of misery, recklessness and deep discontent on the other. Various methods of doing so have been pressed upon them. It has been suggested that they should provide for the treatment of districts or parts of districts on the principle already applied to encumbered estates of tálukdárs and thákurs, settle the debts, pay off the amount, and recoup themselves by various methods, by a rack-rent on the land, by taking produce in kind, by the farming system, &c. They have even been urged to allot an annual sum for charitably discharging the debts of individual needy agriculturists. But the Government of Bombay have rejected all these drastic remedies. 'It would be impracticable in the first place,' says Sir Richard Temple in his Minute of April 14th, 1879, ' and it would be in the second place impolitic, even if it were practicable, for any Government to undertake to deal with the debts of a whole peasantry.' What relief, then, do they wish to provide? For the extreme cases there is the Insolvent Court. But this is an extreme remedy. It involves some expense, some loss of self-respect, and even reasonable current credit, as also the liability of future earnings for a considerable period. A more simple middle path to speedy settlement is most necessary; and this the motion before us provides. It merely requires that, before execution of an old decree can be obtained, the parties shall go to the conciliator, who will endeavour by friendly mediation to effect some reasonable and practicable compromise. That creditors will not object to this, we may infer from their own statements at a public meeting held in Ahmednagar in March last, as also from no exception being taken to the original provision for it in a memorial received from eleven leading natives of Sátára, nine of whom are sowkárs.

"It should, however, be distinctly understood that nothing beyond mediation is intended. The supposition in paragraph 32 of the Select Committee's report, that it is contemplated that a 'decree should be placed on the same footing as an unproved claim,' and that 'the rights of the decree-holder under his decree should be brought in question,' are complete misapprehensions. Nothing of the sort is contemplated, and the words proposed for insertion will have no such effect. What is intended merely is that, if no settlement can be arrived at, the conciliator shall give his certificate. The law will then take its course, and the decree in all its sanctity will be enforced. In all this I submit that there is nothing but what is reasonable, just and absolutely necessary on political grounds in the present state of the country; and I trust that the Council will uphold the recommendation of the Local Government accordingly. Any other course will rob the Bill of one of its essential provisions for the liquidation of existing debt."

His Honour the Lieutenant-Governor said :—"I intend to vote for this amendment, because it seems to me that, if there are any cases in which conciliation is likely to be of any effect, it is in those in which a claim has been already proved, and in which all that remains is to determine the best method of satisfying it with the least trouble to the parties. I understand that the amendment takes away from the decree-holder none of the rights which he possesses under the present law; it merely provides that, before taking out execution, or before the defendant or judgment-debtor is put into the Insolvent Court, a settlement should, if possible, be made by the conciliator; and I consider that it is perfectly reasonable and justifiable that this provision should extend to decrees which have been passed before this Act was passed, as well as to cases which may arise afterwards."

The Hon'ble Mr. Rivers Thompson said :—" I should be sorry to be silent on this amendment, even with the fear of my hon'ble friend Sir Alexander Arbuthnot before me. Whatever be the justice or injustice of the original decree, upon which the Hon'ble Member for Bombay has dealt with some force, the arrangement which this amendment is intended to supply is perfectly harmless and simple to carry out. The principle which permeates the whole of this measure is that, rather than go through a detailed dilatory technical procedure, every attempt should be made, not only for new debts, but as regards those particular sections relating to old debts, to bring the parties together, and try by means of conciliation and adjustment to effect a satisfactory settlement of claims. If a creditor holding a decree against a debtor does not accept that conciliation; if he says, ' I hold a decree from the Court which I can execute any day I choose, and I prefer to stand on my rights,' nothing that this amendment provides need prevent or deter him from doing so. It simply means that a man having a claim, say of Rs. 250, against a debtor should come before a conciliator before he attempts to enforce his decree; and it would be in the conciliator's power to try and explain to him that, if the man against whom he had got a decree was in difficulties, a compromise could be effected and the matter settled in a friendly way. If the judgment-creditor did not accept this, the case would proceed in the ordinary course; and, therefore, this whole section is perfectly harmless—harmless as regards any interference with the rights of the creditor, but still opening a door for a settlement of some kind."

The Hon'ble Sir John Strachey said:—"In regard to the merits of the question involved in Mr. Hope's present amendment I do not wish to say a word. I am perfectly satisfied to leave the case as my hon'ble friends Mr. Hope, Sir Robert Egerton and Mr. Thompson have stated it. I consider their arguments in favour of the amendment to be perfectly unanswerable."

The Hon'ble Mr. Stokes said that, although he was under the disadvantage of speaking when the Hon'ble Financial Member had ruled that nothing could really be said against the amendment, he begged to say that he would oppose it on the broad ground that any legislative provision interfering retrospectively with existing rights was *primâ facie* unconstitutional, and should not be adopted by the Legislature, unless it was proved to be, which certainly was not the case at present, an absolutely overruling political necessity or a clear public gain—such, for example, as establishing a general law of Insolvency. If the amendment were adopted, any one who had undergone the expense and trouble of obtaining a decree against an agriculturist before the proposed Act was heard of, would find himself precluded from executing it, unless he produced a certificate from the conciliator. Practically that requirement would often prevent him from executing his decree at all; for if the judgment-debtor refused (as he was sure to do in many cases) to appear before the conciliator, the decree would not be executed till the lapse of a 'reasonable' time. Well, then, the question would be, how much was reasonable? The answer was, as much as the conciliator (who would, he feared, often be a Government official, with a bias against the sowkár and in favour of the ryot) declared reasonable. The conciliator might not make any such declaration at all, or, as had been pointed out in one of the papers, he might postpone it till the time for presenting an application for execution had expired. He (Mr. Stokes) maintained that any such provision as this would disturb absolute vested rights, against which there was no equity; and he was glad to find himself supported in that view by a gentleman of large experience,—Mr. Naylor, the Legal Remembrancer of the Bombay Government, who said:—

" When the Courts have once passed a decree, their adjudication ought to be, and has always hitherto been, regarded as final. It would be subversive of all recognized principles to allow matters which have been once finally adjudicated upon by the constituted tribunals to be re-opened, especially when the functionary before whom the revision is to take place is an illiterate conciliator. Persons who may hereafter obtain decrees with the knowledge that they will have to take them before a conciliator before being permitted to execute them, will not have so much cause of complaint as the decree-holders who obtained their decrees before the date of the Act. The retrospective effect which it is proposed to give to this section in this respect is, to my mind, altogether inequitable. It is also uncalled-for, because debtors who cannot satisfy all their judgment-debts may, by taking advantage of the insolvency-provisions of the Bill, obtain their discharge on very simple and reasonable terms."

He understood the Hon'ble Mover to say that decrees would not be re-opened during the process of conciliation; but it was impossible to suppose that in an informal proceeding of the kind contemplated the conciliator and the parties would not rake up the whole case from the beginning.

The Hon'ble Mr. Hope said :—" I have very little to say with reference to this amendment in view of the complete statements made regarding it by my hon'ble friends Sir Robert Egerton, Mr. Thompson and Sir John Strachey, concluding with the remark of the latter, which has been fully verified by the result, that the arguments offered have been unanswerable. As I understand it, an argument is called unanswerable when no sufficient answer can be produced to it. The only answer produced is one which I must confess I heard with very considerable surprise—one which was produced on a previous occasion by the Hon'ble the Law Member. I must say that I felt considerable doubt at the time whether he brought it forward seriously, or whether he only used it on the principle that any stick will do to beat a dog with. The statement or suggestion that the decree will be re-opened, made by Mr. Naylor, is simply inaccurate. The decree will not be re-opened, as has been well put by the Hon'ble Members who have already spoken. The creditor will simply be asked, 'You have got a decree for one hundred rupees; will you take fifty down or not?'

If he does, well and good; and if he says 'No, I won't,' there is an end of the matter. It is quite impossible to call that a reopening of the whole case. Still less is it possible to apply to it the totally incorrect language in the report, in which it is said that the decree is placed on the same footing as an unproved claim. I cannot see, either, that it has any retrospective effect, any more than asking a man to make the promise I have just alluded to has. But suppose it was retrospective, I would merely remark that the Council must be aware that retrospective measures with reference to debts are not only passed constantly by this Legislature, but a retrospective measure by which debts may be cut down by one-third of their amount was actually passed in this Council not two months ago, without a single word of objection from, but on the contrary on the motion of, the Hon'ble the Law Member himself; I refer of course to the insolvency-clauses of the Civil Procedure Code."

The question being put, the Council divided—

Ayes.

The Hon'ble T. C. Hope.
The Hon'ble T. H. Thornton.
The Hon'ble Faiz Alí Khán.
The Hon'ble Rivers Thompson.
The Hon'ble Sir E. B. Johnson.
The Hon'ble Sir J. Strachey.
His Excellency the Commander-in-Chief.
His Honour the Lieutenant-Governor.
His Excellency the President.

Noes.

The Hon'ble B. W. Colvin.
The Hon'ble Whitley Stokes.
The Hon'ble Sir Andrew Clarke.
The Hon'ble Sir A. J. Arbuthnot.

So the motion was carried.

The Hon'ble Mr. Hope then moved that in section 38 the words " other than an officer of revenue or police " be omitted.

He said :—" My Lord, these words are an interpolation of the majority of the Select Committee, intended, they say (paragraph 22), 'to guard against the dangers adverted to by the Hon'ble Sayyad Ahmad in his speech.' What the Hon'ble Sayyad Ahmad said was this :—

" 'No doubt, a revenue or a police officer could bring influences to bear on creditors which would induce them altogether to forego their claims; but I need hardly express my conviction that the Government of India would altogether discountenance the exercise of any such influence; and I have no doubt the Council, in order to avoid even the apprehension of its exercise, will see fit to introduce a provision in the Bill prohibiting the appointment as conciliator of any officer exercising revenue or police functions.'

" Now, although no allusion to this subject was made in the letter addressed to the Government of Bombay on the introduction of the Bill (Paper No. 3), these remarks attracted the attention of that Government; and in their reply they stated that 'it is not desirable to exclude from the office of conciliator all revenue-officers, some of whom are capable of exerting a very intelligent and beneficial influence in that capacity.'

" Of the interpolated words, I would premise that they are, in the first place, unnecessary. No reasonable persons, either in this Council or out of it, can, I should hope, seriously suppose that the Government of Bombay would not be as anxious as themselves to discountenance all exercise of undue influence by conciliators, whether they be officials or non-officials. There can be no doubt whatever that any evidence of such misconduct would be promptly followed by deprivation of office, and that, if the offender were official, he would incur the severe displeasure of Government. The words, however, are not merely unnecessary but offensive. They cast beforehand, without a shadow of proof, an unworthy stigma upon the great revenue or executive department by which the bulk of the administration of this empire is carried on. Revenue-officers have in numerous capacities—as magistrates, as surveyors, as municipal councillors, and what not—to intervene in all sorts of disputes between man and man; and in these their general success and their high character are equally undeniable. The words, again, are unprecedented. There is not, as far as I can remember, any page of the Indian Statute-book containing a deliberate expression of want of confidence and an exclusion such as this. The exclusion, moreover, may be most prejudicial, as the Bombay Government point out. It is not likely that in practice revenue-officers, who have much else to do, will be largely employed as conciliators; but occasions may easily arise when they alone can effect what is wanted. If, for instance, meetings such as that at Ahmednagar, to which I have alluded, should result in leading bankers expressing their willingness to compound with all their debtors, a person of considerable position, intelligence and tact could alone carry the transaction through. Why, then, should the aid of such a person, if the parties desired it, be denied merely because he happened to be a revenue-officer? I have known individuals, both European and Native, whose mere appearance on the scene was sufficient to pacify and give confidence to an angry countryside. Of police-officers I need say nothing, because no one dreams of making them conciliators. But, finally, I would urge that where a great and experimental measure, such as that before us, has to be introduced, it is not only fair and reasonable, but indispensable to success, to leave the Local Government free to choose its own instruments. The Local Government have expressed their views and wishes very plainly in this instance; and I rely on the Council to support them."

The Hon'ble Mr. Thornton said :—" I shall vote for this amendment, because, assuming that special Courts of Conciliation are to be established, there appears to me to be no reason whatever why the Local Government should be restricted in its selection of conciliators."

The Hon'ble Mr. Colvin said :—" In speaking upon the amendment which is now before the Council, I cannot help remarking that the statement which we have heard to-day, that the present Bill is only a Local Bill, appears to me to require very large qualification. It is true that the Bill will only be of local application in the first instance; but I doubt if its future consequences will be merely local. If the provisions which this Bill contains are considered to be sound and suitable for relieving agricultural distress in the Deccan, it is not easy to see the grounds upon which the enactment of a similar measure could be refused, if asked for, in order to relieve a like agricultural distress in other parts of the country. It has been said no doubt that the measure is a purely tentative one, and that the experiment need not be repeated if it is not successful. I should be very glad to think that this was so. It seems to me more probable that the admission that an experiment is being made may be lost sight of, and that the results of the measure will not be waited for, but its success assumed. Before the year is out, urgent applications will perhaps be made for a trial of the same experiment elsewhere; and what is now called a local and tentative law, may grow into one of general application, and be treated as if it were a certain specific for the difficulties of the agricultural community everywhere.

"The changes of practice, too, which will be made by the Bill, so far from being in matters of mere technical detail, introduce new principles of very great importance. Much stress has been laid upon the necessity of deferring to local experience upon these points. It could easily be shown, I think, that in the Bill as it stands general experience has been quite sufficiently subordinated to local knowledge. For instance, it is a well-known general principle of law and of common sense that in all suits the best evidence should be obtained. The Bill, on the contrary, insists that the Courts shall go out of their way to look for the worst. It directs them to leave the comparatively safe ground of ascertained and recorded facts, and to trust in preference to the vague, conflicting, and often interested testimony of witnesses deposing to remote and doubtful transactions. They are to do this, moreover, with the express object of discovering fraud where no one has alleged it. Again, it is a matter of almost universal complaint that in India the land is changing hands, or being stripped of all profit to agriculturists by the pressure of their debts. The Bill, if it is passed, will make it almost impossible for the ryots of the Deccan to borrow money at all except on a mortgage of their lands; for it will leave them no other security which a lender can safely accept. It has generally been held, too, that speedy justice is a good thing. Well, under the amendments which have been carried to-day, it is true that the delay caused by appeals has been cut off; but, on the other hand, the Bill will interpose an indefinite delay for the purpose of conciliation before a suit can be taken into Court. For, as far as I can judge from its wording, the delay which a conciliator may cause, if he chooses, has no limit. Further, it has commonly been thought that people should be free to make their own bargains, and that bargains, when made, should be kept. The Bill declares that it is the duty of the Judge, notwithstanding any agreement made by the parties, to alter and arrange the terms of their transaction for them, and, where interest forms part of a bargain, to allow as much or as little as he may think reasonable. The natural effect of this last provision will be to prevent persons from ever foreseeing the result of any transaction in which they may engage. I think that great harm may result from this. I am no advocate for usury-laws; but I would rather have seen a fixed limit to interest prescribed by the law. In that case business could have adjusted itself accordingly, and the borrower and the lender would have been able to make their arrangements. But nobody can foretell what rate of interest may appear reasonable to each individual Judge. The conditions, therefore, on which any loan is made, must always remain uncertain; and constant uncertainty is a risk that people engaged in business cannot afford to run. I have enumerated some of the points upon which the Bill makes great changes, because we have been charged, by implication at least, with a want of proper deference to local authority. My own doubt is whether we have not gone too far in allowing it to override general experience in such important matters. I believe that we might more justly be charged with having given to it too much weight. No doubt the Bill, taken as a whole, ought to have the effect of diminishing the ryot's means of obtaining credit, and of curtailing the large powers which the existing law confers upon creditors, and that these are good ends to aim at. It is true also that the power of the Government in this country is so great that it can hardly ever fail to attain, in part at least, any object towards which it seriously directs its energies. The Judges, too, by whom the law must be carried into effect, and who will be confronted by the practical difficulties of doing so, may be trusted to amend the operation of much in it which (as I believe) is otherwise likely to be purely injurious. Nevertheless I cannot but feel great misgivings as to the prudence of making such very large concessions as have been made to local experience.

" I turn, now, to the particular amendment which is under the consideration of the Council. The question at issue is whether officials should be eligible for the post of conciliator; and it is a most important question in its bearing upon the probable result of conciliation. I think that there is an excellent reason for not entrusting such duties to any officials, even if they be only revenue-officials. Conciliation by such persons is very apt to degenerate into improper pressure. In France, where, as I understand, the system of conciliation originated, no officer of the Government is allowed to discharge these functions; and it is an avowed part of the system that they should not be so employed. I believe that the intended change of procedure is much more likely to succeed in this country if we follow the French practice on this point. As to selecting police-officers for such a post, I can conceive nothing worse or more objectionable. I suppose that in all countries the subordinate officers in the police force must comprise a good many men of doubtful character. It can scarcely be otherwise; and I do not intend to say that the police force in this country necessarily includes more of them than is the case elsewhere. But I think that a man holding an office which makes him the keeper of the door, as it were, through which every claim must pass before it goes into Court, will be strongly tempted in all countries, if he is not an honest man, to make money by it. If a police officer chooses to exert undue influence, there can be little doubt of his power to do so. He can summon, arrest, and search houses. If he is unscrupulous, he can even fabricate a false charge against an innocent man, and possibly have him convicted and imprisoned for years. I think that there can be no Magistrate in this country who has not seen attempts of this kind made, and few Magistrates who would care to affirm that such attempts have never been successful. It should not be possible that men who can bring such influences to bear upon suitors should be appointed conciliators.

" In conclusion, I have only to say that, as the Bombay Government has never expressed any desire to appoint police-officer's as conciliators, and as we have been assured by my hon'ble friend the Mover that there is no intention of doing so, I cannot see any necessity for amending the Bill in the manner which is proposed."

The Hon'ble Mr. Stokes said that he had only one observation to make, and that was that he did not believe that the insertion in the Bill of the words " other than an officer of revenue or police" would be regarded as setting a stigma upon the members of those services. They were not so morbidly sensitive. By the 121st section of the Code of Criminal Procedure police-officers were expressly prohibited from taking confessions; and he had never heard that their feelings were hurt by this suitable prohibition. In this country we all knew how very desirable it was to keep the administration of the law free from any suspicion of executive influence; and he was strengthened in that opinion by the fact that the insertion of words excluding the police was in accordance with the opinion of our wise and experienced Native colleague—the Hon'ble Sayyad Ahmad Khán.

The Hon'ble Mr. Rivers Thompson said:—" I am not going to follow my hon'ble friend Mr. Colvin in his interesting review of the principles of this Bill, because it appears to me that the greater portion of those questions have been already disposed of, and in my opinion been rightly disposed of. The principle which I contend for as regards this amendment is that, in carrying out and giving effect to legislation of this kind, the greatest freedom of action must be left to the local authorities, and that the Local Government might quite well say that, if their hands are tied as to the agents by whom the Bill is to be carried out, they had better give up attempting to carry it out at all. In that view I am quite prepared to support the Hon'ble Mr. Hope in this amendment. I think myself that it would be improved as an amendment if we were only to omit from the section the words 'revenue or' so as to make the exclusion run ' other than an officer of police,' because the only evil contended against is that officers of police might abuse their powers of arrest, and intimidate by an official pressure, which would be injurious. I cannot conceive, however, in what way it would be injurious if the Local Government were perfectly free to employ revenue-officers in discharging the functions of a conciliator. Their ordinary duties amongst the people would especially qualify them for such an office."

The Hon'ble Sir John Strachey said:—" My hon'ble friend Sir Alexander Arbuthnot said to the Council just now, and I think with great truth, that, although it was the duty of this Council to carry out its own views in matters in which important principles were involved, it was equally its duty not to interfere in mere matters of detail, on which the Local Government had expressed a strong opinion. Now, in spite of the remarks which have fallen from my hon'ble friend Mr. Colvin, I can conceive no matter which is more plainly a matter of detail than this. We are not now considering whether the establishment of Courts of Conciliation is a good or a bad thing. That they are to be established is admitted by the Bill as it stands. We are simply asked whether the Local Government shall, or shall not, be at liberty to choose its own agents for this work as it pleases. It seems to me impossible to doubt that the Local Government must be the best judge of such a purely local question as this; it is infinitely more competent to judge than we are.

" In regard to the question of appointing police-officers to act as conciliators, I understood my hon'ble friend Mr. Hope to say— and I hope he will correct me if I am wrong—that it was really unnecessary to talk about the appointment of police-officers, because it had never entered into any one's head to appoint police-officers as conciliators. I quite agree with my hon'ble friend Mr. Stokes in not attaching much importance to the consideration that, if we mention police-officers, we shall be placing a stigma upon them. But if we put in words forbidding the Local Government to appoint a police-officer, we throw a stigma on the Local Government. Although it is highly improbable that a police-officer will ever be chosen as conciliator, still it is conceivable that under some circumstances it will be found desirable to appoint such an officer, and if the Local Government should come to the conclusion that it is proper to do so, I think it should be allowed to exercise its own discretion in the matter.

" With regard to the exclusion of revenue-officers from this duty, I should like to say a few words. If these districts of the Deccan are similar in this respect to those parts of India with which I am acquainted—and I have seen no reason to suppose that they are different—then I say that, of all the men that could possibly be chosen as conciliators in the class of cases with which we have to deal, the revenue-officers would frequently be the best. They know far more about the agricultural classes than any other officers of the Government. Their duties bring them into intimate relations with the people; and the amicable settlement of disputes and the prevention of litigation are, I may say, objects which, without any fresh provisions of law, a good revenue-officer already considers to fall within the sphere of his duties. I myself more than twenty years ago advocated in the provinces of Northern India the establishment of Courts of Conciliation; and the opinions which I held then I hold still. I believe that Courts of Conciliation might be established in the North-Western Provinces with very great advantage. If, when advocating the establishment of those Courts, I had been asked 'Who can you appoint as conciliators?' or if I were asked that question now, I should reply we shall be able constantly to find admirable conciliators in our revenue-officers, who are, I may say, the natural protectors of the people. I am the last person to doubt, or to deny, the immense improvement which has taken place during the last twenty years in the Civil Courts of India. These Courts have been immensely improved, both in the character and in the acquirements of the Judges, and by the very great simplification of their procedure. We cannot be too grateful to the eminent men by whom these benefits have been conferred upon the country; and I hope that my hon'ble friend Mr. Stokes will not think me impertinent if I add that there is no one to whom we owe a larger share of that gratitude for making the procedure of our Courts simple and rational than we owe to him. But, in spite of this improvement which has taken place in the Civil Courts, it still remains as true as ever that every measure by which we can keep the people out of the Courts will be a great blessing to the country. It will be highly interesting to watch the results of this first experiment in India in establishing Courts of Conciliation, which have proved so highly useful in some other countries. It would be a great pity to interfere in any way with any of its chances of success; and I believe we should be so interfering if we were to put any check on the power of the Local Government to choose its own instruments.

" I have only one other remark to make with reference to an observation which fell from my hon'ble friend Mr. Colvin. He said that he believed that the only country in which this system of conciliation had been tried was France, but that in France no officials acted as conciliators. Now, I am sorry to tell him that he has made a great mistake. The truth is that no one who is not an official can act as a conciliator; all the *Juges de Paix* in the country are conciliators, and nobody else. So my hon'ble friend has given an unfortunate illustration in support of his argument."

The Hon'ble Sir Edwin Johnson said :—" I would merely remark that if this amendment is allowed to stand in its present form, I shall have to vote against it; for the objections which have been assigned to the appointment of a police-officer as a conciliator will still remain. I quite agree in the remarks of my hon'ble friends Sir John Strachey and Mr. Thompson as to the advantage of having revenue-officers in the position of conciliators; but I regard it as highly inexpedient to allow police-officers to hold that position, or even to be considered eligible to hold it. I have no doubt that a large number of police-officers would be found perfectly capable of discharging the duties of such an appointment in a very creditable manner; but, irrespective of other considerations, I think that, in justice to the whole body of the police, they should be exempted from the possibility of being placed in a position in which they would be liable to misrepresentation. If my hon'ble friend Mr. Thompson's proposal is agreed to, I shall be willing to vote for the amendment; but if not, I must go against it."

The Hon'ble Sir Alexander Arbuthnot said :—" I cannot say that I attach very great importance to the particular words to which this amendment relates. Those words would not have been inserted in the Bill as revised by the Select Committee, had it not been that our attention was pointedly drawn to the matter by our very able, intelligent and experienced Native colleague—Sayyad Ahmad. It was his remarks that led the majority of the Select Committee to consider it desirable that officers of revenue and police should be expressly excluded from the office of conciliator under this Bill. I must say that, while I do not agree with my hon'ble friend Mr. Colvin in some of the observations which fell from him with reference to that part of the Bill that relates to the subject of conciliation, which appears to me to be the essence of the reform contemplated in the Bill, and from which, though I am not prepared to say that I am extremely sanguine I still hope that some benefits may be obtained, and think that the experiment is one which is amply deserving of a trial, still I agree with my hon'ble colleague in all that he has said as to the expediency of excluding officers possessing the great official authority and the great influence in the eyes of our Native fellow-subjects which is possessed not only by our officers of police but by our officers of revenue. As a matter of fact, I have been accustomed to regard all officers of the Revenue Department in the Presidency in which the greater part of my service has been passed as far the most influential and the most powerful officers we have. They have often infinitely more power than the officers of police. The remark that fell from our Native colleague Sayyad Ahmad about leaving no opening for the appointment of officers of police are, on grounds of principle, unanswerable. I think that, as a matter of fact, the objections to permitting officers of revenue to engage in this duty are very great ; but I for my part shall be quite prepared to agree to the compromise which has been suggested by Sir Edwin Johnson, and which, I think, meets the views of some of my other colleagues, to limit the exclusion to the police."

The Hon'ble Mr. Colvin said :—" My Lord, I should be glad to say a few words by way of explanation, if I may be permitted to do so. My hon'ble friend Sir John Strachey has corrected a statement of mine regarding the office of conciliators in France. I have to thank him for that correction if my remarks were generally understood to apply to judicial as well as executive officers. I know of no objection to the appointment of judicial officers as conciliators. What I intended to say was that no officer invested with executive authority was ever appointed to be a conciliator in France ; and the fact is so. Such an appointment could not, I believe, be made.

" I may take this opportunity of correcting an error which my hon'ble friend himself has made in speaking of conciliation as a novel experiment in India. It appears that Courts of Conciliation have existed under the law in Madras since 1816."

The Hon'ble Mr. Hope said :—" I need not trouble the Council for more than two or three minutes on this matter. I said that no person, so far as I was aware, dreamt of making police-officers conciliators, and therefore while, on the one hand, the Council would be fully justified in omitting the words proposed, on the other I do not see any great objection to leaving them in.

" There is an inaccuracy which seems to me worthy of notice in the remarks of the Hon'ble the Law Member. There is no analogy whatever in the parallel drawn by him between the case of excluding police from taking confessions and the one before us. Originally they used to take confessions; but when in the year 1860 the whole of the police in India were reconstituted—a work with which in my own Presidency I had officially much to do—one of the great things we had to do was to draw distinctly the line between police functions and magisterial functions. At that time Magistrates used to be policemen; but in the course of that re-organization that ensued these two functions were divided. The police were confined to what was strictly their own line of business; the recording of confessions went to the Magistrate. There was, of course, no stigma in this; but a deliberate exclusion like the present was different. However, I am perfectly willing, if the Hon'ble Sir Edwin Johnson and the Council think my amendment should be limited to the exclusion of the words ' revenue or '; and with your Lordship's permission I will alter it to this effect :—

" ' That in section 38 the words " revenue or " be omitted.' "

The motion, as thus amended, was then put and agreed to.

The Hon'ble Mr. Hope next moved that the following clause be added to section 7 (namely) :—

<small>Court to examine defendant as witness.</small> " In every suit the Court shall examine the defendant as a witness, unless, for reasons to be recorded by it in writing, it deems it unnecessary so to do.

He said :—" My Lord, the Bill proposed by the Bombay Government provided against the hearing of suits in the absence of the defendant—a practice which has reached enormous proportions in the Bombay Presidency, and which is proved by the fullest evidence to be often productive of gross injustice. In my introductory speech I said that the proportions in the four districts ranged from 60 to 74 per cent. in 1876, and from 57 to 66 per cent. in 1878. But this was for all suits. In money suits only Mr. Auckland Colvin shows (Minute, p. 30) that it is from 93 to 97 per cent. The Bombay section was substantially reproduced as section 9 of the Bill introduced; but the Select Committee have cut it out altogether. From paragraph 4 of the Report it would seem that they are impressed by the obvious hardship of forcibly dragging a man away from his home and his cultivation, perhaps at a season when every day is of importance to him, merely with a view to 'compelling him to appear in a suit to which he has no defence.' To this it may be answered *in limine* that, as every man is *now* by the law of the land liable to be so dragged, under arrest if necessary, in order to give evidence in the affairs of other people with which he has no concern whatever, there can be no special hardship in obliging him to come up about a matter of primary importance to himself; and as to actual arrest, on the hardships and indignity of which some sentiment has been expended, this penalty is no more likely to be incurred by defendants than by witnesses, of whom arrests are almost unknown. The knowledge that a summons must be obeyed readily ensures attendance. On the other hand, however, the necessity for a defendant's presence is, if possible, greatly enhanced by the present Bill. I do not see how it will be possible for a Judge to comply with the requirements of section 12, to receive the defendant's admission, and weigh it so as to decide whether it is true and made with a full knowledge of his legal rights; to go into the history and merits of the case, to ascertain what defence a man may have, even though he is not aware of it, and to follow up the items of the account, unless the defendant be before him."

The Hon'ble Sir Alexander Arbuthnot here said that he, and he believed those who had hitherto agreed with him, would not oppose this amendment.

The Hon'ble Mr. Hope said that in that case he had no further remarks to make.

The motion was then put and agreed to.

The Hon'ble Mr. Hope then moved that the Bill as amended, be passed.

He said:—"My Lord, in making this motion I wish, on the one hand, to give certain explanations and comments on what it contains, which I hope may be useful to those entrusted with its execution and to the public, as also, on the other, to make remarks on a few important matters not included in it. I shall do so, as far as may be, in an uncontroversial spirit, and the views I express may be taken simply as my own, and not necessitating any rejoinder from Hon'ble Members who may in any instance happen to dissent from them.

" With respect to section 2, doubts have been expressed by the Poona Sabhá, in an able and comprehensive paper which has on some points been most useful, whether the definition of 'agriculturist' covers the important class of agricultural labourers; but it is held by the Hon'ble Law Member that it does so, as of course it is intended to do.

" To section 9 it has been objected that only a defective record, and in some cases no record, is provided for; that Judges will consequently take down just what they choose, and that superior Courts will have nothing to go upon. This is not strictly accurate, since even in cases not exceeding Rs. 10 in amount or value a record of the substance of the evidence is obligatory. And it should be remembered that what is here provided merely follows what is the existing law, either in non-appealable civil cases or in summary criminal trials by a Magistrate or Bench of Magistrates, and in certain trials before a Presidency Magistrate. A mode of record which is found not inappropriate for cases where two years' imprisonment and Rs. 1,000 fine may be inflicted is surely sufficient for the civil suits to which our Bill relates. While thus touching on procedure, I would take the opportunity of repeating and explaining what fell from me when introducing the Bill. I then said that, in view of the fact that 85 per cent. of all suits in British India are for sums under Rs. 100, and 44 per cent. for sums under Rs. 20, 'I cannot but feel, and I think the people feel too, that our Civil Procedure Code, with its six hundred and fifty sections, and all that they involve, is in minor cases a burden almost too heavy to be borne. I trust that the day may come when not only Deccan ryots but all India will obtain some relief in this respect.' I do not dispute that our Civil Procedure Code, whenever its six hundred and fifty sections, just amended as they have been in some one hundred and seventy instances, and still requiring amendment as they do in perhaps as many instances more, shall have been recast with patient judgment into one work, fit to take a permanent place beside such Codes as the Indian Penal Code and Code Napoleon, may then be a suitable machine by which to regulate litigation in which great interests are at stake. But for *minor cases*, of which alone I spoke, it is, and ever must be, an intolerable burden. However refreshing to the legal intellect may be the creation and solution of subtle distinctions and dilemmas, and however noble it may seem to argue and judge with the same care whether five rupees or five lakhs of rupees are involved, the world that has to toil and live can neither wait nor pay for such entertainment. That world in England has long since settled the question by establishing County Courts, which give such satisfaction that their sphere has received, and seems likely still to receive considerable extension. I will repeat my regret that a material simplification of procedure with a view to saving delay and expense has not been found feasible in the present Bill: the rejected sections of the original draft were perhaps not sufficiently thorough to raise the issue with advantage. But, though we seem to have in India an unlucky knack of introducing as improvements what is being abandoned in England as intolerable, I do not despair of the reform I desire being in the end successfully achieved.

" Regarding sections 12 to 15 of the Bill, I also then doubted whether they expressed intelligibly or would secure effectively the action needed for 'going behind the bond.' The objections of the Bombay Government were more fully and emphatically pronounced. In consequence of these I am glad to say that a very great improvement has been effected. But I much regret the absence of an authorization of the Court to award, with or without the aid of a jury or assessors, an equitable sum to the plaintiff instead of nonsuiting him in cases where the Court is satisfied that some money has been lent, but, through the want of books or other evidence, the actual nature and extent of the transactions are doubtful, and the precise sum due cannot be proved. This power has been shown by experience under the Túlukdárs and Thákurs Acts to be most useful in saving the creditor from unreasonable loss, and would have tended to give confidence to the money-lending class. Still, although in this and in some other points the views of the Bombay Government regarding these sections may not have been fully met, I have every hope that the latter will now be found workable and beneficial, especially if the following wise caution of Mr. Justice Maxwell Melvill be kept in view by our Judges:—

" 'I can only express a hope that, in making the experiment, the Government will select men of moderate views, who will not give too loose a rein to the natural feelings of sympathy with the agriculturist and antipathy to the money-lender. These men will, in future, have to determine what rate of interest is reasonable in transactions between the money-lender and the agriculturist; and they will fail to do justice if they forget that the money-lender has many bad debts, that as high interest means bad security, so bad security means high interest, and that the money-lender's security is now more than ever weak, seeing that he cannot touch his debtor's person, nor his house, nor his clothing, nor his cattle, nor (unless the debt be specially secured) his land.'

I may add, incidentally, that it should be observed that chapter III applies to all suits and proceedings to which agriculturists are parties, irrespective of their amount or value.

" To pass on to the question of agriculturists' accounts, it does not seem to have been fully perceived in some quarters that, while sections 65 and 66 ensure to the debtor a statement of his account from the creditor's point of view, section 16 is designed to enable him to get his real liability determined under the provisions for going behind the bond. Section 19 now expresses correctly what was proposed in the Bombay draft Bill : the objections taken to it as it stood when introduced arose merely from accidental oversights in the drafting.

" Considerable criticism has been directed against section 22, which exempts land from attachment and sale in execution of decrees, unless it has been specifically pledged. In my introductory speech I sketched the position of the land-sale question, and explained the reason for the absence from the Bill of any attempt at a final comprehensive settlement of it, and for considering the restriction of sale to specifically-pledged land to be equitable. In the decision of the question I had taken no part, as this restriction had been proposed by the Bombay Government, and accepted by the Government of India and the Secretary of State, before my connection with the Bill commenced. I ventured, however, to express my views as follows :—

" ' I must confess to some misgivings as to how the exemption may work in practice. The money-lender may everywhere make the execution of a bond, laying on the land all his existing unsecured advances, an indispensable condition of further accommodation. At the same time, the exemption rests as to the past upon a perfectly intelligible and reasonable basis, while as to the future the proposed village registration will at least ensure that every ryot when he pledges his land shall understand what he is doing, and insolvency will open to him a loophole of escape when unreasonably pressed by an exortionate creditor, if he prefers that alternative.'

" My doubts have now been more than echoed by Mr. Justice Maxwell Melvill and Mr. Justice West, the former of whom predicts that loans, excepting on mortgage, will soon be unknown; while the latter, concurring in this, adds that the mortgagee will, by the operation of the Bill, be driven on to become a purchaser, and the ryot will have no alternative but to acquiesce in sale, Here I would only observe that the most demonstrably correct economic calculations are liable to be defeated by moral and sentimental causes, and that it by no means follows that mankind will do what logically they ought to do. It may be that the affection which the ryot bears to his land will lead him to defeat his creditor by insolvency; that the competition amongst moneylenders, which the Deccan Riots Commission report, will check the exaction of landed security ; and, best of all, that the difficulties of borrowing will tend to keep the ryot's transactions within his means. The issue can only be known upon experiment. But it seems clear that the course which has been adopted was the best under the circumstances. No solution of the land-sale question generally admitted to be satisfactory is forthcoming. Mr. Justice Melvill candidly admits that he has not got one to produce; the reservation to the ryot by 'a kind and impartial authority' of the 'minimum of land' requisite for 'a decent subsistence,' which Mr. Justice West advocates, has been severely criticized, directly and indirectly, by very competent authorities. To have postponed relief to the Deccan till this question was settled for all India, would have been little less than criminal; to have made no attempt to check the rapid alienation of ryots' lands, by a method equitable in itself and offering the chance of even a limited success, would have been neglectful. At the same time, it is also clear that the land-sale question cannot be put off much longer; and I earnestly hope that what has been written, said and done upon this Bill may accelerate its solution.

"I must now notice the important subject of management by the Collector provided by clause 2 of section 22 and by section 29. In my introductory speech I said that—

'compared with what we mean to compel a man to *pay*, the question of what we shall hold him to owe sinks into insignificance'; and, again, that 'we cannot justly and reasonably legislate for the summary relief of the debtor from unjust and extortionate claims, unless we also give to the creditor full and effective aid in obtaining all that is fairly due to him and reasonably recoverable. A creditor's difficulties when he has got his decree should be reduced to a minimum. If we make the decree a just one, it should be effectively enforceable. Without ample provision on this principle the destruction of the ryot's credit or his bondage to secret and extortionate agreements must ensue, and all our well-intentioned interference will do harm instead of good. With such provision the measure will not injure the ryots' credit, but improve it.'

"In short, I look upon this provision as the keystone or test-point of the Bill. If it works well, the ryot's credit will be secured on a satisfactory basis; if otherwise, his borrowing, even for reasonable purposes, within the limits of his true means will become most difficult, while the alternatives of absolute non-transferability of land, or eviction and a poor-law, will stare us in the face. I note, on the one hand, that the Poona Sabhá, Mr. Moore and Mr. Naylor doubt the Collector's power to manage vast numbers of small holdings, while the Commissioner and the other two Collectors consulted express no misgivings on the subject. I myself consider that there need be no fear of failure, provided it be from the first recognized that the duty is important and difficult, not to be performed by mere perfunctory orders, passed on from the Court to the kulkarni through an intervening chain of little-heeding functionaries. Success will, I anticipate, lie most frequently in a pretty close adherence to the system in Native States, and to the provisions for security and recovery still extant in our law, though of late years little resorted to. If the ryot be retained as cultivator wherever possible,—if a reasonable rack-rent be imposed, personal security exacted, precautions taken against making away with the crop, aid given when wanted in securing a fair price, and payment required at the time means are forthcoming, I see no reason why satisfactory results should not be attained. But careful supervision by Assistant or Deputy Collectors and Mámlatdárs will be indispensable; and possibly the appointment of a special officer for a few months to start the system in the four districts might be advantageous. These, however, are details which will, I doubt not, receive full attention from the Local Government.

The section which enabled the Court to make over moveable property to the creditor at a valuation has been struck out by the majority of the Select Committee. The fact that attached articles of property are constantly sold by auction for a mere song, and often collusively so bought by the creditor, is established beyond dispute. On the section the Poona Sabhá remark:—

" ' We regard the provision as salutary. Forced sales of property under all circumstances prove very ruinous to the debtor classes. We would only recommend that the assessors who are to appraise the property should not be appointed by the Court,' &c.

Messrs. Stewart and Moore approve of it; Mr. Naylor ably defends it; Mr. West apparently objects merely to its present form; and, finally, the Bombay Government, after considering the remarks made in Council, are clear for its retention. Under these circumstances, I am wholly unable to comprehend why, instead of being amended, as it easily might have been, it should have been expunged. On a matter of this kind, and considering the strong favourable evidence, I think more deference should have been paid to the views of the Local Government; and in this case, as in that of summary equitable awards to which I have already alluded, I would have moved the insertion of an amended section, but that I had, unfortunately, to trouble the Council with so many other amendments of even greater importance.

"I am glad to say that section 35, limiting the powers of Subordinate Judges in the punishment of fraudulent debtors, to which I was opposed, has been expunged. The provision in section 33 for an appeal against their sentences is a step towards the separation of punishment for fraud from insolvency, which I advocated. But the punishment of concealment and fraud in the creditor, for which the Bombay draft provided, is still omitted, and must now await the further improvement of the law of Insolvency throughout India, which cannot be long deferred.

"A consideration of the chapter on Insolvency, together with the sections about going behind the bond, suggests the interesting question as to whether their combined effect may not be to destroy credit, put a stop to money-lending, render the revenue irrecoverable, and bring the country to a deadlock. On this point Mr. Justice Maxwell Melvill, who, I hope I may say without offence has treated the problem forced upon us with equal moderation and statesmanship, makes the following remarks :—

" 'I presume that the Government is satisfied that the effect of the measure will not be to destroy the ryot's credit altogether, or to induce the money-lenders to close their shops. If this should not be the result, but if on the contrary, it should turn out that after the agriculturists have been relieved of their existing debts on the easiest possible terms the money-lender will go on lending, not on his own terms but on such terms as may, in the uncertain future, be deemed reasonable by the Judge for the time being, it would indeed be a consummation devoutly to be wished. Regard being had (to use the phraseology of the Evidence Act) to the common course of natural events, human conduct and public and private business, I should be inclined to fear that such happy results as I have last contemplated are not likely to ensue; but it must be admitted that Natives often disappoint our most reasonable expectations, and that the consequences of such a measure as that which is proposed can only be determined by experiment.'

"What Mr. Melvill himself anticipates is tolerably evident; though he qualifies any conclusion very much in the way I myself have done when speaking of the possible effects of the restriction on the sale of unpledged land. But, perhaps, I ought to offer some explanation of the grounds on which, subject always to the same qualification, the Government may be held to be justified in anticipating that the dire results just alluded to may not come to pass, and, consequently, in persevering in the measure before us. It is a truism that a thing is worth what it will fetch, and *per contra* that in the long run, temporary disturbing causes apart, a thing will always fetch what it is intrinsically worth. Now the Bill does nothing to diminish the intrinsic value of land, but rather the reverse. The value of land depends, at bottom, on the net produce, or surplus after three deductions, for the cost of cultivation, the subsistence of the peasant and his family, and the Government demand.* Land is worth as many years' purchase

---

* I of course ignore such extraneous value as the land may now possess through the means a hold on it now gives the creditor of commanding the labour of the debtor and his family and other illicit advantages.—(*Deccan Riots Commission Report, page* 60.)

of this net produce as correspond with the current rate of interest. And this rate of interest ultimately depends upon the facility of recovery. Now our Bill does not alter the Government demand or, consequently, the net produce, but it increases the facility of recovery. It must, therefore, increase the ryt's *sound* credit, instead of diminishing it. I will make my meaning clear by illustration. Suppose a ryot's holding yielding gross produce worth Rs. 100, of which Rs. 50 go for the three deductions I have just named, leaving Rs. 50 as net produce or margin on which the ryot's may borrow. In view of the provision in the Bill for seven years' management of unpledged lands, the money lender would be justified in lending on a money bond Rs. 180 if the rate be 20 per cent., Rs. 228 if it be 12 per cent., and Rs. 252 if it be only 9 per cent. Which of these rates he will adopt, or whether he must exact a higher rate still, obviously depends on his chances of getting paid. But these chances are greatly improved by the Bill; for the ryot will strive to pay punctually rather than come under the management of the Collector, and the Collector's management (if efficient, as it *must be made*) will make loss more improbable still. Notwithstanding all fair allowance for risks, lower rates will thus prove as remunerative as the present high ones. For a loan on mortgage, the principle of calculation and the advantage are the same as for a loan on personal bond; but in the end there is this difference, that in the latter case, if the sowkár lends beyond the limits, he will lose his money, while in the former, if the ryot borrows beyond them, he will lose his land.

"All this, it may be said, is very well in theory, but in practice the conditions of advances depend far more upon 'the degree of simplicity in the borrower and of rapacity in the lender than on any thing else'; and to this existing uncertainty you have added the fresh one as to what rate of interest each individual Judge will think reasonable. I reply that the former uncertainty will be diminished by the Bill; and that the second will prove more imaginary than real. There will be far less temptation to extortionate bargains and frauds, and far more risk in them, now that the whole history and merits of the case are to be laid bare in Court. And the provisions for management and recovery by the Collector, standing behind all agreements, will reduce the factor of uncertainty in credit which arises from individual character, and will assist the Courts in gradually establishing rates of interest varying within but a moderate range. Their decrees will thus in time afford the advantage, without the well-known evils, of usury laws, of which Mr. Justice West has well observed in his pamphlet on 'The Land and the Law,' that 'they set up a standard, and gave fixity to men's vague ideas of what might reasonably be asked for the use of money in those numerous cases in which the loan partook but slightly of the character of a true mercantile transaction.'

"While thus contending that the Government are justified in believing that the ultimate effects of the Bill will prove beneficial, I do not conceal from myself for a moment that a trying time of transition must intervene before all parties have understood and settled down to their new relations. It is to be fully expected that difficulties between debtor and creditor will arise in many individual cases, and even in villages or tálukas generally, and that their effects may appear in the recovery of the land-revenue. But if judicial and revenue officers alike strive to remove misconceptions and fears; if the former are even-handed and temperate in their judgments, and the latter efficient in their management of attached land; and if, I venture to add, the revenue demand can be so timed and adjusted as not to drive the ryot to the sowkár, even temporarily, in order to meet it—then I believe that all trouble will be soon and safely tided over. That the sowkár will permanently cease to lend, there need be no fear whatever. The ryot is just as likely to cease to cultivate. The ryot is as necessary to the sowkár, who can only employ his capital in agricultural dealings and banking, as the sowkár is to him. The pair will not sit down and starve together, with a bag of money between them!

"Another large question, which I cannot pass over without remark, is that of the novel provisions for village-munsifs and conciliators. It has two branches—the one relating to their *personnel*, and the other to their functions. I will first speak of the *personnel* available for each office. As to village-munsifs, it will have been gathered from what I said in my introductory speech that I did not expect that more than a patel here and there would be found qualified to be a village-munsif. If the suggestion which I put forward in 1863, in 1867, and again in 1871, that after a reasonably distant future date no person should be appointed patel who had not received a suitable education, had been adopted, the class would now have stood higher in education and intelligence than they do. But a knowledge of reading and writing is not, after all, indispensable to successful disposal of petty suits, though absence of interest is so; and this is just what will be in patels so rare. Now, however, that the restriction of village-munsifships to patels has been removed and the proposal in the Bombay draft assented to, any person of local influence will be eligible, and the field of selection will be advantageously enlarged. Virtually, it will become nearly the same as that from which conciliators are to be drawn. As to whether competent persons can be found for the two offices, especially the latter, I observe some striking differences of opinion. On the one hand, the Poona Sárvajanak Sabhá, Mr. Byramji Jijibhai in his clear and representative memorial, and a portion of the Native Press appear to have no misgivings. On the other hand, the Collectors of Sholápur and Sátára seem to be pretty much of the opinion of the Commissioner (Mr. E. P. Robertson) that ' too much power will be thrown into the hands of a class *quite incapable* of exercising impartiality, or of resisting local or personal influence and acting independently and uprightly.' One of the principal Native newspapers, too, the *Dnyán Prakásh*, which has produced several very able articles on the Bill, thinks that, though the experiment may well be tried, the difficulties in the way of obtaining proper conciliators are insuperable. Finally, Mr. Justice West appears almost to question whether half a dozen men of integrity and intelligence can be found for conciliators in the whole Deccan tract. Such an opinion, even if not meant to be taken literally, cannot but arrest our serious attention, coming, as it does, from one who is not only a Judge of the High Court, but Vice-Chancellor of the Bombay University. I do not ignore the probability that men qualified in all respects will not be easily met with; but I must confess scepticism as to a population of even three millions and a half (which the four districts comprise) being in a condition verging on that of Sodom and Gomorrah. If it be so, notwithstanding all our education, civilization and vaunted progress, then the inference seems difficult to resist, that our measures for the advancement of Natives to higher positions in the public service are premature. If the population, as a whole, are thus tainted, can our Subordinate Judges, our Deputy Collectors and our Mámlatdárs be utterly different from their caste-fellows and kinsfolk? Without pursuing this interesting dilemma I will only say that, having spent a large share of my time in the Mofussil, and having always mixed freely and confidentially with the people of all classes, I should have no difficulty in finding a sufficiency of competent men in the districts with which I am best acquainted. It is now for those who think similarly to bestir themselves, lest the Native community lose the honourable and beneficent sphere which the Legislature lays open for them, and to make good their opinions by presenting suitable persons to the notice of the authorities. And it is for the latter to strive without prejudice to give the experiment a fair trial, remembering that a knowledge of law is unnecessary, and even reading and writing are not indispensable to a successful discharge of the functions in question, in which the layman of age, influence, shrewdness and good temper may easily surpass the highly-trained Judge. After all, if a competent conciliator cannot be found for any particular local area, no one will be appointed, and the requirement of conciliation before suit will not apply there.

"Turning from *personnel* to functions, I observe considerable confusion and misapprehension of those of conciliators. A conciliator is neither an arbitrator nor a judge, either in our Bill or in France, whence the institution is derived. He is simply a disinterested third party, who is charged to endeavour to bring disputants to an amicable settlement. It so happens that in France the conciliators are *Juges de Paix*, and so have a jurisdiction to try the more petty of the cases (within, say, Rs. 50) in which it is their duty to conciliate. But they conciliate in all the superior cases which they have no power to try. The functions of conciliating and trying are distinct, and have no necessary connexion with each other. Appoint our village-munsifs or Subordinate Judges to be conciliators (there is nothing in the Bill to prevent this), and they will be the exact counterparts of the *Juges de Paix*, except in one particular, to which I will presently allude. Some authorities, including Mr. Justice Green of the Bombay High Court, think that they ought to be so appointed. But others, and especially the Local Government, consider that judicial functions might impart to their recommendations a weight amounting to undue pressure, which parties, and especially the ignorant ryot, might be unable to resist. The one particular of difference from *Juges de Paix* to which I referred is the absence of power to compel attendance. Considering the doubt whether competent conciliators can even be found at all, the Bill follows the opinion of the Bombay Government, thus expressed in Sir Richard Temple's Minute of April 14th, 1879 :—

"'Though he (the Conciliator) would not have the power of deciding, or enforcing his decision if he formed one, still he would, by compelling attendance, be able, if so disposed, to put great pressure on the ryot to admit or to compromise the claim. Such power of applying pressure by an educated man of position upon an uneducated and humble man on a claim preferred by a man generally of some education and wealth is a power that ought not to be conferred upon Honorary Conciliation Judges in the present state of society in the Deccan.'

"I myself doubt whether the want of this power will affect the *status* of conciliators, as some apprehend. If they can settle disputes equitably, the people, debtors as well as creditors, will readily resort to them. But here, as in the case of giving powers of conciliation to Judges, the Bill presents no obstacle to a change hereafter. The Local Government can, under section 37, give power to compel attendance whenever they think fit.

"In connection with chapter VII, some exception has been taken to the cost of the extra Subordinate Judges' Courts to be constituted, and of the supervising officers. The object of bringing the Courts nearer to the homes of the people might, it is said, be as well, or even better, attained by making the Courts move about. The existing Judges, it is added, have not got too much to do as it is; and the new summary procedure, with the temptation to refer difficult points to arbitration, will lead to their having still less. That the Courts should move about to some extent, would certainly be advantageous; and I hope that the hitherto dormant powers of section 23 of Act XIV of 1869 will now be exercised to enable them to do so. But this can never be more than a limited benefit. There are rarely above two or three villages in a táluka containing suitable accommodation for a Subordinate Judge and his clerks, to say nothing of parties and their witnesses; and even these are often not conveniently accessible in the rains. The presence of a considerable body of strangers, too, is always a source of annoyance and expense to the villagers, even if the calls on them do not exceed those of hospitality. Time would likewise be lost in travelling and settling down at each place; pleaders in non-agriculturists' cases would be inconvenienced, and minor practical difficulties would crop up. It is questionable whether, between waiting till the next visit to the locality to begin and adjourning till the next visit to complete, any saving in time would result; while, finally, the ryot would in very many cases be living no nearer to the selected village than to the Court's head-quarters. As to the other statement, it remains to be seen whether the duty of going more fully into cases will not neutralize any saving in time obtained in other ways. But however this may be, I can see no good reason why the judicial unit of administration should be larger than the executive unit. Every táluka ought, in my opinion, to have its Subordinate Judge as well as its Mámlatdár. If the civil work proved insufficient to occupy the Subordinate Judge's full time, he should be invested with criminal powers. The Mámlatdár and his first karkún, being proportionately relieved, could then better overtake the multifarious and increasing duties heaped on them, besides taking back, at a great saving of expense, the registration work, of which they were a few years ago relieved.

"As to chapter VIII on Village-Registrars, I have only to say that I doubt whether kulkarnís, as a class, deserve the abuse which is bestowed upon them by some revenue-officers, and even by one Native newspaper. They perform faithfully a large amount of public business, and their hereditary service emoluments are a security for their conduct. But as to this, and also the objection that they are not sufficiently numerous to save the ryot all trouble in resorting to them, I would point out that many other persons (among whom I may specify village schoolmasters) are eligible, and that clause (*b*) of section 55 will in many cases enable ryots to register their deeds at the places where their sowkárs reside, instead of at their own villages, if they prefer do to so. About chapter IX. I have only to point out that the giving of receipts has been made obligatory ; and of chapter X to say that the provisions regarding appearance by a relative, servant or dependent are copied from the Madras Village-Munsifs Regulation IV of 1816.

"I will now notice three subjects, the entire omission of which from the Bill has been the cause of much adverse comment. The first is that of a modification of the rigidity of our land-revenue system. The Anglo-Indian Press, and seven out of the eleven vernacular newspapers of the Bombay Presidency which have noticed the Bill, have commented more or less emphatically on the absence of provisions in this direction. On the merits of the question in the abstract it is unnecessary for me to add anything to the few remarks which I had to make, for the completion of my argument, in my introductory speech. But as to its omission from the Bill, I may say that it is held that for whatever action (if any) which may be necessary no legislation is required, but that if the fact were otherwise, the Bombay and not the Governor General's Council is the place where it should be undertaken. Legislation is unnecessary, because the question is an executive one. The power of fixing the rates of assessment, original or revised, is given to the Bombay Executive Government by sections 100 to 107 of the new Bombay Revenue Code, as it was by the previous law ; the power of fixing instalments is so given by section 146 ; the granting of remissions is equally an executive matter. The regular mode, therefore, of securing all that the advocates of a change of system desire is by executive order, or by rules made by the Local Government under section 214 of the Code. Supposing, however, that it were thought proper to tie down the Executive Government in these matters more than it is now tied, then the proper course would be to amend the Bombay Revenue Code ; and that is the function of the Bombay Legislative Council, which passed it, not of the Governor General's Council. Our present Bill, I need scarcely say, would not be before this Council at all but that it modifies the Civil Procedure Code, which the local legislatures are precluded by Act of Parliament from touching.

"Another omission which has been censured is that of any reduction of stamp or court-fees, process-fees, batta, &c. Here, again, legislation would have been superfluous. In Act VII of 1870 the Governor General in Council is empowered by section 35 to reduce or remit any of the court-fees mentioned in the schedules; and the High Court, with the sanction of the Local Government, may under chapter IV fix process-fees as it thinks proper. Act I of 1879, section 8, contains a similar power to reduce the stamps to which it applies, among which arbitration awards are included. I am not authorized to announce any decision on this subject; but it will be seen from paragraph 16 of the letter of the Bombay Government, No. 2056 of April 15th, 1879, which was published in the *Bombay Government Gazette* of the 30th of July last, that some reductions are looked upon generally with favour. I may add that the regular inspection of Courts under section 9 of Act XIV of 1869, which is now, as Mr. Naylor remarks, so little practised, is needed, *inter alia*, to check abuses connected with these charges. In 1876 the Judge of Khándesh brought to light a custom of enhancing the amount payable for stamps by requiring, in certain cases, an application on stamped paper before a witness was examined. He also found that in process-serving 'in one Court alone as much as 96 days' pay was obtained for 24 days' work, and 102 days' pay for 26 days' work, of the serving establishment.'

" The last omission I have to explain is that of any legalization of pancháyats or Arbitration Courts—a subject which I mentioned in my introductory speech as still under consideration. A proposal for the definite incorporation of such Courts into our judicial system has been put forward by the Judge of Ahmednagar, Mr. Wedderburn, with the concurrence of a body of Native gentlemen, including some judicial officers, whose position and attainments entitle their views to the fullest consideration. I must say frankly that I look upon as wholly visionary the idea that it is possible now-a-days to find in every village, or even in every small circle of villages, a body of men sufficient in number to allow selection from them by litigants for the formation of a pancháyat, and at the same time qualified to be arbitrators by influence, intelligence and absence of interest. And even were this otherwise, I should expect that the strict regulations, involving checks and delays, which the proposal just referred to comprises, would practically destroy the freedom, simplicity and promptitude supposed to be the chief recommendations of the pancháyat system. That the provisions for arbitration in Bombay Regulation VII of 1827, which succeeded the even more efficient ones of Regulation VII of 1802, had fallen entirely into disuse before their repeal in 1861, and that the present new 'Arbitration Courts' are kept at work chiefly by the exertions of a very small number of disinterested and impartial individuals, are facts not very encouraging to a new departure. At the same time, as there undoubtedly is a popular sentiment, originated probably by aversion to our Courts as now conducted, running in favour of voluntary settlements, I personally can see no harm in aiding them by legislation of a purely permissive kind. We might safely revert to pretty much the position of Regulation VII of 1827. Persons whom the Government deemed of good character and competent, as also the members for the time being of any well-conducted local Arbitration Court, might be officially recognized as arbitrators. Such recognition should have the effect (1) that they should be entitled to the aid in their proceedings of issue of process by the Subordinate Judge of the division; and (2) that any reference for arbitration to them might provide that in the event of any party thereto giving notice, within fifteen days of the date of the award, to the Subordinate Judge of the division that he was dissatisfied with the same, the matter in dispute should be referred back to the same Court or arbitrator, sitting with such Judge as president. This would supply the recognition and control for arbitration which its advocates seem to desire, without putting any pressure on parties to resort to it. But even thus much is considered by the Local Government to be undesirable and likely to lead to prejudicial results. As they are, of course, the best judges of the state of affairs in the Deccan, the law will remain as it is. I may, however, point out that there is nothing to prevent parties appointing village-munsifs and conciliators to be their arbitrators, and that an explanation making this clear has been added to section 43.

"In conclusion, I must observe that it would be premature to indulge in any congratulations upon the passing of this measure, and still more so to attempt to appraise its several parts, to distinguish the several sources whence they may have been derived, and to distribute praise or blame accordingly. It will be time enough to do that, if it need be done at all, when the Act has become an acknowledged failure or success. At present it is the measure of the Government of Bombay (and I am glad to think that through many vicissitudes it has substantially remained so), prepared in general consultation with myself. But I hope that we may augur well for its future from the fact that it not only has the approval of the highest official authorities, but has secured, in a degree quite unprecedented, the substantial support of the Press and the public. It is a sincere and carefully matured attempt to solve a difficult problem and to meet a great emergency. If the course of events should prove that we have erred, we shall have erred in good company, and after all possible precautions to ensure success."

The Hon'ble Mr. Thornton said :—" Having been taunted in the course of this debate with having spoken one way and voted another, I think it due to myself to trouble the Council with a few more words of explanation regarding the course I have pursued. It is true that I have voted for certain provisions in this Bill of the propriety of which I am extremely doubtful; but I have done so on the distinct understanding that the Bill is local, and the measure strictly tentative and experimental. Thus, as regards the abolition of appeals in small-debt cases and the substitution of a revising agency instead, my experience in the Panjáb tells me that in that province such a measure would be exceedingly unpopular; but, while I am not prepared to admit the abolition of appeals in small-debt cases to be a universally appropriate and effective remedy for the misfortunes of the ryot, I am not prepared to object to the experiment being tried in a portion of the Bombay Presidency. Again, my experience tells me that any attempt to exclude legal practitioners from the Courts of a locality where the people have for years been accustomed to forensic agency will positively fail or produce greater evils than those it is sought to remedy. But my opinion, though true of the Panjáb, may not be applicable to the circumstances of the Deccan; and I should certainly hesitate to force the results of my imperfect experience upon the Bombay Government. But it may be urged—'If you are not going to act on your Panjáb experience, why drag it in at all? Why advise the apparently inconsistent course of damning an amendment from your experience, and then voting in support of it?' I answer that I have adopted this course in order to indicate clearly and unmistakeably that, though I am prepared to vote for the measure as a local and experimental one, I do not approve of all its provisions, and am not prepared to adopt it as a triumph of statesmanship or to advocate its extension to other localities until its success has been practically proved.

" There are, moreover, other provisions in the Bill to the success of which my own experience is adverse. Thus, it has been found in the Panjáb that the procedure of Small-Cause Courts is quite unsuited for a rustic population; that the system of forced arbitration provided in section 15 of the Bill is a mistake; and that the system of official interference with the terms of contracts contemplated in chapter III—a system which prevailed, and still prevails to some extent, in the Panjáb—has a demoralizing effect upon the people, raises the rate of interest on money lent, and yet fails to teach prudence to the improvident. It is also my opinion that the extension of the period of limitation in suits on account, besides being based upon a misconception of the present law, will only stave off, and ultimately intensify, the evil it is sought to remedy, and that, while the procedure of all small-debt Courts should be conciliatory, the appointment of special Courts of amateur conciliators will lead only to dissatisfaction and delay. But while I should, for the reasons above stated, object to the extension of these provisions of the Deccan Ryots Bill to the Panjáb, at any rate at present, I should not feel justified on those grounds in refusing to allow them a trial in a locality upwards of a thousand miles away.

"The above explanation will, I trust, remove from the minds of Members of this Council any impression any of them may have received that in the course I have adopted I have acted with inconsistency. I would add that, so far from grudging the Bombay Government its experiment, I shall, whether in India or in England, regard it with the greatest interest, and with the earnest hope that it may work some benefit at least for the much-vexed ryots of the Deccan."

His Excellency the President said:—" I have no doubt that the votes given on these amendments by my hon'ble friend Mr. Thornton were influenced, as my own were, by the importance he attached to the fact that this Bill only comes before the Council at all because it happens to modify the Code of Civil Procedure, which the local legislatures are not competent to deal with. In point of fact, therefore, the Bill, though now about to be passed in this legislature, was, and is, a Bombay measure. As a Bombay Bill it came into our hands, and to me personally it is a cause of no small satisfaction that, notwithstanding the long and careful discussion given to it both in Committee and in this Council, and

'In spite of all temptations
To belong to other legislations,'

it still remains a Bombay Bill."

The Hon'ble Sir Alexander Arbuthnot said:—" The explanation just given by my hon'ble friend Mr. Thornton was, I think, partly elicited by a remark of mine. I am sure that there is no Member of the Council who values more than I do the services and the assistance which have been invariably rendered to us by my hon'ble colleague since he became a Member of this Council; and no one who deplores more than I do the early prospect of his retirement from this Council. I quite see from the explanation with which the Hon'ble Member has now been so good as to furnish us that his course in this matter has been as consistent and straightforward as his course has always been throughout his long and distinguished official career."

The motion was put and agreed to.

The following Act of the Governor General of India in Council received the assent of His Excellency the Governor General on the 29th October 1879, and was promulgated for general information in the *Gazette of India* on the 1st November 1879 :—

Act No. XVII. of 1879.

THE DEKKHAN AGRICULTURISTS RELIEF ACT, 1879.

CONTENTS.

PREAMBLE.

CHAPTER I.

PRELIMINARY.

SECTIONS.
1. Short title.
   Commencement.
   Local extent.
2. Interpretation clause.

CHAPTER II.

OF THE HEARING OF CERTAIN SUITS BY SUBORDINATE JUDGES.

3. Application of this chapter.
4. Certain suits to be instituted in Courts of first class Subordinate Judges.
5. Subordinate Judges not to act as Judges of Small Cause Courts.
6. Jurisdiction of Subordinate Judge and Small Cause Court.
7. Summons to be for final disposal of suit.
   Court to examine defendant as witness.
8. Written statements.
9. Record of evidence.
10. No appeal to lie.

CHAPTER III.

OF SUITS AND OTHER PROCEEDINGS TO WHICH AGRICULTURISTS ARE PARTIES.

11. Agriculturists to be sued where they reside.
12. History of transactions with agriculturist-debtors to be investigated.
13. Mode of taking account.

B 862—46

SECTIONS.

14. Interest to be allowed.
15. Reference to arbitration in certain cases.
16. Agriculturist-debtors may sue for accounts.
    Amount of debts in such cases to be determined according to foregoing provisions.
17. Decree under section 16 may provide for payment by instalments.
    Execution of decrees under this section.
18. Payment into court in cases under section 16.
19. Power to discharge judgment-debtor.
    Power to direct institution of insolvency-proceedings.
20. Power to fix instalments in execution.
21. Arrest and imprisonment in execution of decree for money abolished.
22. Immoveable property exempted from attachment and sale unless specifically pledged.
23. Chapter not to apply to Village-Munsifs' Courts.

CHAPTER IV.

OF INSOLVENCY.

24. Subordinate Judges to have jurisdiction in agriculturists' cases.
25. Agriculturists may apply for adjudication in cases not provided for by Code.
    Modification of section 351 of the Code.
27. Receiver.
28. Proof of debts.
29. Immoveable property not to vest in Receiver, but may be managed for benefit of creditors.
30. Secured debts.
31. Insolvent incompetent to sell, &c., property dealt with under sections 29 and 30.
32. Scheduled debts discharged.
32. Appeals barred.

CHAPTER V.

OF VILLAGE-MUNSIFS.

34. Appointment of Village-Munsifs.
35. Suits triable by them.
    Jurisdiction of other Courts excluded.
    Proviso.

SECTIONS.
36. District Judge's power of revision.
37. Power of Local Government to make rules.

CHAPTER VI.

OF CONCILIATION.

38. Appointment of Conciliators.
39. Matters which may be brought before Conciliator.
40. Procedure thereupon.
Day for attendance may from time to time be postponed.
41. When all parties appear, Conciliator to endeavour to reconcile them.
42. Conciliator to hear statements of witnesses, &c.
43. Any agreement arrived at to be reduced to writing.
44. Procedure when agreement finally disposes of case.
45. Procedure where agreement is for reference to arbitration.
46. Certificate to be given to applicant if conciliation fails.
47. Suit, or application for execution, not to be entertained by Civil Court unless such certificate is produced.
48. Allowance to be made in period of limitation.
49. Local Government to make rules.

CHAPTER VII.

SUPERINTENDENCE AND REVISION.

50. District Judge to inspect, &c.
51. District Judge may withdraw case from Subordinate Judge,
or sit with Subordinate Judge as a Bench for trial of any case.
52. Appointment of Assistant or Subordinate Judge to aid District Judge.
53. Of revision.
54. Special Judge.

CHAPTER VIII.

REGISTRATION BY VILLAGE-REGISTRARS.

55. Appointment of Village-Registrars.
56. Instruments executed by agriculturist not to be deemed valid unless executed before a Village-Registrar.
57. Such instruments to be written by or under the superintendence of a Village-Registrar and executed in his presence.
Attestation of such instruments.

SECTIONS.
58. Registration of instruments by Village-Registrars.
59. Consideration to be fully stated in every instrument executed before a Village-Registrar.
   Previous instruments to be produced.
60. Registration under this Act to be deemed equivalent to registration under the Indian Registration Act, 1877.
61. Village-Registrars to be subordinate to the Inspector-General of Registration.
62. Exemption of instruments to which Government or any officer of Government is a party.
63. Power of Local Government to make rules.

CHAPTER IX.

OF RECEIPTS AND STATEMENTS OF ACCOUNT.

64. Agriculturists entitled to written receipts:
65. To annual statements of account:
66. To have account made up from time to time in a pass-book.
67. Penalty for contravention of sections 64 to 66.

CHAPTER X.

LEGAL PRACTITIONERS.

68. Pleaders, &c., excluded in certain cases.
69. Power of Court to appoint pleader for agriculturist.

CHAPTER XI.

MISCELLANEOUS.

70. Mortgages, &c., to be valid only when written.
71. All mortgages hitherto executed to be registered.
72. Limitation.
73. Decision as to whether person is an agriculturist, final.
74. Civil Procedure Code to apply in Subordinate Judges' Courts.
75. Additional power to make rules.
76. Rules to be published.

An Act for the Relief of Indebted Agriculturists in certain parts of the Deccan.

Preamble.

WHEREAS it is expedient to relieve the agricultural classes in certain parts of the Deccan from indebtedness; It is hereby enacted as follows :—

CHAPTER I.

PRELIMINARY.

Short title.

1. This Act may be cited as "The Dekkhan Agriculturists Relief Act, 1879":

Commencement.

and it shall come into force on the first day of November, 1879.

Local extent.

Sections eleven, fifty-six, sixty and sixty-two extend to the whole of British India. The rest of this Act extends only to the Districts of Poona, Sátára, Sholápur and Ahmednagar.

Interpretation-clause.

2. In this Act, unless there is something repugnant in the subject or context,—

"money":

(1) "money" includes agricultural produce, implements and stock:

"agriculturist."

(2) "agriculturist" means a person who earns his livelihood wholly or principally by agriculture carried on within the limits of the said districts; and every agriculturist shall be deemed to "reside" where he so earns his livelihood.

CHAPTER II.

OF THE HEARING OF CERTAIN SUITS BY SUBORDINATE JUDGES.

Application of this chapter.

3. The provisions of this chapter shall apply to—

(a) suits for an account instituted on or after the first day of November, 1879, by an agriculturist in the Court of a Subordinate Judge under the provisions hereinafter contained, and *(b)* suits of the descriptions next hereinafter mentioned and instituted on or after the same date—

(1) when such suits are heard by Subordinate Judges of the first class and the subject-matter thereof does not exceed in amount or value five hundred rupees, or

(2) when such suits are heard by Subordinate Judges of the second class and the subject-matter thereof does not exceed in amount or value one hundred rupees, or

(3) when such suits are heard by Subordinate Judges of the second class and the subject-matter thereof exceeds one hundred rupees, but does not exceed five hundred rupees, in amount or value, and the parties to the suits agree that such provisions shall apply thereto.

The descriptions of suits referred to in clause (*b*) are the following (namely) :—

(*w*) suits for the recovery of money alleged to be due to the plaintiff—

on account of money lent or advanced to, or paid for, the defendant, or

as the price of goods sold, or

on an account stated between the plaintiff and defendant, or

on a written or unwritten engagement for the payment of money not hereinbefore provided for ;

(*x*) suits for the recovery of money due on contracts other than the above and suits for rent or for moveable property, or for the value of such property, or for damages; and

(*y*) suits for foreclosure or for the possession of mortgaged property, or for sale of such property, or foreclosure or sale, when the defendant, or any one of the defendants not being merely a surety for the principal debtor, is an agriculturist ; and

(*z*) suits for the redemption of mortgaged property when the plaintiff, or, where there are several plaintiffs, any one of the plaintiffs, is an agriculturist.

4. Where a Subordinate Judge of the first class and a Subordinate Judge of the second class have ordinary jurisdiction in the same local area, every suit referred to in section three, clause (*b*), and instituted in such local area shall, if the amount or value of the subject-matter of such suit exceeds one

Certain suits to be instituted in Courts of first class Subordinate Judges.

hundred rupees and does not exceed five hundred rupees, be instituted in the Court of the Subordinate Judge of the first class.

5. Notwithstanding anything contained in the Bombay Civil Courts Act, 1869, section 28, no Subordinate Judge shall be invested with the jurisdiction of a Judge of a Court of Small Causes; and any such jurisdiction heretofore conferred on any Subordinate Judge shall be deemed, except as regards suits instituted before the said first day of November, 1879, to have been withdrawn.

Subordinate Judges not to act as Judges of Small Cause Courts.

6. The Local Government may, from time to time, by notification in the local Gazette, direct that any class of suits which a Subordinate Judge would be precluded from hearing by section 12 of Act XI of 1865 *(to consolidate and amend the law relating to Courts of Small Causes beyond the local limits of the ordinary original civil jurisdiction of the High Courts of Judicature)*, shall be heard and determined by him and not otherwise, and may, by a like notification, cancel any such direction.

Jurisdiction of Subordinate Judge and Small Cause Court.

7. In every case in which it seems to the Court possible to dispose of a suit at the first hearing, the summons shall be for the final disposal of the suit.

Summons to be for final disposal of suit.

In every suit the Court shall examine the defendant as a witness, unless, for reasons to be recorded by it in writing, it deems it unnecessary so to do.

Court to examine defendant as witness.

8. In suits of the descriptions mentioned in section three, clauses (*w*) and (*x*), no party shall be entitled without the permission of the Court to file a written statement.

Written statements.

9. When the subject-matter of any suit does not exceed ten rupees in amount or value, it shall not be necessary to take down the evidence or make memorandum thereof in manner provided by th Code of Civil Procedure; but in cases where the evidence is not so taken down and no memorandum is so made, the substance of the evidence shall be stated in the judgment.

Record of evidence.

10. No appeal shall lie from any decree or order passed in any suit to which this chapter applies.

No appeal to lie.

CHAPTER III.

OF SUITS AND OTHER PROCEEDINGS TO WHICH AGRICULTURISTS ARE PARTIES.

Agriculturists to be sued where they reside.

11. Every suit of the description mentioned in section three, clause (w), may, if the defendant, or, when there are several defendants, one only of such defendants, is an agriculturist, be instituted and tried in a Court within the local limits of whose jurisdiction such defendant resides and not elsewhere.

Every such suit in which there are several defendants who are agriculturists may be instituted and tried in a Court within the local limits of whose jurisdiction any one of such defendants resides and not elsewhere.

Nothing herein contained shall affect sections 22 to 25 (both inclusive) of the Code of Civil Procedure.

History of transactions with agriculturist-debtors to be investigated.

12. In any suit of the description mentioned in section three, clause (w), in which the defendant or any one of the defendants, not being merely a surety of the principal debtor, is an agriculturist,

and in any suit of the descriptions mentioned in section three, clause (y) or clause (z),

the Court shall, if the amount of the creditor's claim is disputed, enquire into the history and merits of the case, from the commencement of the transactions between the parties and the persons (if any) through whom they claim, out of which the suit has arisen, first, with a view to ascertaining whether there is any defence to the suit on the ground of fraud, mistake, accident, undue influence or otherwise, and, secondly, with a view to taking an account between such parties in manner hereinafter provided.

When the amount of the claim is admitted and the Court for reasons to be recorded by it in writing believes that such admission is true and is made by the debtor with a full knowledge of his legal rights as against the creditor, the Court shall not be bound so to enquire, but may do so if it thinks fit.

In other cases in which the amount of the claim is admitted, the Court shall be bound to enquire as aforesaid.

Section IX, clause first, of Bombay Regulation V of 1827 is repealed so far as regards any suit to which this section applies.

Nothing herein contained shall affect the right of the parties to require that any matter in difference between them be referred to arbitraton.

Mode of taking account.

13. When the Court enquires into the history and merits of a case under section twelve, it shall—

notwithstanding any agreement between the parties or the persons (if any) through whom they claim, as to allowing compound interest or setting off the profits of mortgaged property without an account in lieu of interest, or otherwise determining the manner of taking the account,

and notwithstanding any statement or settlement of account, or any contract purporting to close previous dealings and create a new obligation,

open the account between the parties from the commencement of the transactions and take that account according to the following rules (that is to say) :—

(a) separate accounts of principal and interest shall be taken :

(b) in the account of principal there shall be debited to the debtor such money as may from time to time have been actually received by him or on his account from the creditor, and the price of goods, if any, sold to him by the creditor as part of the transactions :

(c) in the account of principal there shall not be debited to the debtor any money which he may have agreed to pay in contravention of section 257A of the Code of Civil Procedure :

(d) in the account of principal there shall not be debited to the debtor any accumulated interest which has been converted into principal at any statement or settlement of account or by any contract made in the course of the transactions, unless the Court, for reasons to be recorded by it in writing, deemed such debit to be reasonable :

(e) in the account of interest there shall be debited to the debtor, monthly, simple interest on the balance of principal for the time being outstanding at the rate allowed by the Court as hereinafter provided :

(f) all money paid by or on account of the debtor to the creditor or on his account, and all profits, service or other advantages of every descripton, received by the creditor in the course of the transactions (estimated, if necessary, at such money-value as the Court in its discretion, or with the aid of arbitrators appointed by it, may determine) shall be credited first in the account of interest; and when any payment is more than sufficient to discharge the balance of interest due at the time it is made, the residue of such payment shall be credited to the debtor in the account of principal:

(*g*) the accounts of principal and interest shall be made up to the date of instituting the suit, and the aggregate of the balances (if any) appearing due on both such accounts against the debtor on that date shall be deemed to be the amount due at that date, except when the balance appearing due on the interest-account exceeds that appearing due on the principal-account, in which case double the latter balance shall be deemed to be the amount then due.

Interest to be allowed.
14. The interest to be awarded in taking an account according to the rules set forth in section thirteen shall be—

(*a*) the rate, if any, agreed upon between the parties, or the persons (if any) through whom they claim, unless such rate is deemed by the Court to be unreasonable; or

(*b*) if such rate is deemed by the Court unreasonable, or if no rate was agreed upon, or, when any agreement between the parties, or the persons (if any) through whom they claim, to set-off profits without an account in lieu of interest has been set aside by the Court, such rate as the Court deems reasonable.

Reference to arbitration in certain cases.
15. Instead of enquiring into the history and merits of a case under section twelve, or if upon so enquiring the Court is unable to satisfy itself as to the amount which should be allowed on account of principal or interest or both, the Court may, of its own motion, direct that such amount be ascertained by arbitration.

If the parties are willing to nominate arbitrators, the arbitrators shall be nominated by them in such manner as may be agreed upon between them: if the parties are unwilling to nominate arbitrators or cannot agree in respect of such nomination, the Court shall appoint any three persons it thinks fit:

Provided that if all the parties reside in the same village, town or city, and, in the opinion of the Court, three fit persons can be found among the residents of such village, town or city, it shall appoint residents of such village, town or city.

The provisions of sections 508 to 522 (both inclusive) of the Code of Civil Procedure shall apply to every reference to arbitration under this section.

16. Any agriculturist may sue for an account of money lent or advanced to or paid for him by a creditor or due by him to the creditor as the price of goods sold, or on a written or unwritten engagement for the payment of money, and of money paid by him to the creditor, and for a decree declaring the amount, if any, still payable by him to the creditor.

Agriculturist-debtors may sue for accounts.

When any such suit is brought, the amount (if any) payable by the plaintiff shall be determined under the same rules as would be applicable under this Act if the creditor had sued him for recovery of the debt.

Amount of debts in such cases to be determined according to foregoing provisions.

17. A decree passed under section sixteen may, besides declaring the amount due, direct that such amount shall be paid by instalments, with or without interest; and, when any such decree so directs, the plaintiff may pay the amount of such decree, or the amount of each instalment fixed by such decree, as it falls due, into court, in default whereof execution of the decree may be enforced by the defendant in the same manner as if he had obtained the decree in a suit to recover the debt.

Decree under section 16 may provide for payment by instalments.

Execution of decrees under this section.

18. The plaintiff in any suit instituted under section sixteen may at any stage of such suit deposit in court such sum of money as he considers a satisfaction in full of the defendant's claim against him.

Payment into court in cases under section 16.

Notice of the deposit shall be given by the Court to the defendant, and the amount of the deposit shall (unless the Court otherwise directs) be paid to the defendant on his application.

No interest shall be allowed to the defendant on any sum so deposited from the date of the receipt of such notice, whether the sum deposited be in full of the claim or fall short thereof.

19. When a decree has been passed, whether before or after this Act comes into force, under which any sum less than fifty rupees is recoverable from an agriculturist, the Court may, either in the course of execution of such decree or otherwise, if it is satisfied that there is no other claim against him and that he is unable to pay the whole of such sum, direct the payment of such portion of the same as it considers him able to pay, and grant him a discharge from the balance.

Power to discharge judgment-debtor.

Power to direct institution of insolvency proceedings. When the sum payable under the decree amounts to fifty rupees or upwards, or when there are other debts due by the debtor which together with such sum amount to fifty rupees or upwards, the Court may direct proceedings to be taken with respect to him as nearly as may be as if he had applied to be declared an insolvent under the provisions hereinafter contained.

Power to fix instalments in execution. 20. The Court may at any time direct that the amount of any decree passed, whether before or after this Act comes into force, against an agriculturist, or the portion of the same which it directs under section nineteen to be paid, shall be paid by instalments with or without interest.

Arrest and imprisonment in execution of decree for money abolished. 21. No agriculturist shall be arrested or imprisoned in execution of a decree for money.

Immoveable property exempted from attachment and sale unless specifically pledged. 22. No agriculturist's immoveable property shall be attached or sold in execution of any decree or order unless it has been specifically mortgaged for the repayment of the debt to which such decree or order relates, and the security still subsists.

But the Court may, when passing a decree against an agriculturist or at any subsequent time, direct the Collector to take possession, for any period not exceeding seven years, of any such property of the judgment-debtor to the possession of which he is entitled, and which, in the opinion of the Collector, is not required for his support and the support of the members of his family dependent on him, and the Collector shall thereupon take possession of such property and deal with the same for the benefit of the decree-holder in manner provided by section twenty-nine.

The provisions of section thirty-one shall, *mutatis mutandis*, apply to any property so dealt with.

Chapter not to apply to Village-Munsif's Courts. 23. No provision of this chapter shall apply to the proceedings in the Courts of Village-Munsifs unless such provision has been specially extended thereto under the power hereinafter conferred.

CHAPTER IV.

OF INSOLVENCY.

Subordinate Judges to have jurisdiction in agriculturists' cases.

24. Every Subordinate Judge shall have the powers conferred by sections 344 to 359 (both inclusive) of the Code of Civil Procedure, as modified by the provisions next hereinafter contained, for the purpose of dealing with applications under the Code of Civil Procedure or under this Act to have agriculturists residing within the local limits of his ordinary jurisdiction declared insolvent and proceedings taken under orders passed under the second clause of section nineteen; and, except as provided in chapter VII of this Act, no such application or proceeding shall be dealt with by any other Court.

Agriculturists may apply for adjudication in cases not provided for by Code.

25. Any agriculturist whose debts (if any) amount to fifty rupees or upwards may apply to any Subordinate Judge within the local limits of whose ordinary jurisdiction he resides to be declared an insolvent, though he has not been arrested or imprisoned, and though no order of attachment has issued against his property, in execution of a decree.

Modification of section 351 of the Code.

26. Notwithstanding anything contained in section 351 of the Code of Civil Procedure, the Court shall declare an agriculturist an insolvent if it is satisfied that he is in insolvent circumstances, and that the application to have him declared an insolvent has been properly made under section 344 of the said Code or section twenty-five of this Act.

Receiver.

27. No person other than the Názir of the Court shall be appointed as Receiver, and no Receiver shall be entitled to commission.

Proof of debts.

28. In determining under section 352 of the said Code the amount of any claim of the nature referred to in section twelve of this Act due by an insolvent agriculturist, the Court shall proceed in the manner prescribed by sections twelve to fifteen of this Act, both inclusive.

Immoveable property not to vest in Receiver, but may be managed for benefit of creditors.

29. No immoveable property of the insolvent shall vest in the Receiver; but the Court may direct the Collector to take into his possession, for any period not exceeding seven years from the date on which the Receiver has been appointed, any immoveable property to the possession of which the insolvent is entitled, and which, in the opinion of the

Collector, is not required for the support of the insolvent and the members of his family dependent on him, and, subject to any rules the Local Government may from time to time make in this behalf, to manage the same for the benefit of the creditors, by letting it on lease or otherwise:

Provided that, if the insolvent or his representative in interest at any time pays into Court the balance of the scheduled debts then unpaid, he shall, subject to any rights created in favour of other persons by the Collector, be entitled to recover possession of such property.

A Collector managing property under this section shall during the management have all the powers which the owner might as such have legally exercised, and shall receive and recover all rents and profits of such property, and for the purpose of recovering such rents and profits shall have, in addition to any powers possessed by an owner, all powers possessed by a Collector for securing and recovering the land-revenue due to Government except the powers mentioned in the Bombay Land-Revenue Code, 1879, section 150, clauses (b), (d) and (e).

Nothing in this section shall authorize the Court to direct the Collector to take into his possession any houses or other buildings belonging to and occupied by an agriculturist.

30. When any scheduled debt is secured by a mortgage of any portion of the insolvent's immoveable property, the Court may direct the Collector, if he can obtain a premium equal to the amount of such debt by letting such property for a term not exceeding twenty years, to let such property and, if he cannot so obtain such premium, to sell such property under section 325 of the Code of Civil Procedure.

Secured debts.

Where property is let under this section, the premium shall be applied to the payment of the debt, and the rent, if any, shall for a period of seven years from the date of such letting be paid to the Receiver and thereafter to the insolvent or his representative in interest.

When property is sold under this section, the sale proceeds shall be applied, first, to the payment of the debt, and the balance, if any, shall be paid to the Receiver.

31. So long as any management under section twenty-nine or letting under section thirty continues, the insolvent and his representative in interest shall be incompetent to mortgage, charge, lease or alienate the property managed or let, or any part thereof.

Insolvent incompetent to sell, &c., property dealt with under sections 29 and 30.

32. When the balance available for distribution among the scheduled creditors under section 356 of the said Code has been distributed, the claims of such creditors shall be deemed to have been discharged, except as regards the right to share in the profits of any property managed by the Collector under section twenty-nine or let by him under section thirty.

Scheduled debts discharged.

33. No appeal shall lie from any order passed under this chapter except orders passed in exercise of the power conferred by section 359 of the Code of Civil Procedure.

Appeals barred.

CHAPTER V.

OF VILLAGE-MUNSIFS.

34. The Local Government may, from time to time, appoint any Patel of a village or any other person possessing local influence in a village to be a Village-Munsif for such village or for such village and for any other villages the sites of which are situate in the same district not more than two miles from the site of such village, and may cancel any such appointment.

Appointment of Village-Munsifs.

35. Every Village-Munsif so appointed shall take cognizance of suits of the description mentioned in section three, clause (*w*), when the subject-matter thereof does not exceed ten rupees in amount or value, and all the defendants at the time of the commencement of the suit actually and voluntarily reside or carry on business or personally work for gain within the local area of which such Village-Munsif is appointed.

Suits triable by them.

Notwithstanding anything hereinbefore contained, a suit cognizable by a Village-Munsif shall not be heard by any other Court:

Jurisdiction of other Courts excluded.

Provided that the District Judge may, from time to time, transfer any suit instituted before a Village-Munsif to his own Court or any other Civil Court in the district for trial:

Proviso.

Provided also that no Village-Munsif shall try any suit to or in which he is a party or is personally interested, or shall adjudicate upon any proceeding connected with or arising out of such suit.

36. The District Judge may, on a petition being presented within thirty days from the date of any decree or order of a Village-Munsif by any party deeming himself aggrieved by such decree or order, set aside such decree or order on the ground of corruption, gross partiality or misconduct of the Village-Munsif and pass such other decree or order as he thinks fit.

District Judge's power of revision.

Except as provided in this Act and in section 622 of the Code of Civil Procedure, every decree and order of a Village-Munsif shall be final.

37. The Local Government may, from time to time, by notification in the official Gazette, make rules consistent with this Act for regulating the procedure of Village-Munsifs and for conferring on them or any of them all or any of the powers for the trial of suits or the execution of decrees exercised by a Civil Court under the Code of Civil Procedure or any other enactment for the time being in force.

Power of Local Government to make rules.

CHAPTER VI.

OF CONCILIATION.

38. The Local Government may, from time to time, appoint any person other than an officer of Police to be a Conciliator and may cancel any such appointment.

Appointment of Conciliators.

Every Conciliator appointed under this section shall be appointed only for a term not exceeding three years, but may on the expiration of the period for which he has been appointed be again appointed for a further term not exceeding three years.

Every Conciliator so appointed shall exercise his functions under this Act in respect of matters affecting agriculturists residing within such local area as the Local Government may, from time to time, prescribe.

39. When any dispute arises as to, or there is a prospect of litigation regarding, any matter within the cognizance of a Civil Court between two or more parties, one of whom is an agriculturist residing within any local area for which a Conciliator has been appointed, or when application for execution

Matters which may be brought before Conciliator.

of any decree in any suit to which any such agriculturist is a party, and which was passed before the date on which this Act comes into force, is contemplated, any of the parties may apply to such Conciliator to effect an amicable settlement between them.

40. If the application be made by one of the parties only, the Conciliator shall take down, or cause to be taken down, in writing a concise statement of the applicant's case, and shall thereupon, by summons or by such other means as he deems fit, invite the person against whom such application is made to attend before him at a time and place to be fixed for this purpose, and shall direct the applicant also to be present at such time and place.

Procedure thereupon.

If such person fails to appear at the time first fixed, the Conciliator may, if he thinks fit, from time to time extend the period for his appearance.

Day for attendance may from time to time be postponed.

41. Whenever all the parties are present, the Conciliator shall call upon each in turn to explain his case regarding the matter in question, and shall use his best endeavours to induce them to agree to an amicable settlement or to submit such matter to arbitration.

When all parties appear, Conciliator to endeavour to reconcile them.

42. The Conciliator shall hear but shall not record the statement of any witness, and shall peruse any book of account or other document produced by the parties, or so much thereof as may be necessary, and, if any party or witness consents in writing to affirm any statement upon oath in any form not repugnant to justice or decency and not purporting to affect any third person, shall provide for such oath being duly taken in the presence of all the parties.

Conciliator to hear statements of witnesses, &c.

43. If on the day on which the case is first heard by the Conciliator, or on any subsequent day to which he may adjourn the hearing, the parties come to any agreement, either finally disposing of the matter or for referring it to arbitration, such agreement shall be forthwith reduced to writing, and shall be read and explained to the parties, and shall be signed or otherwise authenticated by the Conciliator and the parties respectively.

Any agreement arrived at to be reduced to writing.

Explanation.—A Conciliator may be appointed arbitrator under this section.

44. When the agreement is one finally disposing of the matter, the Conciliator shall forward the same in original to the Court of the Subordinate Judge of lowest grade having jurisdiction in the place where the agriculturist who is a party thereto resides;

Procedure when agreement finally disposes of case.

and shall at the same time deliver to each of the parties a written notice to show cause before such Judge, within one month from the date of such delivery, why such agreement ought not to be filed in such Court.

The Court which receives the agreement shall, after the expiry of the said period of one month, unless cause has been shown as aforesaid, order such agreement to be filed; and it shall then take effect as if it were a decree of the said Court passed on the day on which it is ordered to be filed and from which no appeal lies.

45. When the agreement is one for referring the matter to arbitration, the Conciliator shall forward it to the Court having jurisdiction in the matter, and such Court shall cause it to be filed and proceed thereon in manner provided by sections 523 and 524 of the Code of Civil Procedure.

Procedure where agreement is for reference to arbitration.

46. If the person against whom any application is made before a Conciliator cannot after reasonable search be found, or if he refuses or neglects, after a reasonable period has been allowed for his appearance, to appear before the Conciliator, or if he appears but the endeavour to induce the parties to agree to an amicable settlement or to submit the matter in question to arbitration fails, the Conciliator shall, on demand, give to the applicant, or when there are several applicants to each applicant, a certificate under his hand to that effect.

Certificate to be given to applicant if conciliation fails.

47. No suit, and no application for execution of a decree passed before the date on which this Act comes into force to which any agriculturist residing within any local area for which a Conciliator has been appointed is a party, shall be entertained by any Civil Court, unless the plaintiff produces such certificate as aforesaid in reference thereto.

Suit, or application for execution, not to be entertained by Civil Court unless such certificate is produced.

48. In computing the period of limitation prescribed for any such suit the time intervening between the application made by the plaintiff under section thirty-nine and the grant of the certificate under section forty-six shall be excluded.

Allowance to be made in period of limitation.

Local Government to make rules.

49. The Local Government may from time to time make rules—

(*a*) regulating the procedure before Conciliators in matters not provided for by this Act;

(*b*) fixing the charges to be made by Conciliators for anything done by them under this chapter; and

(*c*) determining what record and accounts shall be kept by Conciliators and what returns shall be framed and furnished by them.

CHAPTER VII.

SUPERINTENDENCE AND REVISION.

District Judge to inspect, &c.

50. The District Judge shall inspect, supervise and control the proceedings, under chapter II and chapter IV of this Act, of all Subordinate Judges and the proceedings of all Village-Munsifs and Conciliators.

51. The District Judge may—

District Judge may withdraw case from Subordinate Judge,

(*a*) transfer to his own file any suit or other matter pending before the Court of any Subordinate Judge under chapter II or chapter IV of this Act, and may dispose of the same as if he were a Subordinate Judge; or

or sit with Subordinate Judge as a Bench for trial of any case.

(*b*) stay the proceedings in any such suit or matter, and sit together with such Judge as a Bench to dispose of such suit or matter in accordance with the provisions of this Act.

If the members of any Bench sitting under this section differ in opinion, the opinion of the District Judge shall prevail.

Appointment of Assistant or Subordinate Judge to aid District Judge.

52. The Local Government shall appoint an Assistant or Subordinate Judge to inspect and supervise, subject to the control of the District Judge, the proceedings of all Subordinate Judges, under chapter II and chapter IV of this Act, and of all Village-Munsifs and Conciliators in each of the said Districts of Poona, Sátára, Sholápur and Ahmednagar:

Provided that, if the Local Government thinks fit, the same Assistant or Subordinate Judge may be so appointed for two or more such districts.

Any Assistant or Subordinate Judge appointed under this section may in any district for which he is so appointed, if the District Judge so directs, exercise the powers of the District Judge under section fifty-one of this Act, and transfer any suit under section twenty-five of the Code of Civil Procedure.

53. The District Judge may, for the purpose of satisfying himself of the legality or propriety of any decree or order passed by a Subordinate Judge in any suit or other matter under chapter II or chapter IV of this Act, and as to the regularity of the proceedings therein, call for and examine the record of such suit or matter, and pass such decree or order thereon as he thinks fit;

Of revision.

and any Assistant Judge or Subordinate Judge appointed by the Local Government under section fifty-two may similarly, in any district for which he is appointed, call for and examine the record of any such suit or matter, and, if he see cause therefor, may refer the same, with his remarks thereon, to the District Judge, and the District Judge may pass such decree or order on the case as he thinks fit :

Provided that no decree or order shall be reversed or altered for any error or defect, or otherwise, unless a failure of justice appears to have taken place.

54. The Local Government from time to time may, and if the Government of India so direct shall, appoint an officer, as Special Judge, to discharge in the place of the District Judge all the functions of the District Judge under this Act, in respect of the proceedings of all Subordinate Judges, Village-Munsifs and Conciliators, and may cancel any such appointment.

Special Judge.

Such Special Judge shall not, without the previous sanction of the Government of India, discharge any public function except those which he is empowered by this Act to discharge.

If any conflict of authority arises between the Special Judge and the District Judge the High Court shall pass such order thereon consistent with this Act as it thinks fit.

No appeal shall lie from any decree or order passed by the District Judge under this chapter, or by the Special Judge, or by an Assistant or Subordinate Judge appointed under section fifty-two, or by a Bench, in any suit or proceeding under this Act.

CHAPTER VIII.

REGISTRATION BY VILLAGE-REGISTRARS.

55. The Local Government may, from time to time,—

Appointment of Village-Registrars.
(a) appoint such persons as it thinks fit, whether public officers or not, to be Village-Registrars for such local areas as it may, from time to time, prescribe;

(b) direct the Village-Registrar for any local area to discharge the functions of a Village-Registrar for any other local areas concurrently with the Village-Registrars of such other local areas; and

(c) delegate to any person, by name or in virtue of his office, the powers conferred on it by this section; and may cancel any such appointment, direction or delegation.

Instruments executed by agriculturist not to be deemed valid unless executed before a Village-Registrar.
56. No instrument which purports to create, modify, transfer, evidence or extinguish an obligation for the payment of money or a charge upon any property, or to be a conveyance or lease, and which is executed after this Act comes into force by an agriculturist residing in any local area for which a Village-Registrar has been appointed, shall be admitted in evidence for any purpose by any person having by law or consent of parties authority to receive evidence, or shall be acted upon by any such person or by any public officer, unless such instrument is written by, or under the superintendence of, and is attested by, a Village-Registrar:

Provided that nothing herein contained shall prevent the admission of any instrument in evidence in any criminal proceeding.

Such instruments to be written by or under the superintendence of a Village-Registrar and executed in his presence.
57. When any persons, one of whom is an agriculturist residing in any such local area, desire to execute any such instrument, they shall present themselves before the Village-Registrar appointed by the Local Government for the area in which such agriculturist, or, when there are several such agriculturists, any one of such agriculturists, resides, and such Registrar, after satisfying himself in such manner as he deems fit as to the identity of the parties and receiving from them the fee (if any) prescribed by the Local Government in this behalf and the stamp (if any) which may be required by law, shall write the instrument, or cause the same to be written under his superin-

tendence, and after reading the same aloud or causing it to be so. read in the hearing of the parties shall require them to execute it in his presence.

Attestation of such instruments.

Every instrument so written and executed shall at the time of execution be attested by the Village-Registrar, and also, if any of the parties thereto is unable to read such instrument, by two respectable witnesses.

Registration of instruments by Village-Registrars.

58. Every Village-Registrar shall keep a register of instruments executed before him in such form as shall, from time to time, be prescribed by the Inspector-General of Registration.

As soon as all the parties to any instrument have executed it before a Village-Registrar, he shall make a copy of it or cause a copy of it to be made in his register, and shall deliver the original instrument to the party entitled to the custody of the same, and a certified copy thereof to the other party, or to each of the other parties if there be more than one.

Previous to delivery, the original instrument and each such copy shall be endorsed under the Village-Registrar's signature with the date of registration, the name and residence of the Village-Registrars and the volume and page of the register in which the instrument has been registered.

Consideration to be fully stated in every instrument executed before a Village-Registrar.

59. In every instrument written by, or under the superintendence of, the Village-Registrar, the amount and nature of the consideration, if any, shall be fully stated.

The Village-Registrar shall also endorse upon the instrument a note under his hand, recording whether or not the transfer of the consideration stated therein, or of any part thereof, took place in his presence.

Previous instruments to be produced.

If the instrument modifies, or wholly or partly supersedes, a previous instrument, such previous instrument shall be produced before the Village-Registrar and shall be fully described in the instrument to be executed, and shall be marked by the Village-Registrar under his hand for identification.

Registration under this Act to be deemed equivalent to registration under the Indian Registration Act, 1877.

60. Every instrument executed and registered in accordance with the foregoing provisions shall be deemed to have been duly registered under the provisions of the Indian Registration Act, 1877; and no instrument which ought to have been executed before a Village-Registrar but has

been otherwise executed shall be registered by any officer acting under the said Act, or in any public office, or shall be authenticated by any public officer.

Village-Registrars to be subordinate to the Inspector-General of Registration.

61. The Inspector-General of Registration shall exercise, by himself and his subordinates, a general superintendence over all Village-Registrars, and may, from time to time, with the previous sanction of the Local Government, make rules consistent with this Act for regulating their proceedings and for providing for the custody of their records.

Exemption of instruments to which Government or any officer of Government is a party.

62. Nothing in this Act shall be deemed to require any instrument to which the Government or any officer of Government in his official capacity, is a party, to be executed before a Village-Registrar.

Power of Local Government to make rules.

63. The Local Government may, from time to time, make rules regulating the appointment, suspension, dismissal and remuneration of Village-Registrars, and prescribing the fees to be levied by them.

CHAPTER IX.

Of Receipts and Statements of Account.

Agriculturists entitled to written receipts :

64. The person to whom any agriculturist makes any payment of money in liquidation of a debt shall, at the time of such payment, tender to such agriculturist, whether he demand the same or not, a written receipt for the amount of such payment.

If such payment is made under any instrument executed before a Village-Registrar, the receipt shall, if the agriculturist so require, be endorsed on the copy of the instrument furnished to him under section fifty-eight.

To annual statements of account :

65. Any agriculturist by whom any money is due under any instrument shall, on such date in each year as the Local Government, having regard to local custom, may from time to time, by notification in the official Gazette, fix, be entitled to receive, on demand, from the person claiming under such instrument, a statement up to that date of his account under such instrument.

66. Any agriculturist in whose name an account is kept by any trader or money-lender shall be entitled to receive from such trader or money-lender, on demand, a pass-book, and to require, from time to time, that his account up to date be written therein and authenticated by the signature or mark of the said trader or money-lender.

To have account made up from time to time in a pass-book.

An entry so made in any such pass-book of any payment made to the trader or money-lender shall be deemed to be equivalent, for the purposes of section sixty-four, to the grant of a receipt for the amount so entered.

No person whose account has been written in a pass-book as required by this section shall be entitled also to demand an account under section sixty-five.

67. Any person who, in contravention of section sixty-four, sixty-five or sixty-six, refuses or neglects to tender a receipt or a statement of account or a pass-book, or to write, or cause to be written, any account or any part of an account in a pass-book, or to attest the same when so written, shall be punished for each such offence with fine which may extend to one hundred rupees.

Penalty for contravention of sections 64 to 66.

CHAPTER X.

LEGAL PRACTITIONERS.

68. No pleader, vakíl, or mukhtár, and no advocate or attorney of a High Court, shall be permitted to appear on behalf of any party to any case before a Conciliator or a Village-Munsif, or to any case cognizable by a Subordinate Judge under this Act, the subject-matter whereof does not exceed in amount or value one hundred rupees:

Pleaders, &c., excluded in certain cases.

Provided that any party to any such case may be permitted, on reasonable cause being shown to the satisfaction of the Conciliator, Village-Munsif or Subordinate Judge, to employ any relative, servant or dependent who is not, and has not previously been, a pleader, vakíl or mukhtár, or an advocate or attorney of a High Court, to appear either conjointly with, or in lieu of, such party:

Provided also that a Subordinate Judge may permit a pleader, vakíl or mukhtár, or an advocate or attorney of a High Court, to appear before him on behalf of any party to any case of the description aforesaid in which, for reasons to be recorded by him in writing, he deems it desirable that the party should have such assistance.

When a relative, servant or dependent appears in lieu of a party, he shall be furnished by him with a power-of-attorney defining the extent to which he is empowered to act.

Power of Court to appoint pleader for agriculturist.

69. When in any suit or proceeding before a Subordinate Judge under this Act to which an agriculturist, is a party, any pleader, vakíl or mukhtár, or any advocate or attorney of a High Court, appears on behalf of any party opposed to such agriculturist, the Subordinate Judge, if he is of opinion that such agriculturist has not the means of obtaining proper professional assistance, may, with the consent of such agriculturist, direct the Government pleader or any other fit person (who is willing so to do) to appear on his behalf.

CHAPTER XI.

MISCELLANEOUS.

Mortgages, &c., to be valid only when written.

70. No mortgage, lien or charge of or upon any immoveable property belonging to an agriculturist shall be valid unless it is created by an instrument in writing under the hand of the person creating such mortgage, lien or charge.

Nothing in this section shall apply to any mortgage, lien or charge created by mere operation of law, or in favour of the Government or of any officer of the Government in his official capacity.

All mortgages hitherto executed to be registered.

71. Every instrument executed before this Act comes into force and purporting to create any mortgage, lien or charge of or upon any immoveable property belonging to an agriculturist shall be deemed to be an instrument required by section 17 of the Indian Registration Act, 1877, to be registered; and any such instrument which before the passing of this Act was not so required to be registered may, notwithstanding anything contained in the said Indian Registration Act, 1877, be registered under that Act within one year from the date on which this Act comes into force.

Every Village-Registrar appointed under this Act shall be deemed to be a Sub-Registrar for the purpose of so registering such instruments; and the local area for which he is appointed shall be deemed for such purpose to be his sub-district.

Nothing in this section applies to an instrument purporting to create a mortgage, lien or charge in favour of the Government or of any officer of the Government in his official capacity.

Limitation. 72. In any suit against an agriculturist under this Act for the recovery of money the following periods of limitation shall be deemed to be substituted for those prescribed in the second column of the second schedule annexed to the Indian Limitation Act, 1877 (that is to say):—

(a) when such suit is based on a written instrument registered under this Act or any law in force at the date of the execution of such instrument,—twelve years;

(b) in any other case,—six years:

Provided that nothing herein contained shall revive the right to bring any suit which would have been barred by limitation if it had been instituted immediately before this Act comes into force.

Decision as to whether person is an agriculturist, final. 73. The decision of any Court of first instance that any person is or is not an agriculturist shall, for the purposes of this Act, be final.

Civil Procedure Code to apply in Subordinate Judges' Courts. 74. Except in so far as it is inconsistent with this Act, the Code of Civil Procedure shall apply in all suits and proceedings before Subordinate Judges under this Act.

Additional power to make rules. 75. The Local Government may, from time to time, make all such rules as it may deem necessary for carrying out the provisions herein contained.

Rules to be published. 76. All rules made by the Local Government under this Act shall be published in the official Gazette, and shall thereupon, in so far as they are consistent with this Act, have the force of law.

(Signed) D. FITZPATRICK,
Secy. to the Govt. of India,
Legislative Department.

RULES REGARDING VILLAGE MUNSIFS.

JUDICIAL DEPARTMENT.

Bombay Castle, 17th December 1879.

No. 7635.—In exercise of the power conferred by section 37 of the Deccan Agriculturists Relief Act, 1879, the Governor in Council is pleased to prescribe the following rules for regulating the procedure of Village Munsifs :—

1. Every suit in a Village Munsif's Court shall be instituted by presenting to the Village Munsif in person a written plaint in the vernacular language of the district, which should contain the following particulars—
   (1) The name, religion, caste, profession and place of abode of the plaintiff.
   (2) The name, religion, caste, profession and place of abode of the defendant.
   (3) A statement of the circumstances which have led to the institution of the suit.
   (4) A list of the plaintiff's documents, if any, and of his witnesses, and whether he requires the Village Munsif's assistance to procure their attendance or whether he will produce them himself, on the day to be appointed under Rule 5.

2. If the plaintiff sues upon a document in his possession or power, he must produce it with his plaint.

3. The Village Munsif shall reject the plaint at once in the following cases :—
   (1) If it appears to the Village Munsif that the subject of the plaint is not within his jurisdiction.
   (2) If it appears to him after questioning the plaintiff that the suit is barred by the limitation law.

4. If the Village Munsif admits the plaint he shall number and register it in a Register to be kept for the purpose in the following form :—

Date of presentation.	No. of Suit.	Plaintiff's name, caste, and residence.	Defendant's name, caste, and residence.	Nature of claim.	Final order and date thereof.	How executed.
1	2	3	4	5	6	7

5. When he admits a plaint, he shall fix a convenient day, if possible within seven days from its institution, for the trial of the suit, and he shall require the plaintiff to appear with his documents and witnesses, if any, on the day so appointed. He shall also forthwith, with the least practicable delay, send for the defendant and personally explain to him the nature of the claim informing him of the day fixed for the trial and requiring him to be present in person on that day, unless the defendant admits the correctness of the claim and his own liability, in which case the Village Munsif shall record the admission in full and require the defendant to sign or put his mark to the same, and shall also sign it himself.

6. If the defendant does not admit the claim, the Village Munsif shall require him to name his witnesses, if any, and to state whether he will himself produce them or require the assistance of the Court to procure their attendance, and shall warn him to be present in person with his documents and witnesses, if any, upon the appointed day.

7. Whenever it is necessary to procure the attendance of any defendant or witness the Village Munsif may require the village officers to produce such person before him; and it shall be the duty of the village officers to obey the requisition of the Village Munsif.

8. On the day appointed for the trial, unless the defendant has previously admitted the claim under Rule 5, in which case he may at once pass a final order, the Village Munsif shall first of all examine the parties, or the persons, if any, permitted to appear for them under section 68 of the Act, and shall peruse the documents, if any, produced on either side, in order to ascertain the point or points in issue and whether the defendant has any just answer or defence to the suit; and shall then, if necessary, examine the witnesses on either side; and may also send for and examine any other person who may appear to him likely to be able to give useful evidence as to the matters in dispute; and shall then proceed, at once if possible, to record his final order in accordance with the just merits of the case.

9. If the plaintiff fails without reasonable excuse to attend with his proofs or omits without reasonable excuse to adopt measures to procure the attendance of his witnesses, the Village Munsif shall reject the plaint.

10. If the defendant fails to appear, the Village Munsif shall adjourn the trial to an early day to be fixed by him, and shall meantime take all the measures in his power, with the assistance of the village officers, to procure the attendance of the defendant

on such adjourned date : he shall not decide the suit without examining the defendant unless for special reasons to be recorded by him in writing in his final order.

11. If the witnesses on either side or any of them fail to attend on the appointed day, the Village Munsif may, after taking the evidence of those that are present if he considers it necessary for the purposes of justice and for arriving at a satisfactory decision, adjourn the trial for such period as may be necessary to procure their attendance.

12. The Village Munsif shall examine the parties and their witnesses, if any, orally, and it shall not be necessary for him to take down their evidence in writing or make notes thereof; but if he does not do so, he shall embody in his final order the substance of the evidence, together with the points in dispute, and his decision thereon, specifying the amount, if any, awarded to the plaintiff. Such final order shall be deemed to be the decree.

13. If his decision is in favour of the plaintiff either wholly or in part, he may direct the defendant to pay the amount found due, by instalments not extending over a longer period than twelve months.

14. In no case shall he award more than seems to him on a full consideration of all the circumstances and past history of the debt to be justly and equitably due.

15. The final order shall be written in column 6 of the Register mentioned in Rule 4; and the Village Munsif shall give a copy thereof, under his signature, to either party asking for the same.

16. Every order whether rejecting a plaint or allowing or disallowing a claim shall be endorsed briefly by the Village Munsif on the plaint.

17. If the decision awards the plaintiff's claim in whole or part, the defendant may pay the money due by him under the decree into the Village Munsif's Court and in such case shall be given a receipt for the same : and it shall be the duty of the Village Munsif to cause such money to be paid over to the plaintiff and to require his receipt for the same, and to enter the fact of such payment in the last column of the Register.

18. If the decree is satisfied in whole or in part out of Court, it shall be the duty of the plaintiff to certify the fact to the Village Munsif, and when he fails to do so, the defendant may apply to the Village Munsif, who shall then make enquiries ; and if he finds it proved that the decree has been so satisfied shall refuse to

execute it further. The necessary entry to denote satisfaction under this Rule shall be made in the Register.

19. The decree-holder may at any time within the period allowed by the limitation law apply to the Village Munsif for execution of his decree or such portion of it as may remain unsatisfied; such application must be in writing, and must state that the decree of which execution is sought has remained unsatisfied in whole or in part, as the case may be.

20. In the case of a decree which allows payment by instalments, any default by the judgment-debtor entitles the decree-holder to apply for execution.

21. On application as aforesaid by the decree-holder the Village Munsif may, after making such inquiry as he deems necessary, cause the decree to be executed by the attachment and sale of any moveable property within the local area of his jurisdiction belonging to and in the possession of the judgment-debtor, except such property as is mentioned in the proviso to section 266 of the Civil Procedure Code. Attachment shall be effected by actual seizure, and the property so attached shall be kept in safe custody in or near the village chauri. Provided that no more property shall be attached under this Rule than shall seem to the Village Munsif reasonably sufficient at a fair valuation to cover the amount of the decree remaining unsatisfied.

22. All claims to attached property shall be inquired into without delay and summarily determined by the Village Munsif after hearing such evidence as may be tendered by the claimant and the decree-holder respectively, and after examining, if necessary, the judgment-debtor.

23. If the attached property is subject to speedy and natural decay or when the expense of keeping it in custody shall exceed its value, it may be sold at once, by order of the Village Munsif.

24. In all other cases if the judgment-debtor does not tender the amount of the decree within three days from the date of attachment, the Village Munsif shall issue a notice of the sale of the property, to be posted up in a conspicuous place in the chauri where the property is kept, specifying the property to be sold, the amount for which the sale is ordered, and the day and hour of sale.

25. Except in the case mentioned in Rule 22 no sale shall take place till after the expiration of at least ten days from the date on which the notice has been posted up on the chauri.

26. If the Village Munsif is himself an officiating Patel and if the property is within the limits of his jurisdiction, as such, he

shall himself order and superintend the attachment and the conduct of the sale. In any other case the Village Munsif shall direct his orders for the attachment and sale to an officiating Patel in whose jurisdiction, as such, the property is, and it shall be the duty of such Patel to carry out the execution under the orders of the Village Munsif.

27. The officer conducting the sale may in his discretion for sufficient reason adjourn the sale, reporting the fact to the Village Munsif, who may pass such orders as may seem just as to the renewal of the sale.

28. The proceeds of the sale shall be made over by the Village Munsif to the decree-holder to the extent necessary to satisfy his decree, any surplus being handed over to the judgment-debtor. Receipts shall be taken for any payment made under this Rule: and the necessary entry as to satisfaction shall be made in the Register.

29. The Village Munsif shall be entitled to employ the agency of the inferior village servants for carrying out his orders in any suit or execution matter pending before him under the Act: and it shall be the duty of the Revenue and Police Patels and Kulkarnis throughout the local area of his jurisdiction to render him all the assistance in their power in connection with the discharge of his duties under the Act.

30. No costs shall be awarded by any Village Munsif.

31. The Village Munsif shall be entitled to hold his court in the village chauri.

By order of His Excellency the Honourable the
Governor in Council,

J. R. NAYLOR,
Acting Chief Secretary to Government.

RULES REGARDING CONCILIATORS.

JUDICIAL DEPARTMENT.

Bombay Castle, 17th December 1879.

No. 7636.—In exercise of the power conferred by Section 49 of the Deccan Agriculturists Relief Act, 1879, the Governor in Council is pleased to fix the following Table of Charges to be made by Conciliators and to prescribe the following Rules as to the record and accounts to be kept by them :—

A.—*Table of Charges.*

(1) For forwarding an agreement under Section 44 to the Court. — One-half per cent. of the amount of value or the subject-matter of the agreement.

(2) For ditto ditto under Section 45. — One-half per cent. of the amount or value of the subject-matter of the agreement; provided that the charge shall be in no case less than four annas or more than Rs. 5.

(3) For granting a certificate under Section 46. — Four annas.

The above charges shall not be payable in cash but in court-fee labels which shall be affixed to the documents in respect of which the charges are respectively payable.

If the percentage calculated according to item No. 1 or 2 of the foregoing table amounts to a sum which cannot be exactly represented by court-fee labels of procurable values, the charge shall be enhanced to the nearest amount which can be so represented.

B.—Every Conciliator appointed under the said Act shall keep a General Register in the following form:—

1	2	3	4	5	6	7	8	9	10	11	12	13
Serial Number.	Date of application.	Name, caste, residence and occupation of applicant.	Name, caste, residence and occupation of the person against whom the application is made.	Concise statement of the case.	Date and place fixed for parties to appear.	Date of actual appearance.	Result of the endeavour for reconciliation.	Date of forwarding agreement or reference to arbitration to Civil Court.	To what Court forwarded.	Date of certificate, if any, under Section 46 and to whom granted.	Remarks.	Signature of Conciliator.

Explanations.

(1.) When an application is made to a Conciliator he should immediately fill in the first five columns, giving each application a serial number in the order of its presentation; the concise statement of the case required to be taken down in writing by section 40 of the Act should be written in the fifth column.

(2.) If all the parties to a dispute apply jointly at the same time to a Conciliator, their names should be entered in column 3 as joint applicants, and columns 4, 6 and 7 need not be filled up.

(3.) In the 6th column the adjourned date or dates, if any, should also be shown below the date first fixed, and an entry should be made in the same column showing the mode adopted for securing the presence of the opposite party, whether by summons, message, personal oral communication, or as the case may be.

(4.) If the opposite party fails to appear on the date first fixed or within the time, if any, subsequently extended, this fact should be noted in column 7.

(5.) In column 8 if an agreement finally disposing of the matter is arrived at, an abstract of such agreement should be given, or if a reference to arbitration is agreed to, the name of the arbitrator should be entered, or if the endeavour to bring about an amicable settlement fails, the fact should be recorded.

(6.) The date of the certificate, if any, granted under section 46 should be particularly noted in column 11.

(7.) If cross-applications in the same matter are made at different times, the fact should be noted by a cross-reference in the column of remarks. Any fact connected with the application or dispute which the Conciliator thinks it worth while or important to record may be noted in this column.

(8.) The Conciliator should attach his signature in the last column, when the application is finally disposed of by him.

C.—Every Conciliator shall also keep an account of all fees received by him in the following form:—

1	2	3	4	5	6	7
				FEE FOR WHAT PURPOSE PAID.		
Date.	No. of application as per General Register.	Amount or value of the subject matter.	Fee from whom received.	For forwarding an Agreement to the Court under section 44.	For forwarding an Agreement under section 45.	For granting a Certificate under section 46.
				Rs.　a.	Rs.　a.	Rs.　a.
			Monthly Total ...			

By order of His Excellency the Honourable
the Governor in Council,

J. R. NAYLOR,
Acting Chief Secretary to Government.

RULES REGARDING VILLAGE REGISTRARS AND REGISTRATIONS.

JUDICIAL DEPARTMENT.

Bombay Castle, 7th February 1880.

No. 889A.—The following Rules made, with the previous sanction of Government, by the Inspector-General of Registration, under section 61 of the Deccan Agriculturists Relief Act, 1879, are published for general information :—

PART I.—PRELIMINARY.

Definitions. 1. In these Rules :

(a) " Táluka Village Registrar " means a Village Registrar who is also a Sub-Registrar under the Indian Registration Act, 1877;

(b) " Kulkarni Village Registrar " means a Village Registrar who is also an officiating kulkarni, or a sharer of the kulkarni watan of the village, or of one of the villages for which he is Village Registrar;

(c) " Stipendiary Village Registrar " means any Village Registrar other than a Táluka or a Kulkarni Village Registrar.

2. In case of a Stipendiary or Kulkarni Village Registrar being unable to attend to his duty for a period in excess of 7 days, owing to absence from the village, sudden illness, or other cause, he shall place a competent person in charge of his office, making an immediate report to the Assistant or Deputy Collector in charge of the táluka, through the Táluka Village Registrar, and the person so placed in charge shall, until the receipt of instructions to the contrary, discharge all the duties of the Village Registrar.

Arrangements to be made during absence of Stipendiary or Kulkarni Village Registrars from their offices.

The Village Registrar, by whom any person is so placed in charge, shall be responsible for all his acts as if he were himself still in charge of the office.

PART II.—RECORDS.

(a) Register-Book.

3. The Register prescribed by section 58 of the Deccan Agriculturists Relief Act, 1879, shall be a book kept in the form of Appendix A.

Form of Register Book.

4. A Village Registrar before bringing a new Register Book into use shall count the pages, and satisfy himself that the number thereof corresponds with that given in the certificate on the title page. If the number be found correct he shall certify to that effect on the title page. If there be a discrepancy he shall return the book for correction to the officer from whom it was received.

Examination of new Register Books.

5. The volumes of Register Books in each office shall be numbered in a consecutive series, which shall not terminate with the year but be carried on perpetually. It shall not be necessary to commence a fresh volume at the commencement of a new year. When the amount of copying is great, two volumes of a Register Book may be employed simultaneously, instruments bearing an even serial number being copied into one and those bearing an odd serial number into the other.

Numbering of the consecutive volumes of Register Books.

(b) *Index of Register.*

6. An Index of all entries in the Registers shall be prepared in the form of Appendix B. The Index for all the Village Registry Offices of each táluka shall be prepared by the Táluka Village Registrar at the Mámlatdár's head-quarters, from the memoranda sent to him under Rule 31 as well as from his own Register. In the Index, however, the last column in the form given in Appendix B will be omitted.

Form of Index.

7. The Index should be prepared alphabetically for the entire táluka without reference to the particular office in which the transaction indexed has been registered, and the necessary entry in the Index should be made in each case directly the form referred to in Rule 31 has been received. At the end of the year the Index for the táluka should be bound into volumes.

Arrangement and binding of Index.

8. The rules for the time being applicable to the Indexes of the Registers kept under the Indian Registration Act, 1877, shall be followed in the preparation of the Index under these rules so far as regards:

Certain rules under Act III., 1877, to be observed in preparing the Index.

(a) the method of indexing and transliterating names;

(b) the indexing of an instrument of which there are more executants than one; and

(c) the use of the loose sheets supplied for the preparation of the Index.

(c) *Claim-Note Book.*

Form and use of Claim-Note Book.
9. A book in the form of Appendix C shall be kept by each Village Registrar.

If the registration of an instrument and the furnishing of a copy or copies under the second paragraph of section 58 is completed on the day of attestation of the instrument and before the parties to the transaction leave the office, no claim-note from this book need be granted to any of such parties.

It shall be the duty of the Village Registrar, if possible, to complete the registration and furnishing of copies as aforesaid on the day on which the parties first come to him for the purpose.

If, however, when the parties leave the office any of them have a claim to an original instrument or to a copy, the Village Registrar shall grant to each person having such claim a claim-note, which shall afterwards be taken back and filed when the original instrument or copy to which it relates is delivered to the party who claims it.

(d) *Day and Cash-Book.*

Day and Cash-Book, &c.
10. Every Táluka and every Stipendiary Village Registrar shall keep a Day and Cash-Book in the form given in Appendix D, and in this book shall be entered all fees paid for registration, &c.

Every Kulkarni Village Registrar shall enter his registration receipts under a distinct heading in his ordinary Day Book (Village Form 11).

(e) *General Provisions.*

Local offices of issue for books and forms.
11. The office of every Táluka Village Registrar shall be the local office of issue for books, forms, &c., to the other Village Registrars of the táluka or mahál in which such office is situate.

Transfer of records to office of Táluka Village Registrar.
The office of each Táluka Village Registrar at a Mámlatdár's head-quarters shall be a central office of record for the other Village Registry Offices of the táluka, and the Register Books of the latter Village Registry Offices shall be forwarded to the said Táluka Village Registrar for the purpose of being recorded as they from time to time become complete.

12. All Village Registrars shall provide out of the amount received by them as remuneration such office accommodation as they require, if no public office is available for their use, and also whatever writing materials they require for the work of their respective offices, excepting such blank forms and books as are supplied by Government, and the paper required for the preparation of instruments, or of copies supplied under Rules 29 and 30.

Village Registrars to provide their own writing materials and to be responsible for quality of writing and condition of their records.

They shall be responsible that all instruments written by them, or under their superintendence and all other documents, or books which they are required to prepare are executed intelligibly, legibly and distinctly, and for their records being kept neat and orderly.

13. No Village Registrar may destroy any of the old papers of his office without first having obtained the sanction of the Assistant or Deputy Collector in charge of the táluka for doing so.

Destruction of old papers.

PART III.—PROCEDURE.

(f) *Execution and Registration of Instruments under Sections 57 and 58.*

14. Village Registrars should duly satisfy themselves of the identity of each executant, and should receive the fee for registration and copy before the instrument is written. They should also pay careful attention to the requirements of the Stamp Act.

Preliminary measures to be taken before an instrument is written.

15. Every Village Registrar shall provide himself with specimen forms of all instruments to which agriculturists are ordinarily parties. In drafting an instrument care must be taken to follow the best obtainable form, and whilst fully expressing the intentions of the parties, to avoid repetition or prolixity.

Preparation of instruments.

Above all, the language employed should be simple and clear, and the description of immoveable property, if any has to be mentioned in the instrument, should be such as to enable the property to be unmistakeably identified. When the instrument relates to land to which a survey has been extended the survey numbers should be set forth.

Endorsements to be made on the instrument after its execution.

16. When the instrument has been written, it should be read out to the parties and executed.

(a) The Village Registrar should then endorse upon it a note in the following form :—

	As.	p.
"Fees received as follows :—For preparation, registration, and one copy	4	0
For additional copies (*if any are supplied*) ...		
Total ...As.		"

(b) Immediately below this note should appear the endorsement of attestation required by para. 2 of section 57, in the following form:—

"This instrument written by me (*or* under my superintendence), after having been read aloud within his hearing, has been executed by *A. B.* of *C. D.*, whom I know (*or* of whose identity I have duly satisfied myself), in my presence this day."

If a witness is examined as to identity his name and place of residence should be added in the following form:—
"Witness as to identity *E. F.* of *G. H.*"

The endorsement should be signed and dated by the Village Registrar; and if any of the parties to the instrument is unable to read it, the attestation by two respectable witnesses should immediately follow that of the Village Registrar, in the following form :—

"We, *I. J.* of *K. L.* and *M. N.* of *O. P.*, have witnessed the execution this day of this instrument by *A. B.* of *C. D.*"

(Signed) *I. J.* of *K. L.*
(Signed) *M. N.* of *O. P.*

(c) The Village Registrar shall next endorse upon the instrument the note required by para. 2 of section 59 as to whether or not the transfer of the consideration named therein, or of any part thereof, took place in his presence. This note shall be in one or other of the following forms :—

"*A. B.* of *C. D.* has in my presence this day received from *Q. R.* of *S. T.* the sum of Rs. (*figures*), *i. e.*, in words
                            (*or* the following articles, viz.,
        (being the whole (*or* a part) of the consideration stated in this instrument ;" *or*

"No portion of the consideration stated in this instrument has been paid in my presence to *A. B.* of *C. D.*"

The endorsement should be signed by the Village Registrar.

(*d*) Immediately below such signature should be endorsed a further note showing page and volume of the Register Book in which the instrument is registered.

Finally, at the foot of all these endorsements should be affixed the Village Registrar's signature with his official designation (*i. e.*, Village Registrar of) and the date of such signature.

17. (*a*) If a previous instrument of the nature of that referred to in para. 3 of section 59 be produced at the time of the execution of an instrument before a Village Registrar, the Village Registrar shall write upon the previous instrument the following note :—

Marking of previous instruments for identification.

"This instrument has been modified (*or* wholly, or partly superseded) by instrument No. —— of (year) executed in my presence by *A. B.* of *C. D.* in favour of *Q. R.* of *S. T.*, and attested by me this day."

(*b*) On the new instrument which modifies, or supersedes the previous instrument the Village Registrar shall write, at the top of the document, immediately over the stamp impression, if there be any, the following note :—

"The instrument dated   executed by   in favour of   , which this instrument modifies (*or* supersedes) has been produced before me this day, and a note of such modification (*or* supersession) has been endorsed by me thereon."

But it should be understood that the writing of this note will not dispense with the necessity of a full description of the old instrument being contained in the new one as required by section 59.

(*c*) If in any case it be established to the satisfaction of a Village Registrar that a previous instrument of the nature of that named in this rule has been lost or destroyed, or for other sufficient reason cannot be produced, he shall record on the new instrument, in lieu of the last-mentioned note, a note to the following effect :—

"It has been established to my satisfaction that the instrument dated   executed by   in favour of   , which this instrument modifies (*or* supersedes) has been   , and cannot therefore be produced before me."

To each of the above notes the Village Registrar should attach his signature and official designation, together with the date of signature.

(g) Registration of Old Instruments under Section 71.

[NOTE.—*It should be clearly understood as regards the provisions of section 71 and of Rules 18 to 20 :*

(1) *that they only apply to instruments creating a mortgage, lien, or charge on immoveable property belonging to an agriculturist ;*

(2) *that under the provisions in question no instrument can be registered unless it has been executed prior to the date on which the Dekkhan Agriculturists Relief Act came into force (i. e.,* 1st *November* 1879*) ; and*

(3) *that on and after the* 1st *November* 1880 *the provisions of both section 71 and of these rules will cease to have effect.*]

18. If an instrument of the nature of that named in section 71 be produced before a Village Registrar for the purpose of being registered, the Village Registrar shall satisfy himself that the instrument has been duly executed by the person or persons who purport to have executed it, and also as to the identity of such executant or executants.

Preliminary measures to be taken on presentation of instruments under section 71.

19. The instrument will be presented for registration either by a party who claims under it or by the executant or one of the executants.

Endorsements to be made on such instruments.

(a) The first endorsement on the instrument should therefore be in the following form :—

"This instrument is presented for registration by *Q. R.* of *S. T.*, the party who claims under it (*or* by *A. B.* of *C. D.*, the executant). *A. B.* of *C. D.* whom I, the Village Registrar, know, (*or* of whose identity I, the Village Registrar, have duly satisfied myself,) admits the execution of the instrument which has been read aloud to him by me."

If receipt of any consideration be acknowledged by the executant, the words "and acknowledges having received Rs. (*words and figures*) of the consideration money (*or* the following articles)" should be added to this endorsement, which the executant should then sign, or affix his mark to.

If a witness be examined as to identity, his name and place of residence should be endorsed in the form given in Rule 16 (b).

(b) The Village Registrar should next write the fee-endorsement as follows :—

"Fee received for Registration, 4 annas."

(c) Directly below such endorsement the words "Registration Ordered" should be written.

The Village Registrar should affix his signature with the date of such signature to the foot of these endorsements.

(d) Next he should endorse a further note showing the page and volume of the Register Book in which the instrument is registered.

Finally, at the foot of all these endorsements, the Village Registrar's signature should be once more attached with his official designation and the date of such signature.

(*N.B.—In the case of Registrations under section 71, the law does not require Village Registrars to furnish the parties with copies of the instruments registered; but such copies may be obtained by them under Rule 30*).

20. If the Village Registrar is not satisfied that the instrument was executed by the person or persons who purport to have executed it, he shall refuse to register the same, and immediately below the presentation endorsement prescribed in Rule 19 shall endorse the following words :—

Refusal of Registration.

"Registration of this instrument refused as I am not satisfied that it has been executed by *A. B.* of *C. D.*"

This endorsement should be signed by the Village Registrar, his official designation and the date of such signature being added.

If an instrument be refused for registration it should not be copied into the Register Book.

In dealing with an instrument presented for registration under section 71, the fees should not be received until after it is determined whether the instrument is to be registered or not, and if registration be refused no fees should be levied on it.

(*h*) *Provisions applicable to all Registrations by Village Registrars, whether under Section 58 or Section 71.*

21. No Stipendiary or Kulkarni Village Registrar shall prepare or register any instrument to which he or any member of his family is a party. For the preparation or registration of any such instrument the parties should be referred to a Village Registrar who has concurrent jurisdiction.

Certain Village Registrars not to prepare or register instruments in which they are interested.

22. If in writing an instrument it has been found necessary to make any corrections in the nature of erasures, interlineations, &c., the Village Registrar should require all the parties to the instrument to attest such corrections with their initials or marks, and should also attach his own initials thereto.

Corrections in the original instrument to be attested.

23. If in any case the space afforded by a single piece of paper is found insufficient to contain all the writing of an instrument and it is necessary to attach an extra piece or pieces thereto, the Village Registrar should write his signature across the junction of the two or more pieces of paper of which the instrument consists both on the front and on the reverse side.

Provision where space afforded by single piece of paper is insufficient to contain all the writing of an instrument.

24. A Village Registrar who registers any instrument in the exercise of concurrent jurisdiction, shall forward to the Village Registrar, within whose jurisdiction the executants of such instrument reside, or if they reside in different circles, to the Village Registrar of each such circle a memorandum of the instrument so registered in the form of Appendix B. These memoranda shall be filed in the Village Registrar's office to which they may be sent for one calendar year, subsequent to which period they may, with the sanction of the Assistant, or Deputy Collector in charge of the táluka, be destroyed.

Memorandum of instrument registered by a Village Registrar exercising concurrent jurisdiction to be sent to Village Registrar of circle in which executant resides.

25. In copying an instrument into the Register Book, the endorsements prescribed by Rules 16, 17, and 19 should be copied in column 1, and the contents of the instrument itself should be copied in column 2. When the instrument is stamped, the value of the stamp and the stamp vendor's endorsement appearing on the original instrument should be copied in column 2 of the Register Book at the commencement of the entry.

Mode of copying instruments into the Register.

26. Errors, erasures, or alterations appearing in original instruments, should be copied into the Register exactly as they appear in those instruments, marginal notes being written explanatory of such errors; *e. g.*, "so in the original," or corresponding words in the vernacular with a × over the error and a corresponding mark over the marginal entry relating thereto.

Method of noting errors, erasures, &c., in original instruments in the copies thereof in the Register.

27. On the copy in the Register Book being completed the Village Registrar having carefully compared it with the original should certify under his signature, with his official designation attached, that it is a true copy. Any mistakes made at the time of copying should be corrected by the words written by mistake being underlined and the correct words being written above, or by the words omitted being neatly interlineated, but the Village Registrar should attest all such corrections in the Register Book by attaching his initials thereto.

Attestation of copy of instrument in Register Book and method of attesting corrections in that copy.

The date of the delivery to executants of the copies referred to in para. 2 of section 58 and Rule 29 should, in every case, be shown in the Register Book in column 1 immediately below the endorsements, in the following form : "Copy of this instrument delivered to *A. B.* of *C. D.* on (*date*)."

Date of delivery of copy to executant to be shown in Register.

28. All entries in a Register Book should be numbered in a consecutive series which should commence and terminate with the year, a fresh series being commenced at the beginning of each year. The serial number should appear in column 1 immediately above the first endorsement copied into that column, being distinguished in the case of instruments relating to immoveable property by the letter A and in that of instruments relating to moveable property by the letter B.

Entries in Register Book how to be numbered and marked.

An ink line should be drawn from left to right across the page of the Register Book to show where one entry terminates and where the next begins, such line being drawn immediately below that portion of the copy, whether in column 1 or column 2, which appears lowest down on the page. The entry relating to one instrument in one column should in no case be made alongside of the entry relating to any other instrument in the other column.

Termination of one entry and commencement of next to be shown in the Register Book.

(i) Copies and Searches.

29. Copies* furnished to executants under the provisions of para. 2 of section 58 should contain all that appears on the original instrument, that is to say both the contents of, and the endorsements upon, such instrument; and should, after being compared with the original, be certified to be true copies by the Village Registrar who, below such certificate, should attach his signature and official designation.

Furnishing of copies under para. 2 of section 58 to executants.

Errors, interlineations, &c., appearing in the original instrument should be shown in these copies in the same manner as in the Register-Book (see Rule 26); and mistakes made in preparing them should be corrected as laid down in Rule 27.

30. † Subject to the payment of the fees prescribed in this behalf by Government under section 63, Register Books and Indexes and Memoranda filed under Rule 24, shall be open to the inspection of any person applying to inspect the same, and copies of entries therein shall be given to, or may be taken by any person applying for such copies: Provided that no Register Book or other record of a Village Registrar's Office shall be inspected by any person other than a Government officer, save in the presence of the Village Registrar, and in the place used by him as his office, and that all applications for inspection or for copies must be in writing.

Applications for copy, search or inspection. Receipt for any payment on account of the above to be always given.

Any person permitted to inspect such records may search for any entry therein, or if he shall so desire, such search shall be made for him, subject as aforesaid, by the Village Registrar.

For any payment made under this rule a receipt, in the form of Appendix E, shall be granted by the Village Registrar.

(j) Returns and Pay-Bills.

31. Every Village Registrar, other than Táluka Village Registrars at Mámlatdárs' head-quarters, on registering an instrument, shall at once fill in a printed sheet in the form of

Preparation of Monthly Return, &c.

---

* The stamp-duty leviable on the copies has been remitted by the Government of India's Notification No. 10 of 3rd January 1870 (*Bombay Government Gazette* for 8th idem, p. 40).

† Applications made, and certified copies granted under this Rule, will be subject to the provisions of the Court Fees and Stamp Acts, independently of the copy and search fees leviable under the rules made by Government under section 63 of the Indian Agriculturists Relief Act, 1879.

Appendix B, and shall despatch it at the earliest opportunity to the Táluka Village Registrar at the head-quarters of the Mámlatdár of the táluka.

At the close of each month all such Village Registrars as aforesaid shall forward to the Táluka Village Registrar at the Mámlatdár's head-quarters a memorandum showing the amount of fees collected by them during that month on account of searches and copies granted under Rule 30.

From the returns thus sent, and from the information to be gathered from the books of his own office, the Táluka Village Registrar at the Mámlatdár's head-quarters will prepare a general Monthly Return for the whole of the Village Registry Offices of the táluka in the form of Appendix F, and will submit the same through the Mámlatdár, for the purpose of verification, to the Collector, in whose office again a general district Monthly Return of the same kind will be prepared and forwarded to the Inspector-General of Registration.

Pay of Stipendiary Village Registrars how to be drawn.

32. The Táluka Village Registrar when preparing the monthly return prescribed in the preceding rule will, at the same time, prepare one general bill for the pay of the Stipendiary Village Registrars of the táluka, which bill he should submit to the Mámlatdár's Treasury for encashment. The Táluka Village Registrar on drawing the amount of the bill should take the first opportunity of forwarding, by means of the village mahárs, or otherwise as may be most convenient, to the Stipendiary Village Registrars the amount due to each.

(*k*) *Remittances.*

Remittances to the Treasury how to be made.

33. Remittances on account of registration fees, &c., should be sent as follows to the Treasury :—

by Táluka Village Registrars, to the Táluka or Petta Treasury along with the collections of the office under the Indian Registration Act, 1877 ;

by Stipendiary or Kulkarni Village Registrars, by means of the village mahárs, monthly to the Táluka or Petta Treasury. (The amounts thus remitted monthly should be sent so as to reach a Táluka Treasury not later than the 25th, or a Petta Treasury than the 20th, of each month ; or if these dates fall upon a Sunday or gazetted public holiday, not later than the day preceding such Sunday or holiday. In **March** the remittances may be made so as to reach the Treasury not later than the 31st of that month.)

A remittance by a Táluka Village Registrar should be accompanied by his Day and Cash-Book in which, on the remittance being paid in, the receipt of the Treasury Officer for the amount should be obtained.

Remittances by Stipendiary and Kulkarni Village Registrars should be accompanied by a Chullan specifying the amount remitted.

34. All Village Registrars may appropriate the proportion of the fees due to them at once on such fees being paid to them, the amount so appropriated being shown by a debit entry in the Day Book and the surplus only being remitted to the Treasury.

Percentage payments to Village Registrars how to be drawn.

(*l*) *Correspondence.*

35. Táluka Village Registrars shall, as regards official correspondence, be the medium of communication between the Stipendiary and Kulkarni Village Registrars and the Assistant, or Deputy Collector in charge of the táluka.

Táluka Village Registrars to be the medium of communication between Stipendiary and Kulkarni Village Registrars and the Assistant or Deputy Collectors.

As a rule correspondence from the offices of Stipendiary and Kulkarni Village Registrars should be sent by means of the village mahárs at the first opportunity. If, however, there be any communication of a pressing nature which will not admit of delay it should be sent through the post "bearing."

Correspondence how to be sent.

References from Stipendiary or Kulkarni Village Registrars, regarding matters of procedure, when the point involved is of minor importance and the Táluka Village Registrar to whom the reference is addressed entertains no doubt as to what the answer should be, may be disposed of by the latter without further reference to the Assistant, or Deputy Collector. The reply of the Táluka Village Registrar to a reference of the above nature should, however, be in the shape of advice, not in that of an order. A Register of such references, showing also the manner in which they have been disposed of, shall be kept by each Táluka Village Registrar who will be held responsible for the exercise of due discretion in replying thereto.

References from Stipendiary or Kulkarni Village Registrars how to be disposed of in certain cases.

PART IV.—MISCELLANEOUS.

(m) *Security.*

Stipendiary Village Registrars to give security.

36. Táluka Village Registrars being required to furnish security as Sub-Registrars and Kulkarni Village Registrars being wataudárs, no security for the due performance of their duties need be required. Stipendiary Village Registrars will, however, be required to give security to the extent of Rs. 100. The security bond of a Stipendiary Village Registrar should bo in the form in use in the Revenue Department. The sureties may be one or two in number as the Collector, in whose charge the bonds should be kept, directs.

(n) *Inspection.*

Village Registry Offices subject to the inspection of the Divisional Inspector of Registration and Stamps.

37. The Inspectors of Registration and Stamps will, in the matter of inspection, exercise a general superintendence over the Village Registry Offices within the limits of their respective Divisions.

Local Inspectors of Village Registry Offices.

38. Every Táluka Village Registrar who is a Special Sub-Registrar shall be the Inspector of Village Registry Offices for the táluka or mahál in which his office is situate. Where a Táluka Village Registrar is also a Mámlatdár's or Mahálkari's Aval-kárkún the Inspector-General shall determine what other Táluka Village Registrar shall be Inspector of the Village Registry Offices in his táluka or mahál.

An Inspector of Village Registry Offices shall visit and inspect each of the offices within his charge once at least in two years.

Occasional inspection by other officers.

39. Village Registry Offices shall also be from time to time inspected by each of the following officers, viz. :—

1. The Collector of the District.
2. The Assistant, or Deputy Collector in charge of the táluka.
3. The Mámlatdár or Mahálkari of the táluka or mahál.
4. The Special Judge.
5. The Assistants of the Special Judge.
6. The Subordinate Judges.

40. When examining a Village Registry Office it shall be the duty of an Inspecting Officer to see that the provisions of Chapter VIII. of the Dekkhan Agriculturists Relief Act, 1879, and of these and all other rules framed thereunder, and of the Stamp and Court Fees Acts are duly complied with.

Points to be observed at the examination of a Village Registry Office.

He should also send for some of the parties whose names appear in the Register, and with the aid of the latter question them with a view to satisfying himself that the instrument executed by them has been properly registered, and, if it was written by or under the superintendence of the Village Registrar that it has been correctly and carefully prepared.

The specimen forms of instruments in the Village Registrar's possession should also be examined with a view to substituting improved forms, if any of them are found to be unsuitable.

41. The Inspector of Registration and Stamps will submit a report of the result of his examination of Village Registry offices, sending one copy to the Inspector-General of Registration and another to the Assistant, or Deputy Collector in charge of the táluka. Táluka Village Registrars will also submit similar reports on each office examined by them to the Assistant, or Deputy Collector in charge of the táluka. No Inspector and no Táluka Village Registrar shall issue any order on the subject of his inspection direct to any Village Registrar. Any of the officers named in Rule 39, other than the Collector or an Assistant, or Deputy Collector, who inspects a Village Registry Office will communicate his observations to the Assistant, or Deputy Collector in charge of the táluka.

Reports to be submitted on Village Registry Office inspections. Authentication of books examined.

On receipt of any such report or observations as aforesaid the Assistant, or Deputy Collector in charge of the táluka, will himself dispose of such matters as do not appear to him to require further reference. In more important matters he will refer to the Collector before passing orders.

Every Officer on completing the examination of a Village Registry Office should authenticate the Register Book in current use by making a record therein to the following effect:—

"Examined this day from page   in Volume   to page   in this book."

                            (Signed) *A. B.*

(Registrar, or Assistant or Deputy Collector, or Mámlatdár, &c., *as the case may be*).

42. Inspection reports on Village Registry offices should be as brief as the circumstances of the case will admit of. They should state generally whether the fees are properly levied, whether instruments are properly stamped and carefully drawn, whether the work of registration is done with accuracy (especially with reference to the endorsements of attestation) and despatch, whether the writing in the registers is neatly done, and whether the correct amounts have been remitted to the Treasury. Any matter deserving of special remark should, of course, be specially brought to notice.

Contents of Inspection Reports.

43. Táluka Village Registrars when on inspection tour will be entitled to draw batta at the rates prescribed for subordinates in the Revenue Department, but will not be entitled to draw commission on fees levied in their offices during their absence.

Táluka Village Registrars to be entitled to draw batta, but not fee commission, when on tour.

(o) *Annual Reports.*

44. The Collector of each District in which the Deccan Agriculturists Relief Act, 1879, is in force, shall, shortly after the close of the official year on the 31st of March, submit to the Inspector-General a brief annual report containing such general remarks as he may deem necessary on the work performed during that year by the Village Registrars of his District, with any suggestions which he may have to offer for facilitating, extending, or improving the system of Village Registration. He shall also forward with such report such forms of annual returns as may be called for by the Inspector-General.

Annual Report (and returns if called for) to be furnished to the Inspector-General by Collectors.

APPENDIX A—(*See Rule 3.*)

Endorsements.	Copy of Instrument.

B 862—52

APPENDIX B.

FORM OF INDEX UNDER RULE 6 AND OF MEMORANDUM UNDER RULES 24 AND 31.

Name of Executant or Executants.	Residence.	Nature of Instrument and consideration or value.	Name of Office in which instrument is registered and date of registration and reference to Register-Book.	If instrument relates to immoveables, description of property.	Name of party claiming under the instrument.	Residence.	Total fees paid at time of registration.

APPENDIX C.—(*See Rule 9.*)

FORM OF CLAIM-NOTE BOOK.

On production of this note by the conveyance or mortgage belonging to him attested by me this day will be delivered to him by me (*or a copy of the conveyance or mortgage executed by him and attested this day will be delivered to him by me, or otherwise, as the case may be*).

Village Registrar.

On production of this note by the conveyance or mortgage belonging to him and attested by me this day will be delivered to him by me (*or a copy of the conveyance or mortgage executed by him and attested this day will be delivered to him by me, or otherwise, as the case may be*).

Village Registrar.

APPENDIX D.—(*See Rule 10.*)

FORM OF DAY AND CASH-BOOK.

	Wednesday, 7th January 1880.	Rs.	a.	p.
Fees on entry No. 131 of 1880 at page 88 of Register Book: Registration 4 annas, copy 1 anna		0	5	0
Fees on entry No. 132 of 1880 at page 89 of Register Book: Registration 4 annas		0	4	0
		0	9	0
Portion of above due to Village Registrar	...	0	4	6
Balance to be remitted to the Treasury	...	0	4	6

(Signed) *A. B.*,
Village Registrar of

APPENDIX E.—(See Rule 30.)

Received from for (search, or grant of copy, or inspection).	Received from for (search, or grant of copy, or inspection).
Village Registrar.	Village Registrar.

APPENDIX F.—(See Rule 31.)

INSTRUMENTS REGISTERED DURING MONTH ENDING ———

Name of Office.	Moveables.	Immoveables.	Registration and Copy fees.	Fees under Rule 30.	Total Receipts.	Village Registrar's Pay.	Village Registrar's Commission	Total of columns 7 and 8.	Difference between columns 6 and 9.	
									Surplus of Receipts.	Deficit of Receipts.
1	2	3	4	5	6	7	8	9	10	11

NOTE.—The amount remitted to the Treasury in the case of each office should be represented by the difference between the amount shown in column 6 and that in column 8.

By order of His Excellency the Honourable the Governor in Council,

J. R. NAYLOR,
Acting Chief Secretary to Government.

JUDICIAL DEPARTMENT.

Bombay Castle, 7th February 1880.

No. 890.—In exercise of the power conferred by Section 63 of the Deccan Agriculturists Relief Act, the Governor in Council is pleased to make the following Rules regulating the appointment, suspension, dismissal and remuneration of Village-Registrars, and prescribing the fees to be levied by them:—

    1. Every Village-Registrar shall be appointed, and may be suspended or dismissed by the Collector, or, subject to his orders, by the Assistant or Deputy Collector in charge of the táluka in which such Village-Registrar has jurisdiction:

    Provided that Sub-Registrars who are appointed *ex-officio* Village-Registrars shall not be suspended or dismissed without the concurrence of the Inspector-General of Registration

2. In respect of the suspension and dismissal of Village-Registrars the same provisions, whether as to the reasons for which such persons may be suspended or dismissed, or as to the manner in which an order for suspending or dismissing shall be recorded, or as to the right of appeal against such order, shall apply as are applicable to village accountants.

3. The remuneration to be paid to Village-Registrars shall be as follows :—

    (1.)—To a Village-Registrar who is also officiating kulkarni or a sharer in the kulkarni's watan, ¾ths of the fees.

    (2.)—To a Stipendiary Village-Registrar, a salary of from Rs. 5 to Rs. 10 per month, to be fixed by the Collector in consideration of the work of the office, *plus* ½ of the fees.

    (3.)—To Sub-Registrars who are *ex-officio* Village-Registrars, the same rate as they are entitled to as Sub-Registrars:

Provided always that in case of neglect of duty, carelessness or other official misconduct, the Collector may (with the concurrence of the Inspector-General of Registration, if the Village-Registrar be a Sub-Registrar) withhold payment of such remuneration to such amount or for such period as he shall think fit.

4. The fees to be levied by Village-Registrars shall be at the following rates, (viz.) :—

	As.	P.
For writing, or superintending the writing of, and for attesting and registering any instrument, other than a simple receipt for money, falling within the provisions of section 56, and for making one certified copy thereof under section 58	4	0
Ditto when the instrument is a simple receipt for money	1	0
For every certified copy in excess of one furnished under section 58	1	0
For searching for any entry in the Register, except as hereinafter provided	1	0
For making one copy of any entry in the Register or of a memorandum filed under No. 24 of the Rules framed under section 61 except as hereinafter provided	1	0

Search for or making copy of any entry or of a memorandum filed under the said Rule, if such search or copy is made by the applicant himself or by any person whom he brings for this purpose .... } Free.
Search by Registrar when the applicant can name the actual month in which the registration of the entry required took place ...

By order of His Excellency the Honourable the
Governor in Council,

J. R. NAYLOR,
Acting Chief Secretary to Government.

Bombay Castle, 24th March 1880.

No. 2109.—It is hereby notified for general information that the Rules regarding registration made under Section 61 and 63 of the Deccan Agriculturists Relief Act, 1879, and published in the *Government Gazette* of the 12th February 1880, shall come into force in the four Collectorates of Poona, Ahmednagar, Sholápur and Sátára from the 1st proximo.

By order of the Honourable the Governor in Council,

C. GONNE,
Chief Secretary to Government.

JUDICIAL DEPARTMENT.

Bombay Castle, 19th February 1880.

No. 1226.—With the approval of the Governor General in Council, the Governor in Council of Bombay is pleased to direct, under Section 78 of the Indian Registration Act, 1877, that the Fees prescribed in the following Table shall be leviable in respect of any instrument registered under Section 71 of the Deccan Agriculturists Relief Act, 1879, in lieu of the Fees prescribed in the Table published at pages 881 to 883 of the *Bombay Government Gazette* of the 11th October 1877 :—

Table.	As.	p.
For registering an instrument	4	0
For a copy of an entry, except as hereinafter provided.	1	0
For searching for an entry, except as hereinafter provided	1	0

Search for, or making copy of any entry if such search or copy is made by the applicant himself or by any person whom he brings for this purpose.

Search by Registrar when the applicant can name the actual month in which the registration of the entry required took place.
} Free.

By order of His Excellency the Honourable the
Governor in Council,

J. R. NAYLOR,
Acting Chief Secretary to Government.

REDUCTION OF COURT FEES AND STAMP DUTIES.

JUDICIAL DEPARTMENT.

Bombay Castle, 31st December 1879.

No. 7926.—The following rules made by Her Majesty's High Court of Judicature at Bombay, under Section 20 of the Court Fees Act (VII. of 1870), have been confirmed by the Government of Bombay and sanctioned by the Governor General of India in Council, and are published for general information:—

1. Under the provisions of Section 20 of the Court Fees Act (VII. of 1870), the High Court is pleased to direct that the fees levied for all processes in suits to which Chapter II. of the Deccan Agriculturists Relief Act (XVII. of 1879) applies, except suits of the description mentioned in Section 3, Clauses (*w*) and (*x*), to which an agriculturist is not a party, shall be one-half the fees which would be leviable in similar suits to which the said Act does not apply.

2. The fee leviable for the service of every notice, or other process issued in proceedings taken under Chapter IV. of the said Act (XVII. of 1879) shall be four annas.

3. Nothing contained in these rules, nor in any rules heretofore made by the High Court under Section 20 of the Court Fees Act (VII. of 1870) shall apply to process issued by a Village Munsif under Chapter V. of the said Act (XVII. of 1879).

By order of His Excellency the Honourable
the Governor in Council,

J. R. NAYLOR,
Acting Chief Secretary to Government.

JUDICIAL DEPARTMENT.

Bombay Castle, 7th January 1880.

No. 89.—The following Notifications by the Government of India are republished:—

DEPARTMENT OF FINANCE AND COMMERCE.

The 3rd January 1880.

" No. 10.—In exercise of the powers conferred by Section 8 of Act I. of 1879 (The Indian Stamp Act, 1879), the Governor General in Council has remitted the duties with which the undermentioned classes of instruments are chargeable under the said Act, namely:—

(1) Agreements of the kind described in Section 43 of the Deccan Agriculturists Relief Act, 1879;

(2) Copies of instruments which the Village Registrar has to deliver to the parties under Section 58 of the Deccan Agriculturists Relief Act, 1879;

(3) Powers-of-attorney furnished to relatives, servants or dependants under Section 68 of the Deccan Agriculturists Relief Act, 1879."

" No. 11.—In exercise of the powers conferred by Section 35 of Act VII. of 1870 (The Court Fees Act, 1870), the Governor General in Council has—

(I) remitted the fees payable in respect of powers-of-attorney furnished to relatives, servant or dependants, under Section 68 of Act XVII, 1879 (The Deccan Agriculturists Relief Act, 1879);

(II) remitted in the case of suits instituted before Village Munsifs under Chapter V. of Act XVII. of 1879 (The Deccan Agriculturists Relief Act, 1879), the fees payable in respect of the documents specified in the first or second schedule to the said Court Fees Act annexed;

(III) reduced such fees to one-half in the case of (*a*) suits to which Chapter II. of the said Deccan Agriculturists Relief Act applies, except suits of the description mentioned in section 3, clause (*w*) or clause (*x*) of the said Act to which an agriculturist is not a party; (*b*) proceedings in matters relating to insolvency under Chapter IV. of the said Deccan Agriculturists Relief Act.

(Signed) R. B. CHAPMAN,
Secretary to the Government of India."

By order of His Excellency the Honourable
the Governor in Council,

J. R. NAYLOR,
Acting Chief Secretary to Government.

www.ingramcontent.com/pod-product-compliance
Lightning Source LLC
Chambersburg PA
CBHW030555300426
44111CB00009B/994